# MEDIEVALIA ET HUMANISTICA

# MEDIEVALIA ET HUMANISTICA
## New Series
### Edited by Paul Maurice Clogan

# MEDIEVALIA ET HUMANISTICA

## STUDIES IN MEDIEVAL AND RENAISSANCE CULTURE

*Founded in 1943 by S. Harrison Thomson*

NEW SERIES
NUMBER 4

MEDIEVAL AND RENAISSANCE SPIRITUALITY

Edited by Paul Maurice Clogan

North Texas State University
*Denton, Texas*
1973

# *Editorial Note*

FOUNDED IN 1943 by S. Harrison Thomson and now under new editorship and management, *Medievalia Et Humanistica* continues to publish, in a series of annual volumes, significant scholarship, criticism, and reviews in all areas of medieval and Renaissance culture: literature, art, history, law, music, philosophy, science, social and economic institutions. *Medievalia Et Humanistica* encourages the individual scholar to examine the relationship of his discipline to other disciplines and to relate his study in a theoretical or practical way to its cultural and historical context. Review articles examine significant recent publications, and contributing editors report on the progress of medieval and Renaissance studies in the United States and Canada.

*Medievalia Et Humanistica* is sponsored by the Medieval Interdepartmental Section of the Modern Language Association of America, and publication in the series is open to contributions from all sources. The editorial board welcomes interdisciplinary critical and historical studies by young or established scholars and urges contributors to communicate in an attractive, clear, and concise style the larger implications in addition to the precise material of their research, with documentation held to a minimum. Texts, maps, illustrations, and diagrams will be published when they are essential to the argument of the article.

Individuals, institutions, and libraries may enter standing orders for the new series and receive a 10% discount. Future volumes will be sent to them automatically, and they will be billed when each volume is shipped. Such standing orders may, of course, be canceled at any time. Books for review, manuscripts (which should be prepared in conformity with the *MLA Style Sheet* and accompanied by a stamped, self-addressed manuscript envelope), and all inquiries regarding both *Fasciculi* I-XVII in the original series and standing and individual orders to the New Series should be addressed to the Editor, *Medievalia Et Humanistica,* P.O. Box 13348, North Texas State University, Denton, Texas 76203.

# *Preface*

SPIRITUALITY IS A subject upon which an inordinate amount of nonsense has been and continues to be written. As Don Giuseppe De Luca, founder and first editor of *Archivio Italiano per La Storia della Pieta,* once noted, "orthodoxy and spirituality are not co-terminous and spirituality can produce at the same time erroneous doctrine and authentic devotion." Nevertheless, the subject is still a valid one and with some judicious control the editorial board recommended it for discussion in a symposium of original articles for this fourth volume in the continuing new series of *Medievalia et Humanistica.* Since there are not very many scholars in the United States and Canada whose primary field of research is medieval or Renaissance spirituality, as distinct from literary and intellectual history, though there are obviously a number whose work involves the history of spirituality, the symposium is centered on the subject of spirituality and other aspects of popular religion. Nine scholars from six different fields were asked to examine the significance of *homo spiritualis* in terms of their research and within their disciplines and to relate their original study in a theoretical or practical way to its cultural and historical context. The result is an interesting symposium of significant articles on the subject of medieval and Renaissance spirituality which is designed to indicate current trends and new directions.

Caroline W. Bynum deals with the conception of the Christian life in the Middle Ages and makes an important contribution to our understanding of how that conception was altered in the canonical movement of the twelfth century. Walter L. Wakefield contributes an unusual paper which really penetrates the thinking on religion of some very ordinary people in the thirteenth century without trying to put them into ready-made categories.

In "The Heresy of the Free Spirit and Late Medieval Mysticism," Eleanor McLaughlin offers a major advance in conceptual framework and precision which will interest scholars in a variety of fields. E. Catherine Dunn presents a challenging hypothesis for the interpretation of the Corpus Christi plays as expression of popular devotion which the formal liturgy did not, in itself, accommodate and in fact inhibited. Despite the work of Owst and Prosser, the relationship of medieval drama to new pastoral and spiritual emphases initiated in the thirteenth century, especially the work of the Friars, has not been explored. Sandro Sticca points the way in this direction and argues its necessity. While he suggests that Franciscan Spirituality underlies much of medieval drama, he examines other modes of spirituality and offers a mine of references which will support the continuing work of others in this vein. The role of poverty in Franciscan Spirituality is analyzed by E. Randolph Daniel, who focuses his study on two leaders among the Franciscan Spirituals in the thirteenth and fourteenth centuries. Marjorie Reeves, who is a master of her field, presents a cogent argument for the continuity of medieval and Reformation apocalypticism in England of the sixteenth and seventeenth centuries mainly through the Joachimite tradition. She casts new light on English Protestant thought of the period as well as on some of our general notions of millenarianism and prophecy. Richard C. Trexler's article is part of a larger program of research which aims at comprehensive analysis of religion in Renaissance Florence using insights and methods of comparative religion and anthropology as well as the sociology of religion. Finally, Thomas M. C. Lawler provides a significant essay which could help us to assess St. John Fisher's position in the history of spirituality and relate ascetical and mystical theology as a link between the Middle Ages and modern times.

In addition to the symposium on spirituality, this volume also contains six review articles and sixteen review notices of significant recent publications. The editorial board is pleased to announce that commencing with the publication of this volume, Number 4, subsequent volumes in the new series of *Medievalia et Humanistica* will also be published at North Texas State University. The next volume in the new series will explore from different perspectives the subject of historiography in the Middle Ages and Renaissance. Review articles will examine significant recent publications, and contributing editors will report on the progress of medieval and Renaissance studies in the United States and Canada.

P.M. C.

# MEDIEVALIA ET HUMANISTICA

Paul Maurice Clogan, Editor
NORTH TEXAS STATE UNIVERSITY
Julie Sydney Davis, Managing Editor

## EDITORIAL BOARD

# Contents

*xi*

## REVIEW NOTICES

# MEDIEVALIA ET HUMANISTICA

# The Spirituality of Regular Canons in the Twelfth Century: a New Approach[1]

*Caroline W. Bynum*

## I. The State Of The Question

**H**ISTORIANS OF MEDIEVAL spirituality agree that the years between 1050 and 1215 saw a fundamental change in men's basic conceptions of the Christian life, a change perhaps as deep and as lasting as the Reformation of the sixteenth century or the spread of Christianity in the second to fourth centuries A.D. Central to this change was a new emphasis on the obligation to love and serve one's neighbor, a new sense that Christ wished his followers not merely to worship him and avoid wrongdoing but also to care for their brothers.[2] Scholars are fond of contrasting earlier monastic reforms, characterized by a concern for offering correct worship to God, with the activity and ideas of twelfth-century itinerant preachers, such as Vitalis of Savigny, Norbert of Xanten, Peter Valdes, or Francis of Assisi. But historians have not agreed about exactly when or how this awareness of an obligation to care for one's fellow man emerged. At the moment, a particular stumbling block to the understanding of this development is the lack of a scholarly consensus on the place of the group known as regular canons in the history of twelfth-century spirituality.

General works on medieval spirituality have tended to assume that regular canons formed a separate movement within the religious ferment of the twelfth century, a separate movement that wedded service

3

of others to a life of monastic withdrawal and thereby foreshadowed the friars' concern with love of neighbor. This view sees monks and regular canons as clearly distinguishable because of the centrality granted to service in the canonical movement, and argues that the life led by regular canons was in some way a form of religious vocation that provides a transition from monk to mendicant.[3] Recent, specialized studies on regular canons have continued to assert or assume a similar view of the place of regular canons in the history of medieval religion.[4] But, ironically, the same specialized studies have, over the past thirty years, provided material for questioning these generalizations. And the historian of monastic spirituality, Jean Leclercq, has recently suggested that in the area of conceptions of the cloistered life there is no difference between twelfth-century monks and regular canons, no distinctive canonical spirituality.[5] Although most historians continue to feel that monks and regular canons differed in basic ways, it has become more and more difficult to adduce evidence of widespread and consistent contrasts between the two groups. Recent research does not support the argument that twelfth-century canons and monks differed generally in actual practices, nor has current scholarship established that monks and regular canons diverged widely in the prerogatives they claimed or in the conceptions of the spiritual life revealed in the non-controversial writing of their orders.

Although historians have long known that the second half of the eleventh century saw a general effort to reform existing groups of secular clergy by enforcing on them a life in common and complete renunciation of private property, the research of Dereine has gradually revealed the great diversity of early canonical foundations, some of which were, in their first years, as austere and as isolated as the early Cîteaux.[6] No one would deny that some of the eleventh-century canonical houses in Italy differed from eleventh-century monastic movements in emphasizing the role of every brother as priest. But given the great diversity of the actual life practiced in eleventh and early twelfth-century canonical foundations it is now questionable whether all houses of clerics who renounced private property should be grouped together by historians and distinguished from monastic houses. Indeed, the evidence presented by Dereine and others suggests that an approach that groups together the early Premonstratensians and Cistercians, on the one hand, and, on the other, the Pataria of Milan and the canons for whom the compilation found in MS Ottoboni Lat. 175 was composed[7] may be far more historically valid. Even for the period beginning in the second decade of the twelfth century, when clerics living a full common life came increasingly to be characterized by adoption of the Rule of St. Augustine, historians have found it difficult to identify "canonical characteristics." By the twelfth century, the number of monks in holy orders had increased to the point where some monastic houses had many priests and many brothers in orders.[8] The major historians of the canonical movement agree that pastoral work — that is, service of parish churches and preaching to those outside the cloister — was not an essential element in all canonical life,[9] whereas it was not uncommon in the same period for monks to exercise the *cura animarum,* including preaching.[10] Thus, despite repeated assertions by scholars that regular canons combined monastic practice with a new orientation toward the cure of souls, no evidence has as yet been presented to demonstrate that the actual life lived in most canonical houses in the twelfth century differed generally from the life in most monastic cloisters.[11]

If we turn from the realm of practice to the realm of ideas, we find that, in the later eleventh and twelfth centuries, regular canons and monks engaged in various controversies over the nature and relative superiority of their respective movements, controversies that have sometimes been cited by historians as evidence of distinctive monastic and canonical spiritualities. The existence of such polemical writings certainly indicates that some canons and some monks felt that a distinction existed between their respective forms of the religious life. It also indicates that certain polemical writers desired to underline that difference. A careful consideration of the treatises themselves reveals, however, that in some cases the two groups were claiming the same prerogatives — both the right to the *cura animarum* and a state of spiritual superiority — and this fact suggests that the controversy may tell historians more about new spiritual ideals that touched both monastic and canonical traditions in the twelfth century than about differences between canons and monks.[12] We cannot assume that polemical claims reflect actual practice, nor can we assume that a few polemical treatises represent the opinion of canons in general. Moreover, statements made in the heat of argument are not the best guide to men's ideas about themselves. Polemical defenses of the right to preach do not necessarily reflect a conception shared by canons living together in the cloister that an obligation for one's brother is an integral aspect of the religious vocation.

Although neither polemical claims nor actual practice reveal general and widespread differences between monks and regular canons, historians continue to claim that canons developed a new self-conception, a "new orientation,"[13] that "although all the elements of the apostolic life . . . are found in the monastic order, we must assert that the emphasis is not the same [as in the canonical order]."[14] Only two specific pieces of evidence for a distinctive canonical orientation have, however, been cited.[15] The first is the fact, noticed by several historians, that the Premonstratensian Anselm of Havelberg, changing the traditional exegesis of the story of Mary and Martha, clearly foreshadows the thirteenth-century notion of the "mixed life" of service and contemplation as higher than the life of contemplation alone.[16] The second and related piece of evidence, which has been pointed out most clearly perhaps by Chatillon, is a new emphasis on preaching found in some canonical writings, an emphasis that frequently exists alongside traditional interpretations of the "active and contemplative lives."[17] But Anselm of Havelberg's new exegesis of the story of Mary and Martha does not seem to have been common among regular canons, or even among Premonstratensians;[18] and efforts to increase the importance of the "active life" are not unknown in monastic writings of the same period.[19] Anselm's exegesis differs markedly from interpretations of the passage (and conceptions of the religious life) from the early Middle Ages. It is not clear, however, that his concern is characteristically "canonical." Moreover, Chatillon's suggestion that a new concern with preaching is evidence of a new canonical orientation has been documented only by reference to a single sermon of Richard of St. Victor and a few passages from Philip of Harvengt. In general, as Leclercq has shown, monastic and canonical treatises agree in stressing the soul's obligation to worship and love its Creator as the central aspect of the life of the cloister.[20] On the basis of the evidence presented by recent historians, there is then little reason to argue that twelfth-century monks and regular canons differed in their conceptions of the Christian life.

Current scholarship has adduced increasing amounts of evidence on the actual practices of monks and regular canons, has analyzed monastic and canonical polemic with some care, and has glanced, with less care, at non-polemical writings. None of this evidence, as currently presented and analyzed, proves that there was a general difference between twelfth-century monks and regular canons either in practice or in ideas. And yet, the efforts of canonical authors to defend and define their order in polemic and the few texts cited by Petit and Chatillon do suggest that when a twelfth-century man joined a canonical house he saw in that house a religious ideal somewhat different from the ideals of contemporary monasticism. No historian has shown what that ideal was, and it seems unlikely that further investigation of practice or polemic will reveal a clear distinction between monks and canons. But a survey of recent scholarship leaves us with a nagging suspicion that, in the area of ideas and self-conceptions, the case is not closed. The non-polemical writings of the canons have not been carefully studied. Present arguments about self-conception tend to be based on single texts, single themes, or single authors. More work is clearly needed. If we are to conclude with Leclercq that monastic and canonical attitudes are the same, we must show that, in an extensive body of non-polemical literature, they agree on all aspects of the spiritual life. If we maintain with Petit that they are different, we must be able to show that, in works of similar form and purpose, virtually all canonical authors use language or voice concerns that virtually all monastic authors ignore.

In my effort to answer the question of the difference or similarity of monastic and canonical ideas, I have thus chosen for study the fairly large group of what we might call "works of practical spiritual advice" — that is, works about the soul's spiritual and moral progress within the cloistered life. Such works include treatises on the formation of novices, commentaries on the Benedictine and Augustinian Rules, and certain other works that are clearly parallel to these two genre in form and intention.[21] These works reveal the assumptions of the cloistered about the purpose of their lives much more clearly than abstract treatises of mystical or Biblical theology, works of polemic, or the practical details of custumals. Because each author writes for members of his own order, we need not worry that his unconscious or semi-conscious attitudes toward the Christian life reflect his readers' vocation and status rather than his own. Because the treatises all have the same ostensible subject (to explain the cloistered life to those engaged in its practice), we need not worry that the assumptions of the authors differ because of different purposes in writing. Characteristics that appear in almost all canonical treatises and almost no monastic ones can therefore be related to the self-conception of the canonical authors *qua* canons.

## II. The Canonical Concern With Edification
### A. Edification *Verbo et Exemplo*

Commentaries on the Benedictine and Augustinian Rules and works of advice for novices have usually been studied for their information

7

on actual monastic or canonical practices or for their theories about the soul's relationship to God. In neither of these areas do we find consistent differences between monastic and canonical writings. But if we look at the language, the emphasis, and the specific borrowings with which the two groups of treatises describe the obligations of ordinary cloistered brothers, a revealing contrast emerges: canonical authors see canons as teachers and learners, whereas monastic authors see monks only as learners. What distinguishes regular canons from monks is the canon's sense of a responsibility to edify his fellow men both by what he says and by what he does.

The concern for edification is found in virtually all twelfth-century canonical commentaries and treatises for novices (with the possible exception of the *De questionibus* of Richard of St. Victor) and in virtually no monastic treatises (with the exception of Peter of Celle's *De disciplina claustrali,* Arnulf of Bohéries' *Speculum monachorum,* and Stephen of Salley's *Speculum novitii*).[22] The majority of twelfth-century canonical treatises express this concern in language that links the moral education offered by word to that offered by example and emphasizes both. In several canonical treatises the concern is expressed in descriptions of canons as teachers *verbo et exemplo:* the compilation in MS Ottoboni Lat. 175,[23] the *Regula clericorum* of Peter of Porto,[24] the *De institutione novitiorum* of Hugh of St. Victor,[25] Odo of St. Victor's letters on the canonical life,[26] and Philip of Harvengt's *De institutione clericorum*[27] all use some form of the phrase *docere* (or *instruere,* etc.) *verbo et exemplo* (or *vita et doctrina,* etc.). In addition, a concern with the effects of canonical action and words and a general tendency to link the exhortation to effective speech and to edifying behavior appears in the anonymous *Expositio in regulam beati Augustini,* which has been attributed to Hugh of St. Victor and Letbert of St. Rufus;[28] in the Vienna commentary;[29] and in Adam of Dryburgh's *Liber de ordine, habitu et professione canonicorum ordinis praemonstratensis.*[30] Even in the Bridlington Dialogue and to a slight extent in Richard of St. Victor's *De questionibus* we find, if not the phrase *docere verbo et exemplo* or a linking of word and deed, at least treatments of conduct and speech that reveal an awareness of the obligation to edify.[31]

In a few canonical treatises, the concern for edification is closely and explicitly linked to a conception of the canon as preacher, either to those outside or to those within the cloister. When the prologue of the anonymous compilation found in MS Ottoboni Lat. 175 refers to the task of canons, it is clearly describing preaching:

> Since the order of canons seems to have been established especially for this . . . — that is, to found the life of men in the catholic faith, to instruct according to the laws and morals of the Fathers, to correct, comfort and rebuke disciples by the words of holy doctrine, [and] to establish and nourish [them] for the purpose of guarding it — it is right that they should be moved by fear, broadened by hope, inflamed by charity, adorned with knowledge, outstanding in the light of the faith and in purity of life. And it is fitting that they have in themselves what they preach to others, lest they displease God or become reprobate to men.[32]

Philip of Harvengt's descriptions of clerics, which are directed toward and primarily about regular canons, use the phrase *docere verbo et exemplo* (or the idea behind it) repeatedly in referring to an obligation to preach.[33] Moreover, it is true that canonical commentaries are more likely than monastic ones to include discussions of preaching.[34] But the crucial distinction in focus between monastic and canonical works does not lie in the fact that canons claim for canons the right to preach. Indeed, Rupert of Deutz's monastic commentary claims the right for monks,[35] the commentary in MS Vienna 2207 claims the right for both monks and canons,[36] and Joachim of Flora in his commentary on the Benedictine Rule claims the prerogative for Cistercians.[37] Nor does the crucial difference between monastic and canonical authors lie in the fact that canons discuss preaching more frequently than monks; for many canonical commentaries and treatises do not discuss preaching. Rather the basic distinction is that canons advise canons about the religious life as if an obligation to educate by word and example is a crucial component. More important than the Vienna commentary's reference to preaching is the fact that it refers to canons as responsible for the effect of their words and behavior on others. More important than the fact that Rupert of Deutz and Philip of Harvengt both claim for their constituencies the right to preach is the fact that the monk Rupert generally ignores the educational effects of words and actions, whereas the canon Philip sees the words and deeds of ordinary cloistered brothers as educational.

## B. Canonical and Monastic Views of Conduct

Behind the explicit exhortations to educate *verbo et exemplo* found in many canonical commentaries lies the assumption that an individual living the cloistered life is responsible in whatever he says or does not only for the state of his own soul but also for the progress of his neighbor. This assumption is frequently reflected in canonical discussions of behavior and in canonical discussions of speech or silence even where these discussions are not linked to each other and where words such as *docere* or *instruere* are not used. If we compare passages from canonical works that deal with behavior with similar passages from monastic works, we see clearly the difference in focus of the two groups.

When canonical authors treat conduct, they tend to emphasize its impact on the reader's fellows and to urge him to take care that the impact be a useful and wise one. Monastic authors, however, although they are sometimes aware of reciprocal relationships within the cloister, tend to see these relationships as affecting the reader and to see the reader's behavior as displayed before God. Occasionally they warn their readers to avoid causing scandal, but almost never do they urge them to bring others to good by their behavior. Thus the canon Hugh of St. Victor suggests that behavior may be even more important where it can be seen by men than where it will be seen only by God: "And, although a man ought in no place to desert his discipline, it ought however to be preserved more diligently and more solicitously there where being neglected it will cause scandal to many and being kept will cause an example of good imitation."[38] And Philip of Harvengt informs clerics, among whom he includes regular canons, that ". . . *vita clericorum forma sit laicorum* . . . "[39] In contrast, when the monastic author of the Canterbury *Instructio* discusses behavior, he focuses entirely on personal virtue. In warning his reader against causing a disturbance in the dormitory, for example, he is concerned less with the novice's conduct before his brother than with his conduct before God:

> Therefore we must take care that nothing be done at night that will be shameful to hear in the morning. And if one takes care because of the brethren, what should be done because of God, whom naught can escape and to whom not even the thoughts of the heart are hidden? . . . Let all therefore within and without be done fittingly so that nothing appear which could offend the eyes of our Judge.[40]

Even Bernard of Clairvaux, whose *De gradibus humilitatis* stresses the importance of the cloistered community, nevertheless ignores the individual monk's responsibility for edifying his neighbor. Bernard sees the *cenobium* as providing an opportunity for the individual monk to acquire discipline and to grow in love through identification with his neighbor's joys and sorrows.[41] The monk is urged to love his neighbor, but "love" here means an emotional response, not service, and particularly not educational responsibility. The monk is to love *in order to learn.* Concern for the impression that one's words or deeds make on others is condemned as an element in conceit.[42] Moreover, in Aelred of

Rievaulx's *Speculum caritatis,* where Bernard's conception of the community as teacher of charity is joined to an awareness of conduct as example, we still find a focus on the monk as learner. Although Aelred speaks of other monks as moving or shaping his reader by their example, he does not mention his reader's obligation to teach virtue or love to his fellows.[43]

The concern for appearance before God and union with him that is found in these monastic texts is not, of course, lacking in canonical writings. The new canonical focus on behavior as edification does not replace or shatter older traditions; rather it creeps in unobtrusively alongside them. Aelred's *Speculum* and Hugh of St. Victor's *De institutione novitiorum,* for example, are both studies of the "re-formation" of the image of God in man.[44] To both Hugh and Aelred, the novice is a learner progressing toward God, and the novice's fellows are aids to his learning. In both authors, behavior is often seen as revealed before God. Hugh's emphasis on the novice as educator as well as learner, his emphasis on the novice's behavior as revealed before men, slips quietly into his treatise without any apparent tension or disharmony. Hugh simply pauses, while discussing man's relationship to God, to point out the effects of that relationship on man's fellows.

Canonical authors thus combine the canonical view of conduct with a concern for progress toward God. They are not unaware that offering behavior *coram hominibus* and offering behavior *coram Deo* imply two different intentions in the person behaving.[45] But they show little worry about the possibility of conflict between these two intentions. Indeed, because they move back and forth so naturally between edification of others through virtuous behavior and the offering of that same behavior to God as evidence of love for him, it is sometimes difficult to tell in a given passage exactly what the author's focus is. A description of good behavior that leads to God and a description of good behavior that educates men may, of course, be descriptions of the same behavior and therefore may, on occasion, be the same description, if the question of audience is ignored. An isolated phrase about conduct from Adam of Dryburgh's commentary on the Augustinian Rule and an isolated phrase about conduct from John of Fruttuaria's work for monastic novices may, when compared, seem identical. But the overall impact of the canonical treatises is different from that of monastic ones. Canonical authors assume that canons are not only learners who grow toward God but also pattern *(forma)* and example *(exemplum)* to those who encounter them. Regular canons do not point out that their interest in the educational effects of their own behavior differs from the interests of their monastic contemporaries; but the interest is different nonetheless.

## C. Canonical and Monastic Views of Silence and Speech

Just as canonical and monastic treatises differ in their conceptions of conduct, so the two groups of works differ generally in their treatment of words. With two or three exceptions, monastic authors do not exhort monks to teach each other by word, or even refer to monastic conversation as educational.[46] Moreover, monastic and canonical authors also differ in their treatment of the opposite of words — silence. Whereas canonical authors see silence as preparation for fruitful discourse between men, monastic authors tend to see silence as a good in itself or as a preparation for discourse with God.

The late twelfth-century *De novitiis instruendis,* for example, emphasizes monastic silence as an aspect of self-discipline. The author is concerned, not with the harm that words may do to listeners, but with the soil and temptation that words may arouse for the speaker.[47] Similarly, the anonymous author of the sermons on the Benedictine Rule found in MS Auxerre 50 focuses on silence as a goal and fears speech as an opportunity for sin. In his discussion of chapter vi of the Rule, the author warns monks to guard their mouths, avoid sin, and keep silence so that they may hear God; he interprets Isaiah VI. 5, "Woe is me because I have held my peace," in such a way that "holding one's peace" means "suppressing confession of faults."[48] Even Peter of Celle, whose treatment of behavior (and very occasionally of words) is an exception to the monastic focus, is entirely monastic in his treatment of silence. There are, writes Peter, seven seals with which the book of silence is sealed, seven reasons for keeping silence: tranquility, profession, keeping the peace, quieting the movement and affection of the heart, withdrawing from secular business, scrutinizing the law of God, and contemplation. None of these reasons considers the effect of silence (or of words) on the monk's fellows.[49]

In contrast, when canonical authors set out to treat silence, the discussion frequently evolves into a discussion of useful speech. Philip of Harvengt's *De silentio* begins with the statement that silence is necessary for the cloistered so that they may talk with God, but concludes by concentrating on the dangers of harmful silence and the wisdom of effective speech.[50] And Hugh of St. Victor urges edifying speech as a cure for too much silence.[51] It is not surprising that the Vienna commentary on the Augustinian Rule, which sees regular canons as preachers, should see silence as preparation for didactic speech: ". . . they [the early canons] were silent thus in secret so that they might scatter the word of God in public; they appeared thus free from the acts of the world so that they, being careful, might rule the flock of the people committed to them."[52] It is, however, remarkable that, despite the wide diversity in actual canonical observance, those canonical authors who treat silence all imply that it is preparation for speech. Even Peter of Porto, whose rule allows room for the eremitical vocation and argues for periods of absolute silence in the cloister, betrays a concern for edifying words. Not only does Peter exhort canons to season their words with eloquence; he also states that one practices absolute silence at some periods in order to learn to abstain from lazy or useless words.[53] Peter sees silence less as an ascetic exercise of denial of the will than as a means of assuring that whatever talk takes place between brothers will be useful.

## D. Canonical and Monastic Use of Sources

Monastic and canonical treatises of spiritual advice thus differ in their approaches to both behavior and words. The difference is subtle; often we feel, in reading these treatises, that it is quite unconscious. Regular canons and monks seem to be interested in slightly different things about themselves. Although ostensibly discussing the same topic — the life of the cloister — they shift the focus in different directions. We can see this difference in perspective in the use that certain authors make of traditional texts. When monastic authors borrow texts that describe clerics or preaching, they tend to alter or excerpt those texts so as to remove any emphasis on edifying behavior or speech. When canonical authors draw on earlier texts concerning the cloistered life they tend to add a concern for the educational responsibility of the individual brother.

The monk John of Fruttuaria, for example, borrows extensively from Ambrose's *De officiis ministrorum* in composing his treatise for novices. But his borrowings from Ambrose are taken, not from Ambrose's discussions of clerical functions or of clerical responsibility for the souls of others, but chiefly from chapters on the duties of the young and on modesty, which simply describe the appropriate virtues, and from Ambrose's opening discussion of silence. In almost every case where Ambrose moves from a consideration of silence to a consideration of the useful speech appropriate to clerics, John omits the latter emphasis and adds his own transitional sentences, treating silence as a goal, not as a means toward speech.[54] We can see the same process of selection and adaptation at work in Peter the Deacon's *Exhortatorium*. When Peter borrows from a sermon of Hildebert of Lavardin about the priesthood, he interpolates the words *et monachus* after *sacerdos* where the text refers to individual virtue; where the text refers to service of the altar and preaching Peter does not add *et monachus*.[55]

Canonical authors also tend to borrow from earlier texts what they wish to find, to add to earlier texts what they find lacking, and to emphasize in earlier texts what they see as important. The author of the Ottoboni compilation, for example, goes out of his way to select patristic passages that link life and reputation to effective service of one's neighbor by preaching. In a section entitled *Incipiunt capitula excerpta ex libris sanctorum de edificatione et correctione uite clericorum*, we find among the chapter headings: "(11) *Augustinus*. Ut clerici seruent bonam famam non solum coram Deo, sed etiam coram hominibus;" "(47) *Gregorius*. De his qui uerba legis meditantur et leuiter docent alios, male uerba uiuendo destruunt auditores;" "(201) *Augustinus*. Ut serui dei studeant non solum bonam uitam, sed etiam bonam famam seruare."[56]

Even more interesting than general canonical borrowing is the canonical reaction to the two major rules of the twelfth century: the Rule of St. Benedict and the canons' own Augustinian Rule. The Benedictine Rule itself is almost completely lacking in any suggestion that monks should, or could, offer moral education to one another. It sees in the *cenobium* primarily an opportunity for brothers to defer to, bear with, obey, and love each other in their search for individual salvation.[57] The Rule includes no exhortations to verbal teaching by ordinary monks and contains no references to the helpful effects of the good conduct of ordinary brothers.[58] It treats outward behavior entirely as an aspect of personal virtue. When twelfth-century monastic authors comment upon the Rule, they retain this focus. But when the canon Peter of Porto draws upon the Rule in composing his own rule for the canons of Santa Maria in Porto of Ravenna, he supplements the text with several telling additions. For example, much of Book I, chapter ii of Peter's *Regula clericorum* is borrowed from chapter iv of the Rule of St. Benedict. But in two separate places Peter specifically adds to Benedict's instruments of good works the obligation to bring others to virtue by word and example.[59] It is quite natural that the early twelfth-century *Regula clericorum*, composed before the widespread adoption of some form of the Augustinian Rule by regular canons, draws on the most respected rule for the cloistered life available, the Rule of St. Benedict. But Peter obviously feels a need to add an emphasis that is lacking in Benedict's text, an emphasis on the *cenobium* as a setting within which brothers not only love and obey but also edify each other *vita et doctrina.*

In contrast to the Benedictine Rule, the Rule of St. Augustine itself contains a few traces of concern with edification. Ordinary brothers are not described as teaching by word and example; but the Rule stresses the responsibility of members of the community for each other, implying that brothers ought to aid their fellows by word[60] and that an individual is responsible for the effect of his behavior on the spiritual growth of his neighbors.[61] Furthermore, Augustine's sermon CCCLV on the life of clerics, which was in the eleventh and early twelfth centuries treated almost as part of the *regula beati Augustini,* contains a very important passage that implies that behavior teaches:

> And indeed I do not wish that anyone acquire from you a pretext for evil living. *For we provide good things,* the . . . apostle says, *not only before God, but also before men* (II Cor. VIII. 21; see also Rom. XII. 17). For our sake, our conscience is sufficient to us: for your sake, our reputation ought not to be soiled but it ought to have influence on you . . . Two things are conscience and reputation. Conscience [is] for you, reputation for your neighbor. He who trusting in his conscience neglects reputation is cruel . . . Before all *show yourself an example of good works* (Titus II. 7).[62]

But in commenting on the Rule of St. Augustine and in advising their fellows about the spiritual life, twelfth-century canonical authors do not merely reproduce these vague suggestions of responsibility for edification. Rather, again and again they lay special emphasis on sermon CCCLV and on the sections of their rule that imply educational responsibility. Odo of St. Victor builds his advice about canonical reputation around borrowings from sermon CCCLV;[63] and the author of the *Expositio* uses sermon CCCLV to gloss the portion of the Rule that discusses the impact of gait and bearing.[64] In the *Expositio,* the Bridlington Dialogue, and even in Richard of St. Victor's *De questionibus,* the portion of the Rule that discusses clothing, the gaze of others, and bearing is expounded in such a way as to emphasize the canon's responsibility for his effect.[65] Moreover, Adam of Dryburgh not only glosses this passage in a similar way;[66] he also deliberately returns to the passage several times in the course of his commentary, using it to emphasize the canon's impact on others.[67] It is the only passage from the Rule that he quotes out of order and more than once. The quotation from II Corinthians or Romans that Augustine used in sermon CCCLV becomes a major theme in Adam's treatment of behavior;[68] and he himself frequently joins the phrase *coram Deo, coram hominibus* to the Rule's injunction: ". . . let nothing be done that will offend the gaze of anyone . . . "[69] Just as Peter of Porto chooses to add to the Benedictine Rule a concern for edification, so Adam of Dryburgh chooses to find in his source a similar concern.

The monastic focus on the individual's responsibility for his own salvation appears to have come down to twelfth-century authors from the early Middle Ages.[70] Throughout the century, it proved so powerful that no monastic author broke away. Twelfth-century monastic texts differ greatly in their descriptions of this search for salvation. Some authors see the virtue of the individual monk in completely static terms;[71] others see the monk's search for God as a dynamic process.[72] Some monastic authors feel entirely at home with the focus on the individual.[73] Others seem to feel a tension between love of neighbor and the rise to God. They struggle to retain a focus on individual salvation while allowing some room for man's awareness of his brother.[74] But, regardless of these differences and regardless of some monastic uneasiness over the appeal of love of neighbor as an emotional commitment, no monastic author breaks completely out of the monastic focus to voice unambiguously the idea that a cloistered individual ought to educate his fellow man. In contrast, canonical authors of the twelfth century, although they share with monastic authors the goal of individual salvation, formulate a new understanding of their obligation toward their neighbor. An analysis of twelfth-century works of practical spiritual advice clearly reveals that canonical authors employed distinctive language, focused on new elements in the life of the cloister, and chose texts that would enhance their sense of moral responsibility.

## III. The Canonical Focus: Revival Or New Concern?

At first glance the sources on which canonical authors relied and the fact of the canons' clerical status might appear to explain the canonical perspective, to explain why canons broke away in part from a focus to which monks continued to adhere. Among the sources cited by twelfth-century canons, we can distinguish two groups that suggest the canonical focus: the patristic description of the preacher, and the treatment of reputation in the Augustinian Rule and sermon CCCLV. The first of these traditions, the cliché "teaching by word and example," was a conventional description of the preacher that went back to Gregory the Great's *Pastoral Care* (and before that to the gospels) and appeared regularly in twelfth-century sermons of advice for preachers.[75] Some twelfth-century canonical writings are clearly drawing on this tradition when they connect the phrase *docere verbo et exemplo* to preaching. The second of these groups of sources, Augustine's sermon CCCLV and the section of the Augustinian Rule that treats the effects of behavior, was part of a larger body of material that was especially emphasized by reformers of the clerical life in the late eleventh and twelfth centuries.[76] Quotations from this material are common in twelfth-century canonical writing. These two groups of texts, one might argue, contain in germ the focus that characterizes twelfth-century canonical thought. One might further argue that canons drew on these traditions because they were clerics by definition, whereas monks, who were not always in orders, ignored the "clerical" texts.

Although twelfth-century authors disagreed about what constituted clerical status, there is no question that canonical authors saw regular canons as clerics. Moreover, twelfth-century canons certainly saw the Augustinian Rule and Augustine's sermons on the life of clerics as "clerical" texts and as peculiarly their own. The tradition of advice to preachers undoubtedly also seemed, to some authors, to be a "clerical" tradition. Although clerical status in the twelfth century did not necessarily involve pastoral care or preaching, it is clear that some canonical (and indeed some monastic) authors saw clerical status as including the right to preach.[77] It is therefore likely that some canonical writers felt comfortable borrowing the language of this tradition of advice to preachers exactly because they felt that canons were clerics and, as clerics, preachers. The fact that the secular cleric Stephen of Paris is the only commentator on the Benedictine Rule to emphasize the obligation to teach *verbo et exemplo* or to use the phrase to describe ordinary monks supports the idea that authors who thought of themselves as clerics tended, perhaps subconsciously, to feel close to traditional descriptions of the preacher in a way that authors who were monks did not.[78] Thus it seems possible to argue that regular canons, because they considered themselves clerics, drew on certain "clerical" traditions that suggested both the idea of behavior as a support to effective verbal teaching and the idea of behavior as an agent of moral education in its own right.

This argument implies that canons merely revived, in the context of the older monastic emphasis on individual salvation, a readily available, clerical emphasis on preaching and on reputation. But such an argument is unsatisfactory as an explanation of the canonical concern with edification. The canonical perspective goes beyond anything suggested in the traditions on which regular canons drew. The phrase *verbo et exemplo, vita et doctrina* takes on in twelfth-century canonical authors a broader meaning than its earlier identification with preaching or with leadership. Several of the twelfth-century authors who explicitly use the phrase have in mind not preaching but rather ordinary human intercourse either inside or outside the cloister. They have transferred a sense of responsibility for edification from one role, that of preacher, to another role, that of the canon living a cloistered life (a role that might or might not include the role of preacher). The canonical concern for edification thus does not seem to be simply a union of traditional ideas of the preacher and traditional ideas of the monastic life. Some regular canons, such as Philip of Harvengt and the author of the Ottoboni compilation, borrow the phrase *verbo et exemplo* to describe preaching. But Peter of Porto and Hugh of St. Victor use the phrase to describe other human relationships. And Adam of Dryburgh, who does not use the phrase at all, treats words and actions as if they are agents of edification. The mere existence of a tradition for describing preaching does not explain why regular canons used that tradition to describe almost all human intercourse.

Moreover, the mere existence of certain phrases and ideas in a body of material that canons used for regulating their lives and for meditation does not explain why those phrases took on an importance in canonical writing. The fact that Adam of Dryburgh quotes a passage from the Rule is explained by the fact that he is commenting on the Rule; the fact that he emphasizes certain implications of that passage, and the fact that he returns repeatedly to cite the passage as a vehicle for conveying to others the ideas he sees there, is not explained simply by the commentary form or by the existence of the Rule itself. Twelfth-century canonical authors do not merely voice again a concern present in their sources since the early Middle Ages. Rather they make the Rule's vague references to reputation into explicit statements of an obligation to edify. What in the Rule is basically a concern with avoiding the negative effects of bad reputation becomes in many canonical writers a concern with offering to others the positive effects of good reputation.

The traditional monastic emphasis on individual salvation, the traditional description of the preacher, a few phrases in the Augustinian Rule and sermon CCCLV — we cannot add these three elements together and come up with the conception of obligation that we find in twelfth-century canonical treatises. What twelfth-century canons were voicing was something new: a sense of the individual's responsibility for his fellows, both within and outside the cloister. Because of this new concern, canons turned to traditions that provided language for speaking of the concern, traditions that pointed beyond the monastic focus. Because of their clerical status, they found it easy to borrow from these particularly useful traditions. But the source of the new concern did not lie in the traditions that were borrowed or in the clerical status of the borrowers.[79]

Like most genuinely new concerns in a conservative and traditional society, the shift in focus that we find in canonical, but not monastic, texts is subtle. Canonical authors did not call attention to this change: they spoke in a new way without any clear sense that it was something new. They felt a commitment to educate others that was no longer attached to the role of the preacher or leader, a commitment that gave a new importance to example as well as speech. But the new commitment rested easily alongside the search for individual salvation. The new focus did not replace the old. It did not have to. If speech and action of themselves communicated, then each could be offered *coram hominibus* as well as *coram Deo*. The ordinary brother in the cloister could serve his fellow man and his God by what he was, what he said, and what he did.

The basic distinction between monks and regular canons, which historians have sought in actual practices, in polemical stance, and in articulated conceptions of the spiritual life, thus seems to lie in the area of semi-conscious attitudes and assumptions. Although frequently living similar lives, regular canons and monks understood in very different ways the significance of what they did and the responsibilities entrusted to them. Once we understand correctly the nature of the difference between canonical and monastic spirituality, we realize that the traditional view of the place of canons in twelfth-century history must be revised. Throughout the century, isolated individuals, who sometimes were (or became) both monks and canons, engaged in wandering preaching, in pastoral work, and in the care of pilgrims, the sick, and the poor. There were many such individuals, but we cannot identify them, as a group, as either canons or monks. These actions were new, wherever they appeared; they were not, however, "monastic" or "canonical." The majority of canons, like the majority of monks, only rarely joined actual service of men in the world to the discipline of cloistered withdrawal. What is new and distinctive about the canons as a group is not their actions or the rights they claimed. It is simply the quality of their awareness, their sense of responsibility for the edification of their fellow men. In this awareness we find a note not heard in the older traditions to which twelfth-century monks clung. And it is in this new sense of responsibility for moral education that the writings and thought of the regular canons point to the future.

# NOTES

1. I would like to thank Prof. Giles Constable and Dr. Stephen D. White of Harvard University, who read drafts of this article and made valuable suggestions.
2. See, for example, Marie-Dominique Chenu, "Moines, clercs, laïcs: au carrefour de la vie évangélique," in Chenu, *La théologie au douzième siècle* (Etudes de la philosophie médiévale, XLV; Paris, 1957), pp. 225-251; and Ernest W. McDonnell, "The *Vita Apostolica:* Diversity or Dissent?" *Church History,* XXIV (1955), 15-31.
3. See, for example, Marie Humbert Vicaire, *L'imitation des apôtres: moines, chanoines, mendiants (IVe-XIIIe siècles)* (Paris, 1963), pp. 62-66; and R. W. Southern, *Western Society and the Church in the Middle Ages* (The Pelican History of the Church, II; Harmondsworth, Middlesex, England, 1970), pp. 240-250.
4. C. Dereine, "Vie commun, règle de saint Augustin, et chanoines réguliers au XIe siècle," *Revue d'histoire ecclésiastique,* XLI (1946), 365; *idem,* "L'élaboration du statut canonique des chanoines réguliers spécialement sous Urbain II," *Rev. d'hist. ecclés.,* XLVI (1951), 563-564; *idem,* "Chanoines," *Dictionnaire d'histoire et de géographie ecclésiastiques,* XII (Paris, 1953), cols. 401-403; J. Chatillon, "La spiritualité canoniale," *Saint Chrodegang: communications présentées au colloque tenu à Metz à l'occasion du douzième centenaire de sa mort* (Metz, 1967), p. 120; François Petit, *La spiritualité des Prémontrés au XIIe et XIIIe siècles* (Paris, 1947), pp. 266-267; *idem, La réforme des prêtres du moyen-âge: pauvreté et vie commun: textes choisis . . .* (Paris, 1968), pp. 18-20, 157-159.
5. J. Leclercq, "La spiritualité des chanoines réguliers," *La vita comune del clero nei secoli XI e XII: atti della settimana di studio: Mendola, settembre 1959* (Miscellanea del centro di studi medioevali, III; Milan, 1962), I, 134.
6. In addition to the articles cited above in n. 4, see Charles Dereine, *Les chanoines réguliers au diocese de Liège avant saint Norbert* (Académie royale de Belgique: classe des lettres . . . , Mémoires in-8°, XLVII.I; Brussels, 1952); *idem,* "Les origines de Prémontré," *Rev. d'hist. ecclés.,* XLII (1947) 352-378; *idem,* "Les coutumiers de saint-Quentin de Beauvais et de Springiersbach," *Rev. d'hist. ecclés., XLIII (1948),* 411-442; *idem,* "La spiritualité 'apostolique' des premiers fondateurs d'Afflighem (1083-1100)," *Rev. d'hist. ecclés.,* LIV (1959), 41-65.
7. On the text found in MS Ottoboni Lat. 175, see Appendix under "Canonical treatises parallel to commentaries . . ."
8. Philibert Schmitz, *Histoire de l'ordre de saint Benoit* (Maredsous, 1942-1956), I, 264-265.
9. See John Compton Dickinson, *The Origins of the Austin Canons and Their Introduction into England* (London, 1950), especially pp. 73 and 76; Dereine, in *Dict. d'hist. et de géogr. ecclés.,* XII, cols. 391-395; and *idem, Liège,* pp. 30-31.
10. U. Berlière, "L'exercice du ministère paroissial par les moines du XIIe au XVIIe siècles," *Revue bénédictine,* XXXIX (1927), 340-364; G. Constable, "The Second Crusade as Seen by Contemporaries," "Appendix A," *Traditio,* IX (1953), 276-278; P. Hofmeister, "Mönchtum und Seelsorge bis zum 13. Jahrhundert," *Studien und Mitteilungen zur Geschichte des Benediktiner-Ordens und seiner Zweige,* LXV (1955), 209-273; F. J. Schmale, "Kanonie, Seelsorge, Eigenkirche," *Historisches Jahrbuch,* LXXVIII (1959), 38-63; M. Peuchmaurd, "Le prêtre ministre de la parole dans la théologie du XIIe siècle (canonistes, moines et chanoines)," *Recherches de théologie ancienne et médiévale,* XXIX (1962), 52-76.
11. In "Discussione," *La vita comune,* I, 136-137, Dereine and Leclercq differed briefly over whether the establishment of hospitals might be particularly "canonical." The question has not been explored in depth.
12. On this controversial literature, see Dereine in *Rev. d'hist. ecclés.,* XLVI, 558-564; Peuchmaurd in *Rech. de théol anc. et méd.,* XXIX, 52-76; and Giles Constable, *Monastic Tithes from Their Origins to the Twelfth Century* (Cambridge Studies in Medieval Life and Thought, new ser. 10; Cambridge, England, 1964), pp. 136-185 *passim.*
13. Vicaire, *L'imitation,* p. 62.
14. Petit, *La spiritualité des Prémontrés,* p. 266.
15. In addition, P. Classen has suggested ("Discussione," *La vita comune,* I, 140) that one should distinguish from "monastic theology" a "canonical theology" with a special interest in the sacraments. But, although certain interests are clearly common to a number of Victorines, and certain interests are common to a number of Premonstratensians, I see no convincing reason at the moment for identifying a "canonical" theology.
16. See, for example, F. Petit, "L'ordre de Prémontré de saint Norbert à Anselme de Havelberg," *La vita comune,* I, 476-478.
17. J. Chatillon, "Contemplation, action et prédication d'après un sermon inédit de Richard de saint-Victor . . . ," *L'homme devant Dieu: mélanges offerts au Père Henri de Lubac* (Paris, 1964), II, 89-98. Leclercq in *La vita comune,* I, 117-135, implies that this is true for the late eleventh century. The texts cited in Petit, *Réforme des prêtres,* pp. 77-109, would also suggest this, although Petit does not argue the point.
18. See, for example, Philip of Harvengt, *De obedientia,* xxxi-xxxvi, PL 203, cols. 905-921; Adam of Dryburgh, *De tripartito tabernaculo,* III, xiii-xv, PL 198, cols. 773-780; Richard of St. Victor, *De questionibus regule sancti Augustini solutis,* xiv, ed. in M. L. Colker, "Richard of St. Victor and the Anonymous of Bridlington," *Traditio,* XVIII

(1962), 216; and Richard of St. Victor, *Liber exceptionum*, Part II, Book XIV, chapter v, ed. J. Chatillon (Paris, 1958), pp. 503-504.

19. See, for example, Aelred of Rievaulx, Sermon XVII, PL 195, cols. 303-309.
20. Leclercq in *La vita comune*, I, 117-135.
21. The discussion of canonical and monastic spirituality that occupies the remainder of this article is based on a close analysis of the treatises listed in the Appendix. It is not possible in this article to give a full discussion of problems of dating, authenticity, etc., that pertain to individual treatises, nor is it possible to provide a lengthy justification for the decision to include certain texts as parallel. In my doctoral thesis, *"Docere Verbo et Exemplo:* An Aspect of Twelfth Century Spirituality" (Harvard University, unpub. diss., 1969), which I am preparing for publication, I have analyzed these treatises in more detail and given fuller documentation for the argument summarized here.
22. Peter of Celle's *De disciplina* contains several suggestions that the monk should be concerned about the effect of his behavior or words *(De disc.,* iii, iv and viii, PL 202, cols. 1104D-1107B and 1114A); the most important of these is *De disc.,* iii-iv, PL 202, cols. 1104D-1106A. But Peter's occasional lapses from the monastic focus may be partly explained by the fact that he addresses canons as well as monks. Arnulf of Bohéries's *Speculum* contains one phrase that clearly departs from the monastic focus *(Speculum,* PL 184, col. 1176A). In Stephen of Salley's *Speculum novitii,* the basic perspective is definitely monastic: the author is concerned with virtue as an aspect of the soul's appearance before God; the only relationship discussed at any length is that between the soul and Christ. There are, however, a few references to avoiding the unedifying effects of behavior or enhancing the edifying effects: *Spec. nov.,* i and xviii, ed. Mikkers, *Coll. ord. Cist. Ref.,* VIII, 45-46 and 61.
23. *Studi Gregoriani,* VI, 218-219.
24. *Regula clericorum,* I, ii and xxvii; PL 163, cols. 708C-D, 709C, and 718B.
25. Hugh, *De institutione,* iv, PL 176, col. 928A.
26. Odo, Letter II, PL 196, col. 1404; Letter IV, PL 196, cols. 1406-1408; Letter V, PL 196, cols. 1409-1411.
27. See n. 33 below.
28. *Expositio,* vi, vii, and ix, PL 176, cols. 897C-898C, 901D, 902A-C, 909, 910D, and 912B.
29. Preface, MS Vienna 2207, fols. 11ᵛ and 13 bisᵛ-14ʳ.
30. Adam of Dryburgh, *De ordine,* sermon II and sermon VI, PL 198, cols. 457-460 and 489-494.
31. *Bridl. Dial.,* pp. 39, 112, 130, 141, 173-174, and 187. Richard of St. Victor, *De questionibus,* i, ed. Colker, *Traditio,* XVIII, 203-204; *De ques.,* xiii, *Traditio,* XVIII, 214-215; and *De ques.,* xx, *Traditio,* XVIII, 223. Whatever emphasis on verbal or non-verbal teaching there is in Richard's commentary is very faint. It should be noted, however, that Richard's treatise is not really a work of moral and spiritual advice that ranges over the entire Augustinian Rule, but rather a discussion of twenty questions of a practical nature concerning the daily life of regular canons.
32. *Studi Gregoriani,* VI, 181-182.
33. For example, Philip of Harvengt, *De scientia,* xxiii, xxvii and xxix, PL 203, cols. 695B-C, 699C-700C, and 702A-D; *De justitia,* xlii, PL 203, col. 719A-B; *De silentio,* lxxvi and lxxxviii, PL 203, cols. 1102C and 1123B-1124A.
34. The compilation in MS Ottoboni Lat. 175 *(Studi Gregoriani,* VI, 181-182 and 218), the commentary in MS Vienna 2207 (Preface, MS Vienna 2207, fol. 13 bisᵛ-14ʳ), the Bridlington commentary *(Bridl. Dial.,* pp. 99 and 134-135), Philip of Harvengt's *De institutione (De scientia,* PL 203, cols. 693-708), and Richard of St. Victor's sermon on Gregory the Great (see excerpts in Chatillon, "Contemplation, action et prédication . . .," *L'homme devant Dieu,* II, 89-98) all devote attention to preaching. The only Benedictine commentaries to consider preaching are the commentary of Stephen of Paris, which was written not by a monk but by a secular cleric (see n. 78 below), and Peter the Deacon's odd and derivative compilation, the *Exhortatorium (Bibl. Cas.,* V, *Flor.,* 66b-67b).
35. Rupert, *In regulam,* PL 170, cols. 515-517, 532, 534.
36. Preface, MS Vienna 2207, fol. 14ʳ.
37. Joachim, *Tractatus,* i, xii, xiii-xv, and xxxvii, ed. Baraut, *Anal. sacra tarr.,* XXIV, 42, 61, 63-70, and 105.
38. *De institutione,* iii, PL 176, col. 927C.
39. See Philip, *De dignitate,* ii, PL 203, cols. 669D-670B.
40. *Instructio,* tr. by Knowles, *Constitutions of Lanfranc,* p. 143ʳ, text p. 143ᵛ.
41. Bernard, *De gradibus,* iii, *Opera,* ed. Leclercq, III, 20-21.
42. Bernard, *De gradibus,* xiv, *Opera,* ed. Leclercq, III, 48-49.
43. Aelred, *Speculum,* II, xxiv, PL 195, col. 573B; and III, iv-vi, xii, and xxiv, PL 195, cols. 579-583, 588B-D, and 597A-B.
44. See Aelred, *Speculum,* I, iii-v, PL 195, cols. 507-510; and Hugh, *De institutione,* prologue, PL 176, cols. 925-926.
45. See, for example, *Bridl. Dial.,* pp. 135-136.
46. See above n. 22. The only exception to the monastic approach to silence is Peter the Deacon, who borrows from Smaragdus *(Diadema monachorum,* xxxviii, PL 102, cols. 633C-634A) a passage which states that monks must sometimes speak for the sake of the spiritual health of others and omits the second portion of the same chapter which concludes that keeping silence is safest: see Peter, *Expositio,* Bibl. Cas., V, *Flor.,* 129.
47. *De novitiis instruendis,* MS Douai 827, fols. 77ʳ-78ʳ.
48. MS Auxerre 50, fols. 20ᵛ.b-22ʳ.a. See especially fols. 21ᵛ.b-22ʳ.a.
49. Peter of Celle, *De disciplina,* xviii, PL 202, cols. 1124B-1125D. See n. 22 above.
50. Cf. Philip, *De silentio,* i, PL 203, cols. 945C-946A, with *De silentio,* xiv, PL 203, cols. 969A-970C, and *De silentio,* xxii, PL 203, col. 981D.
51. Hugh, *De institutione,* xiv, PL 176, col. 945B-D.
52. Preface, MS Vienna 2207, fol. 13 bisᵛ-14ʳ.
53. *Regula clericorum,* I, xxxii-xxxvi, PL 163, cols. 720-722. See also *Reg. cler.,* I, ii, xxii and xxiii, PL 163, cols. 709B-C, 716, and 717A.
54. For example, chapter ii of the *De vitae ordine* (PL 184, cols. 562D-565C) is borrowed from Ambrose's *De officiis ministrorum,* PL 16, cols. 43-49, with omissions; chapter iii, PL 184, cols. 567D-568A, is from the *De officiis,* PL 16,

col. 49; chapter iii, PL 184, cols. 568A-B, is from the *De officiis*, PL 16, col. 54; chapter iv, PL 184, the last sentence in col. 568 and the next few sentences, could be derived either from Ambrose's *Exhortatio virginitatis*, I, xiii, paragraph 87, PL 16, cols 361D-362A, or from the *De officiis*, PL 16, col. 43 and col. 26B. Much of chapter iv, paragraph 12, PL 184, col. 569B is from the *De officiis*, PL 16, col. 33A-D; the first few sentences in chapter iv, paragraph 13, are from the *De officiis*, PL 16, col. 28A; other sentences in chapter iv, paragraph 13, are from the *De officiis*, Pl 16, col. 27A.

55. Peter's text in *Bibl. Cas.*, V, *Flor.*, 68a-71a, is borrowed from a sermon of Hildebert, which is numbered 97 in the Migne ed. (PL 171, cols. 786-790), and 9 in André Wilmart, "Les sermons d'Hildebert," *Revue bénédictine*, XLVII (1935), 33. See P. Meyvaert, "The Exegetical Treatises of Peter the Deacon and Eriugena's Latin Rendering of the *Ad Thalassium* of Maximus the Confessor," *Sacris erudiri: Jaarboek voor Godsdienstwetenschappen*, XIV (1963), 145.

56. *Studi Gregoriani*, VI, 190, 191, and 197.

57. See especially Benedict of Nursia, *Regula* (hereafter *RB*), lxxii, ed. R. Hanslik (Corpus scriptorum ecclesiasticorum latinorum, LXXV; Vienna, 1960), 162-163; see also *RB*, lxxi, ed. Hanslik, 161-162.

58. The only references to any kind of verbal aid are the vague reference to the consoling of the sorrowful in the instruments of good works (*RB*, iv, ed. Hanslik, 30, para. 19) and the references to encouraging each other upon rising in chapter xxii (*RB*, ed. Hanslik, 78, para. 8). There is a reference to evil conduct as a scandal in *RB*, xxxi, ed. Hanslik, 89, para. 16. My interpretation of the Rule comes much closer to that of Adalbert de Vogüé, *La communauté et l'abbé dans la règle de saint Benoît* (Paris, 1960) than to the classic interpretation of Cuthbert Butler, *Benedictine Monachism: Studies in Benedictine Life and Rule*, 2nd ed. (Cambridge, England, 1924).

59. *Reg. cler.*, I, ii, PL 163, cols. 708C-D and 709B-C.

60. *Praeceptum*, ed. [Melchoir] Luc Verheijen, *La règle de saint Augustin*, 2 vols. (Paris, 1967), I, 426-428, lines 106-133, especially *La règle*, I, 426-427, lines 115-119.

61. *Praeceptum*, ed. Verheijen, *La règle*, I, 423, lines 78-83.

62. Augustine, Sermon CCCLV, in *Sermones selecti duodeviginti*, ed. C. Lambot (Stromata patristica et mediaevalia, I; Utrecht, 1950), p. 124.

63. Odo quotes from Augustine's sermon CCCLV in Letter V, PL 196, col. 1411; all of Letter V (*ibid.*, cols. 1409-1411) is strikingly similar to sermon CCCLV.

64. *Expositio*, vi, PL 176, cols. 897C-898C.

65. *Ibid.* Also *Bridl. Dial.*, p. 130, and Richard of St. Victor, *De questionibus*, xiii, ed. Colker, *Traditio*, XVIII, 214-215.

66. Adam of Dryburgh, *De ordine*, sermon II, PL 198, cols. 457C-460D.

67. *Ibid.*, col. 459A; sermon VI, PL 198, col. 489C and 492B; sermon X, PL 198, col. 534A. The latter quotation occurs in the normal course of commenting on the Rule. Sermon XIV, PL 198, col. 605A-B, is strongly reminiscent of the same phrases.

68. The words from Paul are quoted in sermon II, PL 198, col. 459A; sermon III, PL 198, col. 463C; sermon IV, PL 198, col. 489B; sermon X, PL 198, col. 534B. The contrast *coram Deo, coram hominibus* is echoed throughout the sermons. See, for example, sermon III, PL 198, col. 461D; and sermon XIV, PL 198, col. 605B.

69. See sermon X, PL 198, col. 534; and sermon II, PL 198, cols. 457C-460D.

70. Jean Leclercq, *Initiation aux auteurs monastiques du moyen âge: l'amour des lettres et le désir de Dieu*, 2nd ed. (Paris, 1963).

71. For example, the commentary on the Rule from Pontigny, MS Auxerre 50, fols. 1ʳ-125ʳ.

72. Bernard, *De gradibus, Opera*, ed. Leclercq, III, 12-59.

73. For example, John of Fruttuaria, *De vitae ordine*, PL 184, cols. 559-584; and Peter the Deacon, *Expositio, Bibl. Cas.*, V, *Flor.*, 82-165.

74. Particularly Aelred, *Speculum*, PL 195, cols. 505-620.

75. J. Leclercq, "Le magistère du prédicateur au XIIIe siècle," *Archives d'histoire doctrinale et littéraire du moyen âge*, XV (1946), 105.

76. Verheijen, *La règle*, II, 215; Dereine in *Rev. d'hist. ecclés.*, XLI, 385-401; and *idem*, *Liège*, pp. 23-27.

77. See n. 12 above.

78. Stephen reveals a non-monastic focus in two ways. First, he wanders away from his ostensible subject to explicit discussions of clerics and preaching (MS Clm. 3029, fols. [63ᵛ.b-64ʳ.a], and [116ʳ.a-118ᵛ.b]). Second, he suggests that *monks* have a responsibility to teach by word and example (MS Clm. 3029, fols. [46ʳ.a-b], [80ᵛ.a-81ᵛ.b], [82ᵛ.a-83ᵛ.a], and [106ᵛ.a-107ʳ.a]).

79. This is not, of course, to argue that regular canons invented the new concern for neighbor that lies behind their concern for edification. As other historians have pointed out, such a concern seems to underlie many of the characteristics of eleventh and twelfth-century religious movements. See n. 2 above.

# APPENDIX:

## Monastic and Canonical Treatises of Practical Spiritual Advice

Unless otherwise noted, the treatises are from the twelfth century and are listed in chronological order within each category (see n. 21 above).

Commentaries on the Benedictine Rule: Rupert of Deutz, *Super quaedam capitula regulae divi Benedicti abbatis,* PL 170, cols. 447-538. Peter the Deacon of Monte Cassino, *Expositio super regulam sancti Benedicti,* 3 books, in the monks of Monte Cassino, *Bibliotheca Casinensis,* V (Monte Cassino, 1894), *Florilegium,* 82-165; and *idem, Explanatio brevis,* in *Bibl. Cas.,* V, *Flor.,* 165-174. Hildegard of Bingen, *Explanatio regulae sancti Benedicti,* PL 197, cols. 1053-1066. Joachim of Flora, *Tractatus de vita sancti Benedicti et de officio secundum eius doctrinam,* in C. Baraut, "Un tratado inédito de Joaquín de Fiore: *De vita sancti Benedicti . . .,*" *Analecta sacra tarraconensia,* XXIV (1951), 33-122. Stephen of Paris, *Expositio super regulam beati Benedicti,* which I have consulted in MS Clm. 3029, fols. 1r-161r. [Commentary on the Benedictine Rule from Pontigny] (late twelfth or early thirteenth century) in MS Auxerre 50, fols. 1r-125r, portions of which have been published in C. H. Talbot, "A Cistercian Commentary on the Benedictine Rule," *Studia Anselmiana,* XLIII, *Analecta monastica,* 5 ser. (1958), 102-159, and *idem,* "The Commentary on the Rule from Pontigny," *Studia monastica,* III (1961), 77-122; my study of this commentary is based on Mr. Talbot's transcript of the entire work, which he very kindly lent to me.

Commentaries on the Augustinian Rule: [Anonymous, attributed to Hugh of St. Victor and Letbert of St. Rufus,] *Expositio in regulam beati Augustini,* PL 176, cols. 881-924 (abbreviated *Expositio* above). Richard of St. Victor, *De questionibus regule sancti Augustini solutis,* in M. L. Colker, "Richard of St. Victor and the Anonymous of Bridlington," *Traditio,* XVIII (1962), 181-227. [Bridlington Anonymous or Robert of Bridlington,] *The Bridlington Dialogue: An Exposition of the Rule of St. Augustine for the Life of the Clergy . . . ,* ed. A Religious of C.S.V.M. [Sister Penelope] (London, 1960). Adam of Dryburgh [or Adam Scot], *Liber de ordine, habitu et professione canonicorum ordinis praemonstratensis,* PL 198, cols. 439-610. Anonymous, Prologue and Preface *in regulam beati Augustini* (twelfth century), MS Vienna, Nationalbibliothek, 2207, fols. 8v-16v.

Monastic treatises for novices: John of Fruttuaria ( + ca. 1050), *Liber de vitae ordine et morum institutione,* PL 184, cols. 559-584, portions of which have been re-edited in André Wilmart, *Auteurs spirituels et textes dévots du moyen âge latin: études d'histoire littéraire* (Paris, 1932), 93-98. Anonymous, *De novitiis instruendis* (twelfth or early thirteenth century), MS Douai 827, fols. 60v-80r, portions of which have been published in Leclercq, "Deux opuscules sur la formation des jeunes moines," *Revue d'ascétique et de mystique,* XXXIII (1957), 387-399. Adam of Perseigne, "Letter to Osmond," in *Lettres,* ed. J. Bouvet, I (Sources chrétiennes, LXVI; Paris, 1960), 110-129 (see also *Correspondance d'Adam, abbé de Perseigne (1188-1221),* ed. J. Bouvet, *Archives historiques du Maine,* XIII, fasc. 4 [1955], 62-77, and PL 211, cols. 583-589); and "Letter to G. of Pontigny," PL 211, cols. 614-623 (see also *Correspondance* in *Archives du Maine,* XIII, fasc. 9 [1959], 503-523). Anonymous, *Instructio novitiorum secundum consuetudinem ecclesiae cantuariensis* (eleventh, twelfth or thirteenth century), MS Corpus Christi College, Cambridge, 441, pp. 359b-391a, portions of which have been published in *The Monastic Constitutions of Lanfranc,* ed. D. Knowles (London, 1951), pp. 133-149. Stephen of Salley ( + 1252), *Speculum novitii,* in Edmond Mikkers, "Un 'Speculum novitii' inédit d'Etienne de Salley," *Collectanea ordinis Cisterciensium Reformatorum,* VIII (1946), 17-68.

Canonical treatises for novices: Hugh of St. Victor, *De institutione novitiorum,* PL 176, cols. 925-952.

Monastic works parallel to commentaries and treatises for novices: Bernard of Clairvaux, *De gradibus humilitatis,* in *Sancti Bernardi opera,* III, ed. J. Leclercq and H. M. Rochais (Rome, 1963), 12-59, and Bernard, *De praecepto et dispensatione,* in *Sancti Bernardi opera,* III, 243-294. Peter Abelard, *Epistola VIII,* in T. P. McLaughlin, "Abelard's Rule for Religious Women," *Medieval Studies,* XVIII (1956), 241-292. Peter the Deacon, *Exhortatorium . . . ad monachos . . . ,* in *Bibl. Cas.,* V, *Flor.,* 61-72. Aelred of Rievaulx, *Speculum caritatis,* PL 195, cols. 505-620. Peter of Celle, *Tractatus de disciplina claustrali,* PL 202, cols. 1097-1146. Arnulf of Bohéries, *Speculum monachorum* (ca. 1200), PL 184, cols. 1175-1178.

Canonical treatises parallel to commentaries and treatises for novices: Anonymous, Compilation of texts relating to regular canons (late eleventh or early twelfth century), MS Ottoboni Lat. 175 of the Vatican Library, portions of which are published in J. Leclercq, "Un témoignage sur l'influence de Gregoire VII dans la réforme canoniale," *Studi Gregoriani,* VI (1959-1961), 181-223. Peter [of Porto] (?), *Regula clericorum,* PL 163, cols. 703-784. Odo of St. Victor, *Epistolae de observantia canonicae professione recte praestanda,* PL 196, cols. 1399-1418. Philip of Harvengt, *De institutione clericorum,* PL 203, cols. 665-1206.

# Some Unorthodox Popular Ideas of the Thirteenth Century

*Walter L. Wakefield*

$A$T THE TIME that the Dominican friars, Ranulph of Plassac and Pons of Parnac, began to act as inquisitors at Toulouse, about 1270-1273,[1] the tribunal was on the way to victory over the great heresies it had been organized to combat. Depositions collected by Ranulph, Pons, and their colleagues from more than eighty persons[2] show that Waldenses were no more to be found in the region and the Cathars were in confusion and disarray. Most of the Good Men had fled the land, leaving their believers to lament the lack of spiritual consolation.[3]

It is not the state of the once flourishing Catharist heresy which concerns us here, but a handful of cases which, perhaps, did not arise from that dualist sect: six in which the suspects could be questioned directly, one in which there was a detailed report from a Dominican colleague, and two in which we know only what was said by informers. They are different from all others in the register of interrogations in that the inquisitors seem not to have seen reason to suspect an active connection with Cathars and also because when the persons involved were directly before them, the judges pressed questions about what they had said or thought. Such interrogation in detail was not a common practice among thirteenth-century inquisitors, who were more interested in guilty associations than beliefs and asked, at most, perfunctory questions about what had been heard from heretical teachers and whether it was believed to be true.[4]

The replies disclosed doubts about orthodox doctrine and practices, gibes that had been uttered about sacred matters, and certain material-

25

istic or rationalistic explanations of natural phenomena. Unfortunately, we cannot know what the inquisitors' conclusions were, for none of their sentences in these or other cases in the register are now known. But we may ourselves raise the question: were the attitudes thus disclosed in the 1270's the product of Catharist propaganda, as has usually been assumed? Or were they, perhaps, indicative of a popular unorthodoxy?

The first case is that of Durandus de Ruffiaco de Olmeria, diocese of Rodez, who was, perhaps, a merchant. Called before the inquisitors on October 9, 1273 on the basis of information received, he denied any recent knowledge of Cathars or Waldenses. Ranulph of Plassac, presiding, did not press that point, but turned to various remarks Durandus was reported to have made. The man at first attempted to avoid answering but eventually gave in, denying the truth of some of the allegations, for others seeking to explain the circumstances and intent of his words.[5] These are the statements attributed to him, with his reply placed in parentheses.

The soul is nothing other than the blood in the body. (This was a jest, made in the marketplace one day, when an acquaintance had jokingly said to Durandus and a companion, "You should pay attention to your souls, for surely you take good care of your bodies." Durandus had replied in like vein, "Do you think there is any soul in the body other than the blood?")

Even if the body of Christ were large as a mountain, it would long ago have all been eaten up by priests. (He had said that once but did not believe it now.)

It is stupid to forego profit out of fear of committing a sin. (He had said that once, in the presence of Grimaldus de Olmeria, a cleric,[6] but now he believed that usury and illicit gain were sins.)[7]

Men had forced the Blessed Lawrence and other saints to go unwillingly to martyrdom. (He had said this once in the presence of the same Grimaldus but now believed that Lawrence had suffered voluntarily for his faith).

Vegetation grows not by the direct act of God but because of moisture and decay in the soil. (What he had said was that grain will not sprout unless first the seed rots.).[8]

His own house had as much virtue as the church of St. Salvina in the diocese of Albi, to which men went on pilgrimage. (He had once wondered aloud to Grimaldus what the pilgrims hoped to find. Why did they not seek out Peter or John, saints who had been closer to Christ?)

When young, he had repeatedly made the sign of the cross without

26

good effect; having foregone the practice as an adult, he enjoyed much good fortune. (Durandus could not recall having said this.)

God's power was by no means as great as preachers claimed it to be. (The reply strikes a poignant note. When Durandus' son traveled with merchants to Alessandria, the father prayed night and day for his return, then learned that the youth was dead. In his sorrow, he had exclaimed that it was of no more use to beseech God for something than not to do so.)[9]

Another man, Gausbertus de Aula, of the diocese of Cahors, was arrested for cruder offenses. Brought from prison on October 31, 1273 and again on November 3, he confessed to making a scatological joke which associated "the gods which make thunder and rain" with parts of the human body. When someone had asked him if he would put his trust in God and His mother, he replied in jest, "Yes, on good security." He also admitted defiling cemeteries, but pleaded weakness of the bladder as excuse. He and his wife had quarreled with their curé about the use of wax candles, and he had said that he "did not give a straw" for the cleric's opinion. He had ridiculed a newly built church as no holier than the implements that built it. He had said he owed no thanks to God or to anyone else for the temporal goods his own labor brought him. He found no virtue in anything but his own tools and strength. Also, he had said that grain and wine and other things come from the rotting of the earth.[10]

Bernardus de Soulhaco, a peasant from the region of Montauban, had been abusive of sacred things, as was revealed in a letter from the Dominican prior of Montauban in October 1276. The inquisitors had asked the prior to investigate for them. Bernardus had derided the consecrated host as nothing but baked dough, such as he had in good supply in his cupboard; if the body of Christ had been as large as Mount Vinhar it would long since have been consumed. Nor would God demean himself by putting himself in the hands of false priests. One need confess sins only to God. Bernardus himself would not confess, even if he had had carnal knowledge of every woman in the village, nor, if he had money to lend, would he think usury a sin. The faith of Saracens and Jews was better than that of Christians. It would be less sinful to kill Christian strangers or all the men of Limoges or Burgundy than to kill three Jews.[11]

Ademarus Galofi was sent to the inquisitors from Castres because he had been heard to say that God did not make human eyes, hands, or other bodily features. On May 25, 1275, he told them that his actual words had been that men's sight, hearing, and perception could not be the direct gifts of God, who, however, permitted them to develop. His reasoning: Nothing God bestows can be lost, the senses are lost at death, therefore, they are not God's gifts. Also, from his own cogitations, he had reached the conclusion that we could not be resurrected in these earthly bodies but would receive others from God. That belief he had already abandoned, after instruction from the Dominican prior at Castres.[12]

Isambardus de Sancto Antonio, in the Rouergue, had been reported to have exclaimed, when a friar announced after Mass that he would say a few words about God, "The fewer the better." Isambertus denied it. He had only said in a whisper to those near him, "This friar preaches a long sermon." He denied knowledge of the Cathars. An accusation that he had impeded collection of offerings in the church he denied also, saying that he only repeated what he had been told by a friar, that it was neither necessary nor lawful to make offerings for the souls of children, since they died in innocence. He had been guilty of employing a worker of spells for his wife, who believed that her barrenness was caused by sorcery, but he had already confessed that.[13]

Petrus Eugrini de Podiodanielis, diocese of Toulouse, on January 10, 1276, told his interrogator that he knew nothing of Cathars or Waldenses. Of "many things" alleged against him, he admitted only having been told by his wife that a man often appeared to her in the guise of a pilgrim, saying he was St. James and assuring her that the souls of the dead, children and saints excepted, did not enter paradise until Judgment Day, but went to a certain place of rest.[14]

The words of certain other men are known only through reports about them to the inquisitors. An archpriest told them of Raymundus Arnoldi de Antunhacho, who had said that if the body of Christ were in the host, it would have been eaten by a century ago. He had ridiculed the Mass as a profit-making invention of priests, but, when reproved, he said he was only joking.[15] Another priest reported that when he was sprinkling holy water in the cemetery at La Garde Pontius de Montibus had ridiculed him, saying, "One donkey could carry all the good that does for the dead." Pontius had argued that only a man's own deeds bring him benefit. Perhaps if children sought the welfare of a deceased parent, some good might result; the acts of others to that end were useless. Furthermore, Pontius had quarreled bitterly with the clergy over their proposal to bury his little granddaughter without candles and at that time had declared himself to be an absolute enemy of the church.[16]

Rather different from any of the foregoing is the case of an elderly merchant of Toulouse, Bernardus Raymundi de Baranhonis. In various appearances in September and November 1274 and in November 1275,[17] he denied knowledge of Cathars or Waldenses other than that fifty years earlier he had known a follower *(amicus)* of the latter and thirty years ago he had heard men speak respectfully of the Good Men. He had never asserted that the pope was neither head of the church nor had power to bind and loose, although he had said publicly what he had been told many years before, that Peter was never pope; rather, Christians had gathered his bones and placed them in the cathedral at Rome. He had also heard that Sylvester was the first pope.

Part of Bernardus Raymondi's troubles arose from the fact that he could read. He admitted possessing a copy of the New Testament with Latin and vernacular texts, which had been passed about for others to make copies. He also owned a life of St. Brandon. Both were handed over to the inquisitors. He denied owning a book containing a famous verse denouncing Rome, but he had heard the poem recited.[18] From his reading, he had drawn mixed conclusions. The vernacular version of John 3:13 led him to believe that no souls but Mary and John the Baptist entered paradise at death, yet because of the Lord's words to the thief on the cross, he thought souls did go to heaven at once. Then he had discovered in the life of St. Brandon that paradise was a place of repose in this world. That belief he gave up after his first confession to the inquisitors four years ago.

Thus, from a number of persons in various places in 1273-1276 come statements of unorthodox attitudes. The witnesses had shown themselves sometimes blunt of speech, sometimes capable of rough humor, often thoughtful, although most of them, no doubt, were illiterate. One or another had shown disrespect for sacred things by dirty jokes, defilement of cemeteries, disparagement of the reputed holiness of saints and shrines, skepticism about the sign of the cross, quarrels with priests over burial practices, restlessness at sermons, and disparagement of conventional attitudes towards Jews and usury. Such anticlericalism runs all through all forms of religious dissent in the Middle Ages. It was surely encouraged by Cathars and Waldenses. It also could easily be generated by peasant skepticism and the frictions of village life.

But these words and acts were also accompanied by more serious divergences from contemporary orthodoxy, statements often tinged with rationalism, skepticism, and revealing something of a materialistic attitude. There are assertions about a terrestrial paradise for souls after death and about the salvation of unbaptized children; the denial that God made human faculties; the derisory quip about the consumption of the host; the identification of the soul as blood; and the attribution of natural growth to the qualities of seed and soil alone. These were not all expressed by any one individual. They do not appear to represent a system or a creed. Most of them had been heard before 1270, and they remained in currency for at least half a century thereafter.

In that connection, a document of uncertain date, perhaps produced about 1300, may be noticed. It is a list of "articles in which modern heretics err," copied from a document once in the archives of the Inquisition at Carcassonne.[19] Sixteen tenets are listed: (1) the body of Christ on the altar is nothing but bread; (2) no priest in mortal sin can consecrate the body of Christ; (3) the soul is nothing but blood; (4) simple fornication is no sin; (5) all men will be saved; (6) no soul goes to a heavenly paradise before the Day of Judgment: (7) to lend at interest is not a sin; (8) a sentence of excommunication need not be dreaded; (9) one may as properly confess to a layman as to a priest; (10) the law of Jews is better than the law of Christians; (11) nature, not God, causes things to spring forth from the earth; (12) the Son of God did not take on true flesh from the Virgin but only its semblance; (13) the observance of Easter, the practice of confession, and penance were instituted only to permit the church to collect money; (14) one who is in mortal sin can neither excommunicate nor absolve; (15) no prelate can give any indulgence; (16) every one born of legitimate matrimony can be saved.

The list is a curious blend of undoubtedly Catharist teachings and others that are foreign to the "classic" Catharism of the early thirteenth century, as exposed by polemicists. We also recognize items similar to the testimony of 1273-1276.[20]

One might, at first glance, conclude that all these are products of Catharist teaching. Yet the inquisitors of 1273-1276 took the witnesses' disclaimers of knowledge of that sect at face value and asked no questions to shake their denial of acquaintance with the heretics. Thus, I undertook to search the literature on heresy, that is, the polemics of orthodox authorship and testimony before the Languedocian Inquisition, for other expressions like these.[21] The results are not conclusive but may justify questioning the extent of Catharist influence on such popularly held ideas.

The idea of a place of rest for souls before the Day of Judgment is said to have already appeared in the ninth century.[22] It was taken up by some of the Cathars, although with various interpretations (a place for all souls before judgment; for souls of the righteous; for Mary, apostles, saints, and the body which Christ had worn on earth, etc).[23] It cannot be limited to them, however. Passagians in twelfth-century Italy approached the same idea, perhaps, by arguing that no soul goes to heaven or hell before the Day of Judgment.[24] That there was a terrestrial paradise for souls after Purgatory has a place in the legends of St. Patrick and St. Brandon.[25] The concept of a terrestrial paradise was advanced by Cathar and non-Cathar[26] in the fourteenth century. Scholars' opinions on its place in Catharist thought are divided.[27]

The conviction that souls of unbaptized children may be saved was expressed outside of Catharist circles,[28] while the dualists insisted that children who did not reach the age of discretion to receive the consolamentum must be damned.[29] That attitude was softened eventually by the teaching that souls of children might pass from body to body until they received that spiritual baptism.[30] Belief in the salvation of children, however, continued to find spokesmen into the fourteenth century.[31]

The assertion that human senses cannot be of God's devising very likely reflects Catharist teaching. I have found it expressed (other than as described above)[32] only in a dualist context, in 1245 and again in the early fourteenth century.[33] Thus, it is probably not a coincidence that Ademarus Galofi also denied the resurrection of bodies, as did the Cathars, even though he claimed to have reasoned it out for himself.

The joking remark that if Christ's body were in the host, it would long ago have been consumed is attributed to Berengar of Tours.[34] Although it may not have represented his actual thought, it was thus heard in the eleventh century before Catharism was widespread in the West, anticipating the materialistic-rationalistic theme in the discussion of the Eucharist in following years. A sermon of 1230 seems to attribute the remark to Waldenses.[35] However, the Cathars had taken it up as early as 1163, as a welcome addition to the arsenal of argument and derison acquired from the Bogomils. It appears repeatedly thereafter in the polemical and inquisitorial literature into the fourteenth century.[36] Undoubtedly, the dualists gave it wide circulation, but it does not follow that all who repeated it, in skepticism or in jest, were also Cathars.

The statement that the soul is no more than the blood in the body did not originate with the Cathars. It has a much longer history;[37] furthermore, their teaching on the origin and eternity of souls was in flat contradiction.[38] Heretics of the middle of the thirteenth century who entertained an opinion perhaps analogous to this, that the soul dies with the body, almost certainly were not Cathars.[39] In inquisitional literature, the equation of soul with blood, in fact, appears relatively late. I have not seen it expressed earlier than 1273. Thereafter it crops up in testimony of peasants of the 1320s, who, however, do not seem to have been Catharist believers.[40] It was still being advanced as late as the fifteenth century.[41] If the Cathars had, indeed, taken it up,[42] it outlived them.

The role of good and evil principles, or of God and the devil, in producing vegetation and fruits of the earth was a matter of disagreement between factions of the Cathars committed either to "mitigated" or "absolute" dualism.[43] The former would admit that the "virtue" which produces growth comes from God.[44] That opinion was to continue to exist, in the early fourteenth century becoming the statement that God does this for the sake of the Good Men.[45] The converse, that natural growth is, like everything pertaining to this world, the work of the devil runs also to the fourteenth century.[46] A middle ground, explaining that vegetation and crops are produced by natural causes appears in the 1240s in Italian and Languedocian sources.[47] This became a formula — *Deus non faciebat florere et granare* — followed by an explanation that growth results from the nature of the seed and soil, moisture and the richness of the earth, or man's labor.[48] Arno Borst explains this conclusion by saying that out of the theological and philosophical problems in conflicting Catharist doctrines of creation of matter was emerging an ethically neutral principle of Nature, and remarks, after citing one such statement from an Italian source of 1280, that one would think he was hearing an eighteenth-century Deist.[49] One might also think himself hearing a peasant keenly aware of the need of good soil, good weather, and hard work, and one might suggest that the naturalistic explanation arose independently of theology and was accepted on its own merits.

Etienne Delaruelle in 1960, advocating a fresh survey of Catharism in Languedoc in its dynamic period, *ca.* 1200, suggested the need to consider heresy not only as dogma and cult but also as a popular movement.[50] Such an examination would be pertinent as well to later days when heresy had been driven underground, survived in little pockets of the urban population or in remote mountain areas, had lost the intellectual leadership of men like those who debated with Diego and Dominic or wrote the "Manichaean Treatise," known to Durand of Huesca.[51]

This brief and inadequate survey has dealt with a few opinions often expressed in that later period. We encounter, chiefly in the words of men and women of a low level of society, some ideas that were in circulation before the Cathars appeared, that sometimes ran counter to the main trends of dualist thought, that were given voice by persons who were not always treated by their inquisitors as believers of the Cathars.

Arno Borst treats these opinions as the result of evolution of Bogomil-Catharist thought in response to western conditions.[52] Jean Vidal sees in them a "disequilibrium" of popular religious ideas resulting from the teachings of the Cathars.[53] Jean Duvernoy admits the possibility of earlier non-dualist heterodox ideas or by-products of contemporary theological speculation penetrating the Catharist milieu.[54] What is proposed here is that a supplemental theory, which does not deny Catharist influence yet does not make it all-pervasive, is also tenable. Before that great heresy appeared, anticlericalism existed, and Catharism profited from it. May we not also see a certain independence of mind and native skepticism,[55] not necessarily dependent on dualist ideas, in the longing to know that children were assured of salvation, in the crude skepticism about the host and other holy things, in the materialistic concept of the soul, in the explanation of natural phenomena without divine action? Such ideas certainly would be encouraged by the anti-ecclesiastical propaganda of the dualists and could even be assimilated by them. But I suggest that the unorthodox opinions which the inquisitors discovered in 1273-1276, which had existed earlier and would persist thereafter, may well have arisen spontaneously from the cogitations of men and women searching for explanations that accorded with the realities of the life in which they were enmeshed.

# NOTES

1. On these inquisitors, see Célestin Douais, *Documents pour servir à l'histoire de l'Inquisition dans le Languedoc* (2 vols., Paris, 1890), I, clxxii-clxxxii. The earliest documents bearing their names are of May 21, 1273 (Ranulph) and November 12, 1273 (Pons), although there is reason to believe, from the statement of one witness, that they had already been in office in 1270 (Paris, Bibliothèque nationale, Collection Doat, XXV, ff. 2-7, 29-35, 200v [hereafter Doat]. Ranulph's name does not appear after March 21, 1275; Pons used the title of inquisitor until November 27, 1277 and thereafter occasionally appeared as deputy *(gerens vices inquisitoris)* or as an official witness to proceedings until 1284 *(ibid.,* ff. 282v-3, 300v, 313v, 318v, 324v; XXVI, ff. 47v-8, 68), although J. L. Biget ("Un Procès d'Inquisition à Albi en 1300," *Cahiers de Fanjeaux,* VI,278) states that Pons and Ranulph were active in the vicinity of Albi from 1274 to 1279 and found a recrudescence of Catharism there. None of their sentences have survived, although one, imposed on a woman not mentioned in the depositions in Doat, Vols. XXV-XXVI, is referred to in the *Liber sententiarum* of Bernard Gui (edited in Philip van Limborch, *Historia inquisitionis* [Amsterdam, 1692], p. 150).
2. They comprise Vols. XXV and XXVI, ff. 1-78 of the Collection Doat, having been copied from a register of the Inquisition at Toulouse in 1679. Some of the material has been exploited in Jean Guiraud, *Histoire de l'Inquisition* (2 vols., Paris, 1935-1938), II, 85-116, 247-94; and in Yves Dossat, "Les Cathares d'après les documents de l'Inquisition," *Cathares en Languedoc,* Vol. III of *Cahiers de Fanjeaux* (Toulouse, 1968).

3. Only one perfected Cathar, Guillelmus Rafardi, was captured and converted in 1278 (Doat, XXVI, ff. 12-45). Guiraud (*Inquisition*, II, 278) is in error in calling Johannes de Torena or den Hug a perfect (Doat, XXV, ff. 126, 128, 129). On the situation in Languedoc at the time, see the works cited in n.2.
4. Cf. Dossat, "Les Cathares d'après les documents de l'Inquisition," *Cahiers de Fanjeaux*, III, 77.
5. Doat, XXV, ff. 20v-24. Durandus was in trouble because one acquaintance had discussed him with another, who wrote to the inquisitors (*ibid.*, ff. 178). Guirauda, his wife, was interrogated on August 6, 1274 (*ibid.*, ff. 181-2v). Her inquisitor did not mention Durandus but sought information about the infidelity of a father and son with whom she and her husband had been on good terms. They were Guiraldus and Grimaldus de Olmeria, who were suspected of receiving heretics in their home, rejecting the last rites, and asserting that there were two gods (*ibid.*, ff. 178, 181-2v).
6. On whom, see n. 5.
7. At this point the text is garbled. Durandus was asked if he ever had said that God did not take away *ea quae credebat ut primum*. It seems likely that *credebat* is a mistake for *creabat* and that this resembles the opinion that God did not take away any human faculties he had bestowed. Whatever it was, Durandus denied making the statement.
8. Another man, Guillelmus Orseti, a year later, was accused of having made a similar statement, but denied it (Doat, XXV, f. 179).
9. As already indicated, we know nothing of the disposition of this or the other cases which will be mentioned.
10. Doat, XXV, ff. 24-6.
11. *Ibid.*, ff. 231-41.
12. *Ibid.*, ff. 203-6v.
13. *Ibid.*, ff. 206v-8v.
14. *Ibid.*, ff. 217v-8.
15. *Ibid.*, f. 214v-5.
16. *Ibid.*, ff. 227-8v.
17. *Ibid.*, ff. 196v-201v.
18. It was a work of the troubadour Guillem Figueras; cf. J. M. Vidal, "Doctrine et morale des derniers ministres albigeois," (Pt. 2), *Revue des questions historiques*, n.s., XLII (1909), 25.
19. Doat, XXXVI, ff. 312-3. Printed in C. Devic and J. Vaissete, *Histoire générale de Languedoc*, ed. A. Molinier, *et al.* (16 vols., Toulouse, 1872-1904), VIII, 984-5. The editors suggest a date about 1300.
20. Jean Duvernoy (*Le Registre de l'Inquisition de Jacques Fournier, évêque de Pamiers [1318-1325]*, [3 vols., Toulouse, 1965], I, 106, n. 40) suggests that it could have been compiled from depositions before Jacques Fournier.
21. Perhaps other sources in which popular ideas might be recorded would disclose pertinent information. Opportunity and facilities for further search were denied me.
22. Arno Borst, *Die Katharer* (Stuttgart, 1953), p. 169, n. 5.
23. For brevity, wherever possible, I shall cite the translations in W. L. Wakefield and A. P. Evans, *Heresies of the High Middle Ages* (New York, 1969), where references to the original sources will be found. In this instance, see pp. 344, 362 (Christ's body, Mary, and the saints are in the "shining sky" or "ether" or they are in a terrestrial paradise); pp. 213 (souls go to a place of refuge); pp. 213 and 697, n. 26 (souls go directly to heaven or hell).
24. *The Summa contra hereticos Ascribed to Praepositinus of Cremona*, ed. J. N. Garvin and J. A. Corbett (Notre Dame, 1958), pp. 200, 283.
25. Paul de Félice, *L'autre monde, mythes et légendes, le Purgatoire de Saint Patrice* (Paris, 1960); Shane Leslie, *Saint Patrick's Purgatory: A Record from History and Literature* (London, 1932).
26. *Le Registre de Jacques Fournier*, I, 133, 138, 139, 538-51 *passim;* II, 463, 483, 491, 498. I write "non-Cathar" because I do not think the deluded Arnold Gelis was as much influenced by Albigensian teachers as is asserted by J. M. Vidal ("Une Secte de spirites à Pamiers en 1320," *Annales de Saint-Louis de Françaises*, II, [1899], 299-300, 307). Both Vidal (p. 304) and Duvernoy (*Le Registre de Jacques Fournier*, I, 133, n. 61) see some connection between the terrestrial paradise and the fourteenth-century discussion of the beatific vision.
27. Duvernoy (*Le Registre de Jacques Fournier*, II, 463, n. 393) calls it a popular tradition foreign to Albigensian thought. For J. L. Riol ("Tels furent les Cathares, d'après les textes de l'époque et les traditions populaires," *Bulletin de la Société des sciences, arts et belles-lettres* du Tarn, XVII [1957], 570) it is "une invention nouvelle." Borst (*Die Katharer*, pp. 168-9); however, he discusses it as intrinsic to Catharist thought, although a western addition to the Bogomil inheritance.
28. See for examples Wakefield and Evans, *Heresies*, pp. 116, 263, 346; cf. *The Summa Ascribed to Praepositinus*, p. 170.
29. Borst, *Die Katharer*, pp. 216-7, esp. n. 12.
30. *Le Registre de Jacques Fournier*, II, 499; III, 229
31. *Ibid.*, II, 110-5 *passim*, 244, 264-5.
32. See p.27-8.
33. Dossat, "Les Cathares d'après les documents de l'Inquisition," *Cahiers de Fanjeaux*, III, 78; *Le Registre de Jacques Fournier*, II, 35.
34. Borst, *Die Katharer*, p. 217, n. 14.
35. C. H. Haskins, *Studies in Medieval Culture* (Oxford, 1929), p. 252.
36. Borst, *Die Katharer*, p. 217, n. 14, giving references to the sources to which a number of others could be added from Doat and *Le Registre de Jacques Fournier*.
37. Borst, *Die Katharer*, p. 371, addendum for p. 150; Duvernoy (*Le Registre de Jacques Fournier*, I, 260, n. 99) regards it as an ancient heresy which had already appeared in Castres in the tenth century and later was adopted by the Cathars.
38. Borst, *Die Katharer*, pp. 148-51.
39. Alan of Lille (*Contra hereticos*, in Migne, *Patrologia latina*, CCX, 328-9) has them defend the tenet by citing the

Old Testament; Peter Martyr (in Wakefield and Evans, *Heresies,* p. 275) refers to such heretics as "predestinati"; and Moneta of Cremona (*Adversus Catharos et valdenses,* ed. by T. A. Ricchini [Rome, 1743], pp. 416-29) says flatly that those who subscribe to this view are not Cathars.

40. *Le Registre de Jacques Fournier,* I, 263-5; II, 129-30.
41. H. C. Lea, *A History of the Inquisition of the Middle Ages* (3 vols., New York, 1888), III, 567.
42. Cf. n. 37. Borst (*Die Katharer,* p. 150) believes they had; he regards this, with other remarks of the time, such as that men die like animals or that the soul withers when the body hungers and dies, as evidence of their philosophical difficulties.
43. Borst, *Die Katharer,* pp. 147-8.
44. Duvernoy (*Le Registre de Jacques Fournier,* II, 462, n. 392), quotes Eckbert of Schönau (A.D. 1163). Cf. Stephen of Bourbon (*ca.* 1250 in A. Lecoy de la Marche, *Anecdotes historiques, légendes et apologues, tirées du recueil inédit d'Etienne de Bourbon* (Paris, 1877), p. 301.
45. *Le Registre de Jacques Fournier,* II, 481-2, 503-4; III, 307. Cf. the prayer (*ibid.,* II, 461-2) to "Payre sant . . . que a poder . . . fa granar e florir."
46. *The Summa Attributed to Praepositinus,* p. 21; Borst, *Die Katharer,* p. 148, n. 19, to whose citations may be added Doat, XXXIV, f. 96 and *Le Registre de Jacques Fournier,* I, 283; II, 58.
47. Moneta of Cremona, *Adversus catharos et valdenses,* p. 122; Dossat, "Les Cathares d'après les documents de l'Inquisition," *Cahiers de Fanjeaux,* III, 78.
48. Cf. Borst, *Die Katharer,* p. 148, n. 19. See also *Le Registre de Jacques Fournier,* I, 230, 457; II, 422; III, 51-2, 347.
49. *Die Katharer,* p. 148.
50. "Le Catharisme en Languedoc vers 1200: Une enquête," *Annales du Midi,* LXXII (1960), 150.
51. Wakefield and Evans, *Heresies,* pp. 494-510, and the references there to the intensive studies of Christine Thouzellier. As for the popular understanding of doctrine, Dossat has remarked (*Cahiers de Fanjeaux,* III, 71, 100) on how superficial it became among believers; "Catharism on the cheap."
52. *Die Katharer,* pp. 143ff.
53. "Doctrine et morale des derniers ministres albigeois," *Revue des questions historiques,* XLI (1909), 369.
54. *Le Registre de Jacques Fournier,* I, 133, n. 61; II, 119, n. 281; 463, n. 93.
55. Cf. Charles Molinier's statement that in such speculation lay the first tentatives of free thought ('Rapport à M. le ministre d'instruction publique . . . Etude sur quelques manuscrits des bibliothèques d'Italie concernant l'Inquisition et les croyances hérétiques du XIIe et XIIIe siècle," *Archives des missions scientifiques et littéraires,* 3d ser., XIV [1888], 231); and the opinion of Duvernoy (*Le Registre de Jacques Fournier,* I, 30), who sees in the examples of a materialistic and critical attitude a rudimentary independence of spirit that would soon be stifled.

# The Heresy of the Free Spirit and Late Medieval Mysticism

*Eleanor McLaughlin*

D ESPITE RECENT SCHOLARLY attention to the history of medieval heresy, there is yet no adequate full-length study of the heresy of the Brethren and Sisters of the Free Spirit. This elusive phenomenon has been variously described as a form of medieval pantheism, or a perversion of the mystical tradition, a kind of *Gassenmystik* resulting from the misunderstanding and misuse of the piety of deification. Many historians today are still quoting medieval reports that the Free Spirits were in theory and practice antinomians and libertines, given to the most crass excesses of sensuality.[1] An obvious reason for the lack of unanimity on the nature of this heresy lies in the absence of a trustworthy body of sources for its history. The bias of inquisitorial accounts confronts every student of medieval heresy, but with the Free Spirits, we are more seriously hampered, for no source material from the hands of the accused is known to exist. We have had nothing but the words of opponents on which to base an analysis of the history and nature of this phenomenon.

This paper offers a partial solution to that dilemma by presenting a new set of witnesses for the history of the heresy of the Free Spirit, an alternative to the typological accounts of inquisitor and chronicler. This new perspective is to be found in the orthodox mystics of the fourteenth and fifteenth centuries, who throw light on the heresy of the Free Spirit in two distinct and complementary ways. First the mystics' own spiritual aspirations, doctrines of deification and spiritual freedom, provide a positive picture of the type of spiritual experience and perfection sought by the heretics, a picture relatively free of the distortions of the inquisitorial mind. The parallels between the highest flower of late medieval mystical spirituality and the heresy of the Free

37

Spirit illustrate the ambiguity of a sharp distinction between the false *vrei geist* and the true *spiritus libertatis* sought by the orthodox mystics.[2] The second justification for looking at the mystics as a new corpus of primary sources for the history of the Free Spirits lies in the fact that the mystical authors were themselves aware that their doctrines of mystical union and freedom from all exteriority could give rise to an heretical false freedom. They wrote extensively, therefore, on the danger of the false free spirit and thus give a direct witness to the nature and origins of this heresy, a witness which is more understanding of the religious motivation of the heretics than the traditional inquisitorial sources. A reading of the mystics by a student of the heresy of the Free Spirit thus has a twofold utility: a more positive and just picture of the intentions of the heretics themselves is revealed and an important methodological point is made — that the student of medieval heresy is well advised to look at this subject in the context of medieval spirituality as a whole. The distinctions "orthodox/heretical" are abstract and institutional and may inhibit our understanding of the concrete historical process. These general propositions will be argued here with reference to a representative sample of the evidence available: the *Mirror of Simple Souls,* an early fourteenth century Beguine devotional treatise, and the sermons of Johannes Tauler. Where appropriate, references will be made to other mystical authors whose discussions of the false free spirit confirm and expand upon the evidence presented here.

The *Mirror of Simple Souls* provides a useful introduction to our problem, for this work is an excellent example of the ambiguous middle ground between an orthodox mystical spirituality and the heresy of the Free Spirit. Also, the *Mirror* has been the subject of recent scholarship which well illustrates the confusion surrounding the identification of the heresy of the Free Spirit. The *Mirror of Simple Souls* has been recently edited in its original French version by Romana Guarnieri, who convincingly attributes the work to the Beguine *clergesse* Marguerite Porete.[3] The history of the text and its presumed author introduces us at once to the complexity of relationship between the heresy of the Free Spirit and orthodox mystical piety, for Marguerite Porete was condemned at Paris in 1310 as a relapsed heretic who wrote a religious tract in the vernacular containing among others the articles of belief:

1. That the annihilated soul must let go of the virtues and no longer be at their service because she has no more use for them, but the virtues obey her.
2. That such a soul has no more concern for the consolations of God nor

> for his gifts and needs not bother herself about them and does not
> know how to do so, for it is God alone who retains her attention and
> those things would prevent that.[4]

These beliefs are clearly set forth in the *Mirror*[5] and are also typical of the heresy of the Free Spirit; there are parallel articles in the catalogue of errors attributed to the heretics of the Swabian Ries of the mid-thirteenth century[6] and in the Vienne decree *Ad nostrum* which laid down the operative definition of the heresy after the publication of that bull in 1317.[7] The contemporary perception of the *Mirror* as heretical is seen also in repeated attempts to supress the book and to associate it with the heresy of the Free Spirit.[8] The English author of a fifteenth-century Latin version of the *Mirror* found it necessary to add to the text extensive glosses to avoid the quietist and antinomian implications he saw in some of its passages.[9] And yet, despite this unequivocal association with heresy, the *Mirror* found wide acceptance in the later Middle Ages as a guide to the heights of the mystical experience, and indeed, in its glossed version was published in a twentieth-century English Orchard Books edition as a work of spiritual edification.[10]

The ambiguity of the *Mirror's* history is echoed in the most recent scholarship on the text: R. Guarnieri argues at length that this tract represents a precious primary source for the history of the Free Spirits and finds in it the characteristic doctrines of deification, antinomian freedom from the virtues, libertinism, and quietism.[11] In the most recent study of the *Mirror,* J. Orcibal argues quite the opposite case, that a close examination of the text in the light of the medieval tradition of mystical spirituality shows the *Mirror* to be a daring, but thoroughly orthodox exemplar of Dionysian, transformational mysticism.[12] Furthermore, in the conclusion of his article, Orcibal makes the useful observation that heresy and orthodoxy are not as rivers which never meet; on the contrary, they frequently rise out of a common source and one stream often flows into the other. The argument which follows substantiates and documents this suggestion to the degree that Orcibal's own judgment on the orthodoxy of the *Mirror* must itself be partially modified. Orcibal remains with the traditional categories insofar as he insists that the *Mirror* is fully orthodox and should be studied in the context of orthodox mysticism ". . . and not with reference to the problematic sect of the Free Spirit."[13] He rejects entirely Guarnieri's suggestion that the *Mirror* was inspired by the doctrines of the Free Spirit heresy. I am suggesting that the conclusions of both Guarnieri and Orcibal with respect to the heretical or orthodox character of the *Mirror* require modification in the light of a more complete understanding of the nature of the heresy of the Free

Spirit. Guarnieri's argument, that the *Mirror* was a Free Spirit source, is weakened by her uncritical definition of that heresy, which in her discussion was a "sect" including virtually every spiritualizing heresy from Tanchelm to the sixteenth-century *Libertins spirituels;* even the English Ranters find their way into the "Free Spirit tradition."[14] Her net is so broad that the subtle distinctions between an heretical and an orthodox mysticism or perfectionism cannot be discerned, and one fears that the sermons of many of the Rhenish mystics would have been included by Guarnieri as "of the Free Spirit" had they not carried the cachet of ecclesiastical approbation.

On the other hand, Orcibal concludes that because there is much that is orthodox in the *Mirror* it cannot be considered part of a corpus of heretical spirituality.[15] The thesis of this paper is that central to the heresy of the Free Spirit is this very ambiguity — an uncertain line between heretical and orthodox claims of spiritual freedom and a large common area between orthodox and Free Spirit piety in the realm of spiritual aspiration. There is no argument with Orcibal's demonstration of the parallels between the *Mirror* and the ofttimes daring spirituality of transformational mysticism. I would add, however, that the *Mirror of Simple Souls* is both orthodox and "of the Free Spirit." This becomes clear if one compares the key doctrines of the *Mirror* with a broad spectrum of Free Spirit confessions, rather than limiting one's reference to the Church's definition in *Ad nostrum,* as Orcibal tends to do. The first task, then, is to take up in logical order the salient teachings of the *Mirror* on deification, freedom from works and external acts of piety, the problem of sin and impeccability, the duality of Nature and Grace and "giving Nature her due," comparing these to relevant passages from a reliable canon of Free Spirit sources.

The *Mirror of Simple Souls,* in a dialogue between Love and Reason, presents a doctrine of deification and freedom for the "Naughted Soul" who belongs to the true Church, Holy Church the Great, but who is at the same time the support and nourishment of the institutional Church, Holy Church the Little. This reformist attitude towards the Church does not appear in the inquisitors' accounts of the heresy of the Free Spirit. The parallels emerge, however, when one examines the spiritual perfection and freedoms claimed by the Naughted Soul.

The relationship between the Naughted Soul and God, the *deificatio,* is clearly a union of wills, not of being or essence, and the final consummation of the *visio dei* lies in the next life, again a mysticism well within the limits of orthodoxy. But the language used to describe this affective union reminds us in its radicalism of numerous accusations brought against the Free Spirits. The author of the *Mirror* lays herself open to a pantheistic interpretation when for example we read, "I am God says Love, and that Soul is God by right of Love."[16] But even here the qualification of the means of union, by right of Love, contrasts with those few Free Spirit sources which are marked by a formal pantheism.[17] More typical of the heresy of the Free Spirit than formal pantheism is the claim to deification through a mystical experience of the divine. The intimacy of union between the soul and God claimed in numerous Free Spirit sources is expressed in words similar to those met in the *Mirror,* that no intermediary stands between God and that soul.[18] A number of Free Spirit confessions include the assertion, "that which God has by nature, the Free Spirit has by grace," a daring description of the highest spiritual state which is expressed in the *Mirror* and by other wholly orthodox mystical writers.[19] The *Mirror* thus shares with many representatives of the heresy of the Free Spirit this claim to deification through a transformation of the soul by grace. The *Mirror* is carefully orthodox in the delimitations of that transformation,[20] but it also contains daring expressions of the *unio dei* that may be found in accusations brought against the heretics.

Even more convincing evidence of the common spirituality of the *Mirror* and the Free Spirits is to be seen in the discussion of the practical implications of the *deificatio,* the "freedom" of the Naughted Soul. This soul takes leave of the virtues, has no concern for the ordinances of the Church, or for any externalities. Furthermore, the soul has no will of its own; God does His work in this soul, without the attention of the soul, so that it remains in a state of *quies,* desiring nothing, not even paradise.[21] Not only is this soul free from concern for the commandments or for its "Even-Christian," but Love is sharply critical of those who live the life of Grace, for the work of any soul is inferior to that which God alone accomplishes in the free soul. The virtues lead only to natural perfection, but God takes the Naughted Soul beyond to the perfection of God Himself.[22] This radical freedom from works and virtues, from all externality, this apparent "quietism" is a principal theme of the heresy of the Free Spirit. The Ries heretics failed to mourn for sin because such acts of sorrow would retard grace,[23] and the sixth article of *Ad nostrum* reports that the perfect soul was free of the virtues.[24] The same theme is found in the confession of Conrad Cannler, of Eichstädt, who held that to exercise oneself in the virtues was for the man who had not yet attained perfection, and Martin of Mainz, who claimed that the *perfectus homo* ought not to pray for liberation from hell or for the attainment of heaven.[25] The inquisitors' accounts of the heresy of the Free Spirit fail to offer any rationale or explanation of the heretics' belief in this freedom from the virtues and external acts of piety. The *Mirror*, by contrast, offers just such a rationale, where the Naughted Soul explains that she is not without virtue, rather the soul who has obeyed the virtues in the lower stages of the spiritual life has passed beyond concern with such matters. But it is important to note that the virtues remain with this soul. It is God, however, not the soul, who carries out the good works and ministers to the neighbor's need. The free soul does not disturb her rest in God with worry about such matters, and yet this soul is not without the virtues.[26] A similar implication is seen in the Ries sentence, ". . . that a man is able to arrive at such a state that God works all things in him."[27] The explanation set forth in the *Mirror* of this doctrine of spiritual freedom avoids the taint of antinomianism or quietism. It is my contention that at least some of those accused of the heresy of the Free Spirit may well have sought a spiritual freedom similar to that of the Naughted Soul of the *Mirror*, only the qualification, "that the virtues are with the soul," was omitted from the inquisitorial record or perhaps not even elicited from the accused. The *Mirror* thus can be seen to present a positive picture of the spiritual aspirations of those accused of the heresy of the Free Spirit.

Indications of the validity of this interpretation are numerous in the Free Spirit sources. For example, Johannes Becker of Mainz qualified the freedoms he claimed. Those who are not yet perfect are bound by the commandments of the Church, and only those who have received the Spirit, who are therefore perfected, are no longer held to the precepts. A distinction is made between the exterior man who looks to the dead letter of the law or Scripture and the interior man who responds to the Spirit, the letter of life. The perfected soul obeys only the Spirit.[28] Such a distinction between the external and the internal spiritual life is a constant motif of Free Spirit confessions. John of Brünn, for example, criticizes those who reverence the Host in order to appear holy before others, but abandon that which is interior,[29] and an article in the Ries collection stated that ". . . man ought to abstain from externals and follow the voice of the Spirit within him."[30] It should be noted that these Free Spirit claims of freedom all assume the perfected soul; only the deified or illumined soul claims this freedom. The teachings of the *Mirror*, open also to 'quietist' interpretation, differ from those of the Free Spirit only in spelling out more carefully the orthodox proviso that despite this freedom from the law granted at the highest stage of the spiritual life, the virtues have not left the soul. Also the important qualification is made that for the soul in this life, the *unio dei* and its accompanying freedoms are temporary and fleeting, a qualification hardly to be found in our Free Spirit confessions.[31]

A recurring theme of the Free Spirit sources is the accusation of claims to impeccability. Here too, the comments of the *Mirror* on the problem of sin can illumine the intentions of those accused of this heresy. One reads in the *Mirror* that this soul is so united with the Trinity that it is able to will or do nothing but the Divine Will, and that when the soul lives in God, no sin may find it, for it has no will.[32] This is similar to typical Free Spirit claims, as, for example, Becker's statement that since he follows the Spirit within him he cannot sin, and that what for other men is sin is not sin for him.[33] The author of the *Mirror* also holds that this Naughted Soul has no malaise from sin, no remorse of conscience, for that would be a fault of charity.[34] This is startlingly similar to accusations made against Free Spirits in the Ries *Determinatio*, "That sins committed ought not to be dwelt upon with bitterness and sadness, because by such grief grace within is impeded."[35] In the sources for the Italian *spiritus libertatis,* Ubertino da Casale warns against those heretics who claim either that they do not sin because grace moves them in all their actions or that they need not mourn their sins because such anxiety is characteristic only of those still in "a carnal state."[36] A similar claim to be free of the necessity of giving attention to sin is seen in the Schweidnitz confessions which speak of a freedom from sin for the perfected souls and also tell of a freedom from "impatient scruples" occasioned by sin.[37]

The *Mirror* illuminates the possible intentions or aspirations of those accused of this heresy in its radical claims for the Naughted Soul of a sinless state and a freedom from worry about sin, claims hedged about with qualifiers and limitations which keep the *Mirror* within the pale of orthodoxy. The author of the *Mirror* limits this freedom to the soul who lives in God, the soul whose will is conformed to God's will. The evidence we possess of Free Spirit beliefs often reveals this same pattern: the claims of impeccability are frequently limited to the perfected soul, the deified soul.[38] Only the modifications set down by the author of the *Mirror* to exclude libertinism — that the virtues are always with the soul — are missing. Again we meet our theme: the doctrines of the *Mirror* coincide with Free Spirit piety, differing primarily in the careful qualifications which were necessary to make a potentially dangerous spirituality acceptable.

A final point of useful comparison between the *Mirror* and this heresy is the problem of nature and the relationship of nature and grace.

Here again we find a similarity of aspiration: to reach beyond the negative, ascetic denial of the natural man to a new encompassing freedom in which the Naughted Soul is able to use what nature has provided and do what pleases her lest she lose her peace.[39] Similar notions are found in Free Spirit confessions, in which the needs of the natural man may be satisfied, for that nature has already been subjected to the Spirit.[40] Freedom from sin in the *Mirror,* the "freedom to give nature her due," presupposes the attainment of a status of the spiritual life in which the Naughted Soul no longer loves temporal things. The ordering of the soul by God is such that it could not demand anything contrary to God's will. A similar conviction is implied in a number of Free Spirit sources, as for example in the Ries sentence which declares, "that to him who is admitted to the divine embrace is given the power of doing what he wills."[41] It is the divine embrace which affords this freedom. However, the *Mirror,* unlike the inquisitorial sources for this heresy, makes explicit that nature, thus freed, never leads the soul away from God.[42] There is good evidence in the Free Spirit corpus that suggests the same kind of qualification, as, for example, the convicted Free Spirit schoolmaster, Wernher of Ulm, who claimed such perfection united to God that he did not *want* to sin. So also, Conrad Cannler, when questioned about a particular form of scandalous behavior, replied that he did not believe God would allow such a sinful act. In light of these statements I suggest that the numerous instances of reported Free Spirit "libertinism," as for example, the assertion that fornication is no sin because it is natural like eating or drinking, may often represent an inquisitor's understanding of an attempt to achieve the same kind of freedom from a scrupulous *concern* with the problem of sin and good works which is described in the *Mirror of Simple Souls.*[43]

The many parallels between the doctrines of the *Mirror* and accusations brought against the Free Spirits are not evidence of the completely heretical character of this tract as Guarnieri and the fate of its presumed author suggest; nor are the clear resemblances between the *Mirror* and earlier orthodox forms of medieval piety grounds for dissociating this work altogether from the heresy of the Free Spirit. The *Mirror of Simple Souls* is both orthodox and "Free Spirit" in its teachings; it represents a spirituality of divinisation and freedom which was common to the orthodox mystical tradition and the heretics, and provides a picture of Free Spirit religious aspirations undistorted by the inquisitors' expectations of extremism and lasciviousness.

This interpretation of the *Mirror* might be hard to sustain if it were not for the corroboration which one finds when looking to other examples of fourteenth-century spirituality. An attentive reading of the leading mystical preachers of this period in the first place confirms the conclusions reached with respect to the *Mirror:* significant parallels exist between Free Spirit and orthodox mystical piety. Secondly, the mystics, after the condemnations at the Council of Vienne and the attack on Eckhart's work in *In agro dominico,* are sensitive to the possibility of misinterpreting their doctrines of *unio* and *spiritus libertatis* and, therefore, unlike the author of the *Mirror,* warn explicitly against the dangers of a falsely understood spirit of freedom. Seuse, Tauler, Rulman Merswin, the author of the *Theologia Deutsch,* Ruysbroeck, Gerard Groote, Gerson, all discuss this dangerous false freedom.[44] By examining this concern we achieve another perspective on the symbiotic relationship between these heretics and the mystics. Their viewpoint can be adequately illustrated by looking at one of these authors, for their understanding of the nature of this heresy showed little essential variation.

Johannes Tauler (1300-1361), a Dominican preacher and spiritual director, unimpeachably orthodox, in contrast to the author of the *Mirror,* belonged to the same Dionysian tradition of *Einheitsmystik* as the *Mirror* and his predecessors Eckhart and Seuse. He was preaching a radical transformational mysticism with strong emphasis on the priority of the inner life and the spiritual freedom granted in the unitive experience. Despite the care he exercised in the expression of those freedoms, undoubtedly a caution sharpened by the Eckhart trial, his spirituality shares certain basic assumptions with that of the Free Spirits. In Tauler, however, we see even more clearly than in the *Mirror,* the qualifications which ensure orthodoxy and distinguish Tauler's piety of inwardness from that of the Free Spirit heresy. Furthermore, unlike the author of the *Mirror,* Tauler was aware of the problem of this heresy, of a false freedom associated with the highest religious aspiration, and preached explicitly against those who followed a false freedom of the spirit. He demonstrates both implicitly and explicitly our thesis, that the followers of the heretical freedom of the spirit sought a religious experience not unlike that advocated by the most orthodox churchmen, and that the mystical preachers provide a more sympathetic and accurate picture of the religious aspirations of the heretics than can be found in the more traditional inquisitorial or chronicle sources.

The general area of correspondence between Tauler and the heretics lies in the shared emphasis on a radically inward religion, accompanied by explicit criticism of the formalism of conventional piety. For example, Tauler often deemphasized the necessity of auricular confession, saying it was not required in the case of venial sins which one could confess directly to God, or even to a good layman. Very similar views were frequently found in Free Spirit confessions, illustrating how the same opinion in one context could be considered acceptable and in another's mouth would be condemned as heretical.[45] Another striking parallel to Free Spirit spirituality is seen where Tauler commented that if a Sister in choir should find that the chants disturb her meditation, she should break off from her choir duties and turn within to God. He wished the spiritual man to limit oral prayer as much as possible.[46] These examples witness to the same impetus to the wholly interior life which is a continual theme of accusations brought against the Free Spirits. See, for example, the eighth article of *Ad nostrum* which deems it an imperfection to disturb one's contemplation by arising at the Elevation of the host at mass, or Conrad Cannler's experience in the church at Eichstädt where the Spirit spoke to him of his freedom from the necessity of confession or the reception of the Eucharist on account of the perfection he had attained.[47] Tauler shared with a number of the accused Free Spirits the conviction that a long tutelage in the ascetic life was the necessary prelude to the true poverty and freedom of the spirit which accompanied the *unio dei*.[48] This union, described as a oneness between soul and God, free of all intermediary, in which the soul lost all *underscheit*, although wholly orthodox, is reminiscent of Free Spirit claims to be so united with God that the angels were not able to discern the difference between God and the soul.[49] However, it is not in the subtle distinctions concerned with the definition of the *unio dei*, but rather in the discussion of the moral and practical results of that union, the *Gelassenheit* or *Armut des 'Geistes* in which the soul becomes free from all that is creaturely, that we find the strongest community between the Free Spirit and Tauler. In this highest state Tauler warned that all "creatures" — acts of piety, the graces of God, visions, feelings, images — are but dangerous distractions of the soul's attention from God. Tauler's radical expression of this freedom from the law is seen in his words:

> "The Pope has no power over those who take this way, for God himself has freed them. St. Paul speaks, those who are led or driven by the spirit of God, they are under no law."[50]

This is not an isolated statement, for Tauler continually attacks the *Werkmenschen* who seem to find pleasure in their acts of piety and good works. He contrasts to their self-regarding religiosity the soul, who in the highest state of the spiritual life, has put aside all its natural works and exercises, ". . . performed through its own powers," so that God alone accomplishes all within that man.[51] This doctrine of freedom from all externality and law, from works and the ordinary acts of religion, is wholly parallel in words and meaning to the beliefs attributed to the Free Spirits. Article three of *Ad nostrum* claimed for these heretics:

> "Those who have achieved this status of perfection and spirit of liberty are not subject to human obedience nor to any precepts of the church, because as they say, where the spirit of the Lord is, there is liberty."[52]

In the confessions of the Schweidnitz Beguines we find the same association of the achievement of the mystical return with this doctrine of freedom. They assert, for example, that when the higher virtues of the interior life have replaced the lower virtues, this *subtilus spiritus* is free of the danger of sin, for whatever happens in charity is not sin.[53] In contrast to the records we have of the heretics, Tauler qualifies this freedom to avoid the errors of quietism and antinomianism. In an explicit discussion of the question, can one rise above the virtues, he answers, "yes and also no." While in ecstasy the soul does not work at the virtues, but as soon as the soul returns to itself, it has to live once more the life of good works and conventional piety. Also, unlike the inquisitorial accounts of the Free Spirits, Tauler, in distinguishing between the higher and lower faculties of the soul, insists that the lower faculties remain ever bound to the law and the practice of the virtues. He dwelt upon the importance of ascetic exercises and the imitation of the life of Christ as preparation for the highest graces. Above all, he stressed the necessity of order in the spiritual life. Nature must be ordered, that God might carry out his work in the soul, and the life of the virtues is the foundation of this order.[54] One senses here a self-conscious provision against a misunderstanding or an exaggeration of the spiritual freedom which he preached.

It should be evident that in no sense do I suggest Tauler was "of the Free Spirits," in this advocacy of a piety of inwardness and freedom. His mysticism is even more unequivocally orthodox than that of the *Mirror*. What is suggested by these parallels between the heresy of the Free Spirit and the speculative mysticism of Johannes Tauler is the possibility that both heretic and preacher sought and advocated a similar religion of inwardness and that accordingly, some of the more extreme claims of antinomian freedom and impeccability recorded by hostile reporters can be better understood if read in the light of the *spiritus libertatis* sought also by the orthodox mystics.[55]

This interpretation is strengthened by explicit references in Tauler to the problem of the heresy of the Free Spirit. First there is the surprising report that Tauler found himself under attack as a member of this heretical movement. In one sermon, he was preaching his customary warning against the "Works-Christians" who point to themselves saying: ". . . we are in a holy order amongst the holiest companions, and pray and read . . . " He followed this description with the complaint that if you warn these people of their peril they scorn you and say: "He is a Beghard," and call you a *"nuwer geist,"* or one of the *"hohen geisten."*[56] Thus the reform preacher did not feel free to carry on his campaign against a dependence on external religious exercises without defending himself explicitly against association with these advocates of an heretical freedom. This is the background of his attacks on the false mystics.

Unlike the author of the *Mirror,* Tauler and many of the other leading mystical preachers of the fourteenth century devoted considerable attention to the problem of these false spirits. The evidence is persuasive that it is the heresy of the Free Spirit to which they refer, for the errors described are identical with those attributed to that heresy, and Tauler in fact refers to these errors as a "perverted false freedom of the spirit."[57] An examination of the passages in which this spiritual phenomenon is described and attacked is doubly useful; it affords a more analytical and even a more sympathetic account than that usually found in inquisitorial and chronicle sources, and it supplies a valuable insight into the mystics' judgment of the origins of this spiritual illness.

The defining characteristic of these people, according to Tauler, is a false freedom or emptiness in which they enjoyed an inner peace and refused to perform good works or seek the virtues, insofar as they had overcome such things.[58] This theme of inwardness and rejection of all external cult is expanded in Rulman Merswin's account to include a disdain for all Scripture as but ink and parchment. Even Christ's mediation is denied, for the Savior is not needed by those who have become one with God. These are familiar Free Spirit themes, including the docetic Christology which Merswin also reports.[59] According to Tauler, this false emptiness is marked by a concentration on self rather than God, a disorderly freedom in contrast to the "true peace and freedom of the spirit."[60] These people claim to be able to do whatever nature prompts without sin, for they have attained a status above law or Commandment and follow the desires of their nature in order that the emptiness of the spirit may remain undisturbed.[61] Important is Tauler's observation that it is difficult to distinguish those who are full of Godly love from those who follow this "natural love," except that the latter, which is love of self, leads to the sins of spiritual pride, avarice, gluttony, and impurity. These themes of antinomianism, libertinism, impeccability are spelled out in his descriptions of these *"frijen geisten"* who in addition to claiming to be free of the virtues, follow the bidding of their natures into acts of unchastity and a claim to be free of all sins. They enjoy these privileges because they believe themselves to have become one with God *"ohne Mittel"* and therefore live without will in a pure state of rest. Whatever they do, good or evil, they claim to be a work of the Holy Ghost. Finally, Tauler offers his analysis of the source of these errors. In one passage of keen psychological insight he suggests that this emptiness is a natural "peace," a self-induced state — we might say a yoga-like inducement of a mystical trance — which comes from man and not God. Another sermon examines the social context of these errors and suggests that this "perverted false freedom of the spirit" is especially to be found among simple or young people who are not sufficiently practiced in the virtues or dead to self, or who have engaged in long and severe penances but without proper love.[62] This latter description fits numerous instances of Free Spirit heresy: the Schweidnitz Beguines, the brothers John and Albert of Brünn, the man who sought spiritual freedom in the (probably autobiographical) *Zweimannenbuch* of Rulman Merswin,[63] and Conrad Cannler, all of whom had submitted themselves to a long and severe ascetic regime before claiming the freedom of the spirit. An association of the false free spirit with the pursuit of the heights of spiritual perfection is a repeated theme in the mystics' accounts. Heinrich Seuse in *Das Buch der Wahrheit* implies that *"das Wilde"* came to his false understanding of the mystic's freedom through a misreading and misunderstanding of Meister Eckhart.[64] The author of the *Theologia Deutsch* finds these heretics to be men who have sought to pass beyond the world of "images" before they have been morally and spiritually prepared.

These authors were unequivocally opposed to "the unrighteous, false, free spirits who are most damaging to the Church."[65] Yet what a different picture of this heresy is revealed in their sermons and treatises of spiritual edification than that which emerges from the more traditional inquisitorial sources. What we see is not simply a sect of amoral libertines, but a religious phenomenon in its origin inspired by the same ideal of deification and spiritual freedom as motivated the great mystics of the Church.

The contribution to our understanding of this heresy made by the use of this new corpus of sources can now be summarized. First we have noted the important parallels between the *spiritus libertatis* advocated by the orthodox mystics, the author of the *Mirror of Simple Souls* and Johannes Tauler, and the heretical *vrei geist*. Although these authors qualify their doctrine of *unio* and freedom from law and creatureliness in such a way that the limits of orthodoxy are observed, nevertheless, especially in the case of the *Mirror,* the line between a freedom acceptable to the Church and the false spirit of freedom of the heretics was often a very fine one. This is not to imply that the mystical preachers of the fourteenth century inspired or caused the heresy of the Free Spirit as one contemporary suggested — that there were no Free Spirits before the time of Meister Eckhart.[66] Nor is there historical evidence that the heretics "infected" the orthodox mystics as some have held.[67] Rather, it seems that the heretics and the mystics shared a common spirituality, a yearning for *Gelassenheit,* that "letting go" which affords the freedom and inwardness of the life of Christian perfection. To study the heresy of the Free Spirit in the context of Catholic mysticism frees us from the sterile debate over the orthodoxy or heterodoxy of a belief and enables us to discern the religious aspirations of the heretics, aspirations which are not readily apparent in the records of the inquisition. The mystics offer us, then, a positive suggestion of what these people really had in mind when they spoke of freedom from all law and from sin or remorse for sin. The inquisitors relayed these beliefs always in the most negative fashion, as an unbridled libertinism or a pantheistic claim to divinization and impeccability. While extremism of this kind undoubtedly did exist, numerous Free Spirit confessions contain a proportion of statements which in another context would have been considered wholly acceptable. The claim to become by grace that which God is by nature is a typical example of the desire for divinization in this life shared by the orthodox mystics and the heretical Free Spirits. A most persuasive example of this ambiguity between the doctrines of Catholic mysticism and those of the Free Spirits is the *Mirror of Simple Souls,* in some passages carefully conservative in its Christ-centered piety, yet daring to the point of heresy in other passages where the freedom from images and creatureliness and works granted the Naughted Soul is under discussion. Both the history and content of this treatise witness to a fundamental confusion among contemporaries as to the definition of the heretical and orthodox *spiritus libertatis.*

A strong confirmation of this thesis is seen in the awareness of the Catholic mystical preachers of the spiritual dangers implicit in their own teachings. The warnings voiced by Tauler of the ease of confusing the true, God-infused *Gelassenheit* with a natural, self-regarding, false emptiness are to be found in substantially similar form in the works of Seuse, the *Theologia Deutsch,* Ruysbroeck, Rulman Merswin, Gerson. Especially interesting in this regard are Gerson's fears that the transformational mysticism taught by William of St. Thierry and his own near contemporary, Ruysbroeck, may have inspired or been associated with the heresies of the Beghards condemned in *Ad nostrum,* the errors of the Free Spirit.[68]

The general conclusions to be drawn from this study follow from this basic insight into the relationship between the heresy of the Free Spirit and orthodox mysticism. First we see the import of studying heresy in the context of the total spectrum of medieval spirituality. A whole new corpus of source material is made available to supplement and often correct the traditional inquisitorial sources. Heresy is placed in its proper perspective as a portion of the total history of spirituality. Secondly, the relationship of the Free Spirits to the mystics, which has been suggested repeatedly by recent historians as well as fourteenth-century observers can be described now more precisely. A popular theory has been summed up in the word *Gassenmystik:* the heresy of the Free Spirit represented the misunderstanding and perversion of Catholic mysticism when it passed from the conventual setting to the illiterate lay groups of the Beghard or Beguine semi-regular. Two sets of circumstance weigh heavily against this theory. First the fact that many of those accused of this heresy appear to have been persons, both clerical and lay, or some religious sophistication.[69] Secondly, and more importantly, the argument of this paper strongly supports the proposition that the possibility of this kind of freedom from all law, externality, sin, and the sorrow for sin was implicit within the apex of the mystical experience as described by orthodox Catholic mystics. The heresy of the Free Spirit thus is seen not as a perversion of medieval Catholic mysticism, but as a latent possibility within that kind of search for Christian perfection.[70] Quietism and claims of impeccability, two defining characteristics of the Free Spirit heresy are the logical expression of certain strains of medieval mysticism.

Finally, the attempts by Guarnieri and Orcibal to allocate the *Mirror of Simple Souls* to the side of heresy or orthodoxy we reject with respect to both method and content. The decision to study the *Mirror* in a narrowly defined tradition, either orthodox or heretical, effectively prevents an adequate assessment of the meaning of this work. When examined without preconception, the teachings of this interesting tract appear to be both orthodox, and, in certain instances when taken literally, heretical. This very ambivalence has been shown to be a prime attribute of the heresy of the Free Spirit, a spiritual phenomenon which reflected the dangers and glories of Paul's words, "Ubi spiritus Domini, ibi libertas."

# NOTES

1. A. Jundt, *Histoire du panthéisme populaire*, Strasbourg, 1875, 55; J. Bernhart, *Die philosophische Mystik des Mittelalters*, Munich, 1922, 167-8; G. Leff, *Heresy in the Later Middle Ages*, 2 vols., Manchester, 1967, I, 314.
2. For the orthodox use of *spiritus libertatis* see M.-A. Dimier, "Pour la fiche 'Spiritus Libertatis'," *Revue du Moyen Age Latin*, III (1947), 56-60; Meister Eckhart, *Die deutschen Werke*, ed. J. Quint, Stuttgart, 1963, V, *Von Abegescheidenheit*, 411.
3. R. Guarnieri, "Il movimento del libero spirito. Testi e Documenti," *Archivio Italiano per la Storia della Pietà*, IV (1965), 353-708.
4. C. Langlois, "Marguerite Porete," *Revue historique*, LIV (1894), 297.
5. R. Guarnieri, *op. cit.*, 412; *Mirouer des simples ames*, ed. R. Guarnieri, *op. cit.*, ch. 9, 527.
6. I. v. Döllinger, *Beiträge zur Sektengeschichte des Mittelalters*, 2 vols., Munich, 1890, II, 395-402, Compilatio de novo Spiritu, "quod homines impediant et retardent perfeccionem et bonitatem per jejunia, flagellationem, disciplinas, vigilias, et alio similia," 402.
7. *CIC* Clem. V, 3, 3: Friendberg, II, 1183 and H. Denzinger, *Enchiridion Symbolorum*, Freiburg, 1960, 221, *Ad nostrum*, 6. "Quod se in actibus exercere virtutum est hominis imperfecti, et perfecta anima licentiat a se virtutes."
8. St. Bernardino of Siena associated the *Mirror* with the heresy of the Free Spirit, Guarnieri, *op. cit.*, 467 and 468-9.
9. Guarnieri, *op. cit.*, 483.
10. J. Orcibal, "Le 'Miroir des simples ames' et la 'secte' du Libre Esprit," *Revue de l'histoire des religions*, CLXXVI (1969), 42; C. Kirchberger, *The Mirror of Simple Souls*, London, [1927].
11. Guarnieri, *op. cit.*, 353, 413-416; "Frères du libre esprit," *Dictionnaire de Spiritualité*, V (1964), 1252, 1264-5.
12. Orcibal, *op. cit.*, 55-58. This author links the *Mirror* for example with the doctrines of William of St. Thierry's *Epistola ad Fratres de Monte Dei;* cf. M.-M. Davy, *Un traité de la vie solitaire . . .*, Paris, 1940, 144, where William speaks of the union with God in which the soul enjoys the *spiritus libertatis.*
13. Orcibal, *op. cit.*, 58-9.
14. Guarnieri, *op. cit.*, 499. Guarnieri herself admits she has not produced an integrated analysis of the nature and origins of the heresy of the Free Spirit.
15. Orcibal, *op. cit.*, 58. He admits a dangerous tendancy towards quietism but notes that Tauler and John of the Cross used similar formulations in speaking of the indifference of the soul to the means of grace, *Ibid.*, 53-4.
16. *Mirouer*, ch. 21, 541.
17. Relatively few Free Spirit sources contain professions of formal pantheism, but some do, as for example the letter of Bp. Johann of Strasbourg, *Urkundenbuch d. Stadt Strassburg*, ed. W. Wigand, Strasbourg, 1886, Abt. I, II, 310; also *Determinationes* of Heymeric of Campo, ed. W. Preger, *Abhandlung d. hist. Kl. d. baverischen Akad. d. Wissenschaften*, XXI (1895), 62.
18. Confession of John of Brünn, W. Wattenbach, "Uber die Secte der Brüder vom freien Geiste . . . ," *Sitzungsberichte d. Preuss. Akad. d. Wissenschaften zu Berlin*, XXIX (1887), 533-4, "Item dicti fratres in spiritu viventes, cum ad perfectum statum libertatis pervenerint, ita totaliter et corporaliter transmutantur quod unum cum Deo efficiuntur, et Deus totaliter et corporaliter est cum eis, quod angeli in speculo Trinitatis non pussunt discernere inter Deum et animam, qui in libertate spiritus vixerit, propter prefatam unionem ipsorum."
19. Confession of Conrad Cannler, H. Haupt, "Ein Beghardenprozess in Eichstädt vom Jahre 1381," *ZKG*, V (1882), 495; confession of John Becker, G. Ritter, "Zur Geschichte des häretischen Pantheismus in Deutschland im 15. Jahrhundert," *ZKG*, XLIII (NF IV) (1924), 156; *Determinationes* of Heymeric of Campo, ed. Preger, *op. cit.*, 63; *Mirouer*, ch. 72, 575; William of St. Thierry, *Epistola*, ed. Davy, I, 146.
20. Full beatitude is known only after death, *Mirouer*, ch. 118, 613. The Free Spirit, Conrad Cannler makes the same qualification, Haupt, *ZKG*, V (1882), 495.
21. *Mirouer*, ch. 39, 553; ch. 9, 527. cf. Martin of Mainz, an accused Free Spirit, C. Schmidt, *Nicolaus von Basel*, Vienna, 1866, 67, "quod perfectus homo non debet pro inferni liberatione ac celestis regni collatione deum orare . . . sed indifferens eius beneplacitum expectare."
22. *Mirouer*, ch. 71, 575; ch. 94, 593; ch. 101, 598.
23. Döllinger, *Beiträge*, II, 398; also Heymeric of Campo, Preger, *Abh. (Bayr.)*, XXI (1895), 63, "Peccat, qui bona opera facit propter aeterna bona vel beatitudines, aut propter deum;" Bp. Johann of Strasbourg, *UB Strass*, 310, "item quod nihil debeat fieri propter premium quodcumque, etiam propter regnum celorum."
24. Denzinger, 221.
25. Conrad Cannler, in Haupt, *op. cit.*, 495, ". . . et quod homo perfectus licenciat a se virtutes per hunc modum, cum non indigeat eis;" Martin of Mainz in Schmidt, *op. cit.*, 67; cf. *Homines Intelligentiae*, "Item de statutis, praeceptis

et ordinationibus ecclesiae non curant nec de orationibus, dicentes quod Deus facit quod disposuit facere et quod vult . . . " P. Fredericq, *Corpus Documentorum Inquisitionis*, 5 vols., Ghent/The Hague, 1889-1906, I, 274.

26. *Mirouer*, ch. 21, 540; ch. 71, 575, ". . . car oeuvre de creature (c'est a entendre oeuvre faicte d'omme) ne peut estre comparee a oeuvre divine, faicte de Dieu en creature de sa bonté pour creature." Eckhart also taught that acts of piety can impede the spiritual man if not done with the proper emptiness, *DW* I, pr. 2, 29.

27. Döllinger, *Beiträge*, II, 396.

28. G. Ritter, *ZKG*, XLIII (1924), 153-4. For example, Becker claimed he was not required to pray aloud, with words.

29. Wattenbach, *Sb. (Berl.)*, XXIX (1887), 531.

30. Döllinger, *Beiträge*, II, 400.

31. The seventh stage of the soul's journey, the life of glory, is reached only after death. *Mirouer*, ch. 118, 613.

32. *Ibid.*, ch. 68, 572; ch. 44, 557.

33. Ritter, *op. cit.*, 155.

34. *Mirouer*, ch. 37, 552, "Car remors ou reprenement de conscience en l'Ame n'est aultre chose que faulte de charité . . ."

35. Döllinger, *Beiträge*, II, 402.

36. *Arbor vitae*, Venice, 1485, IV, vii, f. 153ʳ

37. B. Ulanowski, *Scriptores rerum Polonicarum*, XIII, Cracow, 1889, 240, 244; cf. letter of Bp. Johann of Strasbourg, *UB Strass*, 310, ". . . quod de nullo gaudent, de nullo turbantur."

38. *Ibid.*, 246; *Mirouer*, ch. 109, 604.

39. *Mirouer*, ch. 90, 591, ". . . font les frans tout ce qu'il leur plaist, se ilz ne veulent perdre paix, puisque ilz sont venuz en l'estat de franchise . . ."

40. Confession of John of Brünn, Wattenbach, *op. cit.*, 531.

41. Döllinger, *Beiträge*, II, 399.

42. *Mirouer*, ch. 17, 537. This soul no longer loves temporal things; thus to give Nature its due cannot lead to sinful acts.

43. F. Mone, ed., *Quellensammlung der badischen Landesgeschichte*, 4 vols., Karlsruhe, 1848-67, I, 336, ". . . daz es nit sünd wäre, mer ain notturset alz essen und trinken, und horti der natur zů . . ."; Cannler in Haupt, *ZKG*, V (1882), 495-6.

44. H. Seuse, *Das Buch der Wahrheit*, ch. 6, ed. K. Bihlmeyer, *Deutsche Schriften*, Stuttgart, 1907; Rulman Merswin, *Banerbuechelein*, in Jundt, *Panthéisme populaire*, 211-214; *Zweimannenbuch*, ed. F. Lauchert, *Des Gottesfruendes im Oberland Rulman Merswins Buch von den Zwei Mannen*, Bonn, 1896; G. Siedel, *Theologia Deutsch*, Gotha, 1929, especially ch. 25, 37-41; J. Van Mierlo, "Ruusbroec's Bestrijding van de Ketterij," *Ons Geestelijk Erf*, VI (1932), 304-346; see especially *Kingdom of the Lovers of God, Ornament of Spiritual Marriage, The Seven Cloisters*, in Ruusbroec, *Werken*, ed. Ruusbroec-Genootschap, 4 vols., Tielt, 1944-1948; W. Mulder, ed., *Gerardi Magni Epistolae*, Antwerp, 1933, especially no. 31, 134-136; J. Gerson, *Opera omnia*, ed. L. E. DuPin, 2nd ed., 5 vols., Antwerp, 1706, *Tractatus de dist. verarum visionum a falsis*, *op. cit.*, I, 55, *Admonitio . . . quomodo caute legendi sunt quorumdam libri*, I, 114.

45. F. Vetter, ed., *Die Predigten Taulers*, Berlin, 1910, pr. 40, 165; Döllinger, *Beiträge*, II, 397, "Quod homo unitus deo non debet confiteri etiam peccatum mortale . . . " This view is more extreme than that found in Tauler in specifying the freedom from confessing even mortal sins.

46. Vetter *Predigten*, pr. 63, 342; G. Schneiders, "Die Askese als Weltentsagung und Vollkommenheitsstreben bei Tauler," *Johannes Tauler*, ed. E. Filthaut, Essen, 1961, 202.

47. Denzinger, 221; Haupt, *ZKG*, V (1882), 496.

48. John of Brünn lived for twenty years a life of voluntary poverty and ascetic rigor as a Beghard in Cologne before he achieved the freedom of the spirit.

49. Vetter, *Predigten*, pr. 7, 33; Confession of John Hartmann, Wattenbach, *Sb. (Berl.)*, XXIX (1887), 540.

50. Vetter, *Predigten*, pr. 55, 258.

51. *Ibid.*, pr. 41, 175, ". . . und verlierent ir natürliche werk und übunge nach iren eigenen kreften in natürlicher wise und hant in dem versinkende in disem grundelosem mere weder wort noch wise." Compare with the Schweidnitz Beguines who chastise a sister for remaining too long in church at prayer, ". . . Du mynst dich selbir . . . " instead of rising above self to a true poverty of spirit, Ulanowski, *op. cit.*, 240.

52. Denzinger, 221.

53. Ulanowski, *op. cit.*, 246; 248, ". . . quia spiritus ex hoc stans in arce sua non inficitur, nec mordetur, et tunc licenciant a se virtutum opera . . ."

54. Vetter, *Predigten*, pr. 81, 432; Schneiders, *Johannes Tauler*, 196-7, 200; A. Hoffman, "Sakramentale Heilsweg bei Tauler," *Johannes Tauler*, 217; Vetter, *Predigten*, pr. 48, 218.

55. Compare, for example, the *Homines Intelligentiae*, who claimed, ". . . quod homo exterior non maculat hominem interiorem . . . " Fredericq, *Corpus*, I, 273.

56. Vetter, *Predigten*, pr. 36, 138.

57. *Ibid.*, pr. 30, 195; pr. 48, 218-219, "Dis ist ungeret in der worheit den frijen geisten die in valscher friheit glorierent . . ."

58. *Ibid.*, pr. 48, 218, "In etlichen landen vint man lúte die einer valscher lidikeit phlegent und tůnt sich aller würklicheit ab, und inwendig hütent si sich vor gůten gedenken, und sprechent si sin ze friden komen, und enwellent sich och nút üben an den werken der tugende und si sin der über komen."

59. R. Merswin, *Banerbuechelin*, ed. Jundt, *Panthéisme populaire*, 212; Confession of John Becker, Ritter, *ZKG*, XLIII (1924), 155, ". . . quod distinguit duplicem hominum statum: aliqui sunt qui adhuc subsunt sancte ecclesie, et illi tenentur adorare Christum secundum eius humanitatem propter preceptum ecclesie, cui tenentur obedire; alia pars hominum est sub statu spiritus, sicut ipse est, et illi non tenentur adorare humanitatem illam, sed solum deum sine medio in nuda deitate."

60. Vetter, *Predigten*, pr. 48, 218.

53

61. Cf. Merswin, *Banerbuechelin*, ed. Jundt, *Panthéisme populaire*, 214; Ruysbroeck, *Werken*, I, 232-234; Döllinger, *Beiträge*, II, 402, *Compilatio*, "Item quod peccata commissa non debent recogitare cum amaritudine et dolore, similiter dies elapsos in vanitate, quia per talem dolorem gratia ipsorum plenior retardatur."

62. J. Hamburger, *Johann Taulers Predigten*, Frankfurt, 1864, I, pr. 31, 204-209; *Theologia Deutsch*, ed. Seidel, 162-3, 177.

63. R. Merswin, *Zweimmanenbuch*, ed. F. Lauchert, Bonn. 1896. This interesting tale relates the encounter of the author who seeks the mystical *Durchbruch* with a *Waldbruder* and two *Waldschwestern* whose teachings are those of the Free Spirits.

64. H. Seuse, *Deutsche Schriften*, ed. K. Bihlmeyer, *Das Buch der Wahrheit*, ch. 6; *Ibid.*, 356, n. 26 for Bihlmeyer's comments on the relationship of this work to Eckhart.

65. *Theologia Deutsch*, ed. Seidel, 143, 125.

66. Jan van Leeuwen, "Traktat over de tien geboden," in C.G.N. de Vooys, "Meister Eckhart en de Nederlandse mystiek," *Nederlandsch Archief voor Kerkgeschiedenis*, N.S. III, The Hague, 1905, 192.

67. C. Schmidt, *Theologische Studien und Kritiken*, 1839, 666, 738, cited by H. Denifle, "Aktenstücke zu M. Eckharts Process," *Zeitschrift fur deutsches Alterthum und deutsche literatur*, XXIX (1885), 616.

68. A. Combes, *Essai sur la critique de Ruysbroeck par Gerson*, 3 vols., Paris, 1945-1959, III, 285-292; II, 321-324. Combes edits Gerson's *Epistola prima ad fratrem Bartholomaeum* in which Gerson associates the condemnations of *Ad nostrum* with Ruysbroeck's mystical doctrine as set forth in the *Ornament of Spiritual Marriage*.

69. For example, Franciscan friars were accused of this heresy, L. Oliger, *De secta spiritus libertatis in Umbria saec. XIV*, Rome, 1943, 103-120; Marguerite Porete was known as a Beguine "clergesse," and sent her book to the Bishop for approval, C. Langlois, "Marguerite Porete," *Revue historique*, LIV (1894), 296; Hermann Kuchener of Würzburg was said to have been a priest, *Monumenta Boica*, XL, 415-420; William of Hildernisse of the *Homines Intelligentiae* was a Carmelite friar, Fredericq, *Corpus*, I, 267.

70. It was the essentialist, transformational mysticism of the Dionysian tradition rather than the affective, penitential mystical school which was open to these 'quietist' and antinomian directions. See H. Oberman, "Gabriel Biel and Late Medieval Mysticism, *Church History*, XXX (1961), 259-287, for a good discussion of the varieties of the medieval mystical tradition.

# Popular Devotion in the Vernacular Drama of Medieval England

*E. Catherine Dunn*

MEDIEVAL RELIGIOUS DRAMA in Latin was the flower of the great cultural movement designated as the Carolingian Renaissance, an era that produced a liturgical phenomenon comparable to the celebration of the Dionysiac festival and the tragic drama of ancient Greece. The Latin liturgy of the ninth and tenth centuries was a late expression of Roman classicism revealing the grave and austere sublimity of Mediterranean thought and culture transmitted, from ancient civilization to the early medieval world. The Gregorian chant and the classical Latin idiom that Charlemagne demanded of the clergy in his empire were the imposition of a highly cultivated academic style upon the religious life of a semi-barbaric people. One cannot speak of a popular spirituality finding a vehicle in this liturgical development, but rather of a learned, intellectual worship being required from a people fundamentally alien to the classical spirit of the ritual. The radical shock of this confrontation can be judged by the great effort made over the next few generations to adjust this strange idiom to the popular sensibility. The whole florescence of trope writing was a movement to explain and adorn the highly intellectual Roman sentiments and to make possible an expression of emotion and subjectivity as a kind of descant or interlinear gloss on the authorized text. Out of this compositional activity emerged the drama of the medieval Church.[1]

The cultural conflict that underlies the adoption of the Roman liturgy in France has been remarked by historians since the scholarly study of medieval ritual began in the eighteenth century. L'Abbé Jean

Lebeuf recorded the confrontation of cultivated and primitive tastes, referring to certain forms of troping embellishments as barbaric ("ces morceaux gothiques").[2] F. J. Fétis, writing in the nineteenth century, observed that the Gallican liturgy was yielded up for the Roman only with great resistance because the new regulations abrogated a large measure of popular participation in public worship.[3] Although this contrast between the two rites will remain something of an enigma until a definitive study of Gallican customs appears,[4] recent work by French musicologists supports the older recognition, finding an attempted compromise between the Gregorian chant of the Roman compositions *(cantilena romana)* and the popular melodies of a secular nature used in embellishment *(cantilena vulgaris)*.[5]

Because the liturgical reform, after experimentation by Chrodegang of Metz and Remedius of Rouen, was imposed by royal *fiat* of the Frankish rulers (Pepin and Charlemagne),[6] one easily infers that the conflict involved is simply that of the classical Roman temperament with the Germanic. These are the terms in which F. J. Raby speaks,[7] but the ethnic realities are probably more complicated than he observed. Discussing the Roman Mass as transplanted to a French locale in the eighth century, Joseph Jungmann says that "it was not primarily a Germanic world that it came face to face with, but rather a Romanized Celtic world . . . The features which bring the Celt into bold contrast with the clear logical orderliness of the Roman, with his laconic brevity and stark realism, are hardly to be distinguished from the features we are wont to emphasize in the German. The restlessness and agitation, the strong passionate estheticism which mark the German character, must have been the Celt's too, but only in greater measure . . . [8] In both the Celtic and Germanic expressiveness there are the ardor and subjectivity usually called "romantic" in the history of epoch styles in art, music, and literature. The clash of this quality with the Roman liturgy is a phenomenon by no means confined to the Merovingian and Carolingian eras, but is recurrent even into modern times. Karl Rahner has recently remarked that the Latin liturgy is so cryptic and intellectualized a form of worship that it has needed, again and again, to be interpreted by commentary or by restatement in lyrical and subjective terms.[9]

The Carolingian musical tropes, then, in their lyrical and dramatic forms were such an effort in the history of the Church to adapt the official prayer of the worshiping community to the expressive manner of non-Roman people. The tropes and the dramas were of a *paraliturgical* nature, existing beside the authorized text or inserted between the clauses of the fundamental verbal structure. Originally composed for the clarification and guidance of prayerful expression, they came to possess a rhetorical and sometimes poetic artistry that made them objects of great beauty. They show a wide range of technical accomplishment, from mere prosaic statement to genuine poetry, but the finest of them reveal, along with an intense affectivity, a verbal sophistication in which the classical spirit has been absorbed and recast into transalpine style.

The vernacular mystery plays, coming much later than the Latin dramas, are in this tradition of paraliturgical composition. Although Professor Kolve regards the Corpus Christi play as having been freed from dependence upon the liturgy of any particular feast day,[10] one can nevertheless say that the cycle is still very closely related to liturgical worship as such. Moreover, the Corpus Christi play in the vernacular is simply another step in the process of glossing and embellishing the classical Latin text, this time by translation into a national linguistic idiom like English in order to create a popular version. The drama cycle is of great complexity; yet it is still a descant on the fundamental Latin ritual, as the tropes had been. The vernacular drama, accordingly, is a paraliturgical form of spirituality.

The problem of defining a devotional life is properly that of a theologian and historian; nevertheless, a student of literature may have a contribution to make towards comprehension of the historical forms of spirituality. The literary critic, by profession, works with *style*, i.e., with an author's manner or process of structuring the meaning in an object made of words. Stylistic devices are methods of shaping the materials according to 1) the inclinations or perspective of the writer, 2) his efforts to reach an addressee, and 3) his reflection of the social milieu in which he lives. The style of a dramatic cycle, built up over centuries by a tradition of clerical composition, will consequently be a mirror of numerous individual writers and of the tastes for dramatic entertainment retained by generations of audience-spectators. The manner of expression, though apparently a surface phenomenon, is the product of deeply-rooted tendencies, and is essentially a way of grasping the liturgical meaning and shaping it into beautiful form. A vernacular cycle has something massive, almost monumental, about it, but it is stylistically a key to the type of spirituality that has created the drama and kept it alive in the love of the people.

The first aspect of the spirituality that flowers in these cycles is the Biblical texture. The mystery plays are, in truth, the "peoples' Bible" in the ages when manuscripts of the great book could not be multiplied without enormous cost, and could not be read by the great majority, the general unlettered populace, even if copied. In England, the locale of immediate interest here, there were Latin manuscripts of the Vulgate, and French translations of it, the one kind of text being the province of specialized study in ecclesiastical institutions, and the other kind an answer to the needs of the cultivated Anglo-Norman aristocracy (whether clerical or lay) that ruled England for three hundred years.[11] Neither the Latin nor the French texts could serve the English population of agricultural laborers and bourgeois craftsmen, and when texts in the English vernacular did appear in the very late fourteenth century they were embroiled in Wycliffite controversy and subject to censorship as possibly heretical vehicles of Lollard teaching and interpretation.

This accessibility of the Scriptures to the entire people, not through manuscripts but through the annual Corpus Christi plays, served as a source of information and instruction, like a modern catechetical course in Scripture. It also operated as an indirect control upon the devotional life of those concerned in the enterprise. Although the plays were performed once a year in the early summer, and did not consume more than two or three days, the enterprise involved months of preparation and rehearsal, the whole season of Lent often serving as the interval of long-range training for the great event. Such an immersion in the Biblical narrative and assumption of the roles by actors meant an exposure to the story of creative and redeeming love that must have operated as a theocentric force in the lives of the participants. To say this is not to claim a widespread devotional life as an actual historical phenomenon, for the response of the individual person to the Divine is not automatic and is not always manifested externally. It remains true, however, that the presence of the Biblical material in the midst of daily life served to focus attention on the heart of the Judaeo-Christian message and to shield devotional ardor, when it developed, from peripheral concerns and aberrations.

The vernacular English cycles were built up in several layers, added one after the other from about 1375 to 1450.[12] The earliest *stratum* in each cycle was a small series of plays closely related to Latin liturgical dramas for Christmas and Easter. They were probably translated from Latin texts available in the monastery or cathedral, and expanded with some material that was handled in close imitation of the traditional dramatic texts.[13] I have myself devoted much time to the study of the Towneley and the York cycles in these terms, but cannot here repeat the detailed analyses that are necessary to prove the point. What is relevant to the question of spirituality is the continued presence of this "primitive" layer of dramatic material having the qualities of gravity, sobriety, and reserve that the Scriptural narrative itself possesses and that the Latin plays had preserved in their classical beauty. The later layers of composition are superimposed upon this Biblical material, and they draw freely upon apocryphal literature, legend, and poetry. The expansions, *e.g.* a series of Passion plays, are often expressions of an affective spirituality that is akin to the school of Richard Rolle. They are, however, integrated into the original cycle so that they form a descant or embellishment upon the substratum, just as the Carolingian tropes had been an *obligato* on the authorized Gregorian liturgy and chant. The romantic affectivity is still being controlled by the classical base of the construct, and by a continuous magnetism from the Scriptural center.

An illustration of this surviving presence of the Biblical core can be found in the Towneley Easter play (No. XXVI). Parts of this play are identical with the Easter drama of York (No. XXXVIII), both plays containing exactly the same "Quem quaeritis" scene, in which very little variation has been introduced into the question and answer that had constituted the simple dramatic Latin tropes of the tenth century:

> *primus angelus.* Ye mowrnyng women in youre thoght, here in this place
> whome haue ye soght?
> *Maria Magdalene.* Ihesu that vnto ded was broght, Oure lord so fre.   /noble/
> *Secundus angelus.* Certys, women, here is he noght; Com nere and se. (11.
> 382-87)[14]

The "Hortulanus" scene, the meeting between Mary Magdalene and Christ as "Gardener," appears also in the Towneley play (but not the York correspondent).[15] The scene is probably older than the York Easter play and a surviving remnant of the most primitive layer in the Towneley cycle, a technical matter that need not detain us here. The encounter between Mary and the risen Christ is the most crucial dramatic moment in the entire cycle, for it is the *peripeteia* (in the Aristotelian sense), the recognition and reversal that suddenly transform the Passion catastrophe into a glorious fulfillment. The incident is enclosed within seventy-one lines, a brief interval for the explosive force of this great revelation toward which the whole cycle had been a rising action. The encounter has, however, the simplicity of the Gospel accounts:

> *Ihesus.* woman, why wepys thou? be styll!
> whome sekys thou? say me thy wyll,
>     And nyk me not with nay.                    /deny me not/
> *Maria Magdalene.* ffor my lord I lyke full yll;          /am unhappy/

> The stede thou bare his body tyll  /place to which/
> Tell me I the pray . . . (11.569-74)

After a brief denial that He has removed the body, He asks her what the Lord had meant to her. "He was everything to me," is her laconic reply, to which He answers with his brief but stunning revelation: "Mary, thou sekys thy god, and that am I" (1.585).

The interplay of this simple but sublime Scriptural material with accretions of a later date and in a different style can be seen in the so-called Hegge cycle[16] connected with the city of Lincoln. Here is a scene in the Passion series that is unique in English drama,[17] but typical of fifteenth-century artistic conception and literary technique as found in the latest layer of cycle revisions. It is the "Pietà," the scene of Mary at the foot of the Cross holding the dead body of Christ — a scene later captured in Michelangelo's immortal sculpture. It is essentially a tableau and a lament of the Blessed Virgin. The sufferings of the Redeemer and of His mother are not a feature of Latin drama, probably because the pathos and tenderness involved in their narration exceed the limits of classical taste. Even in the English cycles the Passion play is of late development and shows a "pathetic naturalism" that is regarded by historians of style as a breakdown of the sublimity and abstraction in high medieval symbolic art. The dramatist has designed this scene of the Pietà that the Gospels do not depict, and for which imagination could construct a sad and moving picture.

Joseph and Nicodemus take the body of Christ from the Cross and lay it tenderly in Mary's lap, with concern for the mother's sorrow:

> (Joseph) Loo mary modyr good and trewe
> Here is thi son blody and bloo
> ffor hym myn hert ful sore doth rewe
> kysse hym now onys eer he go.[18] (11. 1140-43)

Mary's lament gathers into itself the universal grief of bereaved motherhood, while simultaneously challenging any woman to make a comparison that can prevail beside her unique anguish:

> . . . ther was nevyr modyr that say this  /saw/
> so here sone dyspoyled with so gret wo
> and my dere chylde nevyr dede A-mys . . . (11. 1148-50)

Although there is deep pathos here and a genuinely feminine touch, the scene is surrounded by the Scriptural business of the request for Pilate's permission to bury the body and the securing of a tomb for it. The tendency to flamboyant or baroque expression of grief is kept within the limits of the controlling Scriptural frame and glows with a mellow light. Even in plays that seem flamboyant to modern taste there is the close juxtaposition of other plays or scenes from the simpler, more austere narratives based directly on the Biblical accounts.

When one seeks in the vernacular English cycles for light on medieval popular devotion, he is likely to discern a second dimension beyond the Scriptural that I have been discussing. It is the liturgical character of the piety that is reflected in the plays, even though one must regard the drama cycle itself as a paraliturgical phenomenon. The English mystery plays were not a body of drama that moved out of the church building and became secularized in the market place or on the pageant wagons.[19] The cycles remained until the sixteenth century a mirror of the ecclesiastical year as the latter was arranged in the sequence of feasts and penitential observances from Advent, through Lent and Easter, and into the Pentecostal season.

"The plaie called Corpus Christi" was integrally related to the liturgical feast that summarizes the Redemptive mystery. It was not simply an annual event placed in early summer when the open and mild weather favored outdoor performance. Although the Corpus Christi procession was separate from the plays, the feast itself was quite meaningful for the Creation-to-Judgment drama sequence, i.e., for salvation history. No matter how much joinery of Christmas, Passion, and Easter plays had to be done to forge a cycle, the totality, in each stage of cyclic expansion, was an entity with logical relationships among the parts and with the Redemption of man as the axis.[20] The feast of Corpus Christi commemorates the sacrifice in both its historical and its timeless reality and focuses attention on the Mass and the Eucharist as the perfect oblation and the sacrament of Divine love. Devotion to the Sacrament fostered by the feast was a corporate, public worship, not the individual adoration before the tabernacle so much more familiar to modern times.

This public, liturgical prayer encouraged by the celebration of Corpus Christi served, like the Biblical narrative, to preserve the devotion of the faithful from frivolous interests and by-paths. The dramatic cycle had a basic interpretative voice, either overtly expressed in an Expositor or more subtly entrusted to characters in the plays. This voice, first given a technical name by Marius Sepet[21] as "la voix de l'Eglise," mediated the import of the Scriptural story as acted and gave to lyrical expression a communal texture. This is not to say that expression was cold or unemotional, but that the affective lyricism was channeled into the modes of the Church's official prayers, the Mass and the Divine Office, which thus served as objective controls over a piety that might easily have found sentimental and unorthodox forms.[22]

The Expositor serving in this directive role is readily seen in the

Chester cycle. Nowhere does he more explicitly fulfill the function than in the Prophet play, the drama in which the figure of Augustine had served as moderator when the *Ordo prophetarum* had been performed as a Latin play of Christmas Matins. (It is more accurate to speak of this interlocutor who summoned the Old Testament prophets to proclaim their testimony to the Messiah as the "pseudo-Augustinian" voice, since the sermon on which the play is based was erroneously attributed to Augustine in the Middle Ages.) The Augustinian *persona* is one of the most important representatives of the Church's viewpoint in the whole range of religious drama, and probably served as a norm for all of the formal expository figures appearing in the cycles (*e.g.,* Contemplacio in the Hegge plays).

The fifth drama of the Chester cycle is its Prophet play, entitled rather inaccurately "Pagina quinta de Mose et Rege Balaak et Balaam Propheta." Several other prophets besides the two named enter into the play, and the lines of Jeremiah with their commentary by the Expositor show the Scriptural material with the voice of the Church closely attached:

IHEREMIA.

Deducunt oculi mei lacrimas per diem et noctem, et non taceant, contritione magna contrita est virgo filia populi mei et plaga et ct.

| | |
|---|---|
| My eyes must run and sorrow aye, | |
| without ceasing, night and daye, | |
| for my daughter, soth to saye, | |
| shall suffer great anye. | /harm/ |
| And my folk shall doe, in faye, | /in truth/ |
| thinges that they ne know may | |
| to that mayden, by many waye, | |
| and her sonne, sickerlie. | |

EXPOSITOR

Lordinges, this prophesie, I wis,
touches the passion nothing amisse . . . [23] (11.329-38).

The interpretative voice continues to explicate Jeremiah's prophecy in detail, point by point.

A more artistic type of exegesis than this formal one was the temporary assumption of an expository voice by a dramatic character within the structure of a play. The Towneley cycle shows this form of "la voix de l"Eglise," one that evades the dangers of an Expositor's rhetorical intrusion into the imaginative world of the play. This phenomenon may be designated as the creation of an *aspect* for the character's voice, a dimension added to his role in the play, and one that may or may not be realistically harmonious with his fundamental dramatic identity. The shepherds who are sent to Bethlehem by the angelic messenger are probably the most dazzling illustration of such a character construct, in the two Nativity plays of the Towneley manuscript.

Although these shepherds are uneducated, rustic men watching their flocks on a Judean hillside and are given a message wholly unexpected, they respond to the announcement of the Incarnation by recapitulating the formal prophecies of the Old Testament. Their manner of speech is alien to their dramatic *personae* at this point, and they have assumed the Expositor's role for the time being. The angelic information had been quite a cryptic revelation, but they respond with a learned discussion of the Virgin Birth. One might argue that they could remember the Messianic prophecies of the Hebraic tradition without showing extraordinary knowledge, but their awareness of Elizabeth, Zachary, and John the Baptist as participants in the prophetic tradition can only mean that they are speaking with an ecclesiastical interpretative voice not their own. One stanza will serve to keynote their role:

/SECOND SHEPHERD/: Abacuc and ely/ prophesyde so,      /Elijah/
        Elezabeth and zachare / and many other mo,       /more/
        And dauid as veraly / is witnes therto,
        Iohn Baptyste sewrly / and daniel also.
        /THIRD SHEPHERD/: So saying,
        he is godys son alon,
        without hym shalbe none,
        his sete and his trone
        Shall euer be lastyng . . .[24] (11. 377-85)

The intellectual level of the expository voice varies from one cycle to another and even within a given set of plays, but generally this dimension of the dramas is remarkably learned, and not ostensibly a condescension to ignorant and unlettered audiences. Indeed, the scholarly books being written today on typological figuration in the plays are a startling (if accurate) revelation of what the playgoers were expected to grasp in the meaning of the cycles. No one who reads the plays carefully, however, will miss the stylistic level of abstract, lofty eloquence that often prevails, played off against the racy colloquialism of certain scenes like Noah's conflict with his wife or the sheep-stealing episode of the rascally Mak. Since the work of Charles Muscatine on Chaucer's relation to the French tradition this abstract, non-representational style has been called "Gothic Idealism," but as a literary mode it is simply the transfer to vernacular speech of the grand style found in Latin medieval poetry, especially of liturgical prayer.

One such passage is the long hymn of praise in the York cycle's play of Christ's entry into Jerusalem (No. XXV). It is a vernacular English "Hail Lyric," a well-known genre of eulogy to the Saviour, here a counterpart of the "Gloria, laus et honor" of the Church's Palm Sunday processional. It is too extensive to reproduce in its entirety, but even a small selection catches the intellectual grandeur holding in restraint the intense affectivity of the lyricism. Each of the eight citizens who have discussed the expected entry of the Lord into the city speaks a stanza of welcome to Him. The fourth one recalls His birth in Bethlehem:

> Hayll! blissfull babe, in Bedleme borne,
> Hayll! boote of all oure bittir balis,
> Hayll! sege that schoppe bothe eveh and morne,   /Person who created/
> Hayll! talker trystefull of trew tales.   /trustworthy speaker/
> Hayll! comely knyght,
> Hayll! of mode that most preuayles   /disposition/
> To saue the tyght.[25]   /the well-disposed/
> (11. 511-17)

In the midst of carefully structured alliterating consonants and rich Northern dialect vowel sounds, the poet here elicits phrases or clauses of theological mystery, greeting Christ as knight and warrior riding into the city, but also as the one who made both the morning and evening (1. 513). In a later line (535) he calls Him "texte of trewthe the trew to taste" (true text for testing the faithful), playing with sound and meaning in a kind of witty paradox such as the Victorine school of lyrical Latin poetry had perfected in the twelfth century.

The final aspect of popular spirituality that strikes me in the cycle plays is a psychological one: the joyous vitality there captured. I am not thinking primarily of the comic spirit so often remarked upon and discussed as occuring in plays like the Second Shepherds' of Towneley. This boisterous, rollicking fun, placed so close to the reverent Nativity scene, never ceases to attract and to baffle the modern reader. It is a genial sense of relaxation in the presence of the holy of which we experience little in the world of today. However, the comic spirit is not necessarily a joyous mood, as the history of literature and of the theater can demonstrate. Comedy, whether crude and rough in its farcical expression or refined and sophisticated in its aristocratic play of "manners," is capable of a mordant satire that often cuts and destroys rather than breathes geniality. Mak and his wife Gyll, for example, fare rather badly at the hands of the shepherds; the tossing of this robber in the sheet is rough punishment for him and has even been interpreted as symbolic death. Comedy has little to offer as a healing process in the confrontation with human foibles and folly. In its more sophisticated forms it is quite merciless.

The joy that pervades the mystery plays, then, is not the comic spirit; nor is it the spirit of "game" that Kolve has recently discussed in his book on the Corpus Christi cycles.[26] Philosophically, the concept of game or play is related both to ritual and to art form, but the distinction between game and religious joy is a crucial one that cannot here be explored. Some of the most delicate questions that cluster around dramatic artistry are involved in this problem, and quite justly have exercised a generation of critics drawing upon Johann Huizinga's concept of "homo ludens." It is not this pattern of mimetic action and fictionalized impersonation that concerns me at the moment.

It is not easy for us to define a spirituality of joy because post-Tridentine devotional phenomena have a different texture from those of the Middle Ages. The spirit of medieval religious drama seems to be an affirmative perspective on the faith, a rich intermingling of intelligence and emotion creating confidence and hope in a vale of tears. Marius Sepet wrote of the liturgical drama in the High Middle Ages as one that flourished when men and women of every condition in life, even in toil and suffering "savaient vivre et mourir dans la plénitude d'une foi joyeuse, sous le regard et le sourire de l'Eglise, qui les avait enfantés, nonseulement à la vie surnaturelle, mais à la vie intellectuelle, et qui les initiait, par les splendeurs de son culte plein d'une divine poésie, aux pures jouissances de l'art."[27]

While this observation of Sepet's was made of the twelfth and thirteenth centuries, it would still be fundamentally valid for the era of cycle plays in the late Middle Ages. Quite naturally there would be many variations in this religious sensibility, each individual having a unique collocation of intellectual and emotional elements in his response to the faith. But the very range of human personalities making up the medieval theater audiences speaks for a core of common experience unfolded in the plays and generally understood by all spectators.

Joy itself can be of many kinds from the naive to the most esoteric, on a scale that is rather clearly perceptible in the cycles. It appears as a luminous quality set off against a contrasting foil of shadow and sadness. One might say that it is modulated through the cycle so as to be a recurrent theme in the midst of an indescribable complexity. Looking at the total construct of any surviving cycle, a modern reader may well repeat what John Dryden said of Chaucer's *Canterbury Tales:* "Here is God's plenty." The sheer variety of character, situation, and event is overpowering; but there is more here than a kaleidoscope of the human condition. There is a rhythmic pattern of returning joy victorious over loss and sadness, of light piercing through somber shadows. Many of the individual plays, especially of the Old Testament, open with a monologue of patriarchal yearning and melancholy, move into

65

an intense conflict, *e.g.,* Abraham's obedience to God's command about Isaac, and then terminate in a burst of relief and joy as deliverance from the sacrifice or conquest of the danger occurs. The play has its own rhythmic undulation of emotional states, over which the victory of Divine power prevails.

There is, as the cycle moves forward, the simple, child-like joyousness of the Christmas story, toward which the Old Testament plays move on a steady course. The longing of the patriarchs and prophets has had about it the melancholy that suffuses the Advent liturgy in the preparation for the great feast, as one dramatic scene after another looks forward to the promised coming of the Redeemer, but ends with fulfillment only in a prefigurative, typological sense. The joy of the Christmas play in all of the cycles is something exquisite, a quality typical of "merry England," the level of which is set by rough peasants offering gifts to a child, who is surrounded by farm animals and tended by a poor couple who have secured transient shelter in a stable. Even though the shepherds become prophets momentarily, as I discussed above, they prevail as characters of rude upbringing, shy, embarrassed, and halting in the effort to be polite and tender. The audience forgets all else about them — that they have quarrelled among themselves, railed against landlords, and stolen sheep. They seem to be personifications of innocent joy, no more reprehensible than small and naughty children.

Then there is in the cycles the joy of Easter, best expressed by Mary Magdalene. This happiness is not that of innocence, but one that has attained maturity after sin and remorse. It has attended upon death but also upon resurrection. Mary, the sinner and yet the first of the Lord's followers to know of His triumph, stands at the crux of the dramatic conflict and as she expresses her relief at finding Christ, sheds the splendor of her happiness over the entire story:

> My blys is commen, my care is gone,
> That lufly haue I mett alone;                /gracious one/
> I am as blyth in bloode and bone
> As euer was wight;
> Now is he resyn that ere was slone,          /slain/
> Mi hart is light.[28] (11. 617-22)

Her joy somehow counterpoises all the weight of the Passion plays that have preceded, even though the physical sufferings of the Crucifixion have been dramatized with a realism almost unbearable to a modern audience.

There are many other degrees and levels of joy throughout the cycles. There is the victory of the dignified Magi eluding Herod and following the star; there is old Simeon hearing the Temple bells ring on their own power as the Christ Child is brought for presentation. Perhaps one may say, finally, that the joy in which the entire mystery sequence is enveloped is that of Corpus Christi Day itself, the time at which a whole town marshalled its resources to celebrate the Eucharistic feast. Although a city might transfer its mystery cycle to some other great festival, like that of Pentecost (as in Chester) or of St. Anne (as in Lincoln), the cycle was still "the plaie called Corpus Christi." The Sacrament instituted on Holy Thursday under the shadow of the coming Crucifixion could not be properly celebrated in Holy Week. The establishment of a special feast of joy in the Eucharist was one of the great achievements of medieval devotional aspiration, and its joy produced a lasting memorial in the plays that bear its name.

The three aspects of medieval popular devotion that have struck me in years of involvement with the religious drama are, in summary, the Biblical texture, the liturgical mode of expression, and the thematic joy that prevails in the developing pattern of narrative line and dramatic conflict. All of these are aspects of a literary *stylistique* that is fundamentally proportioned, measured, and controlled — in a word, classical. Although there is an intense affectivity of lyrical expression and a profound clash of dramatic personalities in the complex story of redemption, the tendency toward embellishments of a romantic or baroque nature is kept within the confines of a Roman spirit that has its origin in the Gregorian liturgy and the communal prayer life of the Church. This literary mode helps define the spirituality of the late Middle Ages and serves as a kind of mirror reflecting much of the inner life and dynamism of popular devotion.

# NOTES

1. The general propositions on the medieval drama in the present essay are based upon several detailed studies that I have made over a period of years. These cannot be recapitulated in the short scope of this paper, but only glanced at in the footnotes as the ideas occur.
2. Lebeuf, *Traité historique et pratique sur le chant ecclésiastique* (Paris, 1741), p. 122.
3. F. J. Fétis, *Histoire générale de la musique* (Paris, 1876), V, 106-7.
4. The "standard" treatment of the Gallican liturgy occurs in L. Duchesne's *Origines du culte chrétien* (Paris, 1902), but Father Johannes Quasten says that it is unsatisfactory ("Gallican Rites," *The New Catholic Encyclopedia* [New York, 1967], VI, 258).
5. Amédée Gastoué, *La Cantique populaire en France* (Lyon, 1924), pp. 6 and 17-20; Jacques Chailley, *L'Ecole musicale de Saint Martial de Limoges jusqu' à la fin du XI siècle* (Paris, 1960), pp. 186-87.
6. Pierre Batiffol, *History of the Roman Breviary*, tr. Atwell Baylay (New York, 1912), pp. 64-65.
7. *A History of Christian Latin Poetry*, 2d ed. (Oxford, 1953), p. 223; Karl Young evades the historical problem, and suggests several explanations as possible for the troping movement. (*The Drama of the Medieval Church* (Oxford, 1933), I, 179-82.)
8. Joseph Jungmann, *The Mass of the Roman Rite: Its Origins and Development*, tr. Rev. Francis Brunner, revised by Charles K. Riepe (New York, 1951), p. 58.

9. *The Christian Commitment: Essays in Pastoral Theology*, tr. Cecily Hastings (New York, 1963), pp. 173-75.

10. V. A. Kolve, *The Play Called Corpus Christi* (Stanford, 1966), pp. 34-44.

11. Grace Landrum gathered statistics of surviving Biblical manuscripts. She says that 5000 copies of the Latin Vulgate survive from the thirteenth century, [apparently in Western Europe generally] of which 300 are in the British Museum. French translations were also easily accessible at that period, before the Wycliffite agitation. "Chaucer's Use of the Vulgate," *PMLA*, 39 (1924), 75-76.

12. F. M. Salter's demolition of the early 1328 date, cherished by the town of Chester as the original year of its cycle, can be studied in his *Mediaeval Drama in Chester* (Toronto, 1955), pp. 29-53.

13. Hardin Craig, in *English Religious Drama of the Middle Ages* (Oxford, 1955), gives considerable coverage to this stratification in each of the chapters on the four surviving cycles. He incorporates the views of Marie Lyle and Esther Swenson, whose doctoral theses he directed. My own position varies fundamentally from Professor Craig's on the York and Towneley cycles, and comes closest to that of Alfred Pollard, which is presented in the EETS edition of *The Towneley Plays*, ed. England and Pollard, Extra Series, 71 (London, 1897), and to that of Martial Rose. See his Introduction to *The Wakefield Mystery Plays* (New York, 1962). I first expressed my view incidentally in "Lyrical Form and the Prophetic Principle in the Towneley Plays," *Mediaeval Studies*, 23 (1961), 80-90, and elaborated it in a yet unpublished monograph *The Prophetic Principle in the Towneley Plays*. It is also active in the dissertations of my students Sister Carolyn Wall and Sister Patricia Forrest.

14. *The Towneley Plays*, ed. England and Pollard, p. 317.

15. York has a separate "Hortulanus" play, not related to the Towneley text.

16. The name is that of Robert Hegge of Durham, who owned the manuscript in the early seventeenth century. (Craig, p. 239.) The cycle is often erroneously referred to as the "Ludus Coventriae," as in the EETS edition.

17. Waldo McNeir, "The Corpus Christi Passion Play as Dramatic Art," *SP*, 48 (1951), 627.

18. *Ludus Coventriae or the Plaie Called Corpus Christi*, ed. K. S. Block, EETS, Extra Series, 120 (London, 1922), p. 311.

19. The best refutation of this commonly accepted idea of secularization is to be found in Salter, pp. 43ff.

20. See Hardin Craig's fine discussion of the Corpus Christi feast and the attachment of the mystery plays to it, pp. 127-50.

21. *Les Prophètes du Christ* (Paris, 1878).

22. See my article "The Literary Style of the Towneley Plays," *American Benedictine Review*, 20 (1969), 481-504, for a discussion of lyricism in relation to liturgical prayer.

23. *The Chester Plays: Part I*, ed. Hermann Deimling, EETS, Extra Series, 62 (London, 1892), pp. 98-99.

24. *The Towneley Plays*, No. XII, "First Shepherds' Play," p. 112.

25. *York Plays*, ed. Lucy Toulmin Smith, 1885; repr. New York, 1963, p. 217.

26. Kolve, Chapters II and VI.

27. Sepet, *Le Drame chrétien au moyen âge* (Paris, 1878), pp. 89-90.

28. *The Towneley Plays*, No. XXVI, pp. 324-25.

# Drama and Spirituality in the Middle Ages

*Sandro Sticca*

CRITICAL AND THEORETICAL studies on the birth and development of the medieval drama have been traditionally concerned with exploring the relation of creed and liturgy to an art form, the drama. The Christian tragic intuition has been looked upon primarily as the issue of the liturgical and paraliturgical ceremonies performed to dramatize and celebrate the tragic and triumphant events in the Christian scheme of the redemption: the Passion and the Resurrection.

This traditional view of medieval drama as an imaginative expression of faith, as a theological statement, possesses an intrinsic validity when applied, in particular, to the liturgical plays. Performed within the confines of Christian worship and subservient to the ends of that worship, they are testimony of the dramatic movement and temper of the liturgy in which they find their origin, and constitute a powerful dramatic and didactic statement on Christian doctrine.

But whereas literary historians have readily recognized the exceptional status of liturgy, Scriptural and canonical, as the primary creative impulse in the inception and development of the medieval drama, they have been, on the other hand, quite reticent in fully ascertaining and assessing the importance of medieval *spirituality* — canonical, mystical, monastic, and popular — which had as much influence on the early beginnings and development of the religious theater. If it was the union of the art of the liturgy and the art of the purely dramatic which created the religious play, it was also the contemporary and in many instances, the antecedent religious *Zeitgeist* and theological attitude which prepared the proper milieu for that play to be articulated and manifested.

It is traditional to characterize medieval spirituality by its three

69

basic manifestations: a practical and affective spirituality removed from intellectual reasoning and interested in emotion, a speculative spirituality concerned with theological preoccupations, and an affective and speculative spirituality which tends to unite and reconcile reason and feeling.

Although my investigation shall be generally concerned with the affective and practical spirituality, I shall not wish to be limited by a consideration of the traditional, rigid, and absolute meaning of *spirituality*. Rather, I shall be guided by a comprehensive view of it, one that takes into account mystical attitudes as well as liturgical, monastic, and popular devotional manifestations. The purpose of this paper will be primarily that of assessing a direct association between that spirituality and the religious dramatic art. I shall try to illustrate to what extent, in the Middle Ages, the actuality of the dramatic theme and the visual realization of scenes and actions is due to the pervasive and inspirational influence of medieval spirituality.

The association between drama and spirituality, in the Middle Ages, will be more easily understood if one realizes the chronological hiatus that normally exists between devotional and popular spirituality and dramatized enactments. Medieval dramatists, more often than not, appear to have transformed only later into coherently acted narratives what medieval spirituality had already declaimed with religious intensity. This lack of spiritual contemporaneity, of historical synchronism had already been remarked, for the visual arts, by Etienne Gilson. Commenting on Emile Mâle's effort to establish a chronological correspondence between religious sentiment and pictorial narratives, Gilson remarked: ". . . y a-t-il nécessairement synchronisme entre l'esprit d'un temps et l'iconographie qui l'exprime, ou n'y aurait-il pas plutôt un certain retard de l'expression artistique sur l'esprit qu'elle traduit en oeuvres concrètes?"[1]

I

The question of chronology is particularly pertinent when applied to the essential element which engendered the religious theater, the tropes. These early religious plays do not demand skill and ingenuity for acting nor a technical dramatic apparatus. Antiphonally sung at first, the only prerequisite is musical competence in liturgical singing. And it is useful to remember at this point that it was partially out of experiment in liturgical music that the liturgical dramatic form was developed in the tenth century.[2] The very birth of that form cannot plausibly be explained without calling attention to the dominant role of music in medieval culture and spirituality and to the persuasive musical explanation of the origin of the Easter play first given by Schwietering 40 years ago and illustrated more recently by competent studies.[3] Behind the flowering of the earliest religious tropes stands indeed the medieval liturgical tradition of the antiphonal chant that had been introduced into Milan from the East by Saint Ambrose in the fourth century.

Antiphonal singing constituted more than a symbolic heightening and intesification of the liturgical ceremony; it fulfilled a distinct devotional function in the worship of God and in the proclamation of the Divine Mystery. One need only recall the emotional and spiritual power, as well as the symbolic significance, attributed to music by Jerome, Augustine, Cassiodorus, and other authors who influenced the form and shape of medieval spirituality. Augustine, for instance, comments thus on the devotional aspect of singing (music?): "Quid est in jubilatione canere? Intelligere, verbis explicare non posse quod canitur corde. Etenim qui cantant . . . cum coeperint in verbis canticorum exsultare laetitia, veluti impleti tanta laetitia, ut eam verbis explicare non possint, avertunt se a syllabis verborum, et eunt in sonum iubilationis. Iubilum sonus quidam est significans cor parturire quod dicere non potest."[4] The *Aetheriae peregrinatio ad loca sancta,* one of the most ancient works describing the ritual of the early Christian Church's *officia,* testifies to antiphonal chanting at Jerusalem in the fourth century: "dicuntur ymni nec non et antiphonae, et fiunt orationes cata singulos ymnos vel antiphonas."[5] The Church of Antioch claimed for antiphonal singing a celestial origin, which was first experienced and put to use by Ignatius:

> consuetudo illa hymnos in ecclesia alternis canendi, initium sumpserit. Ignatius, Antiochiae in Syria episcopus, post apostolum Petrum ordine tertius, qui et cum apostolis ipsis familiariter versatus est, vidit aliquando angelos hymnis alternatim decantantis sanctam Trinitatem celebrantes: et canendi rationem quam in illa visione animadverterat, Ecclesiae Antiochensi tradidit.[6]

St. Basil defended antiphonal singing by stressing its devotional aspect.[7] The fourth century soon saw the birth of a double *ordo psallendi,* that of the clergy and that of the monks. The Justinian Code, dated 529, promulgated the duty incumbent on all the clergy attached to a church to sing Vespers, Nocturns, and Lauds.[8]

Devotional singing became of foremost importance in the liturgy, and schools for chanters were established throughout the Western Church with the approval of various popes. Pope Leo II (682-683), for instance, was renowned for his singing: "cantilena ac psalmodia praecipuus." Pope Benedict II (684-685) distinguished himself "in cantilena a puerile etate." Pope Sergius I (687-701) was recommended for a chant school because "studiosus erat et capax in officio cantilenae, priore cantorum pro doctrina est traditus."[9] And an anonymous liturgical author of the eighth century[10] attributes the creation of many antiphons and responds to several pontiffs: Pope St. Leo (440-461), Pope St. Gelasius (492-498), Pope St. Symmachus (498-514), Pope St. John I (523-526), Pope St. Boniface II (530-532), and last but not least Pope St. Gregory I (590-604). By the early eighth century, monks were chanting in their basilicas the vigil office at night, and during the day, at Terce, Sext, and None. Uniformity of antiphonal chant and psalmody was finally achieved in the middle of the eighth century, 789, when Charlemagne renewed Pepin's decree ordering the adoption of the Roman *cursus* throughout the realm:

> *Omni clero.* Ut cantum Romanum pleniter discant, et ordinabiliter per nocturnale vel gradale officium peragatur, secundum quod beatae memoriae genitor noster Pippinus Rex decertavit ut fieret, quando Gallicanum tulit, ob unanimitatem Apostolicae Sedis et sanctae Dei Ecclesiae pacificam concordiam.[11]

Scholars, moreover, have already remarked on the importance of music in general, and antiphonal chant in particular, in the ninth century, during the lifetime of Tutilo and Notker, at the eve of the birth of the medieval drama.

This brief excursus assessing the importance of music within the confines of medieval liturgy is designed primarily to illustrate that by the beginning of the tenth century, when the earliest antiphonally-sung dramatic tropes appear, chanting had become a perfect means of communal worship, an effective devotional instrument in rendering praise and honor to God. Liturgical chant had become the language of sublime worship as well as an instructive and edifying tool at the service of the liturgy and forming an integral part of it. Centuries earlier, in a beautiful hymn formerly attributed to St. Ambrose, one finds already expressed both the function and purpose of song in the liturgical services:

> Nos ergo nunc confamuli
> Prophetae dicti memores,
> Solvamus ora in canticis
> Prece mixta Davidicis,
> Ut septies diem vere
> Orantes cum psalterio
> Laudesque cantantes Deo
> Laeti solvamus debitum.[12]

Literary scholarship on the history of the medieval religious drama, while recognizing the import and value of music in the embryonic development of drama, has failed to recognize precisely the spiritual and devotional aspect of that music. It has limited itself to generic statements about the crude musical expression which complements and even sustains, phrase by phrase, the dramatic expression. But it has been unable to demarcate decisively the music's ancillary or primary role in the crystallization of the dramatic play from its more traditional and explicit function as the language of worship. The distinction is of capital importance, for the music's devotional and spiritual function did not cease to be part of the religious play with the creation of the tropes, but remained a powerful tool of worship throughout the effective growth of the religious dramatic form, when ecclesiastical playwrights began to create a theater of wide range, embracing the life and Passion of Christ, the stories of the Old and New Testaments, the lives of saints etc. And it is precisely with the devotional, mystical, and spiritual emotion of music that I am concerned, rather than with the psycho-dramatic intention of the musical expression.

Even though in the development of the religious dramatic form music departed often from the stylized solemnity of the liturgy, from the mystic simplicity of the antiphons, by adopting and assimilating melodic forms more decorative and picturesque, more lay, more profane and popular, to reflect and represent the dramatic and human accents of the more grandiose dramatic compositions, music still retained that devotional exaltation, that spiritual jubilation so beautifully summed up by the Apostle Paul,[13] from the earliest dramatic tropes such as in the *Regularis Concordia* to the various *Ludi Paschales,* from the *Jeu d'Adam* to the *Laude* and the *Sacre Rappresentazioni,* from early Latin *planctus* such as the *Victimae Paschalis* and *Planctus ante nescia* to such late compositions as the *Stabat mater* and Cividale *Planctus,* from Latin Passion plays such as the Montecassino and *Carmina Burana* texts, to the grandiose and impressive compositions such as the *Mystères,* Passions, and Mystery Plays of fourteenth and fifteenth-century Western Europe. Music, especially after the role assumed by the Gregorian chant in the responses, the antiphons, and hymns, provided an element of spiritual solemnity, a background of devotional sublimity which contributed to the dramatizing of the Christian mysteries.[14] In the middle of the twelfth century, when the religious drama was in full blossoming, Hidelgard of S. Ruprecht could still write: "Sic et verbum corpus designat, symphonia autem spiritum manifestat."

73

## II

One of the most fruitful associations between drama and spirituality is afforded to the literary historian by the dramatic production of the canoness from Gandersheim, the tenth-century Hrotswitha. Concerned with offering cogent theories for the birth of the Saints' Plays in the late Middle Ages, scholars of the medieval drama have completely ignored the close relation between drama and hagiography in Hrotswitha's work. She is the first medieval dramatist to give dramatic significance to the spirituality of the hagiographical tradition. Indeed, the spirit which animates Hrotswitha's legends as well as the incipient liturgical drama draws its strength from and reflects the profound Christian asceticism which characterizes every literary manifestation of tenth-century medieval life. Hrotswitha found the thematic substance for all her dramatizations in that inexhaustible collection of hagiographical *exempla* known as the *Vitae patrum.* Widely disseminated as early as the sixth century both as single and collective units, the *Vitae* reached the period of greatest florescence in the Carolingian era and in the eleventh century. Together with the *Passiones,* describing the heroic death of martyrs, the *Translationes,* concerned with the translating of relics, and the *Miracula,* compilations of miracles performed by saints, the *Vitae* are constituent elements of that hagiographical genre so prominent in the spirituality of the early Middle Ages. Much more than other hagiographical works, the *Vita* aims to instruct and edify.[15] Although it provided a record of an individual life, it was primarily designed to honor the saint, to exalt his virtues and actions, and to instill and kindle religious fervor.

Among the traditional modes of expression, in the tenth century, it is the hagiographical genre that achieves prominence; acquiring a fresh vigor and amplitude through the influx of new oriental legends, Byzantine and Syriac, hagiography becomes an effective means of religious instruction and edification. In this it follows a well-established tradition: the providing of moral exhortation by means of an *exemplum.*

The *exemplum* as a pedagogical instrument is not indigenous to Christianity. It was taught by the Latins in their schools and it figures in manuals on rhetoric. It suffices to remember Seneca's "longum iter per praecepta, breve et efficax per exempla."[16] In the Christian era it is Tertullian who first envisions the religious potentialities of the *exemplum* as a catechizing vehicle, even though, in his writings, it is difficult to separate polemic from religious exhortation.[17] Although he did not hesitate to make use of *exempla* taken from profane history *(ad vxorem, de exhortatione castitatis, de monogamia, ad martyres, ad nationes)*, Tertullian left an especially rich patrimony of *vetera exempla,* culled from the Old Testament, and of *nova documenta* selected from the New Testament to illustrate the ideal of the Christian life.

Beginning with Ambrose, however, one observes a definite change in the *exemplum* tradition. The immediate aim of the early Christian moralists is to find manifestations of exemplary living in Biblical or contemporary Christian sources; they will very seldom rely on classical *exempla* and only as a *provocatio* to the Christians.[18] St. Jerome in his *Vitae*[19] and St. Augustine in the *Confessions* (VIII, 1-7) provide evidence of the popularity of the hagiographical *exemplum.* And it is the Patristic period, in particular, with the *Vitae Patrum,* the *Collationes Patrum,* and the *Acta Sanctorum,* that confers on the *exemplum* an effective salvic potency as a catechistic medium aimed not at erudite knowledge but at intelligent living of the Christian mystery. Hagiographical narratives deal primarily, at this time, with *exempla* furnished by the martyrs of the Christian faith; Leo the Great finds them the most edifying: "ad erudiendum Dei populum, nullorum est utilior forma quam martyrum. Sit eloquentia facilis ad exhortadum, sit ratio efficax ad suadendum, validiora tamen sunt exempla quam verba."[20] With the end of the persecutions, it is the life of the ascetic, hermitic and monastic, that becomes the most widely disseminated hagiographical *exemplum.* It continues its effective growth after the Patristic period, recommended by St. Gregory the Great in his homilies and *Dialogues,* becoming, in successive centuries, a powerful and persuasive means of religious instruction in the homiletic works of Odo of Cluny (d. 942), Rathieu of Verona (d. 974), Aelfric (d. 1020), and St. Wulfstan (d. 1095), and in the hands of Benedictine and Cistercian spiritualists such as Peter Damian (d. 1072), Peter the Venerable (d. 1156), Herbert of Torres (d. 1179), and others.

Hrotswitha's dramatization of legends taken from hagiographical accounts seems not to be attributable, therefore, to personal choice alone, but appears to have been dictated primarily by a consideration of the popularity of the hagiographical *exemplum* within the tenth-century ascetic and monastic spirituality,[21] which saw in martyrdom and hermitic life the two perfect realizations of the Christian ideal. Indispensable in the understanding of the fundamental religious purpose of Hrotswitha's sacred legends is an awareness of the medieval culture of which they are a genuine expression. As the distinguished medievalist Franceschini cogently observes, "l'opera di Rosvita . . . è schietta-

mente e squisitamente medievale, i suoi drammi non differiscono che
per la forma dai poemetti agiografici e dalle vite dei santi della
tradizione."[22] The supreme testimony of the vitality of monastic life
and spirituality as providing the best exemplification of how to achieve
the complete sanctity of a perfect Christian life is offered by the subject itself of Hrotswitha's plays. Of her six legends, two, *Dulcitius* and
*Sapientia*, are *passiones: Gallicanus, Callimachus, Abraham,* and
*Paphnutius* are *conversiones* brought about by the personal perfection
and sanctity of holy men. The last three stories culminate in a spiritual
epiphany that takes place in the very cell of holy hermits. To be sure,
the clearest manifestation of the resurgence of the hermitic movement
within the medieval monastic spirituality emerges towards the end of
the eleventh and the beginning of the twelfth century,[23] but the
embryonic rebirth of interest in hermitic life must be found in the
tenth century. Hrotswitha's interest in hagiography is illustrated not
only by her hagiographical poems celebrating St. Gongolf, St. Pela-
gius, St. Theophilus, St. Basil, St. Dionysus, and St. Agnes and the
poems consecrated to the first cenobites of Gandersheim, but also by
the fact that all her dramas are visibly inspired by this ascetic spiritual
tradition with its qualities of absolutism and complete dedication. In
accordance with the paradigmatic meaning and value of the hagiographical accounts, Hrotswitha closely adheres to the monastic and
spiritual atmosphere of the times when she, too, expresses the purpose
of her dramas as that of glorifying God and of proclaiming wherever
possible the virtues of Christ working in His saints: "Christi, qui sanc-
tis operatur, virtutem quocumque ipse dabit posse cessem
praedicare."[24]

## III

One of the clearest examples of the close association between music
and spirituality on one side, and drama on the other, is afforded by the
Italian *Laude*. The *Laude* were indeed born out of the encounter of the
evangelical texts with the lyrical and religious effusions of the people,
for the "piety of medieval Italy was an evangelical one, but so also,
was it a singing one."[25]

As a dramatic form the *Lauda* began as a lyric chant, sung by the
*flagellanti* through the city streets, or in church and in the confraternity's oratory. The original nucleus of the *Laude* must be found in the
*Laude* of Holy Week, for the Passion of Christ and the laments of the
Virgin were, from the start, the events most intensely felt by the

Umbrian poets. While the liturgical drama found its germinal point in the dramatic office of Easter, the *Laude* concentrated their poetical energy on the Passion of Christ, reflecting the penitential and Christocentric spirit of the *flagellanti* and of the spiritual aspirations of the thirteenth-century society, which, perhaps more than any other, accentuated the sorrowful aspect of the divine mystery. And it is the spirituality (popular and especially monastic) of the time which provides the religious background for the birth and development of the *Lauda*.[26] The *Lauda* cannot be understood without referring to the great spiritual currents of thirteenth-century Umbria, in particular those emanating from the monastic orders, the Dominicans in Perugia and the Franciscans in Assisi.

It is generally known that the *Laude* passed from their simple lyrical state to actual dramatic representation towards the middle of the thirteenth century. Some scholars view this change as a reflection, chronologically, of the *Laude's* passing from the uncontrolled lyrical exuberance of the *flagellanti* to the more disciplined stability of the *disciplinati,* which allowed a movement towards representation. But although the penitential movement of 1260 marks a definite historical moment illustrating the dramatic tendency of the *Lauda,* it would be misleading to derive from that movement any *post hoc* argumentation in the active development and dissemination of the dramatic *Lauda*. The penitential and dramatic character of the flagellant *Lauda* was inspired by monastic piety, particularly the Franciscan, which antedates the flagellant movement.[27] Scholarship on the *Lauda* had generally dismissed the impact of Franciscan piety by basing its evidence on erroneous chronological premises. The priority in the birth of the *Lauda* was in fact accorded to the *lauda perugina,* which is the expression of a popular, Dominican, and liturgical atmosphere.

Sporadic attempts at illustrating the flourishing of the *Lauda* in terms of Franciscan spirituality have been made. Recently, in a convincing study, Arnaldo Fortini has evaluated the influence of that spirituality on the *Lauda* by demonstrating that the *laudari* from Assisi are the oldest extant, at any rate, older than the ones from Perugia. He concludes by claiming for the Assisi *Laude* and the Franciscan movement the birth and formation of the Italian vernacular theater.[28]

A more plausible and cogent argument than the philological for the priority of the Assisi *Laude* can be made in terms of monastic spirituality. The Christocentric intensity of the *cantio penitentium* of the earliest *flagellanti* did not originate with them, for the Passion of Christ had been intensely felt and expressed years earlier by St. Francis (1181-

1226). Indeed, St. Francis and his movement provided for the *Lauda* both its spirituality and its social and popular character.

The spirituality of St. Francis is distinctly affective, and fundamentally devotional and popular,[29] exhibiting a most human and intimate approach to the divine mysteries, the Passion in particular. Love for Christ crucified stirred St. Francis' soul, and it was a love which, governed by compassion, incited him to a participation in His sufferings. Participation in Christ's Passion was a cherished ideal for St. Francis,[30] and indeed the sufferings of the Redeemer upon the Cross are for every Franciscan "the centre of all man's hope of salvation, his only consolation, his sorrow and his delight."[31] Of immediate and pertinent concern in defining the genesis of the dramatic *Lauda* is St. Francis' distinctive interest in stressing, in his writings, the joy and the "delight" to be found in the contemplation of Christ's Passion. The "giullare di Dio" had himself piously sung, at different occasions, Jesus' Passion[32] and exhorted his followers to such devotional practice. In its intense lyricism and catechistic impulses, the practice was intended to promote a more general participation in and apprehension of the human suffering of the Christocentric mystery, the Passion and the Virgin's lament at the Cross. As such, it possessed a distinct theatrical tendency, for the lyrical element, outside the immediate confines of the liturgy, was demonstrative, demanding an immediate and positive response from the audience. We have actual record, for instance, of *laudi assisane* which were directed to the spectators.[33] It was precisely out of the encounter of these two converging tendencies, the lyrical and the Christocentric, that the dramatic *Lauda* was born. Franciscan piety provided the new and essential spirituality, with its desire to understand the abstract through the concrete, the divine through the human, and to secure a more human and dramatic visualization of the Christian mysteries. In his desire to give immediate expression to the inner impulses, to make concretely accessible the religious message, St. Francis "was the first to awaken the dramatic powers of Italian feeling and of the Italian language."[34] His dramatic legacy is especially apparent in his dramatization, in 1209, of the Nativity, which was instrumental in popularizing this devotional practice.[35]

The actuality and emotional content of Franciscan spirituality, so removed from sacramental tradition and theological symbolism, were soon given wider propagation and diffusion through the dissemination of the Franciscan friars in the Western World. Of particular significance is the contribution of Franciscan spirituality to the early English drama. The first group of Franciscan brethren reached England in

1224. Within five years of their arrival, they had established a dozen houses, and by 1240 there were thirty-four houses of the Order of Friars Minor. More impressive still is the fact that by 1282 the Franciscan Order possessed 1,583 houses in Europe. The Franciscans' early contact with the English drama took place at the behest of Bishop Grosseteste of Lincoln, who, concerned over the irreverent character acquired by the religious plays, encouraged the friars to take charge of them. And it appears that as long as the religious plays were acted in the church or the churchyard, the Franciscans first and the regular orders of friars and secular clergy later exercised a distinct governing function in the performance of the plays.[36] *MS. Cotton Vespasianus D. VIII,* the manuscript preserving the Coventry cycle of plays, points to the Franciscans' role in their performance: "Videntur olim coram populo sive ad instruendum sive ad placendum a Fratribus Mendicantibus representata." Their active role in the production of the York plays has also been noted. Recent scholarship has placed in its proper perspective the Franciscans' contribution to early English drama by evaluating available material and by a detailed study of the verse satire *On the Minorite Friars,* of Wycliffite authorship, which expressly treats of the Franciscans and their activities in religious drama.[37] Evidence indicates that the early religious dramatic activity in England developed, to a great extent, within the confines of Franciscan spirituality, against the background of the spirit of joy, song, and drama inherited from the Order's holy founder.[38] We shall have occasion to examine later the more lasting and pervasive influence exercised on the medieval religious drama by the spirituality of a more famous Franciscan, St. Bonaventure.

## IV

A really momentous development in the complementary relationship of drama and spirituality took place during the eleventh and twelfth centuries, and is reflected in the appearance of new mystical forces, with their emphasis on the personal and emotional implications of the Passion. Although serious attempts at rendering accounts of Christ's Passion appear in the fourth, fifth, and sixth centuries, they lack sensitive human accents. Iconography and liturgy are primarily interested in celebrating the *Verbum,* the triumphant Divinity, the source of life and salvation; in literature, such works as Ambrose's *De Passione Domini,* Sedulius' *A solis ortus cardine,* and Fortunatus' *Vexilla regis prodeunt* celebrate ontologically the atemporal and eternal meaning of the Passion. They celebrate Christ *in sancta cruce* rather than *in parasceve*. Their theme was not the Passion, but the stupendous triumph: *Pange lingua gloriosi proelium certaminis*. The new forces at work were the mystical concentration on Christ's human sufferings as articulated primarily by St. Anselm and St. Bernard. To be sure, the heralds of this Christocentric piety can be found early in the eleventh century in monastic figures such as St. William of Volpiano (d. 1031), St. Richard of Verdun (d. 1046), and especially Volpiano's nephew and favorite disciple, John of Fécamp (d. 1078).

It was left to St. Anselm (1033-1109), however, to supply the theological and theoretical justification for Christ's sufferings through a new interpretation of the necessity of the Redemption. In the *Cur Deus Homo*, a Christological treatise reminiscent of those of the second to fifth centuries, St. Anselm emphasizes the true significance of the humanity of Christ by stressing that the redemptive act took place on a human level.

The devotion to Christ's Passion that stirred in the souls of pious monks early in the eleventh century and was fostered in the same generation by the delicate sensibility of St. Anselm finds its greatest expression in the concentrated pathos devoted to it by St. Bernard (1091-1153). An unremitting love for Jesus crucified was the focal point of St. Bernard's life and the guide for his interior feelings and emotions: "haec mea sublimior interim philosophia, scire Jesum, et hunc crucifixum."[39] St. Bernard's treatment of Christ's suffering founded a new strain of spirituality, for as Pourrat points out, his writings "dès le XIIe siècle, orientèrent les coeurs vers les mystères de la vie terrestre, en particulier vers ceux de sa naissance et de sa passion."[40]

The Christocentric mysticism of St. Anselm and St. Bernard soon acquired a religious universality by being incorporated into the common body of Christian opinion. By virtue of their examples and personal reputation — St. Anselm as the Primate of England and the so-called Father of Scholasticism and St. Bernard as the renowned *doctor mellifluus*, the founder of the Cistercians, the preacher of the Second Crusade, and both through the efforts of their various pupils and monastic orders that fostered the perpetuity of their teachings — medieval spirituality came to know Christ with a more delicate intimacy and dwelt primarily on his Passion. These theological and devotional considerations necessarily had literary consequences, one of which, as it has recently been shown, was the dramatization, in the twelfth century, of Christ's Passion.[41]

The two most important Latin works in understanding the spirituality of the Middle Ages are Anselm's *Dialogus Mariae et Anselmi de Passione Domini* and Bernard's *Liber do Passione Domini.*[42] Although they were originally intended for contemplatives, manuscript tradition attests to their popularity and to their rapid diffusion and dissemination. By the middle of the thirteenth century, copies of the *Dialogus* could be found in practically every monastic library in Europe. An even greater popularity was enjoyed by the *Liber de Passione* in nearly every western European country; in England alone, the *Liber* survives in at least twenty-three manuscripts.[43] Examples of this popularity are provided by the persuasive influence they exercised on the English medieval religious lyric and on the iconography of the Passion.[44]

The tracts of Anselm, Bernard, and their followers not only provided dramatists with a textual tradition of a theology and Christology of suffering, but, in their narrative realism and immediate and concrete description of the details of the Passion, they offered also rich potentialities for imaginative and dramatic realizations of those details. The peculiar feature of this spirituality with its new sensitivity to the sufferings of Christ is its preoccupation with the tangible and immediate rather than with the symbolical and theological, a desire to embrace and express the divine by emphasizing the actual and the concrete. This Christological spirituality, for instance, supplied both medieval dramatists and artists with definite visual suggestions in their endeavour to reconstruct, dramatically and pictorially, the historical reality of the Crucifixion. Two basic accounts were available to any medieval artist setting out to represent the Crucifixion. Based on Anselm's *Dialogus,* the one sees the Crucifixion accomplished *jacente cruce,* that is, with the cross already on the ground.[45] The other account, the Crucifixion *erecto cruce,* is derived from a concise description in Bernard's *Liber de Passione.*[46] A complete description of the harrowing details relating exactly how Christ was stretched and nailed to an already erect cross are found in the *Meditationes Vitae Christi* of the pseudo-Bonaventure.[47] Although the influence of the *Meditationes* was the most pervasive one in the Middle Ages, extending both in drama and iconography to virtually every incident in the Passion story, it is the Crucifixion *jacente cruce* as described by Anselm that became the favorite version, preferred by the compilers of Passion plays.

The simple narrative realism of Anselm's *Dialogus* and Bernard's *Liber de Passione* was enormously popular with English, French, and German dramatists who translated into appropriately rudimentary and at times sophisticated dramatic terms the Passion details contained in these spiritual and devotional texts. A few examples will suffice. In the *Arras Passion* and in the *Frankfurt Passion,* Pilate hopes that the flagellation of Jesus may move the Jews to take pity on Him. The detail and the humane motive are found in Anselm's *Dialogus:* "Pilatus autem sperans crudelitati Judaeorum satisfacere . . . "[48] In the *Alsfeld, Donaueschingen, Eger, Heidelberg,* and *Tyrol* German Passion plays, Simon is summoned to carry the cross because Jesus is too weak. The source again seems to be the *Dialogus:* "Quod fecerunt non causa miserationis, sed quia prae debilitate id facere non poterat."[49] All of the four English cyclic dramas, the *York,* the *Towneley,* the *Ludus Coventriae,* and the *Chester* dramatize Jesus' meeting with the women of Jerusalem. Although the incident had been recorded by Luke (xxiii:28), the dramatists could find a more detailed and graphic description of it in the *Dialogus.*[50] The *York* and *Towneley* plays commemorate at length Mary's lamentations at the foot of the Cross; it has been shown that the influence of mystical writings, Anselm's and Bernard's in particular, dominate this dolorous scene in the English plays.[51]

Particularly important in transmitting the influence of St. Anselm, St. Bernard, and St. Francis are such mystics as St. Bonaventure (1221-1274) and St. Bridget (1304-1374), whose writings constitute the culmination of a homiletic trend towards pietism and human realism. The *Meditationes Vitae Christi,* in particular, long attributed to St. Bonaventure but now ascribed to the Franciscan monk Joannes de Caulibus, had a profound influence on the drama and plastic arts of the later Middle Ages.[52] By enlarging the bare outlines of canonical narrative, by inventing and investing new scenes of the Passion with concrete detail, the *Meditationes* pass over dogma in order to represent a personal and poignant human experience for the pious to contemplate. Profoundly influenced by the *Meditationes* were later mystics and preachers such as Jacopone da Todi, Jacopo da Voragine, St. Bridget, Robert Manning of Brunne, Nicolas Love, Richard Rolle, John Mirk, Ludolf of Saxony, Jean Tauler, Henry Suso, Roberto di Lecce, Bernardino de Bustis, and others, who in turn influenced the religious drama.

Of far greater significance in the study of the relationship of drama and spirituality in the Middle Ages are the means by which the mystical influence continued to be effective through the centuries. One of these is represented by the current of mysticism and homiletic literature of the fourteenth and fifteenth centuries and expressed in the works of people such as Rolle, Mirk, and John Gregory. The principal effect of the comprehensive dissemination of homiletic literature of the

Passion was to establish a popular taste which found natural expression in the drama. Moreover, such works as Voragine's *Legenda Aurea,* Vincent of Beauvais' *Speculum Historiale,* the *Speculum Salvationis,* and the *Biblia Pauperum* are mines of information for medieval dramatists, treating the common fund of Biblical material and Catholic dogma, but modifying it to popular ends and along the lines of mystical attitudes rather than theological interpretations. Mystical themes and attitudes are especially evident in that impressive number of vernacular religious poems written in Europe from the thirteenth to fourteenth and fifteenth centuries. The influence on the religious medieval drama of such works as the *Cursor Mundi, A Stanzaic Life of Christ, The Northern Passion, The Southern Passion, La Passion de Jongleurs,* the *Erlösung,* the *Alt Passional,* and the *Passión Trobada* has been either demonstrated or suggested.[53] Like the devotional and homiletic, the poetical tradition, too, passed on that Christocentric sensibility which had been so beautifully and emotionally illustrated by St. Anselm, St. Bernard, St. Francis, and St. Bonaventure. And it is under these influences that the Passion plays of Western Europe were taking form.

V

Any investigation of drama and spirituality would be incomplete without a consideration of Mary's role in the Passion plays and the religious attitudes that made it possible. Just as the impetus to an awakened sensitivity to the Passion was supplied by the Christocentric mysticism of the eleventh and twelfth centuries, so too the embryonic nucleus in the redaction of Mary's role in it sprang out of the meditations on the sorrows of Mary, which, beginning in the eleventh century, reach their climax in the twelfth, and by virtue of their pathetic commentary on the sacrifice on the Cross show the natural ties that exist between the *Passio* and the *Compassio.* Although some scholars have anachronistically suggested that the *Mariae Compassio* begins in the West, in about the fourteenth century, there is clear evidence for the fact that the theme began in the eleventh.[54] Comments on the suffering and compassion of the Virgin at the foot of the Cross are found in the writings of St. Anselm of Canterbury, John of Fécamp, St. Anselm of Lucca,[55] and in the following centuries in the writings of St. Bernard, Arnauld of Bonnevalle, Eadmer, the most famous of Anselm's English disciples, Richard of St. Victor, and St. Bridget of Sweden. The tradition culminates in the lyric accents of the *Medita-*

83

*tions Vitae Christi.* And the medieval religious drama chronologically reflects mystical comments on Mary's *compassio* by realizing dramatically the vision of the grieving figure of the *mater dolorosa* from the Latin Passion plays of the twelfth and thirteenth century to the vernacular Passions of the later Middle Ages.

From the *Cursor Mundi* to the *Northern Passion,* from the *Southern Passion* and *A Stanziac Life of Christ* to the English cyclic plays, one witnesses the popularity of the Mother's supreme expression of love and compassion for the Son. Equally important is the role assigned the Virgin in the French vernacular Passions, from the *Passion du Palatinus* to the *Passion d'Arras,* from the *Passion Semur* to the *Passion d'Autun.*[1] In the German vernacular dramatic tradition the role of the Virgin was generally even more developed than in the French or English vernacular Passion plays. In such German Passion plays as the Tyrol *Passion,* the St. Gall *Passion,* the Frankfurth *Passion,* and the Alsfeld *Passion,* the Virgin occupies the center of the stage throughout the scene on Mount Calvary. In Italy, in the vernacular Passions, *Sacre rappresentazioni,* and particularly in the *Laude,* the Virgin achieves prominence by playing a significant dramatic role in the culminating moments of the divine tragedy. In all these dramatic expressions one perceives the mystical method of emphasizing the concrete, the human; the desire to stress the immediacy rather than the historicity of the scene, and to arrive at the intensification of emotions through the evocative power of the thing seen is clearly and primarily the expression of a readily definable religiosity: the peculiar gift of the spirituality of the medieval mystics.

Modern essays on the history of the medieval drama have given prominence only to the timeless themes and literary dimension of that drama; since, however, that drama is very much the product of the main-stream of medieval religious spirituality rather than an isolated example of drama *per se,* its history will not be complete until full investigation is undertaken of the spiritual modes within which that drama was expressed.

# NOTES

1. Etienne Gilson, "Saint Bonaventure et l'Iconographie de la Passion," *Revue d'Histoire Franciscaine,* I (1924), 405-424, p. 406.
2. Ferdinando Liuzzi on p. 105 of his "L'espressione musicale nel dramma liturgico," *Studi Medievali,* n.s. 2 (1929), observed that "la musica è . . . nel teatro medievale, l'elemento propriamente, squisitamente estetico. Ne è anzi in un certo senso il solo: certo il più puro." Helena M. Gamer, "Mimes, Musicians, and the Origin of the Mediaeval Religious Play," *Deutsche Beiträge zur Geistigen Überlieferung,* V (1965), 9-28; William L. Smoldon, "The Melodies of the Medieval Church-Dramas and Their Significance," *Comparative Drama,* II (1968), 185-209.

3. J. Schwietering, "Uber den liturgischen Ursprung des mittelalterlichen geistlichen Spiels," *Zeitschrift für deutschen Altertum und deutsche Literatur,* 62 (1925), 1-20.
4. *Enarr. In PS, XXXII, II, S. I, 8-9,* in *Corpus Christianorum,* XXXVIII (1956), p. 254.
5. Hélène Pétré, ed. *Ethérie. Journal de Voyage* (Paris, 1948), p. 194.
6. *Socratis Historia Ecclesiastica,* Lib. VI, Cap. 8, in Migne, *P.G.,* LXVII, col. 691.
7. *S. Basilii Magni Epistola,* CCVII, e, in Migne, *P.G.,* XXXII, col. 763.
8. *Codex Justinianus,* 1.3.41.
9. *Liber Pontificalis,* I, pp. 359, 363, 371.
10. Pierre Battiffol, *History of the Roman Breviary* (Paris, 1893; trans. by A. M. Y. Baylay, London, 1912), pp. 114-119.
11. *Monumenta Germaniae Historica, Leges* 2, ed. Boretius, I (1883), 61.
12. *Hymni S. Ambrosio Attributi, P.L.,* XVII, cols. 1211-13. The editor doubts that St. Ambrose wrote this hymn: "hic hymnus . . . in dubium non immerito revocari potest, num vere ab Ambrosio fuerit compositus."
13. *Ad Ephesios,* V, 19: "Implemini Spiritu sancto, loquentes vosmetipsos in psalmis, et hymnis, et canticis spiritualibus, cantantes, et psallentes in cordibus vestris Domino."
14. Commenting on the juxtaposition of word and music in the liturgical drama, Michel Mathieu refers to the music's *lyrisme pieux* and stresses the fact that "la musique . . . catalyse l'effusion communautaire, . . . la musique reliait le plan liturgique au plan dramatique." See pp. 100-03 of his "Distanciation et émotion dans le théâtre liturgique au moyen âge," *Revue d'Histoire du Théâtre,* XXI (1969), 95-117. William Noomen has pointed out the structural and thematic significance of the chanted liturgical lessons in the *Jeu d'Adam:* "Le *Jeu d'Adam.* Etude descriptive et analytique, "*Romania,* LXXXIX (1968), 145-153; Carolyn Wall, in the "York Pageant XLVI and Its Music," *Speculum,* XLVI (1971), p. 697, remarks on the solemnizing values of music.
15. J. de Ghellinck, *Littérature latine au moyen âge* (Paris, 1939), pp. 64 and 68; J. W. B. Zaal, *A Lei Francesca* (Paris, 1962), 46. See also Joseph N. Garvin, ed., *The Vitas sanctorum patrum* (Washington, 1946).
16. Seneca, (*Ep.* 6, 5).
17. Tertullian stresses the efficacy of the living *exumplum* in his *Apologetica, P.L.,* I, 535-536.
18. St. Jerome, for instance, will often turn to profane literature to find *exempla* which might justify a theological truth or Christian virtue. Commenting on virginity he had occasion to write: "Quoniam intellexi in commentariis adversarii [Jovinian] provocari nos ad mundi sapientiam . . . percurram breviter graecas et latinas barbarasque historias et docebo virginitatem semper termine pudicitiae principatum." *Adversus Jovinianum I, 41, P.L.,* XXIII, col. 270ab.
19. Pierre Labriolle, *Histoire de la littérature latine chrétienne,* 2 vols. (Paris, 1947), II, 506-509.
20. *Sermo LXXXV, 1, P.L.,* LIV, 435b.
21. René Aigrain, in *L'hagiographie* (Paris, 1953), stresses, p. 238, the influence in the later Middle Ages of the famous tenth-century *Passionarium maius* of St. Gall, a compendium of *Passiones* and *Vitae.* Beginning with the eighth century the *Passiones* began to be read in the divine office. (Cf. Salmon, *op. cit.,* 155-157)
22. Ezio Franceschini, "Per una revisione del teatro latino di Rosvita," *Rivista Italiana del Dramma,* Anno II, Vol. 1, (Rome,1938), 315. Enrico Panzacchi expressed the same idea in his *Critica spicciola* (Rome, 1886), when he spoke, p. 245, of the "spirito . . . asceticamente religioso" of Hrotswitha's plays. As early as 1847 Victor Chasles, in "Hrotsvita, naissance du drame chrétien au X*e*me siècle," *Etudes sur le Christianisme et sur le Moyen Age* (Paris, 1847), identified the background upon which Hrotswitha grafted her plays, p. 278, as that *fonds* of "vies des saints et les pathétiques ou merveilleuses légendes dont l'histoire chrétienne se compose."
23. Jean Leclercq, "Deux opuscules médiévaux sur la vie solitaire," *Studia monastica,* IV (1962), 24.
24. Paulus de Winterfeld, *Hrotsvithae Opera* (Berlin, 1965), 134.
25. Sister M. Cyrilla Barr, "The Popular Hymnody of Medieval Italy and Its Relationship to the Pious and Penitential Confraternities," *Studies in Medieval Culture,* III (1950), 151.
26. Scholars such as Angela Terruggia have stressed unduly the importance of the *Confraternite,* instead of the spirituality that guided them. Cf. her essay on "Lo sviluppo del dramma sacro visto attraverso i codici di Assisi," *Atti del Centro Studi Origini del Teatro Italiano,* estratto dall' *Annuario XI, Accademia Etrusca di Cortona* (Cortona, 1960), 171-198.
27. Fernando Ghilardi, "Le Origini del teatro italiano e San Francesco," *L'Italia francescana,* XXX (1955), 341-352; XXXI (1956), 81-87; Arnaldo Fortini, *La lauda in Assisi e le origini del teatro italiano* (Assisi, 1961), and Paolo Toschi, *Le Origini del teatro italiano* (Torino, 1955), pp. 677-8.
28. Fortini, p. 480; G. Galli had already affirmed the priority of the Assisi *laudari* in his "I Disciplinati dell'Umbria del 1260 e le loro *Laudi,"Giornale Storico della Letteratura Italiana,* Supplement VII-IX (1904-06), 69.
29. Alfonso Pompei, in "L'influenza religioso-sociale di S. Francesco e della sua primitiva fraternita nel secolo XIII," *Miscellanea Francescana,* LXVI (1966), writes on p. 200, that "la forma di vita francescana si rivolse, nella sua pieta, soprattutto al popolo."
30. A most extended and learned analysis of St. Francis' Passion piety is found in P. Oktavian von Rieden, "Das Leiden Christi im Leben des HI. Franziskus von Assisi. Eine Quellenvergleichende Untersuchung im Lichte der zeitgenössischen Passionsfrömmigkeit," *Collectanea Franciscana,* XXX (1960), 5-30; 129-145; 241-263; 353-397.
31. F. J. Raby, *A History of Christian Poetry* (Oxford, 1927), 423; Amedée P. De Zedelgem, "Aperçu historique sur la dévotion au chemin de la Croix," *Collectanea Franciscana,* XVIII-XIX (1948-49), 45-142.
32. Fortini, p. 380. In Bonaventure's *Legenda Sancti Francisci* one reads: "Dumque per silvan quandam iter faciens, laudes Domino lingua francorum vir Dei Franciscus decanteret cum iubilo." In *S. Bonaventurae Opera Omnia* (Ad Claras Aquas, 1898), VIII, p. 509.
33. Galli, pp. 120-42.
34. Erich Auerbach, *Mimesis* (New York, 1957), p. 151.
35. St. Francis was clearly influenced by the religious and immediate antecedents of this dramatization, which finds its roots in the meditative devotions of Cistercian spirituality, particularly St. Bernard's, on the Christ-Child. (Cf.

St. Bernard's *In Epiphania Domini*, i. 2, *P.L.*, CLXXXIII, 183; also his *In Nativitate*, i. 3, *Ibid.*, 116.)

36. Harold Goad, *Greyfriars* (London, 1947), pp. 168 ff. Glynne Wickham, *Early English Stages 1300 to 1660*, 2 vols. (London, 1959), I, 124-128.

37. Lawrence G. Craddock, O.F.M., "Franciscan Influence on Early English Drama," *Franciscan Studies*, X (1950), 383-417.

38. Craddock, p. 417.

39. *P.L.*, CLXXXIII, St. Bernard, *Sermones in Cantica*, Sermo XLIII, 4, 995. St. Bernard appears to be echoing St. Paul's "Non enim iudicavi me scire aliquid inter vos, nisi Iesum Christum, et hunc crucifixum." (*Ad Corinthios*, I: 2-3).

40. P. Pourrat, *La spiritualité chrétienne*, 2 vols. (Paris, 1947-51), II, 481; Felix Vernet, *La spiritualité médiévale* (Paris, 1929), p. 18; Salmon, *op. cit.*, p. 243. On the history of the devotion to the humanity of Christ, see P. C. Richstämmigkeit in ihrer historischen Entfaltung. Ein quellenmässiger Beitrag zur Geschichte des Gebetes und des mystischen Imenleben der Kirche (Cologne, 1949); L. Génicot, in *La spiritualité médiévale* (Paris, 1958), p. 73, refers to the fact that "la passion du Christ" and the "tendresse pour la vierge" are "les éléments essentiels de la spiritualité des XIᵉ et XIIᵉ siècles."

41. See my *The Latin Passion Play: Its Origins and Development* (Albany, 1970).

42. For the *Dialogus*, see *P.L.*, XLIX, 271-290; for the *Liber*, *P.L.*, CLXXXII, 1133-1142.

43. Rosemary Woolf, *The English Religious Lyric in the Middle Ages* (Oxford, 1968), p. 247.

44. For the lyric consult Woolf, especially Chaps. II and VII; for the iconography see F. P. Pickering, *Literature and Art in the Middle Ages* (Florida, 1970), Chap. V.

45. *Dialogus, op. cit.*, cols. 282-82: "Cum venissent ad locum Calvarie . . . nudaverunt Jesum . . . Post hoc deposuerunt crucem super terram, et eum desuper extenderunt, et incutiebant primo unum clavum adeo spissum quod tunc sanguis non potuit emanare, ita vulnus clavo replebatur. Acceperunt postea funes et traxerunt aliud brachium filii mei Jesu, et clavum secundum ei incusserunt. Postea pedes funibus traxerunt, et clavun acutissimum incutiebant . . . Post haec erexerunt eum cum magno labore, et fuit adeo alte suspensus."

46. *Liber, op, cit.*, col. 1135: "Ante oculos ejus fuit in cruce levatus, et ligno durissimis clavis affixus . . . "

47. A. C. Peltier, ed., *S. Bonaventurae Meditationes Vitae Christi*, in *Opera Omnia*, XII (Parisiis, 1868), *Caput LXXVIII*.

48. *Dialogus, op. cit.*, col. 279.

49. *Ibid.*, col. 281.

50. *Ibid.*

51. The problem of textual correspondences and of influence of mystical writings on English cyclic dramas and on the French and German Passion plays has been partially investigated, respectively, by Sister John Sullivan, *A Study of the Themes of the Sacred Passion in the Medieval Cycle Plays* (Washington, 1942), and by Hadassah Posey Goodman, *Original Elements in the French and German Passion Plays* (Bryn Mawr, 1944); Paul Marie Maas, *Etude sur les sources de la Passion du Palatinus* (Tiel, 1942).

52. I will limit myself to a few references on the subject: P. Keppler, "Zur Passionspredigt des Mittelalters," *Historisches Jahrbuch*, III (1882), 285-315; IV (1883), 161-188; Emile Mâle, *L'Art religieux de la fin du moyen âge* (Paris, 1946); P. Livario Oliger, O.F.M., "Le *Meditationes Vitae Christi*," *Studi Francescani*, VIII (1922), 18-47. Studies on the similarities and parallels between drama and religious art are numerous, especially for English. Cf. for instance, Christopher Woodforde, *The Norwich School of Glass Painting in the Fifteenth Century* (Oxford, 1950); Otto Pächt, *The Rise of Pictorial Narrative in Twelfth-Century England* (Oxford, 1962), especially Chap. III; W. L. Hildburgh, "English Alabaster Carvings as Records of the Medieval Religious Drama," *Archaeologica*, SCIII (1949), 51-101; M. D. Anderson, *Drama and Imagery in English Medieval Churches* (Cambridge, 1963); J. W. Robinson, "The Late Medieval Cult of Jesus and the Mystery Plays," *PMLA*, LXXX (1965), 508-514.

53. In her introduction to the *York Mystery Plays* (Oxford, 1885), p. xliv, Miss L. Toulmin-Smith finds general resemblance between the *Cursor Mundi* and the York cycle of *Corpus* plays, and so does J. S. Purvis, *From Minster to Market Place* (York, 1969), p. 6. In her edition of *The Northern Passion* (London, 1916), EETS, OS, 145, p. 8, Miss Francis A. Foster comments on the influence of the poem on the English cycle plays. More specific information is provided in her "The Mystery Plays and *The Northern Passion*," *MLN* XXVI (1911), 169-171. She finds similarities of details between the plays and *A Stanzaic Life of Christ* (London, 1926), EETS, OS, 166, p. xxviii. Grace Frank stresses the significance of vernacular sources such as the *Passion des Jongleurs* for medieval French drama in "Vernacular Sources and an Old French Passion Play," *MLN*, XXXV (1920), 257-269. On the importance of the *Erlösung* and the *Alt Passional*, see R. M. S. Heffner, "Borrowings from the Erlösung in a Missing Frankfurt Play," *JEGP*, XXV (1926), 474-497; in a most recent and learned study of the medieval German drama, Wolfgang F. Michael, *Das Deutsche Drama des Mittelalters* (Berlin, 1971), affirms, p. 145, that "das Verhältnis der *Erlösung* zum Drama is Uberhaupt grundlegend."; see also passages on the subject in George Duriez' *La théologie dans le drame religieux en Allemagne* (Lille, 1914). Dorothy Sherman Severin in " '*La Passion Trobada*' de Diego de San Pedro y sus relacions con el drama medieval de la Pasion," *Anuario de Estudios Medievales*, I (1964), 451-470, points out the influence on this poem of Ludolf of Saxony's *Vita Christi*, which is based on the pseudo-Bonaventure's *Meditationes;* she feels that the *Passion* was represented. On this poem see also Humberto Lopez Morales, *Tradición y creación en los Orígines del teatro Castellano* (Madrid, 1968), 77-78.

54. Angelus Luis, "Evolutio historica doctrinae de Compassione B. Mariae Virginis," *Marianum*, V (1943), pp. 274-76; Lutz Machensen, "Mittelalterlichen Tragödien. Gedanken uber Wesen und Grenzen des Mittelalters" in *Festschrift für Wolfgang Stammler* (Berlin, 1953), p. 99. Peter Damiani (988-1072), commenting on the prophecy of Simeon, appears to be the first to have introduced the term *Compassio* in the sense which will be predominant in later centuries: "te etiam transfiget *gladius compassionis* in mente" (*In Nativitatem B. M.*, I, in *P.L.*, CXLIV, col. 748A). On the sorrows of Mary, see Yrjö Hirn, *The Sacred Shrine* (Boston, 1957), Chap. XIX; on the theological and religious sources of the *compassio* see Don Denny, "Notes on the *Avignon Pietà*," *Speculum*, XLIV (1969),

213-233; also my *The Latin Passion Play*, Chap. V.

55. For St. Anselm of Canterbury consult his *Dialogus, P.L.,* CLIX, 271-290 and his *Oratio XX, P.L.,* CLVIII, 902-905; for John of Fécamp, his "Ardens Desiderium ad Christum" in *Analecta Monastica,* XX (1948), p. 103; St. Anselm of Lucca states that Mary "non potuit sine incomparabili dolore uidere in crucis patibulo gloriosissimum filium clavis affixum." (Quoted in H. Barré, *Prières ancienne de l'Occident à la mère du Sauveur,* Paris, 1963, p. 229.)

# Spirituality and Poverty: Angelo da Clareno and Ubertino da Casale

*E. Randolph Daniel*

FRANCISCAN SPIRITUALITY IS well-known to those interested in the history of the Order of Friars Minor, but it has traditionally been treated as a subsidiary theme while poverty, regarded as a polemical and legal issue, has held the center of the stage. This applies especially to the controversy between the Franciscan Spirituals and the Conventuals. The accepted view holds that this dispute grew out of drastic modifications of the ideal of St. Francis in favor of learning, preaching, clericalization, and legalism. The Rigorists refused to accept the modification of poverty which the Conventuals regarded as necessary, and, instead, the Spirituals insisted on strict adherence to the letter of the *Regula bullata* as interpreted by the *Testamentum*. Within this framework, spirituality could only function as a subplot, tangential to the flow of the action.[1]

This examination of two of the Spirituals, Angelo da Clareno and Ubertino da Casale, will show that the accepted interpretation of their position rests on the application to them of a set of alien values, the consequence of which is a distortion of their views. The Spirituals, however, valued the inner life more highly than the outer and, therefore, viewed poverty as primarily an interior, spiritual virtue which formed an integral part of the spirituality of those who, in assuming the habit, had vowed to search for conformity to Christ. The expression of this imitation externally required poverty both for individuals and for the Order itself, but this outward conduct remained secondary, albeit necessary. Both Ubertino and Angelo emphasized Spirituality as the crucial issue, and saw their struggle with the Conventuals as a conflict between the Franciscan spirit and a carnal desire for worldly honors which took external form in disputes about papal bulls, buildings, tunics, books, etc. To them, polemics concerning legal issues were only outward manifestations of an interior war.[2]

Angelo da Clareno and Ubertino da Casale were both leaders among the Spirituals. Angelo (d. 1337) was originally named Peter of Fossembrone from his native village in the March of Ancona. He joined the Order in 1270, and about 1278 was imprisoned along with other Spirituals from the March by the provincial minister. Raymond Gaufridi, then minister general, freed them in 1289 and sent the little group of friars to work with King Hayton of Armenia. They returned to Italy before 1295, when Pope Celestine V separated them from the Order of Friars Minor and authorized them to call themselves the "Poor Hermits." After Boniface VIII revoked Celestine's acts, the Spirituals fled to the island of Trixonia in the Gulf of Corinth. Two years later they moved to southern Thessaly, where Angelo probably acquired his knowledge of Greek.[3] He was again in Italy from 1305 until 1311, when he went to Avignon to participate in the controversy before Popes Clement V and John XXII. After 1318 he lived in Italy, at Subiaco, where he wrote his *Expositio regulae* (c. 1321) and his *Historia septem tribulationum* (finished after 1320).[4]

Ubertino (born 1259, died before 1341) entered the Order in 1273 and, after completing his novitiate, spent nine years as a student in Paris. He was already interested in contemplation, but he fully developed his spiritual life only after his return to Italy, where he became acquainted with Blessed Angela of Foligno and John of Parma. While serving at Santa Croce in Florence, he became a disciple of the leader of the Spirituals of Provence, Peter John Olivi. Ubertino's main activity was preaching until he was sent to Mount Alverna, where, during 1305, he wrote his *Arbor uitae*. When Pope Clement V agreed to hear the controversy between the Conventuals and Spirituals, Ubertino emerged as the leading spokesman for the latter, and his polemical treatises give us a detailed and skillful defense of their case. After John XXII crushed the Spirituals' hopes, Ubertino apparently became a Benedictine. Later he joined forces with Emperor Louis of Bavaria, and the end of his life is shrouded in mystery.[5]

The spirituality of Angelo and Ubertino was not novel. In valuing the inner life more highly than the outer, they merely expressed the traditional emphasis of monasticism. A favorite text of medieval writers was 2 Corinthians 3:6: "The letter kills, but the spirit makes alive."

For an exegete this text demonstrated that the spiritual senses hidden beneath the letter of scripture possessed much greater value than the letter itself. The monastic life, however, paralleled its hermeneutic. The monks esteemed the spiritual, interior, and invisible quest more highly than the literal, the exterior, and the visible routine. The semi-eremitic orders of the eleventh century and, more importantly, the Cistercians and the canons of St. Victor in the twelfth century interiorized and systematized monastic spirituality.[6]

The twelfth century also saw renewed emphasis on poverty within the framework of monastic spirituality. Both the Cistercians and the Premonstratensian Canons placed renewed emphasis on manual labor. Among those circles of laymen who sought to lead the evangelical life, poverty had an important place.[7]

Franciscan spirituality developed along the lines already laid out in the twelfth century. The newness of the Friars Minor lay primarily in their external observance and function rather than in their interior life. Mendicancy, the refusal to possess more than the minimal necessities even in common, and the insistence on mission distinguished the friars from the monks. Franciscan spirituality was closely related to the friars' eschatological understanding of their mission. Christ himself had called St. Francis and his brothers to be the spearhead of the *renouatio euangelicae perfectionis.* The divine mission of the Order of Friars Minor was to prepare the church and the world for Christ's final coming in glory by setting an example of apostolic spirituality and conduct. Their behavior and their preaching had to express their inner desire to conform themselves to Christ. Self-renunciation required visible poverty and humility.[8]

St. Bonaventure developed Franciscan spirituality theologically by his exemplarism. His insistence that Christ is the archetype of all things and that the latter, properly conceived, point back to him is a theological statement of a value system which focuses all acts and entities toward a single goal, according greater value to an individual step by placing it nearer on a line toward the center. Since the archetypal Christ can only be perceived by beginning from sense phenomena and moving inward, so the viator who wishes to approach Christ must develop within himself the spiritual virtues, and these are more important than the external because they are closer to the goal.[9]

For Angelo and Ubertino, conversion was first of all a total renovation of the interior man. He must re-orient his entire self, emotional, intellectual, volitional, and spiritual, toward complete conformity to the crucified Christ. Exterior behavior necessarily followed from this inward transformation. A friar, directed by prayer, meditation, and contemplation toward the passion, expresses this internal movement in his dress, goods, dwelling, relationships with his brothers and with people outside the Order. His mode of life is, therefore, examplaristic of his spirituality. His conduct flows from within him and simultaneously reveals symbolically to the outside observer that interior state which would otherwise be unknowable. While this outward expression is necessary and important, its value remains for him secondary to that of his spiritual quest.

The Spirituals followed Thomas of Celano and St. Bonaventure in discerning this configuration in St. Francis himself. Angelo drew directly on the *Legenda maior* when he made the vision of the crucifix at St. Damian's the critical moment in Francis' conversion. After this experience, Francis was continually preoccupied by thoughts of Christ and the cross. Periodically he retreated to hermitages where he gave himself completely to prayer, meditation, and contemplation. From these periods of solitude, he drew the strength to travel and to teach men both by example and words the true nature of evangelical perfection. The stigmata are at once the culmination of Francis' quest and the divine seal on his holiness. In the *Itinerarium mentis in deum* and the *Legenda maior,* Bonaventure had made the stigmata the key to understanding the life and mission of St. Francis, but in doing so, he only elaborated a pattern already suggested by Thomas of Celano, and one that implicitly, if not always explicitly, is present in the series of works which emanated from Brother Leo and the Companions. Angelo stood here in the tradition of St. Bonaventure.[10]

For both Angelo and Ubertino, *cupiditas* and *superbia* were the roots of sin. Avarice and pride were the cause of the fall and the factors which had led to the corrupt state of mankind. Poverty and evangelical perfection were the divine remedy which could lead men back to the kingdom of God. Angelo envisioned the followers of St. Francis as a society in which all its members, having rejected greed and adopted poverty, would be united with Christ and each other in a brotherhood of love. By its stark contrast to the world, this society would prepare the way for the coming of Christ, drawing the elect toward evangelical perfection and casting the harsh brightness of a spotlight on the sins of the worldly.[11]

Humility and poverty almost invariably appear together, and where only one is mentioned, the other is implied. They expressed the reorientation of the self by which the friar stripped himself of all pride and possessions, thus denying his carnal desires and beginning to despise mundane things and honors. Such contempt for worldly values is a necessary corollary of the desire to conform himself to Christ and of the thirst for celestial delights. The archetype of this quest was Christ, surrendering himself for the redemption of mankind. Frequently Christ's nudity on the cross is cited as the supreme example of poverty, the standard for which a brother ought to strive in denying himself. Poverty, therefore, in its external form, is the expression of this interior search to suffer with Christ and of the transvaluation of values which directs the Franciscan to God rather than to possessions. Longing to attain union with Christ and to teach other men evangelical perfection by his example and words, he will use only the barest necessities.[12]

Study and the necessary use of books and convents for schools could therefore be reconciled with poverty so long as this study was conducive to the development of spirituality. If, however, study led in a different direction, then even conformity to poverty might make it questionable.[13]

According to both Angelo and Ubertino, the virtues of humility and poverty express themselves in the form of a minimal use of housing, clothing, food, books, etc., but not all men who practice poverty are inwardly disciples of St. Francis. Spirituality necessarily seeks to become visible in behavior consonant with itself. Nevertheless, the visible symbol could exist without the spiritual sources. Men who inwardly continued to want possessions or desired mundane honors, could outwardly act like true friars. Even malignant men, hostile to the Order, could hypocritically adopt its mode of conduct. Ultimately, however, these false friars will betray their inner attitudes.[14]

Since poverty is the expression of spirituality, the latter became the chief norm by which to judge poverty. Angelo and Ubertino recognized Scripture, the text of the *Regula* and the *Testamentum,* the weight of outside opinion, whether religious, clerical, or lay, the authority of the church and the papacy, and ultimately Christ himself as standards, but they refer most frequently to the inner quest in discussing questions about poverty. Possessions contradicted humility and self-denial for the sake of Christ. How could a brother claim that he wanted to conform to Christ, but simultaneously demand and enjoy luxuries?[15]

In the eyes of the Spirituals, the development of the legal distinction between *dominium* and *usus,* while it established the friars position vis-a-vis their critics among the seculars, did not erect a suitable standard for poverty among the friars themselves. How could unrestricted use be reconciled with the interior spirituality of the friars? Was it not true that only that use was acceptable which expressed self-denial, mortification, and contempt for mundane attractions? From interior quest to outward behavior, from the spirit to the letter was the context within which the Spirituals viewed the question of poverty. The *usus pauper,* even when phrased in doctrinal or legal terminology, was in their eyes the only acceptable corollary of the Franciscan spirit. The *renouatio euangelicae perfectionis* or *imitatio Christi crucifixi* could not be reconciled with superfluity or abundance.[16]

The Spirituals, therefore, viewed the controversy over poverty as, in fact, a conflict between Franciscan spirituality and carnal unconverted men who wanted to call themselves friars while they retained only the husk of the Franciscan life. This is clearly the view of Angelo da Clareno in his *Historia septem tribulationum.*[17] He began by introducing the stigmatized Francis as the exemplar of *cruciform,* Christlike perfection.[18] Using the device of having Christ himself speak in the first person, Angelo emphasized that Christ had called Francis and his brothers to initiate the *renouatio* of evangelical perfection; that the *Regula bullata* and the *Testamentum* came from Christ himself; and that the conformity of Francis and his friars to Christ is first of all one of the interior spirituality and thence a mode of behavior.[19] For Angelo this was the beginning of the party to which the Spirituals adhered. Angelo described his opponents' origin as a conference called by Satan who, fearing that the Order of Friars Minor would succeed in calling the church back to the perfection of the Gospel, adopted a demonic suggestion that the best way to combat Francis and his disciples would be by "fifth-column" tactics. The demons were to begin persuading their own men to enter the Order and to pose as sincere brothers. They were to behave at first like the true friars in order to corrupt the Order gradually.[20]

Angelo made his division of the Order tripartite by placing a middle group between the Spirituals and the Conventuals:

"Many will want to enter this religion, who will begin to live for themselves, not Christ. They will follow carnal prudence more than the observances of faith and the Rule. They will devote themselves mostly to the flesh and will give only a little of themselves to the spirit. They will give in to the weaknesses of nature and deafen their hearts to grace. Thus, they will neglect to grasp the strength which grace could give them and will be unable to seize hold of the kingdom of God. From this time, there will be a decline from perfection and the religion will slide downwards and the brothers will begin to cool the ardor of their perfect love."[21]

Angelo described the seven persecutions in terms of this schemata.

Each persecution is instigated by enemies of Francis within the Order whose carnality, envy, malignancy, pride, etc. induce them to attack those friars who, despising mundane allegiances, desire only to adhere to the crucified Christ.[22] The instigators of these persecutions are able to persuade the middle group, usually by deceptions, to side with them against the rigorists. Angelo almost never named a friar he regarded as a true instigator. The minister-generals of the Order, for example, St. Bonaventure or Johannes de Murrovalle, are left in the middle group. Angelo believed that the final result of this struggle would be the purification of the Order and the full realization of the *renouatio evangelicae perfectionis,* not only in the Order but also in the church.[23]

Angelo never identified the *carnalis ecclesia* with the papacy or the leadership of the Order. He did not directly attack the papal bulls which sought to clarify the observance of the Rule and could, in fact, argue that *Exiui de paradiso,* if it had been implemented, would have promoted the true observance.[24] The traditional explanation of the struggle as a conflict between the need for modifications in order to serve the church and a zealous literalism is one that Angelo would not have accepted, since he saw no inherent conflict between the Rule and the mission of the Order. For him the controversy was a conflict between evangelical spirituality and carnal malignancy, with the majority of brothers and the papacy caught between the two opposing forces.

Ubertino's view of the struggle did not differ substantially from that of Angelo. The *Arbor uitae* is on one level a theological exposition of exemplarism centered on Christ. Simultaneously it is a series of guides to meditation on the life of Christ from his eternal origins to the final climax of history. Throughout the work, the focus of Ubertino's christology is the passion. He developed interior spirituality around this central point, and constantly reiterated the demand that this spirituality express itself in humility, poverty, and love. For example, in chapter eleven of book one, *Jesus Maria natus,* Ubertino included a lengthy attack both on the friars and on the secular clergy. He accused them of claiming to live according to the Gospel, while they in fact were moved by a spirit wholly contrary to that of Jesus. According to Ubertino, some argue that contemplation is aided by a well-fed body, a comfortable cell, a spacious convent, etc. For these people moderation is necessary for the contemplative life. "Discretion is the mother of virtues." Ubertino replied that "carnal discretion is not the mother of virtues, but the nurturer of all vices. Carnal prudence produces death, spiritual prudence life and peace." This passage gives us a clear insight into

Ubertino's thought. Exterior virtues are expressions of evangelical spirituality, while any other spirit will come to the surface in hypocrisy or in vice. Against a seemingly Aristotelian theory of moderation, Ubertino defended his concept of evangelical perfection as both spiritually and ethically focused on poverty.[25]

Both Angelo and Ubertino regarded the *uita franciscana* as a spirituality centered on the passion of Christ which must express itself in exemplary behavior. Thus, they saw the struggle between the Spirituals and the Conventuals as a conflict on the spiritual level which manifested itself in disputes over the *usus pauper.*

The traditional opinion about the "literalism" of the Spirituals needs, therefore, to be modified. This portrayal of them as fanatical advocates of the extreme practice of poverty has long created difficulties, because the conduct of the Spirituals did not conform to their putative demands. Peter John Olivi was trained at Paris and taught at Montpellier, Florence, and Narbonne. Ubertino was a lector at Santa Croce. Although Angelo never held this post, his translations from Greek indicate that he was a learned man. Certainly the Spirituals did not reject all use of convents or books. In fact, the Spirituals' insistence that observance must be consonant with the inner norm permitted them to accept such behavior as could be reconciled with their spirituality. Studies which promoted spirituality could be legitimately encouraged, even though this required the use of books and buildings, while any learning which inspired a mundane spirit was totally unacceptable.

The importance of spirituality suggests a reason for the Spirituals' use of Joachim. The development from the letter through the combination of letter and spirit to the full *spiritualis intelligentia* was a prominent theme in Joachim's thought. He looked also for the coming of *uiri spirituali* who would pass through a purifying period of tribulation. The Spirituals found in Joachim a description of their Order as initiating and spurring the renewal of evangelical perfection through suffering and tribulation. Their eschatology, however, remained Franciscan, since they preserved a christological focus.[26]

In their spirituality and their concept of poverty as its expression, the Spirituals stood in the mainstream of the development of the Order in the thirteenth century. The Spirituals, however, represented only one side of the controversy, and both sides deserve a hearing. More work needs to be done on the program of the Conventuals, particularly on their concept of the relationship between spirituality and poverty, before the controversy can be fully explained.[27]

The purpose of this paper has been to demonstrate that spirituality was central, not incidental in Ubertino da Casale's and Angelo of Clareno's defense of poverty. They consistently understood the *usus pauper* as the expression of self-denial and the quest for conformity to Christ. Conversely, spirituality was the norm by which they judged observance. The apparent inconsistencies in their behavior disappear if they are judged within their own frame of reference, since conduct which promoted spirituality was legitimate. Spirituality may also have been the force which attracted them to the Abbot Joachim's prophecies of *uiri spirituali*. Although Ubertino, in particular, was an able legal and theological polemicist, his approach was not that of a fanatical legalist. Without further study of other important Spirituals and, as pointed out above, of the Conventuals, a full re-evaluation of Ubertino and Angelo is impossible. At the least, however, such a re-examination must begin by understanding the Spirituals within their own frame of reference, the tradition of Franciscan spirituality.

# NOTES

1. For a traditional treatment of Franciscan spirituality, see Jean Leclercq et. al., *A History of Christian Spirituality*, vol. II: *The Spirituality of the Middle Ages*, trans. by the Benedictines of Holme Eden Abbey, Carlisle (London, 1968), pp. 283-314, which interprets the Conventual-Spiritual controversy as a conflict between poverty and obedience and inserts the history of Franciscan spirituality into the development of medieval spirituality rather than into the development of the Order. John Moorman, *A History of the Franciscan Order from its Origins to the Year 1517* (Oxford, 1968), pp. 256-272, treats spirituality under Franciscan literature. The most recent detailed treatment of the development of poverty is by M. D. Lambert, *Franciscan Poverty* (London, 1961). Lambert interpreted the development of Franciscan poverty with reference to the transformation of St. Francis' devotional doctrine of the absolute poverty of Christ into a legal and polemic position. Decima L. Douie, *The Nature and Heresy of the Fraticelli* (Manchester, 1932), pp. 50-152, remains the best treatment of Angelo and Ubertino. Cajetan Esser, *Origins of the Franciscan Order*, trans. by Aeden Daly and Irina Lynch (Chicago, 1970), pp. 228-240, is the best treatment of poverty in English, but confines itself to the period of origins.

2. In this paper I have used spirituality to refer to the inner, in contrast to the external, life. The *lectio divina, meditatio, oratio*, and *contemplatio* formed interlinked parts of the spiritual life for the Franciscans as for the monks. It is difficult to separate spirituality from mysticism, since the latter category must include such figures as Giles of Assisi, St. Bonaventure, Jacopone da Todi, and Angela of Foligno, but *imitatio Christi* or *conformitas* did not necessarily include the unitive, mystical experience of God. Thus, spirituality is a broader term, and in the case of Angelo and Ubertino a more accurate one. Poverty in this paper refers both to an inner spirit of self-denial or renunciation and to the outward expression of this in conduct. The Franciscan concept of *paupertas* seems to me to include both these dimensions and, in fact, the key to understanding Angelo's and Ubertino's treatment of poverty lies in grasping the intimate connection which, for them, existed between poverty as a component of spirituality and the observance of poverty both by individual friars and the Order as a whole. Their determined defense of the *usus pauper* derived directly from their conviction that the inner life must necessarily assume a visible dimension which fully and accurately reflects its source.

3. Douie, pp. 50-59, 69-70. Angelo translated the *Scala paradisi* by St. John Climacus, the Rule of St. Basil, and the "Dialogues of St. Macarius." His knowledge of Greek and his acquaintance with the Greek fathers and Basilian monasticism is clearly reflected in his *Expositio regulae fratrum minorum* (Edited by Arsenio Frugoni [Quaracchi, 1912]). The principle sources for Angelo's life are the *Historia septem tribulationum*, tribulations five and six (edited by Franz Ehrle, "Die Spiritualen: ihr Verhältnis zum Franziskanerorden und zu den Fraticellen," *Archiv für Literatur-und Kirchengeschichte des Mittelalters*, II [1886], 125-149, 287-327), and Angelo's *Epistola excusatoria* (edited by Ehrle, ibid., 1 [1885] 521-533).

4. Douie, pp. 59-69.

5. Douie, pp. 120-132. Frèdègand Callaey, *L'Idealisme franciscain spirituel au xiv* *siècle* (Louvain, 1911), pp. 2, 3, 7, gives a quite different reconstruction, dating Ubertino's birth to 1249 and his entrance into the Order to 1273 but placing him at Genoa through 1285 and postponing his study at Paris until 1289-1298. After 1325, the reliable evidence about Ubertino's activities and death is extremely meagre. His early career must be reconstructed from his *Arbor uitae crucifixae Iesu* (Venice, 1485; reprinted with an introduction by Charles Davis [Turin, 1961]), Prologus primus, pp. 3-5.

6. For an example of this use of II Cor. 3:6, see Abbot Joachim of Fiore, *Aduersus Iudeos,* Arsenio Frugoni, Fonti per la storia d'Italia, no. 95 (Rome, 1957), pp. 68, 98. On the spirituality of the twelfth century, see Leclercq *et al.,* pp. 127-220, and R. W. Southern, *The Making of the Middle Ages* (New Haven, 1955), pp. 222-240. The latter views St. Francis as the climax of the developments of the twelfth century.
7. Leclercq *et al.,* pp. 127-128, 145-150, 187-200, 257-261.
8. On Franciscan eschatology, see P. Ilarino da Milano, "L'incentivo escatologico nel riformismo dell'ordine francescano," in *L'attesa dell'età nuova nella spiritualità della fine del medioevo,* Convegni del centro di studi sulla spiritualità medievale (Todi, 1962), pp. 283-337. In my opinion, Franciscan eschatology differed considerably from that of Joachim, especially in its emphasis on a *renouatio* of evangelical perfection as a preparation for the second coming of Christ, while Joachim envisaged a series of *status* culminating in the monastic, millenial *status* of the Holy Spirit. The role of this eschatology in the formation of the mission of the Order has been treated in my unpublished manuscript, "Martyrs, Mystics and Missionaries: The Ideology of the Medieval Franciscan Mission." The single clearest statement of Franciscan eschatology is found, in my opinion, in the Prologue to the *Legenda maior* of St. Bonaventure (edited PP. Collegii s. Bonaventurae, Analecta franciscana, 10 vols. [Quaracchi, 1885-1941], X: 557-559. Hereafter cited as AF). On Ubertino's eschatology of renewal see the *Arbor uitae,* Book 2, chp. 2, p. 92; Book 2, chp. 5, pp. 113, 119; and Book 2, chp. 7, p. 130. For Angelo, see his *Expositio Prooemium,* pp. 3-4; chp. 1, pp. 16, 44-48, chp. 4, pp. 99-102, chp. 12, pp. 222-228; epilogue, pp. 231-236.
9. On exemplarism and Bonaventure, see Ewert Cousins, "Mandala Symbolism in the Theology of Bonaventure," *University of Toronto Quarterly,* 40 (1971), 185-201. The *Itinerarium mentis in deum* (edited PP. Collegii S. Bonaventure, *Opera theologica selecta,* [Quaracchi, 1964], V: 179-214) indicates in its use of symbols Bonaventure's christocentric exemplarism. Theologically, Ubertino seems to adhere to the school of Bonaventure in his *Arbor uitae.* A study of exemplarism in the *Arbor uitae* might prove valuable in establishing the relationship between Ubertino and Bonaventure and would also throw light on Ubertino's eschatology.
10. Thomas of Celano, *Vita prima sancti Francisci,* Book, 2, chp. 2, section 91, AF X: 69-70; idem, *Vita secunda sancti Francisci,* Part I, chp. 6, section 10, AF X: 136-137; Bonaventure, *Legenda maior,* chp. 13, AF S: 615-620; *Legenda trium sociorum,* edited by Guiseppe Abate, "Legenda s. Francisci Assisiensis tribus ipsius sociis hucusque adscripta," *Miscellanea francescana,* 39 (1939), Prologue and chp. 5, pp. 276, 387. Angelo, *Expositio,* chp. 1, pp. 12-13. Angelo's dependence on the *Legenda maior* is demonstrated by his use of the phrases ". . . totus absorptus . . . ueluti cruci confixus . . . ;" the reference to Mt. 16:24; and the failure of Angelo to name St. Damian as the place of the vision (cf. *Legenda maior,* chp. 1, AF X: 562).
11. Angelo, *Expositio,* chp. 6, pp. 133-136, 176-177.
12. Ubertino, *Arbor uitae,* Book 1, chp. 11, pp. 61-68; Book 2, chp. 8, pp. 131-135; Book 5, chp. 1, pp. 423-428. Angelo, *Expositio,* chp. 1. pp. 13-17, 23-24, 41-43; chp. 2, pp. 56-57, 69; chp. 3, pp. 82-83; chp. 6, pp. 129-132, 157, 175-177.
13. *Ibid.,* Book 2, chp. 2, pp. 87-88, 93; Angelo, *Expositio,* chp. 9, pp. 195-197; chp. 10, pp. 208-215. On the attitude of Bonaventure and of the Spirituals toward learning, see David Burr, "The Apocalyptic Element in Olivi's Critique of Aristotle," *Church History,* 40 (1971), 15-20; Tullio Gregory, "Eschatologia e Aristotelismo nella scholastica medievale," in *L'attesa,* pp. 262-282.
14. Ubertino, *Arbor uitae,* Book 1, chp. 11, p. 64; Book 2, chp. 3, p. 94. Angelo of Clareno, *Historia,* De legenda antiqua, edited by F. Tocco, "Le due prime tribolazioni dell' ordine francescano," *Rendiconti della r. accademia dei Lincei* (Roma, 1908), pp. 26-27.
15. In Ubertino's strictures on the religious it is not the text of the Rule which he cites but the incompatibility of the conduct of both clerics and religious with the spirituality they profess to seek. Cf. Ubertino, *Arbor uitae,* Book I, chp. 11, pp.61-64; Book 2, chp. 3, pp. 94-95.
16. Ubertino, *Arbor uitae,* Book 2, chp. 6, pp. 120-121; Book 2, chp. 8, pp. 132- 133; Book 3, chp. 9, pp. 184-188.
17. The *Historia septem tribulationum* was edited by Ign. v. Döllinger, *Beiträge zur Sektengeschichte des Mittelalters,* 2 vols. (Munich, 1890: reprinted New York, 1960), II: 417-526. Franz Ehrle edited tribulations three through seven in his *Die Spiritualen,* 2 (1886), 125-155, 256-327. Subsequently Tocco edited the *De legenda antiqua* and the first two tribulations in his *Le due prime tribolazioni.* The edition of Döllinger was made from a text which contained numerous omissions and lacunae. Subsequent references to the *Legenda* or the first two tribulations are to Tocco, and references to tribulations three through seven are to Ehrle.
18. Angelo da Clareno, *Historia,* De legenda antiqua, pp. 7-8.
19. *Ibid.,* pp. 8-16, 25-31.
20. *Ibid.,* Prima tribulatio, pp. 49-52.
21. *Ibid.,* De legenda antiqua, p. 19.
22. *Ibid.,* Prima tribulatio, pp. 33-34, 48-49; Secunda tribulatio, pp. 70-71; 81-83; tertia tribulatio, pp. 256-258; Quarta tribulatio, pp. 271-274; Quinta tribulatio, pp. 287-295; Sexta tribulatio, pp. 127-129.
23. On St. Bonaventure, see Angelo da Clareno, *Historia.* Quarta tribulatio, p. 277. On Johannes de Murrovalle, ibid., Quinta tribulatio, p. 296. On the future realization of the *renouatio,* see ibid., Nota de forma habitus, edited Ehrle, *Die Spiritualen,* 2 (1886), 153-155.
24. Angelo da Clareno, *Historia,* Sexta tribulatio, p. 139. See also idem, *Expositio,* chp. 10, p. 207.
25. *Ibid.,* Book 1, chp. 11, pp. 65-66.
26. On Joachim and the future *uiri spirituali,* see Marjorie Reeves, *The Influence of Prophecy in the Later Middle Ages: A Study in Joachimism* (Oxford, 1969), pp. 135-144, 191-228.
27. The sources apparently pose a problem since, apart from their share of polemical works, the identifiable Conventuals have left us little evidence from which to reconstruct their position. In the latter half of the thirteenth century and the first half of the fourteenth century, the friars produced a considerable number of mystical and spiritual writings, but much of this is either anonymous or from men about whom we know too little to link them with the Conventuals.

# History and Eschatology: Medieval and Early Protestant Thought in Some English and Scottish Writings

*Marjorie Reeves*

Eschatology means discourse about "last things." It is often used in association with the word "apocalyptic," which literally means an unveiling of things usually hidden, but, since the hidden things men desire to know most are future things, has come to mean revelation of the future. Recently interest has focused on attitudes of men in the sixteenth and seventeenth centuries towards their future. The adjectives eschatological, apocalyptic, prophetic are applied somewhat indiscriminately to their hopes and expectations which, it is recognized, form a significant thread in the pattern of ideas in this period. Together these words carry the implication of knowledge which is revealed, not natural, and of expectation which is placed in the context of a divinely-ordained end to history. With them are associated the terms millennial and millenarian which embody the dream of a final blessedness. In studying such hopes there is an important distinction to be made which has not, in my view, been sufficiently noticed: the final age of gold can be expected to fall either within history or beyond it. There are, that is to say, two kinds of "millennium," one the apotheosis of history, the other, an extra-historical state of being. When historians describe millenarians as "escapists" with a minimal concern for historical development, they are usually thinking of the second type.[1] Yet many of those who studied eschatology in the sixteenth and seventeenth centuries were concerned as much with the pattern and direction of history and its final stage as with its dissolution.

The importance of this point was implied by E. Tuveson in his significant book *Millennium and Utopia*.[2] He connected millennial dreams of a last golden age of history with the origins of the idea of progress. The two stand, of course, in sharp juxtaposition: the idea of progress, as understood by the modern mind, is generated by observation of natural phenomena and seen as an endless historical process. A millennium as the final act of a divine drama with a definite beginning and ending is a very different concept, yet Tuveson thinks that the expectation of such a triumphant final act probably assisted the growth of more naturalistic ideas of progress. To reach this point, he suggests, Protestant thought had to turn from an earlier attitude of pessimism towards history to a more hopeful view of its progress and climax. He does not ask whence this new optimism was derived. Had it antecedents or was it self-engendered? There was a whole history of medieval expectation on which to draw. The purpose of this essay is to examine prophetic expectations in a limited group of English and Scottish Protestants during Elizabethan and early Stuart times, to discover how far, if at all, they drew on medieval sources for their eschatological interpretations of history.

Medieval prophecy obviously bequeathed to men of the Renaissance the expectation of Antichrist as the precursor of Last Things, for there was to be no uninterrupted royal road of progress to a more glorious life. Even those Renaissance scholars who expected the return of the age of gold somehow held this together with a Christian belief in a final climax of evil.[3] The crucial question concerned the relation of Antichrist to history. Could the forces of goodness triumph over those of evil in the men and institutions of this world, so that between the defeat of Antichrist and the end of history there ensued a period of triumphant living on this earth? Or must all men and institutions crumple before the onslaught of Antichrist, so that the victory could only be won by heavenly forces sent to wind up history and herald the Last Judgement? The main current of Christian thought has tended to see the victory of good over evil in terms only of individual souls won, while expecting a deterioration of institutions and society generally as a presage of the approaching end. The text from Matthew, xxiv, 12, "And because iniquity shall abound, the love of many shall wax cold," was frequently quoted in support of this pessimistic view. In such a view history had no final apotheosis. The drama of Last Things was one of cosmic forces in which human agencies were of small significance and the victory was won above, rather than in, history. The fate of history was simply to be dissolved.

An alternative view, however, sought to give significance to events in time by linking this cosmic conflict to a developing pattern in history itself. Medieval Christians who sought such a pattern believed that it was built into history by God the Creator: it was therefore not natural, but ordained to a divine end, not cyclical, but lineal. Certain Biblical symbols were used to support the conception of a significant structure in history and to feed the expectation of a final triumph within it. Some of these were, however, ambiguous and could be read either in support of the optimistic or the pessimistic view of history.

In the first place there was a figure of the Week of Creation, read as a symbol of the progression of history towards its Sabbath Age.[4] This Seventh Day could be viewed as a final blessedness within time and distinguished from the Eighth Day of Eternity. But it could be placed on the other side of the great gulf fixed by the Last Judgement, a symbol of the supernatural order, not the historical. A second sequence of sevens was derived from the Book with Seven Seals in the Apocalypse. This was generally used to plot out the Church's history from the Incarnation, often in a sequence of conflicts with the forces of evil. Joachim of Fiore had converted it into a double sequence of Seals and Openings in which the Old and New Dispensations ran in parallel lines through their appointed conflicts to the climax of their seventh or Sabbath age. Joachim had found a powerful symbol of this in the "silence in heaven about the space of half an hour" at the opening of the seventh seal (Apoc., viii, 1). Although a historical interpretation of the Seven Seals is by no means peculiar to Joachim, his use of it was widely known in the later Middle Ages and Renaissance period.

The most unambiguous symbol of a progression in history towards a higher plane was found by Joachim in the concept of the Trinity itself. Following innumerable Biblical clues, he proclaimed a Trinitarian structure in history in the three successive dispensations of the Father, Son, and Holy Spirit. Although he held that all three Persons were operative in all three ages, although the dispensations overlapped mysteriously, yet Joachim prophesied a decisive change in history when, after the crucial victory over Antichrist was won, the Holy Spirit would be given to men in a fuller revelation and a new dispensation of history would begin. This expectation of the ascent of man to fuller knowledge and greater illumination has affinities with the idea of

101

progress, but is based, not on man's innate capacity to achieve higher things, but on divine will embodied in the nature of history. It sets a high value on historical event, however, and interprets the working of divine will through human agencies. Although placed within the context of Last Things, the Age of the Spirit is seen as a triumph of humanity between the defeat of Antichrist and the winding up of history at the Second Advent.

In medieval speculation on last things certain further Biblical clues were in common use. The conversion of the Jews was expected before the end of the world: this could be viewed pessimistically as a mere prelude to crisis, or enlarged to include the entry of all unbelievers into a glorious, universal Christendom. The promise of John, x, 16, — There shall be one fold and one shepherd — prompted the same dream of a united and universal Church. The strange prophecy in Apocalypse xx, 2, of Satan bound for a thousand years gave rise to the millennarianism which was, strictly speaking, derived from this text. But whereas some, especially Joachim and his disciples, placed the millennium within history and equated it with the future sabbath age and opening of the seventh seal, others saw it as an extra-historical stage, beyond the Last Judgement. Others again robbed it of expectation by locating it in the past, or identifying it with the whole Christian era. In support of a historical millennium were the arguments that it is conceived as a time sequence, with a terminus when Satan will be loosed briefly, a stage which must surely precede the Last Judgement.

Finally, as an inheritance from medieval tradition, we must note the legends of the last world emperor and angelic pope. A miraculous ruler would arise (or return from death) at God's summoning, to subdue all peoples, exterminate or convert the infidel, and reign in peace over a united world. Again there was an ambiguity here. In the original form of the legend the triumphs of the emperor culminated in a period of material peace and prosperity which was rudely shattered by the onslaught of Antichrist. Historical institutions were expected to go down in ruin and divine intervention to establish a wholly other regime. In later forms — under the influence of Joachimism — the last emperor is often allotted the role of destroying Antichrist and reigning afterwards in an apotheosis of history. When he is partnered by an angelic pope, or series of them, this regime represents a higher spiritual plane of history to be achieved before the end of the age.

Such in brief was the main stock of prophetic ideas on the last age inherited from the Middle Ages. It could be argued that Protestantism represented too much of a break with the past to make a use of this heritage likely. Yet one finds developing in Protestant thought first a belief that this is a new age in a unique sense, and then a colviction that the whole of history has been leading up to it and that in history one can read the prophetic signs pointing forward. Medieval prophecy chimed with this mood in several ways. First, it affirmed a pattern in history which by God's providence was leading to a climax: this enhanced the reformers' sense of significance in the present moment. Secondly, it dramatised the conflict with evil, heightening the tension of the battle with cosmic forces now being fought out. Thirdly, Joachimist prophecy in particular proclaimed that history was about to culminate in a new and final dispensation. This was precisely what some Protestants believed they were witnessing in their own age, citing the new learning, the new preaching, the development of printing, the opening up of the new world, as proofs. Although their Christology taught them that there was only one turning-point in history — the Incarnation — and therefore only two dispensations, the tremendous sense of happening in the Protestant Revolution almost created a second turning-point and so a third dispensation. Although few expressed this in fully Joachimist terms, the sense of a new age, the fruition of history, was frequently present. Moreover, the Joachimist prophecies that God would summon new human agencies to bring about this *renovatio mundi* could underline their own sense of mission.

How far did English and Scottish Protestant scholars in the sixteenth and seventeenth centuries draw on the armoury of the Middle Ages for ammunition? Some of them undoubtedly knew the great compilations of medieval material made by Mathias Flacius Illyricus, the Magdeburg Centuriators, and Johann Wolf.[5] John Bale and John Foxe were in touch with Flacius when in exile, and he is cited by a number of writers. From such a store of material they could read history prophetically, that is, pick out the "signs" placed therein by God. An almost standard procession of prophetic witnesses was formed:[6] Hildegarde of Bingen, Joachim of Fiore, Cyril the Carmelite, Robert Grosseteste, William of St. Amour, Gerard Segarelli and Fra Dolcino,[7] Dante, Marsilius of Padua, William of Occam, together with more recent prophets such as Wyclif, Hus, and Savonarola. The first function of these prophets was denunciation of the Roman Church and identification of Antichrist. Here Joachim stood out as a major prophet of Antichrist, particularly because of his statement that Antichrist was already born in Rome, made to Richard Coeur de Lion at Messina in 1191.[8] This was widely used as a story told with telling dramatic effect. Bale had it,[9] and Foxe was sufficiently impressed to cite it three times, once in the *Rerum Ecclesia Gestarum Commentarii* and then twice in the *Actes and Monuments,* once in the usual Hoveden version, and once in a peculiar version which I have not met elsewhere.[10]

To John Knoxe, Joachim — "a man sometymes of great authoritie and reputation among the Papistes"[11] — was a prime witness to the identification of Rome with New Babylon. Knoxe knew Joachim's *Expositio in Apocalypsim* and quoted several passages from it in Latin and in English in his *Answer to a Letter of a Jesuit Named Tyrie.*[12] Knoxe says that he will refute Master Tyrie from Catholic writers, but in order not to cause him too much pain he will limit himself to two, of whom one is Joachim.

> The great hoore he (i.e. Joachim) sayes, the Universal Fathers affirmed to be Rome. Not, sayes he, as concerning the Congregations of the just, which sometymes was a pilgrimer in it, but as concerning the multitude of the reprobate who be their wicked workes blaspheameth and inpungeth the same Kirk.

The kings of the earth who fornicate with Babylon are the prelates to whom the regiment of souls is committed. "And least that any should thinke yᵗ such a sentence had recklessly eschaped him, he dowbles the same wordes over againe." The merchants of the earth are "yᵉ brutish Preastes that knowe not these thinges yᵗ apperteane to God." In concluding his appeal to Joachim, Knoxe states plainly the view that God had provided such prophets that in these latter days men might read and learn from history:

> If Maister Tyrie or any other of that sect blame us of rayling . . . Then let him and them consider that we learned not of Martyn Luther, what kind of men the papistes were: but that which we speak and affirme now, we have received of the Papistes themselves. For this hath bene the mercyfull provydence of God towardes his lytle flock ever from the beginning. That when a universall corruption began to spred the self, then wer rased some as it wer one or two amonges yᵉ hole multitude, till admonishe the present age and the posterities to come, how far men had declyned from the originall puritie: that at least God might have some testimonie, that yᵉ veritie of God was not altogether buryed in the earth.

A little later an English theologian, William Perkins, makes a slightly different selection from the same pages of Joachim's *Expositio.*[13]

As we shall see, John Bale had an interesting collection of prophetic manuscripts, including several pseudo-Joachimist ones. Another Irish bishop, Edward Stillingfleet, probably possessed several of the Venetian editions of genuine and spurious works of Joachim.[14] The famous prophecies of the popes were imported into England under disguise and published by Walter Lynne as *The Begynninge and Ende of Poperie.*[15] Later, Archbishop Laud possessed a manuscript, probably of Italian provenance, containing these and other pope prophecies in an anthology of text and pictures.[16] In 1582 an interpretation of the Apocalypse by a latter-day Joachite, Iacopo Brocardo, was published in London under the title *The Revelation of St. John reveled, Englished by J. Sanford.* This was full of prophecies of the new age to come.[17] Among unusual references to Joachim is Dr. John Dee's to *Joachim the Prophesier,* citing him on the beauty and prophetic power of numbers.[18]

The information which has been pieced together about John Bale's library shows that his passion for history was at least partly rooted in the medieval prophetic tradition.[19] He possessed the *De periculis novissimorum temporum* of William of St. Amour, as well as two other prophetic works of his; *De principio et fine mundi* attributed to Methodius and a work entitled *De ortu et vita Antichristi;* prophecies of Mechthilde, the Sibyls, and John of Bridlington. He had two pseudo-Joachimist manuscripts; the commentary on the supposed oracle of Cyril the Carmelite and a prophecy entitled *Ioachim abbas contra pullulantium fraterculorum ordines.*[20] In addition, most unusually, he possessed Peter John of Olivi's works on the Apocalypse and on Genesis,[21] while another Joachite, Arnold of Villa Nova, was represented by five items, of which the *De mysterio cymbalorum Ecclesiae* and the *De consummatione saeculi* are directly prophetic.[22] Another interesting entry in his book list reads: *Prophetia de Antichristo per fratrum Columbinum.*[23] Although it does not appear in his list, Bale must have possessed the *Compilationes Vaticiniorum* of John Erghome, a fourteenth-century English Austin Friar, which seems to have contained a good deal of Joachimist material.[24] Finally, there is one piece of evidence which suggests that Bale did link Joachimist prophecy with the Reformation. In *A Brefe Chronycle concernynge the Examynacyon and death of . . . Syr Johan Oldecastell,*[25] Bale collected material on one whom he saw as a precursor of the Reformation. At the end, in a section headed *Prophecyes of Joachim Abbas,* the doctrine of the three *status* is clearly summarized, culminating in a statement on the Age of the Spirit which must have appealed at once to the Reformers:

In the latter dayes shall apere a lawe of lyberte. The Gospell of the kyngedome of Christ shall be taught, and the church shall be pourged as wheate is from chaff and tares. More clerely shall menne than be lerned. The kyngedome of the fleshe shall be done awaye, and these thynges shall be fulfylled towarde the ende of the worlde. The holy ghost shall more perfyghtlye exercise his domynyon in convertynge peoples by the preachers of the latter tyme, than by the Apostles. . . . The churche of Rome shall be destroyed in the thyrde state, as the synagogue of the Jewes was destroyed in the second state. And a spirituall churche shall from thens forth succede to the ende of the worlde.

This summary of Joachimism was adapted from the hostile account of Guido of Perpignan, and since Bale possessed a copy of his *Summa de haeresibus,* it seems fairly certain that he selected and linked this prophecy to Lollardy.[26]

With Bale we have moved beyond the negative aspect of medieval prophecy as evidence for the identification of Antichrist to its positive expectation of a new age at the end of history. Here, quite clearly, Joachimist prophecy was the principal source inherited from the Middle Ages. From the passage quoted above we might have expected Bale to develop the theme of the third age, but in his main work on prophecy, *The Image of Both Churches,* he does not go as far as this. *The Image* is buttressed by an impressive array of medieval, as well as Biblical and Patristic, sources. Joachim's *Expositio* figures in the opening list of authorities, with the note: *Quia profunda liber huius.*[27] There are eight references to Joachim in the *Image.*[28] From these it would seem that Bale's attention was mainly directed towards the prophetic past rather than the future. His chief concern was to show how God's providence had shaped history to His grand design which was yet to be completed. The driving force to this interest was, no doubt, expectation of the last stages about to be unfolded, but these he was content to leave in vague outline. Although Joachim was by no means unique in interpreting the Seven Seals as stages of history, Bale probably drew his use of this symbol directly from the Abbot, since in two passages on the seals he gives Joachim as his sole reference.[29] Like Joachim, Bale makes the seven ages of the seal-openings cover the whole of the Church's history, treating the later sequences of seven in the Apocalypse — trumpets and vials — as running concurrently with the seals. Like Joachim, he sees the various angels of the Apocalypse as human agencies of God's will in history rather than supernatural ones. Of particular interest is his interpretation of the angel flying through the midst of the heaven (Apoc. viii, 13):

> Which betokeneth certayn peculiar servauntes of God, illumined with some knowledge, and leadying on hygh conversacion in the church. Such were Joachim Abbas, Cirillus of carme, Angelus of Hierusalem, Theolosphorus of Cusencia, Rainhardus and other. And sens their time Petrus Johannis, Robertus de usecio, Johannes de rupescissa, Arnoldus de Villa nova, Hieronymus Savonarola with such lyke . . . with a loud voyce they cryed, ernest wrytynges they sent the worlde over, under the tytell of revelacion and prophecy.[30]

Almost all those named besides Joachim were his disciples or have been linked with him. Bale names one of his authorities for this list as Joannes Erghom, and it seems clearly to have been drawn in part from the latter's *Compilationes Vaticiniorum.*[31] Again, in the commentary on ch. xviii, 4, he repeats a list of godly men which includes Joachim, Cyril, Ubertino da Casale, Petrus Johannis, and Arnold of Villanova.[32] He draws his interpretation of the Angel with right foot in sea and left on land (Apoc. x, 1, 2) directly from Joachim and applies the prophecy to the new opening of the Gospel by the true preachers, for "everywhere shall truth be opened." Although he does not link it with the third *status,* Bale does follow Joachim in identifying a sabbath age on earth with the silence of the seventh seal-opening, when — after the Fall of Babylon and the binding of Satan — peace and concord will reign and God's word shall be held in estimation. "In the tyme of this swete silence shall Israell be revived, the Jews shal be converted, the heathen shal come in again. Christ will seke up his lost shepe . . . that they may appere one flock, lyke as they have one shepeherde."[33] He is insistent that this sabbath is to be "in the pleasaunte land of the lyvyinge," for there are two sabbaths: "the mystical sabbath of his people here and the eternall sabbath after."[34] Of the first sabbath he says: "In this latter tyme wyl the true christian churche, when all the worlde shall confesse his name in peace, be of hyr full perfyghte age."[35] Thus John Bale, though moderate and cautious, does join those medieval prophets who had looked for a fulfillment of history itself before the great Eighth Day of eternity.

In his latest and unfinished work, *Eicasmi seu Meditationes in sacram Apocalypsim,* Foxe reveals a similar preoccupation with history as prophecy. He interprets the successive sequences of sevens in the Apocalypse historically, and in the intricate calculations of the times which fascinate him Joachim is cited twice as the authority.[36] His general pattern precludes the use of the figure of Satan bound as a symbol of the beatific age to come, for he divides the Church's history into three periods: three hundred years of persecution to Constantine; one thousand years of peace to 1300, the period of Satan bound; the persecution of Antichrist, Satan being loosed, which has lasted until the present day.[37] In this last phase there have been ten persecutions from Wycliffe to that inflicted on Spain and Flanders by Philip II.[38] Again, we find the symbols of the Apocalypse interpreted in terms of human agencies. Foxe quotes Joachim's *Expositio* on the interpretation of the star falling from heaven: "Clericum tamen fuisse, et imbutum scientia literarum";[39] he attributes to Joachim (with others) the identification of the angel "amictum nube" (Apoc. x, 1) as "aliquem ordinis angelici nuncium" and knows that Joachim interprets the sea and land on which his feet are planted as the Old and New Testaments.[40] The weight of his meditations, so far as they had proceeded, was mainly on reading the pattern of prophecy fulfilled. As he leaves it, this pattern appears to lead directly to the Last Judgement, for the work breaks off before he reaches the culminating vision of the New Jerusalem. Yet even so, he gives a sense of history rising to a positive climax before the end, rather than of dissolving into failure. This hope centers, once again, on the new preaching of the Gospel. It is first seen in the heading *De Tempore Restituendi Evangelii,* relating to the Book carried by the angel of Apoc. x which St. John is commanded to devour.[41] Twice Foxe gives lists of the great new evangelists raised up by God to renew evangelical doctrine, ranging from Arnold of Villanova to those "quos recentiori hac mundi aetate ad repurgandam saniores doctrinae lucem excitavit dominus."[42] In particular he sees this *renovatio* symbolized in the resurrection of the two witnesses (Apoc. xi), linking this with the new opportunities of his day:

> . . . quo primum nova haec mireque opportuna facultas Typographica, singulari Dei consilio orbi patefacta eluxerit. Quo factum est, ut paulatim salutaris doctrinae et religionis reformatio magis magisque efflorescere, errores deprehendi, in fide, in cultu corruptelae corrigi, velutque . . . nova quaedam lucis aurora oculis se inspargere occoeperit.[43]

Here Foxe echoes the theme of latter-day Joachites such as Guillaume Postel.[44] Though no millenarian, he used the prophetic tradition to read the signs of the new age dawning. This impression of the *Eicasmi* is reinforced by two Joachimist quotations in the *Actes and Monumentes.*[45] One is a well-known sentence from the pseudo-Joachimist Super Hieremiam: "Also Abbas Joachim in the exposition of Jeremy saith that from the yere of our lord 1200, al times be to be suspected." The other concerns Olivi: "Peter John Aquitane a Franciscan frier in Uasconia who after all the rest proficied that in the latter daies the lawe of libertie shoulde appeare."

Although in this case there is no direct evidence of drawing on Joachimist prophecy, John Napier, in his *Plaine Discovery* (1593), approaches the Apocalypse from the same viewpoint, as an interpretation of history leading up to his own day and thence forward into a positive new age. While he understands the seals as covering the first period of Church history only, he makes the Trumpets and Vials run concurrently: the last Trumpet and Vial began in 1541 and should end in 1786.[46] At the blast of the Seventh Trumpet Christ's kingdom "shall bee spread and enlarged over all. And this can no other wayes come to passe, but by the preaching of the Evangell, which was of newe opened up and preached at the comming of the first Angell, whome the Text saith, to have the *Evangelium aeternum.*"[47] Only now, "in this our seventh age," is the Sealed Book really to be opened.[48] Napier faces the old dilemma encountered by Joachites of reconciling his conviction that a new level of illumination is about to be attained with the centrality of revelation in the Incarnation. Christians, he argues, could not instantly after Christ's crucifixion know Him truly, but only after "a certaine progress of time." Now is the time:

> This prophecying over againe by the open booke meaneth that besides John's first prophecying and writing of this Revelation, in closed and darke language, it must be prophecied, preached and opened over againe by the whole Church in the name of John in these our daies of the seventh age.
> . . . without all question, this is the time of knowledge, even presentlie . . . [49]

Thus the last age of history, which Napier sees as beginning c. 1541 "in the mouths of Luther, Calvin and other his ministers,"[50] is conceived as one of triumph, a triumph symbolized by the tremendous number Seven so dear to Joachim. Yet — like Joachim too — he distinguished it from the great day of eternity. The throne of God and His temple, Napier argues, describe, not the majesty of God in heaven, but His Church among His heavenly Elect upon earth: "it meaneth God's true Church to be visible, his trueth and true religion preached and opened up, and finally the Majestie of God to be knowne."[51] To distinguish this age of history from the final timeless beatitude, he introduces the concept of two resurrections, the first from Antichristian errors, the second, the General Resurrection at the end of history.[52] His final felicity is clearly beyond time: "for seeing this is the time of eternall rest, all heavenly motions and earthly vicissitudes must have an ende: yea, seeing the motions of the Spheares, Planets and Starres were made for the distinction of times . . . as also forth from this shall be no time."[53] In a passage which might almost have been written by Joachim, he sees the perfect dimensions of the New Jerusalem as symbolizing the Trinity and the Unity of the Godhead.[54] Napier, like Foxe, is not a millenarian, nor does he use Joachim's concept of three *status* in history, but his conception of a seventh age in history as one of fulfillment through further illumination clearly links him with the Joachimist tradition.

The full force of an optimistic expectation concerning history is first felt in Thomas Brightman's *Revelation of the Revelation* (1615), with its great message that "after this storme [of Antichrist] has blowne over, there shall followe presently gawdy dayes."[55] This hope is the climax of an interpretation of history which is rooted in the medieval prophetic tradition. As in medieval number symbolism, the number seven is central to this interpretation:

> Moreover the number of seven is an universall number, by whose revolu-

tion all tymes are framed, al ages beinge in like manner wheeled about upon this Pole, as the whole frame of heaven is turned about upon the seven starres of Charles-wayne. For which cause this nomber as beinge full of mystery, is used throughout the Booke afterwards.[56]

As in Joachimist thought, the angels of the Apocalypse are seen as symbols of God's human agents. Thus the angels of the seven churches represent historical churches down to Philadelphia, Geneva, and Laodicea, England.[57] The four *animalia* are servants of God ("for . . . it is playne that they are men"), and he links them with a scheme of four ages: the first, the Lion, extended to Constantine; the second, the Ox, to Wycliffe; the third of the Man began with the Gospell reviving, while of the fourth he writes:

> Wee doe as yet looke for Eagles to come into the World, which the callinge of the Jewes shall at last bringe in, when as the Gospell shalbe fully restored and brought to his due and glisteringe beautie . . . Then shall the Bishoppe looke wishly and with fixed eyes upon the Sunne, and they shall search out with a mervailous sharpenes of witt, whatsoever part it is of the truth of God that shall lye hidden to that day . . . they shall soare aloft, havinge all there conversation in the heavens.[58]

The association of the *animalia* with periods of history might well have been taken from Joachim's *Expositio,* while the Eagle figuring the soaring illumination of the age to come is precisely Joachim's symbol.[59] A direct connection is possible, for at one point Brightman clearly is using Joachim as a source. Rather surprisingly, he interprets the angel (or eagle) who flies through the heavens uttering the threefold Woe as Pope Gregory the Great.[60] He himself feels the need to justify this identification, and the presumption that he took it from Joachim is strong, since in dealing with the next verse of the Apocalypse he cites Joachim directly.[61] The right and left feet of the descending angel of Apocalypse x, 2 are good medieval teachers, and Brightman's list of these includes two Joachites, John of Roquetaillade, and Arnold of Villanova.[62] The angel's "little book" signifies the restoration of the gift of prophecy now, in the time of the sixth trumpet, when "a more full prophecy and more plentiful knowledge shined forth."[63] Once again he finds this fulfilled in Reformation history and the development of printing.[64]

So Brightman sees in the immediate past and the present all the signs of history working towards its climax. The Son of Man seated upon a cloud (Apoc. xiv, 14) is a worthy prince, perhaps a German reforming ruler.[65] The angel with the sickle (Apoc. xiv, 17) was Thomas Cromwell and the second angel, Thomas Cranmer.[66] The harvest was begun to be reaped in Germany in 1521 but the vintage harvest will be reaped in "our own Realme of England."[67] A peculiar position of importance is accorded to Elizabeth, who was given the role of pouring a vial on the popish bishops.[68] All this is still very much human history, not divine intervention: "It is not to be thought that Christ will come forth in any visible forme; these things that are nowe in acting are farre off from the last comming of Christ."[69] Three moments in the final act of the drama can be distinguished: the first before the battle with the Beast and Dragon; the second, the battle itself; the third, the space between victory and Christ's coming in Judgement.[70] Like the Joachites, he believed himself to be standing on the threshold of these things: "And indeed we waite now every daye, while the Antichrist of Rome and the Turks shal be utterly destroyed. Till this victory be obtained the Church shal be still in her warfaring estate, she must keepe in Tents."[71]

In placing his last age of history so clearly between victory over Antichrist and world's end, Brightman ranges himself with the Joachites, and, indeed, he uses many of the old ideas to delineate this time: it will see the final destruction of the Turks and the calling of the Jews, indeed, the whole world, into the one sheepfold; it will be a time of tranquillity and perpetual peace; it will be the New Jerusalem coming down to earth.[72] He plants this emphatically in history: ". . . not that Citie which the Saintes shall enjoy in the Heavens, . . . but that Church that is to bee looked for upon earth, the most noble and pure of all others that have ever bene to that tyme."[73] His expectation is confident: ". . . then shall be indeed that golden age, and highest top of holy felicity and happinesse, which mortall men may expect or think of in this earthly and base habitation."[74] Again, he uses the concept of two resurrections to make the distinction between this age and the eternal felicity. The first resurrection is "a blessednesse to be attained unto in this life . . . This Resurrection belongeth onely to those who, forsaking the Romish Synagogues of Satan, become the true cittizens of the reformed Churches."[75] With his attention focused on this apotheosis of history, Brightman has little to say on the second, or general, resurrection. This kingdom of Christ will at length be translated from earth into heaven, "but I finde no mention in this Booke of the time into which this translation shall fall . . . This Prophecy proceeds no furder then to the finall and universall slaughter of all the enemies and the full restoration of the Jewish Nation . . . as also of the whole Church in all nations wheresoever; it telleth us that shalbe most happy, but it setteth downe no certaine point of time wherein it shall depart hence from the earth and shall take possession of the heavenly inheritance thereof."[76]

111

Brightman does not use the symbol of the millennium for his golden age,[77] nor does his contemporary, Hugh Broughton, who, in his interpretation of the Apocalypse, also follows the idea of placing the thousand years of Satan bound in the past.[78] His belief that history is moving toward a positive climax is, however, clear. The seven angels of Apocalypse xv, 6, represent "what God by men will doe upon earth."[79] The opening up of the new world is a sign of God's will at work: "Now God driveth us to both (East and West) Indians, not for Pepper and Tobacho: but in tyme, to shew his name."[80] Equally the growth of knowledge and illumination over the last hundred years is a sign of progress towards the climax: "All reformed Countries flow with learned men."[81] The Rider who is called faithful and true (Apoc. xix, 11) is already at work, as a marginal note points out: "This is made famous in 1588 and 1605 for our Albion."[82] Above all, Broughton believes passionately that the conversion of the Jews is imminent and that this will set the seal on the fulfillment of history.[83]

This point emerges clearly in Broughton's vision of the New Jerusalem as *the* climax of history. "A city so high, so long and so broad would hold an infinite companie of men." If envious men had not obstructed the "opening up of both Testaments in Ebrew and Greeke . . . which others might translate into many tongues, many poore Jewes and Turkes had seene the xii tribes over our gates . . . and had taken Chambers in the large building of our square Jerusalem."[84] Albion, France, and the martyr of Spain now hold the three western gates of the city, for here the Hebrew and Greek Testaments are studied as never before.[85] The pearls of the gates, that is, the words of the New Testament, which, when buried in Latin "had lost their gaynesse," will now be brought back to their pristine beauty. The pure gold of the streets represents the "open lawes" and rules of faith now being made clear and "agreeable to the soules frame."[86] Broughton uses traditional symbols for his hopes, but his passion for pure texts makes his New Jerusalem a scholar's paradise. He ends with a plea for help in preparing material for the Jews and a threat that he will "leave all hinderers, as murtherers of soules, out of Jerusalem the holy Citie."[87]

The examples so far selected[88] draw mainly on the tradition of Apocalypse-commentary, but medieval prophecy offered also a literature of oracle, verse, and political prognostication which charted a future darkened immediately by the onslaught of Antichrist, but ultimately illumined by the great world emperor and the angelic pope who would preside over the apotheosis of history. In a remarkable collection of *Admirable and notable Prophesies,* published in 1615, James Maxwell exploited this story to the full, delineating a future which owed little to the periodisation of Apocalypse-interpretation, but much to pseudo-Joachimist prophecy. He invokes twenty-four famous Roman Catholic witnesses to "the Church of Rome, Defection, Tribulation and Reformation."[89] To these he attaches a large number of other witnesses or anonymous oracles, drawn from an impressive range of carefully named sources which demonstrate his wide-spread researches. He appears to have had many of the chief prophetic works and anthologies published in Europe from the late fifteenth century onwards. These include J. Lichtenberger's *Prognosticatio,* W. Ayitinger's *Tractatus de revelatione beati Methodi,* the *Mirabilis liber,* W. Lazius' *Fragmentum vaticinii,* the compilations of M. Flacius Illyricus and J. Wolf, and the *Pleiades* of Sire de Chivigny.[90] Altogether Maxwell's small book forms a commentary on the whole history of medieval prophecy from Hildegard to Nostradamus.[91] The Abbot Joachim holds pride of place, and Maxwell has collected a good deal of material in his praise.[92] With him are grouped Cyril the Carmelite and the Sybil Erithrea (both connected with pseudo-Joachimist writings), as well as the two Joachites, Johannes de Rupescissa and Telesphorus of Cosenza.[93]

Maxwell's viewpoint is extremely interesting, for he shares the full reformer's zeal for proving the iniquities of Rome, yet he is so steeped in medieval prophecy that he accepts all its categories of future reformation. Thus, although the prophecies of denunciation, tribulation, and chastisement are fully represented, the thrust of the book is towards the future *renovatio* which Maxwell finds so prominent in all his oracles. All these hopes cluster round the two medieval figures of the holy last emperor and the angelic pope under whom Christians will enjoy a golden peace. Typical of many passages is this summary from Telesphorus of Cosenza:

> A certaine Angelicall Bishop or Pope, together with a King of France chosen Emperor and crowned with a crowne of thorns, shall reforme the Church and make the Gospell to be preached through the whole world: so that from henceforth the Romaine Bishops shall renounce their temporal state and power and onely meddle in spirituall matters . . . And then at last (saith he) the best Cocke that ever was shall crowe, to wit the Angelicall Bishop.[94]

The political figure is supported chiefly by the Second Charlemagne prophecy in various forms and by the Lily prophecies, as thus:

> Among the lilies shall arise a comely Prince . . . and unto him shall the whole world do homage. He will strike down the prickly bear (the Turk). Happy and blest shall his yeares bee from West to East. . . . This flourish-

ing or flourie Prince, bearing the new name, shall plant the vine of our
Saviour: unto him all Nations shall submit themselves and the crowne of
the East shall be given him to keepe.[95]

For the portraits of the Angelic Pope and his successors Maxwell uses
pseudo-Joachimist prophecies.[96] Thus there is an exceptionally Catholic tone to Maxwell's expectations due to the medieval mould in which
his hopes are cast. Indeed, the value of the Catholic past to Protestants
is directly affirmed when, in introducing his twenty-four witnesses, he
says: "And though that the Iurie bee called from Rome, yet the verdict
thereof is very likely to find credite with the reformed (for few of them
bee of the opinion that no good thing can come from Rome)."[97] He
rebuts, however, the charge of favouring Rome, and is devoted to the
house of King James VI and I.[98] Indeed, though cautiously, his commentary on the prophecies points to a particular quarter whence the
world may see the holy emperor and angelic pope appearing:

> The Good Bishop or Pope that should thus reforme the Church is com-
> monly called Pastor Angelicus, Angelicall Pope, and who knoweth but
> that he may even be a Pastor Anglicus, a Pastor or Bishop sent forth from
> the Countrie of England. The English have been more fertile converters of
> Nations . . . then any other Land else; . . . And that as there is in no
> other Countrie or Nation of the world to be found so many learned and
> eloquent Preachers, not so many complet Divines, for Iudiciousnes,
> Ingeniousnes and Moderation . . . as there is in England, so it may well
> be that God will honour this same Island with the reformation of the
> Church of Rome and her daughters . . .[99]

Again, he picks up a pseudo-Joachimist prophecy beginning *Flores
Rubei* and interprets it thus: "The red Roses shall send foorth the
sweet waters that shall purify and cleanse the Church from all her cor-
ruptions." This refers, he believes, to a "rosie Prince," and he hopes
that the Rose of England will be a chief instrument in the propagation
of the Gospel and the source from which will spring the reformation of
the Church.[100] To support this claim Maxwell traces the English royal
line back to Constantine and announces an unpublished treatise
described thus:

> A Discourse of Gods especiall providence for . . . the Monarchie of great
> Brittaine: wherein is shewed by divers probabilities, olde Predictions and
> Prophecies, that from thence is likely to spring the last Imperiall Mon-
> archie, which should subvert Mahometisme and Iudaisme, convert both
> Iewes and Gentiles . . . and restore both Church and Empire to the integ-
> rity they once had in the happy daies of Constantin the great borne in
> great Brittaine: therein likewise . . . is laid open the vertuous inclination
> . . . and happy education of Prince Charles, with a briefe of his most
> noble descent from forty-nine Emperours, of Romaines, Greeks and Ger-
> maines, besides Kings . . .[101]

Surely this is a pointer to Charles I as the Second Charlemagne?
Turning finally to a group of mid-seventeenth century visionaries,

we find their own experience engendering a forward-looking hope. England in the 1640s appeared to be on the verge of a new dispensation in history, and in their excitement these visionaries turned naturally to symbols and concepts which expressed their expectation. If a new dispensation, then what more appropriate than to see it as a third, the Age of the Holy Ghost? This concept particularly fitted the thought of William Saltmarsh who clearly saw the divine pattern of all history "folded up in" three dispensations of "Law, Gospel and Spirit, or of letter, graces and God, or of the first, second, and third heavens."[102] The design of God, he believed, had been to lead out His people "from age to age, from faith to faith, from glory to glory, from letter to letter, from ordinance to ordinance, from flesh to flesh, and so to Spirit, and so to more Spirit and at length into all Spirit . . ."[103] In tracing this progress of the people of God towards the goal of history, Saltmarsh used many Biblical figures in the way Joachim had done, as, for example, the Exodus from Egypt, the passage of the Spiritual Israelites across Jordan into the Promised Land, the fire licking up Elijah's sacrifice seen as a type of the Spirit's baptism to come.[104] The entire thrust of history is towards its conclusion and thus, just as the ministry of the Gospel was more glorious than that of the Law, so the ministry that is to destroy the ministry of iniquity must be more excellent, glorious, and powerful than that of the Gospel, exceeding it in gifts of miracles and other gifts. The present ministry through Christ's people "who are his Angel" runs through the channels of Arts, Sciences, and Language acquired by natural power and industry, according to any appearance of the Spirit of God. It marks progress in the long passage from "lower ministrations to higher," but is still not that ministry of "more Spirit" which will embody the last glory of life in the flesh, and is still to be distinguished from the "last and more full and rich ministration and most naked" which belongs to the presence of God Himself beyond time.[105] Thus Saltmarsh's Age of the Spirit is clearly within history, reached through divine operation on human agencies, and always to be distinguished from the state of eternity.

Here we meet a doctrine of progress — not of Man's achieving, but of God's ordaining — which is very close to the Joachimist belief in progressive revelation. Yet Saltmarsh shows no knowledge of Joachim, and the problem for us is whether, as has been suggested,[106] his threefold dispensation does derive from this most obvious source, or whether the new experience of the age could spontaneously have engendered a similar concept of history through the working of a similar type of Biblical exegesis. In the absence of any direct evidence of

Joachimist influence, one must assume the latter. Yet this kind of exegesis stems back to a strong medieval tradition. In a general sense Salt-marsh belongs to this tradition, but the parallels with Joachimism seem to me to spring from a particular type of religious experience and hope common to both Joachites and Puritans, rather than from the direct influence of the one on the other.[107]

The same conviction concerning a third dispensation in history about to dawn is central to William Erbery's thought. The first two were those of Law and Gospel, but this third dispensation "which we are now entering upon" is of a different constitution: it is a discovery of God differing from Law and Gospel, yet "tis mixt of both, for both were glorious and the glory of both . . . is joyned together in this third."[108] There is a clear parallel here with Joachim's thought, for he insisted that, just as the Spirit proceeded from Father and Son, so the third age must grow out of, overlap with, and take into itself, the first two. Moreover Erbery's three dispensations are specifically Trinitarian in significance: "God under the Law . . . was known as the Father. In the Gospel God was known as the Sone . . . The third will be pure Spirit, when nothing but Spirit and power shall appear, when God shall be all in all."[109] Again, in many ways his exegesis parallels Joachim's: the Exodus and Red Sea crossing as type of the passage from the second to the third age; the teaching of St. John on the coming of the Spirit as prophesying a further dispensation in history; the third heaven of St. Paul's vision as the third age; the concept of the Sabbath when words will cease.[110]

Erbery's new age is clearly a dispensation within history, active through human agencies, and transforming secular as well as religious institutions. Again and again he insists that the glory of God will be manifest in and through the Saints. "In this third dispensation God in the Saints restores all things . . . things spiritual and civil also, renews the forms of Kingdomes, of outward Government and Order, as well as things in the Spirit, in and by the Saints . . . First the glory of God returns into his Temple, that is, all spiritual things are restored . . . and then there follows restitution of civil power."[111] Where Maxwell still saw his age of peace and tranquillity in terms of world emperor and angelic pope, Erbery centres his expectation on the Saints and the Nation, affirming "that these wars and wranglings will shortly cease in the Nation, in which God will so appear with power and glory that all the Nations about us shall be broken, or brought in with us at last to the Government of Jesus. That is, when God alone shall reign in Men and Men reign in Righteousness, and Righteousness arise in truth, then shall the Royal Law and Rule of Christ in love be followed: That Men and Magistrates shall do to all as they would be done unto, or rather, do to Men as God would."[112]

We have already encountered the problem of how a further dispensation of new knowledge could be squared with the orthodox Christology of a once-for-all revelation. The Spiritual Franciscans of the thirteenth century, seeking to erect St. Francis into the harbinger of the third age, fastened on the concept of three advents of Christ — once in the flesh, a second or intermediate advent in St. Francis, and a third in final judgement.[113] Some Puritans had the same overwhelming sense that the new stage about to begin in history had the quality of a new advent. Thus both Saltmarsh and Erbery postulated an intermediate advent, calling the final and full manifestation of Christ the third advent. Alternatively, they speak of three resurrections: the first of Christ in His Flesh; the second, the spiritual resurrection of the saints to rule in the new dispensation; the third, the General Resurrection of the dead.[114] This doctrine, proclaimed by Joachites and Puritans alike, carried the implication that men in the new dispensation would be granted more illumination than the Apostles and saints of earlier ages.

Other Puritans, writing or preaching in the same great period of the 1640s, express a similar expectation. John Archer looks for a "middle coming of Christ": "For Christ has three commings. The first was when he came to take our nature. . . . The second is when he comes to receive his kingdome. A third is that when he comes to judge all and end the world: the latter commings are two distinct commings, not one (as it hath beene thought)."[115] He deduces from the Scriptures a threefold state of Christ's kingdom, describing the third thus:

> I call this last state of his Monarchicall because in this, when he entreth upon it, he will governe as earthly Monarches have done, that is, universally over the world . . . and in a worldly visible earthly glory; not by tyranny, oppression, and sensually, but with honour, peace, riches and whatsoever in and of the world is not sinfull, having all Nations and Kingdomes doing homage to him, as the great Monarchies of the World had.[116]

He proves the inevitability of his golden age by the historical pattern of kingdoms and, although some of the details of his visionary future have the features of a supra-historical millennium, he clearly sees it as a period in time before the Last Judgement: "a time of restoring all things . . . which cannot be meant of the world's end, and heaven which follows it, for at the world's end, the earth ends, and shall not be made new . . . therefore it must be meant of a time and a state to be in this world."[117] Robert Maton similarly uses Daniel's "propheticall image" of the successive kingdoms to show that Christ's kingdom must succeed them all in time and space.[118] In proclaiming his final age he uses traditional ideas: the conversion of the Jews, the hope of one shepherd and one sheepfold, the symbol of Satan bound for the millennium — as well as the concept of an intermediate resurrection.[119] From a mass of Biblical texts he proves that this kingdom must be on earth, arguing that the words "My kingdom is not of this world etc." do not literally mean another world, but "such an alteration over the whole frame of nature and such a change of government on the Earth, that this time shall then as well be accounted the time of another world, as the time before the Flood is now taken for the old world by us."[120] Again, John Brayne in *The New Earth, or the True Magna Charta of the past Ages, and of the Ages or World to come,* uses the figure of the three tabernacles in the Transfiguration story (Luke ix, 33): "The service of God under Moses and under the law is meant under the tabernacle for Moses. The service of God under Christ and grace is meant by the tabernacle for thee or Christ. Which administrations falling, in the hiding of the Church, are again to be restored in our dayes by that Elias, in that tabernacle attributed to him."[121] This is strikingly reminiscent of Joachim's writing, and, we may recall, the figure of the returning Elias was to Joachim and the Joachites the harbinger of the third age.

Yet, for all the echoes, none of the mid-seventeenth-century writers quoted above show any direct use of medieval sources. In one case, however, we have such evidence. William Dell cites among other medieval writers Joachim, William of St. Amour, Mathias of Janov, Wycliffe, and Hus. Of particular interest is the long passage he quotes and translates from the pseudo-Joachimist *Super Hieremiam* which, of course, he attributes to Joachim.[122] Here the locusts loosed from the bottomless pit in Apocalypse ix are interpreted as *Scholastici et Magistri,* leading to a great diatribe against the idols of carnal learning. The significant thing is that Dell carries the quotation on from denunciation to prophecy of the true illumination to come when the preaching of the Cross has destroyed "all Philosophical Doctrine and Humane and secular learning." At that time "the children and youth and men of all ages, sorts and conditions shall be taught no other Doctrine . . . than that which is found in the Scriptures . . . and that not according to any humane and philosophicall understanding, but according to the teaching and mind of the Spirit." I have not met this passage quoted by any other writer of the period, so one may presume that Dell selected it for himself straight from the work. He had already expressed, in a sermon preached in 1646, his expectation concerning the spiritual Church now being born. Its hall-mark is that "where Christ sends the Ministration of the Spirit, there many *young* people are brought to Christ, as being most free from the forms of the former age."[123] He believes that "the Lord must build this spirituall Church and set it up in the world . . . and cause it to increase till it fills the world."[124] In this hope he can conclude: "Goe and tell the Foxes that we will walk without feare in the world both today and tomorrow, and the third day we shall be perfected."[125]

Within the scope of this article it has only been possible to examine a sample of the English writers in this period who were concerned with a prophetic future within history.[126] But certain points emerge. There was a conscious use of medieval sources on the part of some but by no means all. Joachim and the Joachites, who expected a triumphant apotheosis of history, are drawn on considerably, but — curiously enough — not in connection with the concept of a three-fold dispensation leading to an Age of the Spirit. We cannot be sure that they derived this notion from Joachimism. While no conscious link is made, however, the symbols and images used, drawn mainly from the Bible, are interpreted in strikingly similar ways. In postulating a "middle advent," these Puritans solved the Christological problem of reconciling progressive illumination with a once-for-all revelation in the same way as some Joachites. In their approach to the future these writers use a tradition of historical interpretation which is rooted in the medieval belief that God has provided clues to the pattern which His Providence is working out. In relating history and prophecy these Protestant thinkers still follow a medieval way of thought. It was, perhaps, this historical approach which led a significant group to place their age of beatitude within and at the climax of the historical process. Some certainly use the symbol of the millennium for this, but — as we have seen — by no means all. It is clear that the term millenarian, used indiscriminately, is misleading, both when applied to those who — while expecting a future golden age — placed the period of Satan bound in the past, and when no distinction is made between the hope of a millennium within history and that of a post-historical state of being. Here I have confined my attention to those who, in placing their golden future within time, made an optimistic affirmation concerning the historical process, because they are perhaps the more significant group. They were, it is true, making an affirmation about further revelation from God, not about the innate capacity of men to progress; furthermore, it would seem that they expected change to stop in the final stage of immutable beatitude. Nonetheless, their ideas could become a seedbed for future hopes: a new illumination of the Spirit, a reign of peace, an ecumenical gathering into one sheepfold, a blossoming of the gifts of men, a richer yield from the earth, all these expectations, detached from their eschatological setting, could be translated into purely human hopes within history.

# NOTES

1. See, for instance, W. Haller, *Foxe's Book of Martyrs and the Elect Nation* (London, 1963), p. 130: "To seek escape from history like the millenarians . . . was to reject Christianity." M. Walzer, *The Revolution of the Saints* (Cambridge, Mass., 1965), pp. 297-298, contrasts "the chiliast's dream" with the "minimum programme" of more sober Puritans. But W. Lamont, *Godly Rule: Politics and Religion 1603-60* (London, 1969), p. 13, makes a point similar to mine: "What if millenarianism meant not alienation from the spirit of the age but a total involvement with it?"

2. E. Tuveson, *Millennium and Utopia* (Berkeley, 1949), pp. 45 ff.

3. M. Reeves, *The Influence of Prophecy in the Later Middle Ages* (Oxford, 1969), pp. 429-431, (hereinafter, *Influence of Prophecy*).

4. For the following four paragraphs, see Reeves, *Influence of Prophecy*, passim.

5. See, for example, R. Abbott, *Antichristi Demonstratio* . . . (London, 1603), p. 63; H. Broughton, *A Revelation of the Holy Apocalyps* (London, 1610), p. 88: T. Brightman, *A Revelation of the Revelation* (Amsterdam, 1615), p. 315: J. Maxwell, *Admirable and notable Prophesies* . . . (London, 1615), pp. 57, 60, 80, 83; E. Stillingfleet, *Discourse on the Idolatry of the Church of Rome* (London, 1672), p. 137.

6. For the most popular medieval witnesses, see J. Bale, *The Image of Both Churches* . . . (London, 1550), sig. H. iv^v, (Pt. 3) sig. Aa.v^v-vi^r; J. Foxe, *Actes and Monumentes* . . . (London, 1563), pp. 135-136; *Rerum in Ecclesia Gestarum Commentarii* (Basle, 1559), p. 57; Brightman, *op. cit.*, pp. 64-75, 337, 488-92; Maxwell, *op. cit.*, passim; W. Dell, *The Tryall of Spirits* (London, 1653), pp. 25, 33.

7. For the pseudo-Joachimist prophecies associated with the name of Cyril, see Reeves, *Influence of Prophecy*, p. 57. For Segarelli and Dolcino, *ibid.*, pp. 242-248.

8. *Ibid.*, pp. 6-10.

9. J. Bale, *The First two parts of the Actes or unchast examples of the English votaryes* . . . (London, 1551), f. cviii^v; *Scriptorum Illustrium maioris Brytanniae* . . . *Catalogus* (Basle, 1558), p. 233.

10. Foxe, *Rerum in Ecclesia*, p. 57; *Actes and Monumentes*, pp. 70, 135. For other English references to this episode, see J. Jewel, *A Defence of the Apologie of the Churche of Englande* (London, 1567), p. 434; R. Abbott, *op. cit;*, p. 62; N. Bernard, *Certain Discourses* (London, 1659), p. 122. A second famous episode which brought Joachim's name into prominence was the scandal of the Eternal Evangel which is cited against the Roman Church by J. Bale, *Acta Romanorum Pontificum* . . . (Basle, 1558), p. 441; Foxe, *Actes and Monumentes* (London, 1570), p. 403; Brightman, *op, cit.*, p. 315; J. Donne, *The Sermons of John Donne*, ed. E. Simpson and G. Potter (Berkeley and Los Angeles), viii, pp. 264-5; E. Leigh, *Foelix Consortium* (London, 1663), p. 115; E. Stillingfleet, *op. cit.*, pp. 238-246.

11. J. Knoxe, *An Answer to a Letter of a Iesuit Named Tyrie* (Saint Andrews, 1572), sig. D. vi^r. I owe this reference to Mrs. K. Firth.

12. *Ibid.*, sig. D. vi^r-D. viii^r, cf. Joachim of Fiore, *Expositio in Apocalypsim* (Venice, 1527), ff. 190^r, 194^r, 198^v-199^r, 200^v, (hereinafter, *Expos,*).

13. Reeves, *Influence of Prophecy*, pp. 488-489.

14. The Marsh Library, St. Patrick's Cathedral, Dublin, which contains Stillingfleet's books, has Joachim's three main works in the sixteenth-century Venetian editions, as well as the pseudo-Joachimist *Super Hieremiam* (Cologne 1577), and *Vaticinia de summis pontificibus* (Venice 1589) and the rare biography by Gregorio de Laude, *Magni Ioachimi Prophetae* . . . *Joachimi* . . . *Hergasiarum Alethia Apologetica* (Naples, 1660). I owe this information to Mr. Warwick Gould.

15. On these prophecies see Reeves, *Influence of Prophecy*, pp. 453-462 and 'Some popular prophecies from the Fourteenth to the Seventeenth Centuries' in *Popular Belief and Practice*, ed. G. Cuming and D. Baker (Cambridge, 1972) pp. 107-134. Lynne's version, published in London in 1548, was dedicated to Edward VI and Edward, Duke of Somerset. It consists of selected pictures without original captions or text, but with an anti-Papal commentary translated, he says, from the German. In 1527 Andreas Osiander had published a German version of the full prophecies. Lynne's text does not derive from this, yet he may well have had a connection with Osiander since he also published an English version of Carion's chronicle with an appendix by J. Funck, Osiander's son-in-law. Lynne's edition of the pope prophecies was first pointed out to me by Mr. Bauckham.

16. Oxford, Bod. Lib., MS. Laud Misc. 588; see Reeves, *Influence of Prophecy*, pp. 461-462.

17. On Brocardo, *ibid*, pp. 494-499. He is cited as an authority by J. Foxe, *Eicasmi seu Meditationes in sacram Apocalypsim* (London, 1587), Preface. For other English translations of works on prophecy in this period, see C. Hill, *Antichrist in seventeenth-century England* (London, 1971), pp. 15-17.

18. Preface by John Dee to H. Billingsley, *The Elements of Geometrie of the most ancient Philosopher Euclide of Megara* (London, 1570), f. 2ᵛ.
19. For the following list of Bale's books, see H. McCusker, *John Bale, Dramatist and Antiquary* (Bryn Mawr, 1942), pp. 35-47.
20. This is a problem. The only text I know which is at all unfavourable is the pseudo-Joachimist prophecy beginning *Erunt duo viri, unus hinc, alius inde* (see Reeves, *Influence of Prophecy*, p. 527) which expresses animosity towards the *Saccati* but favours the Friars Preacher and Minor. There is, however, in Trinity College, Dublin, MS. 347, f. 35ʳ⁻ᵛ, a *Prophecia Joachim de Ordine Fratrum Minorum et Praedicatorum.* Could this have been Bale's, which he somehow interpreted in a hostile sense? In his *Acta Romanorum Pontificum . . .* (Basle, 1558), p. 440, under the heading *Defectio a Christo . . . per fraterculos Mendicantes,* he associates a pseudo-Joachimist prophecy on the *tempus periculosum futurum* with the rise of impostor friars, so clearly there was a link in his mind. Mr. Bauckham first drew my attention to Bale's Joachimist MSS.
21. On Olivi, see Reeves *Influence of Prophecy*, pp. 195-201, 407-8.
22. On Arnold of Villa Nova, *ibid.,* pp. 221, 314-317.
23. A prophecy attributed to frater Columbinus which contains echoes of Joachimist texts exists in MSS, London, Brit. Mus., Cotton, Cleopatra C.x, ff. 157ʳ-158ʳ; Oxford, Bod. Lib., Ashmole, 393, f. 80ʳ⁻ᵛ; Dublin, Trinity College, 516, (according to J. Bignami-Odier, *Etudes sur Jean de Roquetaillade* (Paris, 1952), p. 149).
24. See Reeves, *Influence of Prophecy*, pp. 255-256, for a further explanation of this point.
25. Published in 1544.
26. For Guido of Perpignan, see Reeves, *Influence of Prophecy*, pp. 69-70, 475, n.l. When I wrote the latter note I did not know that Bale possessed Guido's work.
27. Bale, *Image of Both Churches,* sig. A. ivᵛ. In this list of authorities Bale includes 'Sylvester Meuccium, Venet. li.i. Pro maiori intelligentia' (sig. A. vʳ). This is the *incipit* of a short section with which Meuccio prefaced his edition of Joachim's *Expositio.* For this Venetian editor of Joachim's works, see Reeves, *Influence of Prophecy*, pp. 262-268.
28. *Image,* sigs. E. ivʳ, E. viiᵛ, H. ivᵛ, K. viiᵛ, Lʳ, L. iiʳ, (Pt. 3) Aa. viʳ, Ll. iiʳ.
29. *Ibid.,* sigs. E. ivʳ, E. viiᵛ. In the first passage Bale gives seven pairs of godly men to whom in each age God has opened the truth, very much in the style of Joachim (cf. *Liber Concordie* (Venice, 1519), ff. 18ʳ⁻ᵛ, 26ʳ⁻ᵛ) (hereinafter, *Lib. Conc.*).
30. *Ibid.,* sig. H. ivᵛ. For the Joachites in this list, see Reeves, *Influence of Prophecy*, as follows: Cyril the Carmelite (name connected with pseudo-Joachimist writings), pp. 57, 226-227, 522-523; Telesphorus of Cosenza, pp. 57-58, 325-331, 343-344, 423-424; Reinhard, p. 340, Petrus Johannis (Olivi), pp. 194-205; Robert d'Uzes, pp. 167-169; Johannes de Rupescissa (Roquetaillade), pp. 225-228, 321-325, 416-417; Arnold of Villa Nova, pp. 221-222, 314-317.
31. See Reeves, *Influence of Prophecy*, pp. 255-256.
32. *Image,* (Pt. 3) sig. Aa. viʳ. For Ubertino da Casale, see Reeves, *Influence of Prophecy*, pp. 207-209.
33. *Image,* sig. H. ivʳ⁻ᵛ; Also (Pt. 2) Bviiᵛ.
34. *Ibid.,* sigs. E. viʳ, (Pt. 3) Ggᵛ.
35. *Ibid.,* (Pt. 3) sig. C. ivᵛ.
36. Foxe, *Eicasmi,* pp. 85 (citing *Expos.,* f. 131ᵛ), 90. Other references to Joachim occur on pp. 83, 100-101, 120, 143, 149, 379.
37. *Ibid.,* pp. 5-6.
38. *Ibid.,* p. 55.
39. *Ibid.,* p. 83, cr. *Expos.,* f. 130ᵛ. The opposition of Joachim and the Joachites to scholastic learning suited Protestants very well.
40. *Eicasmi,* pp. 100-101, cf. *Expos.,* f. 138ᵛ.
41. *Eicasmi,* p. 107.
42. *Ibid.,* pp. 108, 144; see also pp. 149-50, 284-285.
43. *Ibid.,* p. 144.
44. See Reeves, *Influence of Prophecy*, p. 481. Brightman, *op. cit.* p. 93, also expatiates on the wonderful art of printing.
45. *Actes and Monumentes,* pp. 175, 136. The first is taken from a sermon preached at St. Paul's Cross in 1388 by Thomas Wimbledon who quotes from the pseudo-Joachimist *Super Hieremiam* (ed. Venice, 1516), f. 1ᵛ (hereinafter, *Super Hier.*). The second has an echo of Bale's addition to the Oldcastle chronicle, and Foxe also mentions Guido of Perpignan, but appears to have substituted Olivi for Joachim as the author.
46. J. Napier, *A Plaine Discovery of the whole Revelation of St. John . . .* (Edinburgh, 1593), pp. 2-12.
47. *Ibid.,* p. 14.
48. *Ibid.,* p. 142.
49. *Ibid.,* p. 144.
50. *Ibid.,* p. 142.
51. *Ibid.,* pp. 30-31.
52. *Ibid.,* p. 19.
53. *Ibid.,* p. 250.
54. *Ibid.,* pp. 255-257. The similarity emerges strikingly in Napier's insistence that while the length, breadth, and height are distinct they are inseparable and can only form one city. Joachim used a series of metaphors in a similar way against what he conceived to be the quaternity of Peter Lombard: for instance, fire, flame and heat which are only one fire; *radix, stipes, cortex* which are only one tree; three interlaced circles in which a common central segment expresses the unity which does not exist outside the three circles; three channels which are one water; *aĕr diffusus, aĕr conspissatus, aĕr motus* which are one air. See *Expos.* ff. 36ᵛ-38ʳ; *Il Libro delle Figure dell' abate Gioachino da Fiore,* vol. II, ed. L. Tondelli, M. Reeves, B. Hirsch-Reich, Pls. XI, XXVI. For Joachim's

treatment of the number-symbolism of the New Jerusalem, see *Expos.*, ff. 217$^r$-220$^v$.

55. Brightman, *op. cit.*, Preface.
56. *Ibid.*, p. 6.
57. *Ibid.*, pp. 109, 125.
58. *Ibid.*, pp. 181-185.
59. See *Expos.*, ff. 24$^r$, 106$^r$-108$^v$, 162$^v$; *Psalterium decem chordarum* (Venice, 1527), f. 268$^r$.
60. Brightman, *op. cit.*, p. 283: Cf. *Expos.*, f. 130$^r$, interpreting *Apoc.*, viii, 13.
61. Brightman, *op. cit.*, p. 287, commenting on the star falling from heaven (*Apoc.*, ix, 1): "Ioachimus Abbas wil have him to be some Clergyman and one endued with the knowledge of learning." Cf. *Expos.*, f. 130$^v$: ". . . clericum tamen fuisse et imbutum scientia litterarum."* This same passage is used by Foxe, *Eicasmi*, p. 83.
62. Brightman, *op. cit.*, p. 337, see also p. 488.
63. *Ibid.*, p. 348.
64. *Ibid.*, pp. 343-349, see also p. 93.
65. *Ibid.*, p. 499.
66. *Ibid.*, pp. 503-504.
67. *Ibid.*, p. 502.
68. *Ibid.*, pp. 390-391, 528. On the idea of England's divine mission, see Lamont, *op. cit., passim.*
69. Brightman, *op. cit.*, p. 820.
70. *Ibid.*, p. 827.
71. *Ibid.*, p. 852.
72. *Ibid.*, Preface, pp. 13, 122, 185, 255-256, 517, 559, 814-816.
73. *Ibid.*, p. 121.
74. *Ibid.*, p. 966 (Misnumbered), in an exposition of Daniel appended to the *Revelation.*
75. *Ibid.*, pp. 848-851.
76. *Ibid.*, p. 559.
77. He places the period of Satan bound in the past, but he does interpret the text "And they lived and reigned with Christ a thousand years" (*Apoc.*, xx, 4) as the blessed age of the "first resurrection" (*ibid.*, p. 851).
78. Broughton, *op. cit.*, pp. 278-279.
79. *Ibid.*, p. 43.
80. *Ibid.*, p. 141.
81. *Ibid.*, p. 271.
82. *Ibid.*, p. 273.
83. Broughton had a passion for Hebrew learning and for better understanding with both Jew and Turk, see pp. 50, 264, 269.
84. *Ibid.*, pp. 315-416.
85. *Ibid.*, p. 314.
86. *Ibid.*, p. 329.
87. *Ibid.*, p. 339.
88. I must stress the fact of selection, since I have necessarily omitted some important writers for lack of space.
89. J. Maxwell, *Admirable and notable Prophesies uttered in former times by twenty-four famous Roman Catholicks, concerning the Church of Rome, defection, Tribulation and reformation* (London, 1615).
90. For these compilations, see Reeves, *Influence of Prophecy*, as follows: Lichtenberger, pp. 347-351; Aytinger, pp. 352-354; *Mirabilis liber*, pp. 379-380; Lazius, pp. 369-372; Flacius Illyricus, p. 487; Wolf, pp. 487-488, Chavigny, pp. 385-386.
91. It deserves a proper study of its sources.
92. Maxwell, *op. cit.*, pp. 17-18, 131, 135.
93. For Cyril, Rupescissa, and Telesphorus, see references above, notes 7, 30; for Sibyl, see Reeves, *Influence of Prophecy*, pp. 56, 147, 307-308.
94. Maxwell, *op. cit.*, pp. 43-44. For the last emperor and angelic pope, see Reeves, *Influence of Prophecy*, parts III and IV.
95. Maxwell, *op. cit.*, pp. 45-46. For the Second Charlemagne prophecy, see Reeves, *Influence of Prophecy*, pp. 320-331.
96. Maxwell twice cites Joachim on the Angelic Popes in the *Lib. Conc.* (pp. 67, 142). The first (and longer) passage is in fact derived from Lichtenberger's *Prognosticatio* (Strasbourg, 1488), Pt. 1, cap. 36, or perhaps from the *Mirabilis Liber* (Paris, 1522), f. xxv$^v$, quoting the former. It cannot be traced in the *Lib. Conc.*, not directly in any of the known pseudo-Joachimist works. His one mention of the *Expos.* (p. 53) is followed immediately by a paraphrase of a passage from the *Super Hier.* which he cites often: pp. 42, 51, 53-54, 64, 115, 132, 138-141, 143. The commentary on Sibyl Erithera appears twice (pp. 53, 64) and the *Vaticinia de summis pontificibus* is used (pp. 69-72, 136-137), but Maxwell questions Joachim's authorship of this.
97. Maxwell, *op, cit.*, p. 7.
98. *Ibid.*, pp. 121-123, 148-151.
99. *Ibid.*, p. 84.
100. *Ibid.*, pp. 86-87. See also pp. 149-150.
101. Preface.
102. W. Saltmarsh, *Sparkles of Glory or Some Beams of the Morning-Star* (London, 1648), p. 52.
103. *Ibid.*, pp. 54-55.
104. *Ibid.*, pp. 22, 46, 53-54. For Joachim's use of Elijah's sacrifice as a key symbol, see *Lib. Conc.*, ff. 7$^r$, 103$^r$.
105. *Ibid.*, pp. 37-50.
106. W. Schenk, *The Concern for Social Justice in the Puritan Revolution* (London, 1948), p. 87: "This idea (i.e. a future

Age of the Spirit) belonged to a theological scheme of history going back to Joachim of Fiore."
107. This view is taken by G. Nuttall, *The Holy Spirit in Puritan Faith and Experience* (Oxford, 1946), p. 104.
108. *The Testimony of William Erbery, left upon Record for the Saints of Succeeding Ages* (London, 1658), p. 36.
109. *Ibid.*, p. 66.
110. *Ibid.*, p. 36-38, 88.
111. *Ibid.*, p. 39.
112. *Ibid.*, p. 192.
113. See Reeves, *Influence of Prophecy*, pp. 198, 208, 291-292. On similar ideas among continental reformers, *ibid.*, pp. 482-483, 494-495.
114. Saltmarch, *op. cit.*, pp. 39, 89; Erbery, *op, cit.*, pp. 9, 23, 40-41, 94, 188, 236-238, 248.
114. (a) This conviction comes out strongly in the writings of Gerrard Winstanley, e.g. in *Truth Lifting up its Head above Scandals, Works*, ed. G. Sabine (New York, 1941).
115. J. Archer, *The Personall Reigne of Christ upon Earth* (London, 1642), p. 15.
116. *Ibid.*, pp. 2-3.
117. *Ibid.*, p. 10.
118. R. Maton, Israel's Redemption or the Prophetical History of our Saviour's Kingdome on Earth: That is, Of the Church Catholicke and Triumphant (London, 1642), pp. 51-52.
119. *Ibid.*, pp. 5-6, 29-30, 43, 50, 60-64.
120. *Ibid.*, pp. 64-65. J. Burroughs, *An Exposition of the Prophesie of Hosea* (London, 1643), i, pp. 80, 131-133, 183-187, writes in a similar vein.
121. J. Brayne, *The New Earth, or the True Magna Charta of the past Ages, and of the Ages or World to come* (London, 1653), p. 92.
122. W. Dell, *A Plain and Necessary Confutation of divers gross and Antichristian Errors . . .* (London, 1654), pp. 17-18, cf. *Super Hier.*, f. 43ᵛ. His translation, paraphrase, and extension of this passage are most interesting. I owe this reference to Mrs. G. Lewis.
123. W. Dell, *The Building and Glory of the truly Christian and Spiritual Church . . .* (London, 1646), p. 3. This recalls a Joachimist idea that the third dispensation would be characterized by boys, see Joachim, *Tractatus super Quatuor Evangelia*, ed. E. Buonainti (Rome, 1930), p. 92; *Super Hier;*, f. 1ᵛ.
124. Dell, *Building and Glory*, p. 25.
125. *Ibid.*, p. 31.
126. An obvious omission is Joseph Mede. I have also left on one side the question of Milton's position, since this is dealt with by M. Fixler, *Milton and the Kingdom of God* (London, 1964).

123

# Ritual Behavior in Renaissance Florence: The Setting

*Richard C. Trexler*

IN PRE-REFORMATION Europe public religious ritual afforded an avenue to religious experience for the majority of men. The present essay will examine the setting for such behavior in late medieval and Renaissance Florence. It is intended to be less a description of behavior than an analysis of the nature of the sacrality of place, objects, and time upon which the religious ceremonies of an urban center rested during periods of stability. The article is in a sense a study of civic religion, for it finds that the Florentines perceived the sacred as a union of the cosmic and the particular. What was sacred? When? Where? And how did the Florentines utilize the power of the sacred?

I

There was no holy land in Florence. The city's perimeter of walls and gates were lustrated, and nunneries were to be found near most entrances to the city. But within this enclosed space, there were only holy relics, images, and persons. Nunneries, churches, and government buildings were revered as houses for these sacred objects. The Florentines altered their behavior as they approached the narrow confines of power: the altar, cloister, and throne.

Within the city these three buildings were the fixed locations of ritual behavior important to the whole of society.[1] All were covered by laws prohibiting gambling and whoring, as well as drinking in the ambient.[2] Blasphemy was prohibited to protect their inhabitants.[3] All three had some right of asylum or immunity attached to them.[4] Sacri-

125

lege within them sullied not the ground, but the sacred presences.[5]

Nunneries were peculiar in that they stood apart from society. Secular patrons might support the nuns and compete to affix familial coats of arms to monastery walls. Nunneries created merit-making opportunities for laymen, who received prayers in return. Yet laymen afforded this help in order to keep the houses apart from the world, and not to absorb them into it. The constant ritual sacrifices performed in these sanctuaries were thought to guarantee the continuity of public life. These were the city's holy enclaves. Monastic life was a stable rite of passage, a generational or biological phase converted into a durable social entity. The women's sacrality was located in their ritual activity more than in their persons or nunneries. Utility to the commune depended on their ceremony being carried out in seclusion.

Churches on the contrary were public places, the departure and terminal point of most manifestations of public unity. A wide range of activities was carried out there, including preaching, meetings of public commissions, and the sale of religious objects. But none of these activities was limited to churches. Fundamentally, the church was a shrine containing powerful objects near altars. One did not so much "go to church" as "go to see the body of Christ" or of some other sacred personality.[6] Indeed, the word "altar" was used interchangeably with "church" or "chapel." The church's main business was the articulation of social and transcendental order. Through participation in sacrifice, men bound themselves to various saints and to each other in the presence of the saint. From the solemnization of an international treaty "over the host," "over the altar," "over the relic," or "over the bible," to the simple promise of the individual to his image-saint, the church served as a nexus of obligations, patronage, contract.[7]

The dignity of a church depended upon the number and quality of its relics, images, and *ex votos*. All major churches kept lists, and visitors mentioned relics first in describing a church. The honor of the Florentine government required that the store of sacred objects in the cathedral and in the church of its Protector, St. John the Baptist, be superior to those of any lesser church. The value attached to these objects did not, however, transfer itself to the physical area of the church. The main occasions for their demonstration were in fact outside the church, when they were carried in procession through the city. Inside or out, it was proximity to the holy object which modified behavior.

Before the construction of the city hall, the priors of Florence had met in churches and had used their altars as the backdrop and seal of their executive actions. The new city palace (started 1298) articulated the location and fledgling independence of the communal power, but it heightened rather than eliminated the need for an altar of submission, communion, and contract. The city hall had to be partly church. The sacramentals of political power, the myriad of flags, the high towers, seals, chairs, and batons, functioned in one sense to "frame" the exercisers of power, to define and limit communal power without extinguishing it. The raised platform added to the building in the 1320s gave the effect of an altar, and it commonly served as such during festive occasions, with mass, displays of relics, and sermons making it the main outdoor shrine of Florence.[8] Upon these steps each successive Signoria took its oath or "sacrament" of office in full view of the *popolo*. On the rare occasions when civic turmoil made it necessary to solemnize this contract out of the people's view, chroniclers of local events recorded such privacy as never having happened before.[9] These altar-steps were also the stage where the subjects of Florence displayed their annual signs of submission to the public authority.

Inside the palace, a chapel was built to St. Bernard which served the brother priors for their obligatory divine services. Predictably, the saint's altar soon acquired importance as one of the sacred stones upon which communal contracts were sealed.[10] New subjects of the Signoria made their offerings on Bernard's altar and feast day as well as on that of the city's patron, the Baptist.[11] When the steps of the palace became a regular stopping place on the standard processional route — the priors were joined to the procession much as the relics fetched from churches — the building had definitely become one of the centers of ritual activity within the city.

Within the confines of these three places, the behavior of Florentines took on a ritual nature distinguishable from the forms of the marketplace. The meeting halls of the religious confraternities, private homes, and hospitals were not areas associated with socially significant ritual behavior. Unlike the *palazzo* or the church, they were not on the processional route. Unlike the monastery, the special prayers and cultic activity of their inhabitants were not sought out during crisis. It was primarily these places' lack of power objects which accounted for their inconsequential ritual position in the city.

The city was a unified whole. No boundary processions marked off its sectors, and no administrative subdivision of the city had its own divinity or saint, its own particular sacrality. The standard processional route in Florence was a *via sacra* only when the processional day and its activity were underway. This route was intended to touch most

of the signal buildings of the city. If for political reasons a sector of the
city was purposely omitted, the insult consisted in depriving it of the
presence of the sacred objects in the procession.[12] One of the purposes
of the procession was, in fact, to *de*sacralize the public areas of the city.
By concentrating offerings and obeisance to the sacred objects in the
procession, the populace marked itself off in the passage of the processional group from the world of the holy; the procession once past, the
areas of the city returned to an unconsecrated state.[13]

## II

The common charisma of nun, city governor, and the religious
object properly speaking, is more significant as a social fact than their
obvious differences. All three demanded and received a formalized
behavior.[14] No sacrality was perceived as resident only in its own
material, but rather as mediated and heightened by patronage. Ritual
behavior was provoked by the combined authority of heaven and
earth. Originally and persistently, chapels and churches in the city
belonged to certain families which had built them, posted their arms
upon them, and installed their relatives in them as priests and clerics.
Relics were imported. Previously passive images started to perform
miracles. In order to increase their resources, families obtained indulgences for those who visited their churches. It was a fortunate family
indeed which possessed such a piece when it first showed signs of holiness. Otherwise, an object which began to gain attention would be pur-
chased by the families for installation in their churches. The result was
that every significant holy object had patronal associations. The *tavola*
of Impruneta was the Buondelmonte's, a nunnery was associated with
the Adimari, a relic of the cross was the Pazzis', and so on. This con-
sorterial association with valuable religious objects penetrated deeply
into Florentine life. The new bishop on first entering the city afforded
the chance for an ostentatious display by his family and those of the
*vicedomini* of the see. The Cerchi enhanced their fortune by housing a
saintly recluse in their palace. The Palagi and the Soderini patronized
holy persons. The Ruspi possessed renowned relics. The list could be
extended. But the point is made: possession of valuable religious
objects was one of the most important signs of honor and dignity.[15]

The developing commune had to compete with this tradition,
increasing its own dignity by acquiring communal relics and images,
combating the accumulation of sacred objects by family groups. When
the Medici in the 1420s and 1430s started to inflate the number of dig-

nitaries in their parish church of St. Lorenzo, it was a sign that the family sought to challenge the charisma of the commune. Determined that no single family should exceed its honor, the commune responded by increasing the dignity of the cathedral.[16] In time-honored fashion, the commune also took under its protection many of the religious entities in the dominion and city, and as part of the contract, it obtained a promise from the religious that only the communal herald would be posted on the building or near a shrine.[17]

This rivalry to bestow terrestrial authority upon the sacred had important implications for the social perception of holiness. Relics, first of all, were an important agent in particularly solemn contracts, protecting and patronizing agreements. Matteo Villani told how the prior of the Dominican friary in Florence, seeing his church tower repeatedly struck by lightning, removed the images from the tower and replaced them with relics, apparently a superior protective agency.[18] The power of the relic was personal. When one received a relic into the city, one took in part of the saint himself.[19] These saints aided civic and cosmological continuity; images, on the other hand, enabled the city to bend and change bad fortune, heal ruptured contracts between it and the cosmos.

Florentine society preferred relics of ancient saints already venerated in the city for political reasons. Thus in 1311 the commune went to lengths to obtain the relics of St. Barnabas (associated with the Guelphic victory at Campaldino in 1289),[20] in 1362 some of its patron St. Reparata,[21] and in 1393 and ca. 1415 those of its advocate St. John the Baptist.[22] The only reference in the chronicles to the relics of a modern saint came in 1502, when the commune obtained the cloak of St. Francis.[23] In general, then, political groups sought relics of those saints who had already proven their protective power and whose feasts had already been incorporated into the communal festive calendar.

In 1331 the head of the patron of the Florentine church, St. Zanobi, was found buried near the cathedral. Giovanni Villani tells us that this skull was put in a reliquary of silver "in the likeness of the face and head of the said saint, in order that on his feast it could be shown annually to the people with great solemnity."[24] This passage cautions us from separating the relic too decisively from the image. Relics became images and, as Villani suggests, anthropomorphism and verisimilitude fostered devotion. Further, the silver and gold of the image and the precious stones which surrounded it, to Villani's mind, "fostered the piety of the faithful." Physical likeness and precious surrounding combined to provide a setting encouraging adoration.

Descriptions of relics visited or touched in this age usually put as much emphasis on the jewels and casing as on the object itself. At times, the word "relic" was used indiscriminately to refer to the relic itself, its simulacrum, or the jewels or other signs of esteem attached to it.[25]

Most miracles in Florence which achieved publicity were associated with images. Two of the great Madonnas were fixed and could not be borne about, while several others were portable. The figures were charismatic because they *saw,* and dozens of minor miracles resulted from the image having viewed something pleasing or displeasing. Their public utility consequently depended on their being given sight only when and where something edifying was to be viewed, namely a ritual activity sanctioned by public authority. Veiled and unveiled, dressed and disrobed, given gifts, struck and caressed,[26] carried under the baldachin of her patron(s), the image was encouraged to cause patterned behavior rather than incalculable acts. The value of image or relic depended on the value set upon it by a patron. Patronage determined what was institutionally holy just as surely as it bestowed fame upon an artist.[27] By vouching for value, patronage prevented idolatry, and this clarity as to what was venerable contributed to the articulation of social bonds.

This dual personality of the object of religious devotion, incorporating the charisma of the saint and of the patron, was one of the prime facets of the Florentine perception of the holy. In passing the gates into the city, the indiscriminate, anarchic holy was transformed into a cult instrument. The same may be said of the host, the living God himself. Feared precisely because of its unitary charismatic power, it was accompanied with the marks of authentification. Decorated and engraved hosts were displayed in homes.[28] In the church a special architectural enclosure was developed for it which, often enough, bore the herald of the donor.[29] The altar cloths beneath the sacrifice of the host were donated by testators and fitted out with coats of arms.[30] In Corpus Christi processions, the living God was surrounded with the safer files of the civic order. Nearness to the host in procession was a mark of signal prestige. The coats of arms of recognized civic and familial authority hung from the baldachin under which the host was carried in its precious monstrum.[31] A main reason for these accompanying paraphernalia was a desire of the group or individual involved to partake of the sacred power of the host. Here again, the sacred was perceived as an amalgam of charismas.

*Ex votos* are the clearest expression of this mixture; these relics of promises and contracts kept were separated from the image or relic they accompanied. As authentication of the power of a relic or image, *ex votos* increased the devotion of the visitor even though they were neither flesh nor clothing of a saint. The more striking their size and quality, the more honored the church. Indeed, in 1502 life-sized votive figures in the Servite church were jokingly said to be "adored" in a manner usually reserved to the cult object.[32] *Ex votos* became part of the total reaction to the sacred object. Like secondary relics, they partook of the sacrality of the holy objects themselves by their nearness to them. Yet unlike them, the votives were nothing apart from the ambient of the sacred object. They were profane. In civic revolutions one of the first actions of a victorious faction was to remove and destroy votive representations of the defeated politicians, a sign of disrespect designed to diminish the influence of the vanquished with the populace and with the sacred object.[33]

Patrons used sacred objects to increase their authority over the whole. Conversely, the fame of an object once sacralized ennobled the patron. The relation between them may seem to have its origins in the power of the family or government which valued the sacred objects. It was not the object which ennobled the family, but familial and social power which ennobled a cold, material instrument. Before the scientific revolution, however, holy power was conceived to exist beyond social or familial force. It resided in those objects and persons which could massively affect the whole body of humans.

The urban religious experience, then, is one of a holiness captured, veiled, framed, and manipulated. The logical but unstated object of public urban religious ritual was to create a continuity which would make the miraculous unnecessary. Holiness was liturgical. Cult objects did not lose their sacrality in the process of manipulation, but rather increased it. The power enclosed in a church was activated through contact and manipulation by priests or devotees. Those many objects in a church which were efficacious only for individuals were open to view, but framed by flowers, *ex votos,* and the like. Objects of communal power were veiled, and their activity was closely supervised.[34] The political powers enclosed in the church were restrained by being surrounded by frames or houses of precious stones. Individual devotion and submission to these objects were accomplished while the veil covered the object. Its unveiled display was a sociopolitical, even cosmological act done only on certain days, only to certain persons, and only when the commune contracted or supplicated in the process of manifesting the power and the unity of the republic.[35] Indiscriminate and repeated unveiling of social and divine power by random individuals decreased the devotion of the people and therewith the social efficacy of the object. The less dignified the viewer of the unmasked image, the less devotion it could command.[36] Those whose faces were recklessly shown to the masses could cause crowds, disorders, scandal, incalculable crowd actions.[33] The objects in a church were meant to be predictable. They were a resource of power which when exposed acted to bind men together, not tear them apart. It would be unjustified to say that the signs of public authority *became* the relic, even though contemporaries often failed to distinguish. Yet the accompaniment of relics, images, and hosts cannot easily be distinguished from the objects themselves as causes of ritual behavior.

Spontaneously drawn or etched images (a cross, an IHS) were akin to the objects used by the magicians. Manipulated only by creator and private utilizer, these unframed objects were essentially uncontrollable. Such random creations and drawings created outlets for power without the authentication which would simultaneously engender devotion while rendering the images of positive value. Outdoor images or symbols thus had to be enshrined, fitted out with candles, frames, and altars; they became objects with constitutional authority. They bore the authoritative marks of the politically accepted division of labor; they had been blessed by the priest, fitted out with indulgences by the pontifical authorities, and adored by respected groups or individuals. Spontaneity had been harnessed, and the objects now radiated the power of the political order. Their desecration meant the defilement of that order. To hurl mud at a corner shrine meant not only to curse the figure represented, but as well the altar and frame of social authority.[38]

Among secular individuals, only the communal power affected the whole and can thus be included under the category of sacred objects. Like the image, the Signoria had to be kept concealed from sight as much as possible, for constant viewing of the civic authority would diminish its charisma.[39] Again, the days on which the Signoria entered office were among those feasts on which, according to law, the population should behave better.[40] Most important, the city's industry was shut down, and debts were suspended on the days the priors took office for the same reason they were curtailed when a particular saint was festively honored: so that the people of the city could accompany such venerable objects.[41] The analogy has already been drawn between fetching the Signoria from the palace during procession and solemnly proceeding to a church along the processional route to incorporate its main relic to the parade. In all these forms the populace saw its government accompanied and exalted in the same fashion as its more strictly religious objects.

The Signoria was exalted not as a priest, but as a holy object. With the nuns excluded from manifestations of public religiosity, the priors of Florence functioned as sacred but lay monks whose holiness was in their activity. They had acceded to their office (short-term in Florence) through ceremonies resembling rites of passage.[42] In this liminal state they offered the city to its protective powers in a manner not unlike the nuns, who also recommended the commune to the divine power through their activity.

Here the analogy to the monastic life ends, and the fundamental distinction between the power of the Signoria and that of other objects appears. The power of the church was manipulated, while that of the nunneries was continually formalized. The public power within the city hall was basically incalculable and intended to be so. Within their palace — which they could not leave except for ceremonial purposes — the city priors in defending the whole were expected to punish in an anormative, wondrous fashion those who violated accepted norms. The chroniclers narrate these horrible punishments as if proving the solidity of the commune by the terrible vengeance visited upon those who stepped outside. The penalties of the Italian municipalities were creatively frightening, for executive violence of an imaginative nature was one of the instruments for retaining the whole. The public officer, unlike other cult objects, exercised a continual power often beyond control, power without mask or veil: ceremonial spontaneity. The public power was, so to speak, the solemn magician whose power, if not his person, was always exposed to the public view. The paraphernalia accompanying that power was meant to limit it and heighten it, but never to extinguish this flame of authority. The commune, said the Florentine merchant-historian Dati, was an authority which did not die.[43] Machiavelli realized that in order to perpetuate authority, *terribilità, ferocità*, incalculability had to be the portion of the Prince alone.

### III

In a curious "ship's log" kept during the early quattrocento, the Florentine merchant Luca Albizzi recorded along with his daily position the name of a particular saint to whom he seems to have dedicated the day and place.[44] The saints were not recorded on their liturgical feasts, and the basis of Albizzi's system remains a puzzle. It is clear, though, that for this man of affairs, the times through which he was passing

133

were qualities of unequal value and not clock-like abstractions. It is not surprising to find Albizzi bestowing his saints upon time. Like place and objects, time's power was interpenetrated with divine and earthly authority. Renaissance Florentines continued to keep time by saints' days. They assumed almost without question the idea that time was civic-minded, and that its normal rhythms had to respond to communal authority and private utility.

Segments of time were sacred to certain powers.[45] Most commonly, a day was associated with the saint whose feast was being celebrated. But mixed with the influence of the saint was the moral configuration of the stellar sphere, which exerted either a malevolent or friendly influence upon the city. While morally and temporally at variance with each other, the fixed liturgical calendar of the saints and the shifting rhythms of astral events were in ritual melded together. Florentines often scheduled military and other governmental actions to coincide with both conjunctions and saints' days thought to be friendly to the public weal.[46] In one case, a clerical astrologer of the commune scheduled the dates of religious processions.[47] In another, three days of solemn clerical processions preceded the astrologically determined time of the consignment of authority to a military leader.[48] Priests and laymen stood in the service of the Christian saints, but their movements were geared to those of the planets as well.

When unexpected events occurred, a cosmic causality had to be determined, for there was no accident. Post factum searches for the causes of unfortunate events usually blamed the sinfulness of the Florentines, which had provoked the ire of God. Accompanying this voluntaristic explanation, rational astrological explanations competed for favor.[49] It does not seem that the saints were blamed for social or political misfortune.

When, on the contrary, the causes of fortunate communal events were sought out, the day's saint usually earned the laurels, and a favorable astrological conjunction was only occasionally proposed as an explanation. In the normal view, the saint had noticed the supplication and interceded to a God who responded automatically.[50] In the Florentine republican calendar, all but one commemorated event was tied to the intercession of a particular saint.[51] God's delight at the Florentines' good fortune seldom emerged as a casual factor; only his wrath was directly casual. Nor did any favorable astrological conjunction ever enter the communal memory: such a memory could not, with the exception of the solstices, be converted to any fixed date on the calendar.

A second conception of time was built on the belief that the world was full of intelligences. Each act had a *telos,* a meaning or goal, a direction inherent in itself. The significance of two actions occurring in different areas in the same instant of time depended on the inherent goal of the actions themselves. If, for example, a procession to pray for a victory took place at the same instant that the battle began whose aim was the same victory, the history of the events of that instant recorded both events together as part of the same causal net. Rather than the history of a period resting solely on a series of terrestrial causes, the immanent goal or *telos* of two disparate actions might be more historically significant. Acts with identical goals when performed synchronically were more powerful than when performed without such synchronication. Time was an absolute only in the sense that there was a teleological "same instant" throughout the universe.

This principle was manifested most clearly in the propitiation of a divine power at the same time that some crucial political or individual event was taking place. Thus Michelangelo asked that masses be said in Florence at the same time that he was pouring a bronze statue in Bologna.[52] The Florentine mercenary Vitelli requested that a procession propitiating the miraculous *tavola* of Impruneta be advanced to coincide with the day on which he was to attack Pisa.[53] The Signoria of Florence minutely described to the Volterran and Pistoian governments the plans for processions in Florence and their three purposes, ordering the subject communes to do the same in their cities in the same time and order.[54] When the Signoria discovered that the feast of St. Rossore had been celebrated "with the most wondrous devotion" in the church of Ogni Santi on the same day the Florentine forces had defeated the Visconti, it was believed that this conjunction of intents had caused God to give victory.[55]

It might seem that the principle behind such arrangements was simply the belief that the saint's attention was more easily caught by simultaneous supplication. But the understanding of this chronological sympathy was much more intellectual and teleological. In this conception, the emphasis was not so much on the eyes of divine powers, but rather on a direct sympathy between the goal inherent in the acts themselves. We see this at work, for example, in the chroniclers' post factum discovery that the government's idea of sending for a miraculous Madonna, its decision to do so, and finally the Madonna's entry into the city of Florence had each coincided with a fortunate political event.[56] These associations were quite as historical as the ship's voyage or the Virgin's descent upon the city.

These two time conceptions incorporate both voluntaristic and intellectual explanations of events. In the first, the tension, if there is one, is between the intercessionary explanation and the astrological. In the second, the basically magical assumption of sympathetic *telea* competes with the idea of a propitiatory manipulation of the saint. Even though the chronicler Landucci described a teleological sympathy between two sets of events occurring in different spaces, he ended by imputing personal will to these happenings. For him, these events did not prove the existence of an impersonal magic whose force lay in the *telos* of events, but rather showed that the Virgin Mary had intended to perform this set of three miracles. For him, the "miracle was evident."[57]

This contemporary "difficulty" in differentiating between saint's time and astrological time, in discerning the inconsistency between a belief in magical, intelligent sympathies and the ritual propitiation of personal forces, presented no practical problem.[58] Any calendarization of power is inconsistent with the voluntarism of divinities, and it is just as unreasonable to propitiate or manipulate intelligent but will-less *telea*. In practice, however, both will and intellect were imputed to personal divinity and astral configurations. Then as now individuals ritualized their social behavior to disarm an incalculable force whose effect on them seemed at times malevolent and willful, at times indifferent to their individual desires. Through this activity they moved ahead through a predictable and manipulable life experience. Personal ritual aimed at a self-assertion through submission, which an urban culture calls civility.[59]

Collective ritual aimed at the same goals for the political groups which participated in common ceremonies. It is in the nature of the city especially to manipulate the power of time and objects to reasonable ends. The city pits its concentrations of political authority against the chaotic sacrality which hovers above and outside it, and which threatens to appear within the walls itself in the varied social and familial groups which threaten its unity.[60] Human experience proved how subject cities were to the incalculable. Civic and diplomatic order were not truly natural. They required the genius of men applied to the infinity of the sacred to make them so.[61] To Machiavelli's mind, human ability was tested by man's capacity to defeat and "acculturate" fate, to use the interstices of freedom between the fields of implacable and mysterious force. Was it not this principle which led the astrologers to attune processions to the conjunctions of the heavens? Certainly in the Middle Ages as well as during the Renaissance, processions were timed astrologically, and saintly geniuses were intermingled with astral personalities and forces to predict, explain, and manipulate events.

All students of the Renaissance know how preoccupied contemporaries were with astrological calculations. Scarcely a battle could be fought, a cornerstone laid, a military baton consigned without the consultation of an astrologer. Such ceremonialization of auspicious time had to include the organization of the political and social body in public manifestations of religion. This was especially true in a republic such as Florence, where sovereignty was public, and was constituted in the processional parts. The procession in the republic reflected a potent order which that of a principate could not. Certainly Machiavelli, like all other observers of the processions of the Savonarolan period, must have been impressed by their discipline and solidarity. It is interesting to speculate that the young chancellor may have had them in mind when he went about organizing the civic militia which was to be the salvation of his beloved republic.[62] Yet the value of such ruminations is limited. Like Machiavelli, we must turn repeatedly to the principles underlying the actions of the men who determined social, political, and military policy.

In a universe of intelligences, one cannot be sure of the true meaning of any act, the real nature of any moment. The festive calendar of the commune helped to clarify the ambiguity of individual and communal actions. Like most men of the age, Florentines believed that their actions might mean something *in specie aeternitatis*. The Florentine historian Goro Dati described how, when spring came, the thoughts of the Florentines turned to games, dances, and a long preparation for the feast of their patron, St. John. It seemed, he said, that they had nothing else to do but feast and make merry.[63] He understood no better than we just why certain points on the calendar were associated with group behavior which deviated from social and divine norms. What did Dati mean, for example, when he described how wedding banquets were postponed until the feast of the patron "so as to do honor to the feast"?[64] An examination of communal laws and institutions relating to time will help to answer this question. The uncertainty of actions *in specie aeternitatis* was alleviated by framing them *in specie civitatis*.

Calendrical feasts achieved group solidarity in urban Florence through behavioral deviations toward both ends of a continuum from dance to procession. Two examples from the Florentine tradition may serve as illustrations. A confraternity's anniversary mass for its dead was attended by all the brothers. After solemnly attending divine services, they participated in a fraternal meal which was all other than solemn. Mass and meal, the propitiative and assertive aspects of the affair, were viewed as equal parts of the total honor paid the deceased.[65] The same extremities can be observed in the feast days celebrated in Florence. Foot and horse races, singing, buffoonery, and floats balanced the solemn offering to the saint and the procession of the clergy with their relics, images, and crucifixes. Both were in honor of the saint.[66]

Legal norms were not for all days; behavior depended on time. This was a fundamental principle of communal law, and not just a datum of special experience. Sumptuary laws were not enforced during celebrations.[67] Prohibited games were legal on some days of the year.[68] And, what might seem oddest in a city so dedicated to merchandising, debts were suspended during several feast days.[69] It was a commonplace that people behaved worst on feast days and that ease was conducive to sin. Some felt that the fewer feasts there were the better. Still, the principles of such deviant behavior were rooted in a calendar of behavior sanctioned by the communal law itself.

Thus, prohibited activities *which might lead to sin or which were sinful on occasion* were relaxed.[70] On the other hand, the solemnity of the feasts caused the commune to suspend activities such as usury which were licensed in everyday life although they were in violation of divine law. *Sinful activities per se* were forbidden. The exchange tables of the usurers and pawnbrokers were closed, but also removed from the public — and divine — view.[71] The feast displayed opulence without the workaday sin which had produced it.

The commune complemented this licensed behavioral deviancy by rigorously prosecuting those who committed grievous crimes on the same feast days. To murder or scar the face of an adversary on such days was to risk double punishment for the crime in question.[72] It has always been important to prevent the sacrificer from becoming the victim. How dishonored the saint was if one of his supplicants were severely wounded or murdered while publicizing his devotion![73] St. John and the other Florentine divinities desired to see the full face of the supplicant, both his formal obeisance and his creative licentiousness, within the framework of overriding order.[74] In the confraternity or the commune, the social and political frame was the setting for atypical behavior. Incorporating elements of play to the purified representation proved the vitality of the transmitted order. A commune at peace displaying to the world its cohesion and its spontaneity: how pleasing to any ruler:

> God requests and desires from man the accustomed and triumphant cere-
> monies at every step and grade of the spiritual and temporal. Through
> both sacrifices and vows and solemn diversions and the adornments of his
> people, a delighted God becomes a placable friend and the benefactor of
> cities . . . [75]

Through games and sacrifices the Lord becomes a friend. Expected behavioral deviancy, time's possession by particular sacred forces, and the teleological homogeneity of events in time are all attempts to reduce the sacred to an order which then can be subjected to manipulation.

Yet this is not enough. After all, the simplest agricultural communities have organized time to use it. In the city the sacred was subjected to a process of political authentification which left its mark on the citizen's perception of the holy. Far from the rural wood where unsuspected power resided, the city afforded a perception of the holy which, though seen as a unity, was in fact an amalgam of social and divine power. In turn, each city compartmentalized its sacred time in accordance with its own history and traditions.

Several aspects of the political impress upon sacred time have already been mentioned. The days on which the Signoria entered office were included among the sacred feasts upon which "men should conduct themselves more modestly." The populace was released from work and debt collection on those days so that they could accompany the Signoria, just as on other days they accompanied the relics and images of the commune. The festive calendar was dotted with recollections of events in the communal past. Yet the best way to determine the nature of the communal impact upon time is to find how often and why celebrations of feasts were stopped.

The answer is, quite often. Ritual activities were commonly postponed or cancelled. Moreover, our sources reveal little anxiety at these departures from the ordinary. The chroniclers regularly record when St. John's Day was not at all or only partly celebrated, yet they give no indication that such postponement was a matter of great concern. When the baton could not be bestowed upon a Florentine mercenary captain at the moment the communal astrologers had planned, the Signoria assured those responsible that they should not be concerned by the situation.[76] Clearly, time was no more exempt from social authentification than object.

The most common reason for postponements or cancellations was a disunity of the city which under public circumstances might precipitate disorders. The danger that a gathering might display the weakness of the public authority was, however, only one part of a larger whole. For public scandal would not have pleased the honored saint. The power of a saint was in part measured by the devotion shown him. Disorder was in some sense a demonstration of divine weakness as well as a challenge to divine and temporal authority.[77]

While the festive celebration as a whole was a setting for rearranging and renewing civic order, an order which in the stable commune was as indivisible as the sacred amalgams carried in procession, the solemn offering was more important than the assertive and spontaneous part of the proceedings. If the community were not at peace with itself, its government at least had to be at peace with the Protector. Further, it was extremely important that communal tensions not disturb the obligatory annual submission to St. John of Florence's subject communities. Consequently it was this part of the general festivities the observance of which was most zealously guarded. If, on the other hand, there were *no* res publica to successfully stage these submissions, as happened during the Ciompi revolt, then the whole festival was postponed till a later date. "In reverence to St. John," read the law of September 28, 1378, the Protector's feast was to be celebrated on St. Luke's Day (October 19) in the same way that it was traditionally celebrated in June.[78] When October came, civic tensions still did not permit the traditional festivities. Therefore the floats and the parade of the sections of the city were suppressed, and only the submissions of the subjects and those of the knights sworn to defend the shaky commune were carried out.[79] Without a civic order capable of containing luxury and buffoonery, only the ritual submission could be carried out of those of whose allegiance there had to be no doubt.

A second reason for failing to hold festive activities on the correct day was that through a postponement the participation in and audience to the celebration could be increased. In 1289 a delay of some days permitted the victorious Florentine troops near Arezzo to return and participate.[80] In 1402 the celebration of St. John was held off until the French ambassadors arrived to see it. During the Council of Florence the date was again modified so that a greater number of visiting prelates could view it.[81] The more Florentines participating, the greater the honor paid the saint. The more foreigners who saw the power, unity, and opulence of Florence on display, the more imposing the honor accruing to the patron and the commune.

Government did suppress or postpone celebrations which might not redound to the greatest honor of the saint and the commune. Timely celebration increased the power of solicitation only when the commune was stable, and only if the maximum publicity could be achieved. The liturgical calendar obeyed a communal dynamics.

Still, the yearning for festival imposed limits on the government's ability to postpone or suppress a public manifestation of power and unity. And the political authority had to be sure that its motivations in postponing these events were credible. Neglect of the saint was no more readily condoned than the needless suppression of festive joviality. The Dominican rigorist Savonarola had to learn this the hard way. For him, the traditional horse races, masks, and spinning firewheels so much a part of the Florentine festival were little more than the devil's handwork, and were suppressed.[82] Yet by 1497 he had to yield to popular pressures, and the rollicking of the Florentines was again offered to their saints. Savonarola failed for many reasons, not the least of which was his inability to convince the Florentines that his opposition to the buffoon was based on genuine spirituality. To some of his opponents, his reasons were more sinister:

> He wants to impede our divine and annual ceremonies and triumphs and feasts and praises and illuminations, which reach to the feet and soles of the glorious God . . . He hopes that our patron and benefactor St. John the Baptist and the other saints, deprived of their accustomed honors, will, justly, turn against us, and then ruin will follow.[83]

The cosmology behind these words is eminently local. Social and political welfare depended upon honoring the time and the person of saintly benefactors, while ruin followed the neglect of the city and the political and familial traditions which had hallowed the patrons. Savonarola promised a New Jerusalem. Florentines chose to retain a religion impregnated with local values, and a political and social life suffused with sacred meaning.

# NOTES

1. Such formalized behavior was thought to affect the well-being of everyone in the city whether they participated in or were directly related to that behavior. It is a premise of this paper that there was a peculiarly urban religious mode. See the pathfinding work by J. Comblin, *Théologie de la Ville* (Paris, 1968), esp. pp. 457-68; see also G. van der Leeuw, *Religion in Essence and Manifestation* (New York, 1963), pp. 268-72. On the concept of sacred space and the city, see *ibid.,* pp. 392-402.

2. For prohibitions concerning the city hall, see *Statuti della repubblica fiorentina,* ed. R. Caggese, vol. I: *Statuto del capitano del populo degli anni 1322-25* (Florence, 1910), p. 238 (taverns and alimentation); *Archivio di Stato, Firenze* (hereafter *ASF*) Provvisioni 65, f. 71v (22 June 1377) (prostitution); *Statuto del podestà dell'anno 1325* (Florence, 1921), pp. 379f (actors and buffoons in the Palace).

3. The chronicler Stefani complained in 1376 that the laws against blaspheming the Signoria were not enforced, while persons blaspheming the Guelphic *Parte* came off worse than those blaspheming God; *Cronica fiorentina di Marchionne di Coppo Stefani,* ed. N. Rodolico, *Rerum Italicarum Scriptores* (hereafter *RIS*), new edition, XXX (Città di Castello, 1903-55), rubrica 767. Statutes against those vilifying the Signoria are in *Statuto. . . . capitano,* p. 90; *Statuta populi et communis Florentiae* (1415), (Friburgi, 1778), I, p. 257f.

4. On the asylum problem in Florence as it concerned churches and monasteries, see *Statuta,* I, pp. 360f; R. Trexler, *Synodal Law in Florence and Fiesole* (Città del Vaticano, 1971),p.60. The judicial immunities of the religious need

no comment. As to the Signoria, those offending them were punished two or three times the normal rate; on their immunities, see *Statuto . . . capitano,* pp. 89-91.

5. M. Douglas, *Purity and Danger* (New York, 1966), p. 61, cites Thomas Aquinas to the effect that it was not the blood defilement which desecrated a church, but the sin of injuring another. For a statue of the Virgin weeping from the crimes she saw daily, see Luca Landucci, *Diario Fiorentino dal 1450 al 1516,* ed. I. Del Badia, (Florence, 1969), p. 279 (1506).

6. A Franciscan who decried this customary usage in Florence was arrested by the Inquisition; Franco Sacchetti, *Il Trecentonovelle,* ed. V. Pernicone, (Florence, 1946), pp. 161f (*Novella* LXXIII).

7. For examples of the use of the host and bible, see G. Villani in *Croniche di Giovanni, Matteo e Filippo Villani* (Trieste, 1857), XII, 2, 3; *La vita del beato Ieronimo Savonarola,* ed. attrib. P. Ginori Conti, (Florence, 1937), p. 74. For the "sacred stone" of the cathedral, see F. Guicciardini, *The History of Florence* (New York, 1970), p. 100. According to church law, every altar had to have a relic in it. On oaths over relics, see F. Del Migliore, *Firenze Citta' Nobilissima Illustrata* (Florence, 1684), p. 487. For contracts of Peace, see N. Rubinstein, *The Government of Florence Under the Medici, 1434 to 1494* (Oxford, 1966), p. 163; Dino Compagni, *Cronica delle cose occorrenti ne' tempi suoi* (Milan, 1965), p. 73 (II, 8).

8. For an extensive description of the platforms and the arrangements on them for a propitiative procession in 1390, see *Biblioteca Nazionale, Firenze* (hereafter BNF), *Fondo Panciatichi* 158, f. 160r (12 Oct. 1390). My thanks are due to Anthony Molho for permitting me to read his transcription of this anonymous chronicle.

9. G. Villani, *Cronica,* XII, 8 (1342); *Cronache e memorie sul tumulto dei Ciompi,* ed. G. Scaramella, *RIS* new edition XVIII, part 3 (Città di Castello, 1917-34), p. 17 (1378).

10. Compagni, *Cronica,* pp. 77, 203f (II, 12); Rubinstein, *Government,* p. 157 (1466).

11. *ASF, Prov.* 153, ff. 163v-165r (27 Oct. 1462).

12. Compagni, *Cronica,* p. 79 (II, 13).

13. On the process of desacralization in an agrarian setting, see H. Hubert and M. Mauss, *Sacrifice: Its Nature and Function* (Chicago, 1964), pp. 57, 71, 95; see also Comblin, *Théologie,* pp. 211f.

14. For an illustration of the similarities as they were perceived by the Florentines, see my article "Florentine Religious Experience: The Sacred Image," *Studies in the Renaissance* XIX (1972), nn. 30, 31. Charisma is the quality of certain places, objects, and times which attracts a ritual clientele because of their latent ability to reconstitute all fundamental relationships. By sacrality I refer to the "other," conceptualizable apart from all relations and influence. Unlike charisma, sacrality may dissolve order without replacing it. For an equating of Weber's charisma of office (*Amtscharisma*) with Durkheim's collective sacred, see Talcott Parson's Introduction to M. Weber, *The Sociology of Religion* (Boston, 1963), p. XXXIV.

15. See R. Davidsohn, *Storia di Firenze,* 8 vols. (Florence, 1956-68), II, pp. 180-88; VII, pp. 115ff. The patrons of hundreds of these objects can be found in Richa, *Notizie istoriche,* in Del Migliore, *Firenze . . . Illustrata,* and in W. and E. Paatz, *Die Kirchen von Florenz,* 6 vols. (Frankfurt am Main, 1940-54).

16. In 1419 Giovanni di Bicci de' Medici with other parishioners had undertaken the refurbishment of the church; D. Moreni, *Memorie istoriche dell'Ambrosiana reale basilica di San Lorenzo* II (Florence, 1804), pp. 341-45. In 1427 the Signoria increased the number of canons in the cathedral; *ASF, Prov.* 117, ff. 119r-120r (26 July 1427). But the commune could not keep pace with Medici largess, and in 1432 the Signoria protested the diminution of the honor of the cathedral; *ASF, Missive* 34, ff. 56v-57r (15 Oct. 1432). In 1532, just after the Medici regained control of Florence, the pope sent over one hundred relics to S. Lorenzo, one of many signs of Medici disdain for the republic; see Luca Landucci, *Diario,* p. 370.

17. In the church of S. Marco, for example, there were to be "arma et signa populi et comunis florentini et Partis Guelfi, et non alterius . . . "; *ASF, Prov.* 107, ff. 52v-53r (26 Apr. 1417). See also *ASF, Prov.* 30, ff. 49rv (8 Feb. 1340sf); E. H. Gombrich, "The Early Medici as Patrons of Art," in *Italian Renaissance Studies,* ed. E. F. Jacob, (London, 1960), p. 299.

18. Matteo Villani, *Cronica,* VIII, 46 (1358). The prior who had decided on the change was the learned canonist Fra Piero Strozzi.

19. See for example the speech of welcome made to St. Andrew by the humanist pope Pius II when the saint's relics entered Rome; *Memoirs of a Renaissance Pope. The Commentaries of Pius II,* ed. L. C. Gabel, (New York, 1959), pp. 240-49, esp. 246.

20. G. Villani, *Cronica,* IX, 13.

21. M. Villani, *Cronica,* III, 15-16.

22. *Cronica volgare di anonimo fiorentino dell'anno 1385 al 1409, già attributa a Piero di Giovanni Minerbetti,* ed. E. Bellondi, *RIS,* new edition, XXVII, part 2, p. 172 (May, 1393); *ASF, Prov.* 110, ff. 204rv (27 Jan. 1420sf).

23. *Diario fiorentino di Agostino Lapini* (Florence, 1900), p. 54. The political preference for saints of sacred history seems to contrast sharply with the individual and social penchant for the recent relics of saintly neighbors; E. Delaruelle et al, *L'Eglise au temps du Grand Schisme et de la crise conciliaire (1378-1449),* (Fliche et Martin, XIV, 2), Paris, 1964), pp. 789f.

24. G. Villani, *Cronica,* X, 168.

25. See for example *Cronica . . . Minerbetti,* pp. 172f.

26. For the dressing and undressing of one image, and for accounts of unveiling, see Landucci, *Diario,* pp. 198, 270, 281, 287.

27. The Florentines of course often determined that relics were hoaxes; see for example M. Villani, *Cronica,* III, 15-16. But there were plenty of indisputably genuine relics which had no particular social dignity, in part because they had not been "ennobled" by a valuable person. For Giovanni Dominici's complaint that adorned figures were preferred to those darkened with age, see his *On the Education of Children,* ed. A. Coté, (Washington, 1927), p. 35.

28. This is still done in Poland. I have not encountered the custom in Italy, but for an early sixteenth century example in Germany, see *The Autobiography of Johannes Butzbach,* eds. R. F. Seybolt and P. Monroe, (Ann Arbor, 1933),

142

p. 108.

29. H. Caspary, "Kult und Aufbewahrung der Eucharistie in Italien vor dem Tridentinum," *Archiv für Liturgie* IX (1965), pp. 102-130.

30. The cloth covering the body during a funeral was often used to such ends. As many as three such communion cloths were used at one time; Trexler, *Synodal Law*, p. 55.

31. A well-known example is the famous baldachin of Venice. The coats of arms suspended from its edges can be seen in Bellini's "Procession in Piazza San Marco."

32. See a letter to a Gonzaga of 1502, printed in A. Warburg, *Gesammelte Schriften* (Leipzig, 1932), I, p. 349.

33. For the removal of that of the *gonfaloniere a vita* Piero Soderini in 1512, see Landucci, *Diario*, pp. 330f. On the removal and destruction of those of the Medici in 1527, see Bernardo Segni, *Storie Fiorentine di messer . . .* (Milan, 1805), I, p. 41.

34. On the limits of unveiling the Madonna of Or San Michele, see S. La Sorsa, *La compagnia d'Or San Michele overo una pagina della beneficenza in Toscana nel secolo XIV* (Trani, 1902), p. 189. Veiling of the Madonna de' Servi is discussed in Del Migliore, *Firenze . . . Illustrata*, pp. 288f. The "exposure to public view" or unveiling of civic monuments practiced today still retains something of the old psychology. Often enough, monuments or buildings long in use are re-newed so that a public figure can then officially unveil the structure.

35. Del Migliore, *Firenze . . . Illustrata*, pp. 288f. For the effects of repeated unveiling at Venice, see B. Pullan, *Rich and Poor in Renaissance Venice* (Cambridge, Mass., 1971), p. 158.

36. Showing the Belt of the Virgin of Prato not to nobles and dignified men, but vile individuals of dishonest life, caused a decline of devotion, according to *ASF, Prov.* 139, ff. 196v-197r (30 Dec. 1448).

37. Del Migliore, *Firenze . . . Illustrata*, p. 289.

38. For an example of the fate of such a defiler, see Landucci, *Diario*, p. 233.

39. *ASF, Prov.* 151, ff. 242r-243v (14 Sept. 1460). For governments "spirati da Dio," see E. B. Garrison, *Studies in the History of Medieval Italian Painting* IV (Florence, 1960),pp.31,33,39(Siena, 1260). See also Landucci, *Diario*, pp. 193, 250

40. *ASF, Prov.* 79. ff. 238v-239v (26 Oct. 1390); see also *Statuta*, I, pp. 250f; II, p. 440.

41. The shops were ordered to close in 1383 and everyone was ordered to take part in the procession; *BNF, Panciatichi*, f. 148r (4 Oct. 1384). In 1465 the entry days of the Signoria, for a long time days on which shops were closed, were declared days of debt suspension so that many more people would be able to accompany the Signoria; *ASF, Prov.* 155, ff. 243v-244r (11 Mar. 1464sf). The same step was taken for St. Zanobi's feast so that he could be accompanied; *ibid.*, 172, ff. 132r-133r (21 Dec. 1481).

42. On rites of enthronement as rites of passage, see A. Van Gennep, *The Rites of Passage* (Chicago, 1960), pp. 110-15.

43. G. Dati, *Istoria di Firenze di Goro Dati dall'anno MCCCLXXX all'anno MCCCCV* (Florence, 1735), p. 69. On the ambiguity in the notion of sacrality between the disordered and the ordered, see the analysis of Robertson Smith's views by E. Durkheim, *The Elementary Forms of the Religious Life* (New York, 1915), pp. 455-61.

44. *ASF, Signoria, Dieci di Balia, Otto di Praticha; Legazioni e commissarie, Missive e responsive* 5, ff. 47r-50v (1429-30); see M. Mallet, *The Florentine Galleys in the Fifteenth Century* (Oxford, 1967), pp. 204f.

45. H. Hubert and M. Mauss, "Etude sommaire de la représentation du temps dans la religion et la magie," in their *Mélanges d'histoire des religions* (Paris, 1909), p. 200. On the concept of sacred time, see van der Leeuw, *Religion in Essence*, pp. 384-92.

46. For examples in military actions, see G. Uzielli, *La vita e i tempi di Paolo dal Pozzo Toscanelli* (Rome, 1894), pp. 214-17; E. Casanova, *L'Astrologia e la consegna del bastone al capitano generale della repubblica fiorentina* (Florence, 1891). For a case of processions planned ahead for the feast of St. Martin because it was believed that this saint would hear prayers to end a plague, see *ASF, Prov.* 154, ff. 227v-228v (8 Nov. 1463). In at least one case, the *bastone* was given to the mercenary captain on the feast of St. John Baptist. Whether this was due to solstitial or liturgical considerations is unknown; C. Guasti, *Le Feste di San Giovanni Battista in Firenze* (Florence, 1884), p. 18.

47. *BNF, Panciatichi*, f. 150r (11 June 1385). This same astrologer had just determined the auspicious times for a new electoral scrutiny. For private prayers timed to auspicious moments, see E. Garin, *Medioevo e Rinascimento* (Bari, 1966), p. 165 (1509).

48. *BNF, Conventi Religiosi Soppressi C-4-895, Prioritsta di Paolo di Matteo Pietrobuoni*, f. 116r (16-18 March 1426sf).

49. See the classic Florentine exposition of both causalities in G. Villani, *Cronica*, XI, 2 (Flood of 1333).

50. Astrologers felt that miracles attributed to the saints often resulted from astrologically determined actions; T. O. Wedel, *The Medieval Attitude Toward Astrology* (New Haven, 1920), p. 74 (citing Roger Bacon). For Florentine attributions of civic fortune to saints, see U. Dorini, "Il culto delle memorie patrie nella repubblica di Firenze," *Rassegna Nazionale* CLXXIX (1911), pp. 3-25.

51. This was the Parliament of 11 Aug. 1458, an innerpolitical victory of the Medici; see Dorini, "Il culto," p. 21.

52. *Le Lettere di Michelangelo Buonarotti*, ed. G. Papini, (Lanciano, 1913), p. 27.

53. Landucci, *Diario*, p. 199 (24 Aug. 1499).

54. *ASF, Missive* 22, f. 139v (3 June 1391).

55. *ASF, Prov.* 123, ff. 112v-113v (13 June 1432).

56. Landucci, *Diario*, pp. 139f; Schnitzer, *Quellen und Forschungen zur Geschichte Savonarolas*, 4 vols., (Munich, Leipzig, 1902-10), IV, p. 146 (account of Piero Parenti); Guicciardini, *History of Florence*, p. 122. Another teleological, non-intentional event of this type was the concurrence of the city's offerings to St. John in 1403 with the beginning of civil war in Milan; Dati, *Istoria*, p. 77.

57. Landucci, *Diario*, p. 140.

58. M. Douglas, *Purity and Danger*, p. 80.

59. The "creative formality" of personal ritual calls for a formalized behavior of the patron as well as the client. Much modern research on this phenomenon is conveniently available in J. Huxley (ed.), *A Discussion on Ritualization of Behavior in Animals and Man*, *Philosophical Transactions of the Royal Society of London*, ser. B, CCLI (1966), pp.

247-524.

60. However different in form personal ritual may have been from political or societal, their rationales were similar. Jack Goody tends to edge his definition of religion and ritual toward the private and *gemeinschaftlich*, while using the word "ceremonial" to describe the public activity of a *Gesellschaft*; J. Goody, "Religion and Ritual: The Definitional Problem," *The British Journal of Sociology* XII (1961), pp. 145ff, 157ff; E. R. Leach, "Ritualization in Man in relation to Conceptual and Social Development," in Huxley, *Ritualization*, pp. 403f. Here are two usages of the word "ceremony" during the quattrocento: "Fu una cirimonia, e stimasi atto di poco pondo"; Rubinstein, *Government*, p. 174; "Con bella cirimonia, e simulata ipocrisia sotto gran santità per mettere paura a essi frati"; L. Randi, *Frate Girolamo Savonarola giudicato da Piero Vaglienti* (Florence, 1893), p. 40.

61. "Ritual recognizes the potency of disorder"; Douglas, *Purity and Danger*, p. 94. See also P. Berger, *The Sacred Canopy* (Garden City, 1967), pp. 40f.

62. Processions had originally had a military character, of course, and in Florence the offeratory processions of the *gonfaloni* were those of originally military societies. Not only did battles and other military operations start to become part of Florentine festivals toward the end of the quattrocento; a military terminology was used to describe the discipline and organization of the Savonarolan processions. On the processions of the revivified *gonfaloni* in the Last Republic, see P. Gori, *Le feste fiorentine attraverso i secoli. Le feste per San Giovanni* (Florence, 1926), pp. 216-20.

63. Guasti, *Feste*, pp. 4f.

64. *Ibid.*

65. On polar behavior at funerals, see E. De Martino, *Morte e pianto nel mondo antico* (Turin, 1958), pp. 225ff. In Florence, meals accompanied many other solemn acts, such as the consecration of nuns and the ordination of clerics. For episcopal regulation of these meals, see Trexler, *Synodal Law*, pp. 61f, 114.

66. By no means was this whole range of behavior considered "spiritual" by the Florentines. They made a distinction between the spiritual and secular parts, both of which were delighted in by the saint; Savonarola called the dances within the procession "holy madness"; Schnitzer, *Quellen*, I, p. 377; see also below, p. 140.

67. On the feasts of St. John the women lined the streets in their richest finery. In such cases the vice of feminine presumption could not be suspected, and no sin was committed. On special days, such as when a dignitary entered a city, the sumptuary laws were officially suspended; see for example the suspension of 30 Apr. 1459 when Pius II entered the city; *Ricordi di Firenze dell'anno 1459, RIS*, new ed. XXVII, part 1 (Città di Castello, 1907), pp. 19, 55.

68. See the excellent article by L. Zdekauer, "Il giuoco in Italia nei secoli XIII e XIV," *Archivio Storico Italiano*, ser 4, XVIII (1886), pp. 20-74, esp. p. 33.

69. Reasons included attempts to attract tourists seeking indulgences available in the city, increasing attendance at communal ceremonies, etc. The first case I have encountered in Florence is in *ASF, Prov.* 96, ff. 23rv (29 Apr. 1407); see also *Statuta*, I, pp. 190f. But the practice doubtless was old and ubiquitous. In 1296, for example, such safe-conducts vs. debt collectors were given for those *contadini* who wanted to visit a doctor in Siena; W. Bowsky, *The Finance of the Commune of Siena, 1287-1355* (Oxford, 1970), p. 32. Debt suspension for indulgences is found in Milan in 1480; E. Cattaneo, "I 'Libri Indulgentiarum' di Milano nei secoli XIV-XVI," *Studi in onore di Carlo Castiglioni*, (Milan, 1957), pp. 264f.

70. Games of chance and rich clothing were not sinful in any general sense, but were prohibited because of non-inherent factors, for example that they led to drink or that they could mirror vices.

71. *Statuto . . . podestà*, pp. 367f; *Statuta*, II, pp. 440f. Comblin notes that St. John Evangelist sees the New Jerusalem as a great carnival, "a pure gift of human life in its pure state"; *Théologie*, p. 213.

72. *ASF, Prov.* 137, ff. 79v-80v (13 June 1446).

73. The battle scenes enacted on the feast of St. John in 1513 brought death to some of the participants; Landucci called this type of celebration "bestial"; *Diario*, p. 340. For Giovanni Cambi, these deaths were part of a general diabolism which dishonored the saint; Guasti, *Feste*, p. 28.

74. Mikhail Bakhtin contrasts the "monolithic seriousness" of political processions with the parodic laughter of the "popular-festive form." This does not square with the Florentine evidence. Parody can make the Gods laugh, and there is no reason to believe that popular festivities were only "externally related" to the liturgical calendar; M. Bakhtin, *Rabelais and His World (Cambridge, Mass., 1968), pp. 6-10.*

75. Francesco Altoviti, *In defensione de Magistrati, et delle leggi et antiche cerimonie al culto divino della citta di Firenze contro alle invettive et offensione di Fra Girolamo* (Florence, 1497), f. a-v recto. The writer was an opponent of Savonarola.

76. Uzielli, *Vita . . . Toscanelli*, p. 214.

77. See for example the description of the Bianchi processions of 1399, which appeared to emanate from God because of their perfect order and disposition; *Cronica . . . Minerbetti*, pp. 241f (1399). The same attitude informed Florentine reactions to the "miraculously" ordered processions of the Savonarolan years. One of the better known postponements was one of 1512, when a plot was underfoot to bar the Signoria from the Palace after it left to go to the church of the Servi to unveil the Madonna; see Benedetto Varchi, *Storia fiorentina di messer . . .* (Milan, 1805), I, pp. 180-85.

78. *ASF, Prov.* 67, ff. 45rv (28 Sept. 1378).

79. *Cronache . . . Ciompi*, pp. 85f.

80. Davidsohn, *Storia*, III, pp. 465, 468.

81. Gori, *Feste*, p. 16, with a list of such suspensions and cancellations.

82. Ginori Conti, *Vita . . . Savonarola*, p. 123.

83. Altoviti, *In defensione*, f. a-v recto.

# Fruitful Business: Medieval and Renaissance Elements in the Devotional Method of St. John Fisher

*Thomas M. C. Lawler*

ALTHOUGH THEOLOGICAL POLEMICS on Reformation controversies make up the bulk of St. John Fisher's writings, one strand of his work is private and devotional in character: a Latin tract on the method of prayer (S.T.C. 10888); a *Treatyse,* or series of ten sermons on the penitential psalms; two spiritual exercises which he wrote in the Tower for his sister Elizabeth, a "Spirituall Consolation," and "The Wayes to Perfect Religion;" and an undated Passion sermon, *Lamentationes, Carmen, et Vae.* After Fisher's death, the Passion sermon was printed with the Tower works to form a little book of three spiritual exercises.[1] Father Ong has noted the parallel between "The Wayes to Perfect Religion" (in the anonymous Latin translation) and Erasmus' famous method book on the study of scripture, the *Ratio seu methodus compendio perveniendi ad veram theologiam:*

> Method seems to have had considerable currency in the Hertogenbosch piety of Erasmus' circle, where one finds also the *Methodus perveniendi ad summam Christianae religionis perfectionem* of the martyred Bishop of Rochester, St. John Fisher. The later Sixteenth and Seventeenth century spate of method books has not yet flooded Europe, but evidently something is in the air. Strangely, it seems to be something humanistic rather than scholastic, rhetorical and devotional rather than dialectical and speculative.[2]

In this paper I will analyze the structure of Fisher's meditations and point out some possible sources which illustrate the continuity between medieval and Renaissance elements in his devotional method.

145

Fisher seems to have been jointly influenced by the systematic spiritual exercises of medieval writers like Henry Suso and Walter Hilton and the humanistic emphasis upon suasive sacred rhetoric and methodical piety which Father Ong mentions above. Both traditions cultivated an affective, interior spirituality as an antidote to the excessive rationalism of scholastic theology and the externalism of the *ex opere operato* attitude in some practices of popular piety. Intrinsically valuable as religious literature, Fisher's meditations are historically interesting as precursors of the *Spiritual Exercises* of St. Ignatius Loyola and the devotions of the Counter Reformation which drew in a similar way upon medieval and Renaissance traditions.

In *On the Copia of Words and Ideas,* Erasmus explains how to acquire a "copious" prose style by imitating figures of speech culled from ancient writers and "stored in the memory" for later use.[3] This technique of rhetorical amplification is analogous to the art of meditation which Fisher practices and, indeed, teaches the reader in the three exercises I will examine. In both techniques an image, motif, or precept is imprinted in the memory and then elaborated with original variations. Each of Fisher's meditations appears to have been initially inspired by a notable passage from another spiritual writer which he amplified into a full discourse. His "copious" prose style, rich in imagery and rhythmical sentence patterns, stirs the soul's affections to bring about the inner conversion of the will to God which is the final goal of meditation.

The Tower meditations, written in old age, infirmity, and truly pitiable circumstances achieve an austere serenity which testifies to the quality of Fisher's spiritual life. On December 22, 1534, after he had been in prison eight months, he asked Cromwell for warmer clothes, a better diet, and "sum bowks to styr my devotion mor effectuelly thes hooly dayes for the comforth of my sowl."[4] No one knows if Cromwell complied, but Fisher was probably allowed a few books of devotion until his correspondence with More was discovered, after which stricter conditions must have been imposed. This supposition is strengthened by several parallels, which have not been noticed previously, between "A Spirituall Consolation" and a famous spiritual guide by the fourteenth-century German mystic Henry Suso, *The Little Book of Eternal Wisdom* (c. 1328) or *Horologium Sapientiae* (c. 1334), as he entitled the expanded Latin version.

The *Horologium Sapientiae* was translated widely into the vernacular languages, and about 1491 William Caxton printed the abbreviated English version, the *Seven Poyntes of Trewe Loue and Wisdame.*[5] "A

Spirituall Consolation" is an example of the "Spectacle" method of meditation on death, a tradition derived from an exercise that was often imitated or circulated separately from the rest of the *Horologium,* in which Christ as Eternal Wisdom, places an Image of a Dying Man before the Disciple who is advancing in the spiritual life. Thomas Hoccleve's "Lerne to Dye" (1421) is in part a direct translation of the meditation, and on the continent Jean Mombaer recommended it in the *Rosetum,* the book of systematic devotions for the Brethren of the Common Life.

Like Donne's sonnet, "This is my play's last scene," Fisher's "Spirituall Consolation" exemplifies the way a Renaissance writer creates a new work by improvising in an old tradition. In Suso's exercise, the Disciple carries on a dialogue with the Dying Man as he laments his plight while death approaches. Fisher's meditation is a monologue overheard as it were by Elizabeth, who is equivalent to the Disciple. The tone and technique of dramatization is very similar, however, for in both meditations the Dying Man's pitiful ejaculations disorder his train of reflection. Fisher accumulates fresh details to fix the scene vividly in the imagination, and lingers over some motifs in rhythmical periods of increasing emotional intensity. In addition, he arranges the themes he borrows somewhat differently from the original. The following outline of the dramatic movement of the "Consolation" lists the main parallels with Suso's meditation.

To stimulate fervent devotion, withdraw the mind from outward business and imagine a man "suddenly" ravished by death (*Works,* p. 351, 1.21-p. 352, 1.7; *Seven Poyntes,* p. 358, 1.20-31).

The Dying Man wonders where his soul will "lodge this night" in the "unknown country" of death (*Works,* p. 352, 1.21-25; *Seven Poyntes,* p. 362, 1.43-45).

He doubts the sincerity of his forced deathbed repentance (*Works,* p. 353, 1.28-p. 354, 1.5; *Seven Poyntes,* p. 360, 1.29-32).

Neither friends nor riches can persuade death to "spare" him time for repentance (*Works,* p. 354, 1.18-26; *Seven Poyntes,* p. 358, 1.45-p. 359, 1.6). The Dying Man "cloathed" himself in earthly rather than spiritual riches, and did not spend "one hour or day" properly in holy works. He counsels the living to study his plight and use their remaining time "fruitfully" (*Works,* p. 354, 1.26-p. 355, 1.22; *Seven Poyntes,* p. 359, 1.23-p. 360, 1.3).

The Dying Man's five senses deteriorate *(Works,* p. 356, 1.4-7, 24-26; *Seven Poyntes,* p. 363, 1.4-6), and he decries his past sensual indulgences like fine "cloathing" and "soft bedding" (*Works,* p. 358, 1.28-32; *Seven Poyntes,* p. 364, 1.13-16).

Now the Dying Man imagines himself before the seat of judgment where he will have to "answer" for not "expending one day" in "pleasing service" to God. (*Works,* p. 359, 1.6-12, 31-36; *Seven Poyntes,* p. 360, 1.35-43).

Every man must keep "before the eyes" the danger of an unprepared death since his final hour is "uncertain" (*Works,* p. 360, 1.28-p. 361, 1.1-3;

*Seven Poyntes,* p. 364, 1.20-24, p. 365, 1.14-15). At the last moment there is no hope except the "mercy of God" (*Works,* p. 360, 1.25; *Seven Poyntes,* p. 364, 1.30).

The sinner cannot count on the prayers of his friends, since they will seek their own "profit." He must imagine that his soul is already in purgatory, crying to him as his own "best beloved friend." This is the essential device of the spectacle method of the art of dying well (*Works,* p. 360, 1.1-7 and p. 362, 1.24-31; *Seven Poyntes,* p. 361, 1.25-34).

The fact that Fisher's exercise is not an "original" work in our modern sense, but derived instead from established meditative traditions, clarifies its value as a personal testament of the "Spirituall Consolation" he received from the ancient ways of the church. Relieved of the official burdens of Reformation polemics, he reconsiders the contested doctrines of purgatory and the necessity of good works for salvation in a private devotional mode. In his Tower writings More withdrew from the world into the comforts he discovered as a young man in the Carthusian Charterhouse. Similarly, Fisher's final recollections afforded him a means of confessing to his closest relative that his works of humanistic reform had distracted him from the spiritual good works of prayer and meditation which constitute "fruitful business." On the last page of the "Consolation," Fisher sets aside the persona of the Dying Man and stands before Elizabeth as the Image of Death in his own person:

For in this hangeth all our wealth, for if a man dye well, he shall after his death nothing want that he would desire. . . . And therefore delay it not as I haue done, but before all other buzinesse put this first in suertie, which oughte to bee chieefe and princypall buzinesse. Neyther buildyng of Colleges, nor makyng of Sermons, nor giuing of almes, neyther yet anye other manner of buzynesse shall helpe you without this (*Works,* pp. 361-362).

In the first Tower tract Fisher embraces his particular situation and the thoughts he cannot avoid, but he designed the second as a special gift for Elizabeth and her business as a nun "in this life here" (*Works,* p. 365). The initial biblical texts announce the transition to a hopeful meditation on life, 2 Cor. 2:16, Christ is the "sent of the verie lyfe" for those on the path of salvation, and Cant. 1:3, "we shall runne after the sent of thy sweete oyntmentes." These biblical metaphors lead into the exordium, pointedly separated from the subsequent meditation by a title, "A comparison betweene the lyfe of Hunters, and the lyfe of religious persons." This analogy was probably inspired by a passage in Walter Hilton's *Scale of Perfection,* a classic of English devotional literature which Elizabeth may well have known. Quite appropriately, the figure Fisher imitates in his "Wayes to Perfect Religion" deals with the art of meditation. Hilton is warning novices not to attempt the advanced techniques practiced by the adept:

> An hound that runneth after the hare, only for he seeth other hounds run, when he is weary he resteth him or turneth home again. But if he run for he seeth the hare, he will not spare for weariness till he hath gotten it.[6]

Adding visual details, Fisher amplifies the correspondences between the physical hardships endured by the hunter and the austerities of a nun's daily routine (*Works,* pp. 365-367). Just as the hunter who does not see the hare wearies of the chase, the religious who does not acquire an interior love for Christ through mental prayer will tire in the external round of fasting, ritual, and charitable works:

> the cause why that so many religious persons so diligently pursue not the wayes of religion as doe the hunters, is the want of the obseruation of their game, which is nothing els but the lack of loue (*Works,* p. 368).

In his essay on "The Continuity of English Prose from Alfred to More and His School," R. W. Chambers notes that "The Wayes to Perfect Religion" is the last work in the genre of the *Ancrene Riwle* and the *Scale of Perfection,* the medieval devotional guide for cloistered nuns.[7] The tract should also be viewed in relation to humanistic method books like the *Enchiridion* and the *Ratio Verae Theologiae.* The ten "common considerations" which follow the exordium are equivalent to the canons and principles of biblical interpretation which Erasmus prepares for the layman and theology student to provide a practical and "compendious" way of "arriving at a mentality worthy of Christ," the *scopus.* The same etymological metaphor appears in each of these tracts, the idea of method as a true "way" which guides the student who would otherwise wander.[8] Absorbing past and present as does its title, "The Wayes to Perfect Religion" supplements Erasmus' method books for laymen and theology students — it is a "ready" way to an old art for Elizabeth and her community.

The idea of method was closely allied to the commonplace tradition of rhetoric and dialectic, and from classical times through the Renaissance the hunting metaphor had been applied to the process by which the orator searches the places of invention stored in the memory to "find" the arguments for his discourse. In the *Advancement of Learning,* V, v, for instance, Bacon sums up the usefulness of the figure in a discussion of the artificial memory which stores the places: "you will more easily remember the image of a hunter pursuing a hare . . . than the mere notion of invention."[9] The relationship between method and the commonplace tradition explains the rhetorical basis of the technique of mental prayer Fisher teaches Elizabeth. The ten "common considerations" which follow the hunting similitude in the exordium are theological *loci* which he twice advises Elizabeth to "imprint" in her "remembraunce" so that she can "resorte" to them when she wishes to "inflame" the love of Christ in her heart (*Works*, p. 368, 386). Like Suso and Hilton, Fisher stresses that all the faculties must be recollected from outside distractions and focused on the present object of meditation. The hunter is Fisher's emblem for the intellectual and emotional wholeness of true prayer:

> All hys mynde, all his soule, is buzied to knowe where the poore Hare may be founde. Of that is his thought, and of that his communication (*Works*, p. 366).

Though the considerations form a logical sequence, each is a self-contained rhetorical set piece with a final exhortation that "this one consideration" should inflame a love for Christ (*Works*, pp. 369, 372, 374).[10] The first reminds Elizabeth that God created her out of "naught," and the second surveys the different kinds of being he might have given her if he had not elected her "to beare hys Image and lykenesse" (*Works*, 371). The three succeeding considerations review the purifying gifts of baptism, penance, and the cloistered life, which have restored her to the "cleanenesse of . . . first innocencie" (*Works*, p. 374). The purgative half of the *via* refurbished the divine image in the soul tarnished by the fall. In the sixth consideration the mystical garden of Canticles, hinted at in the opening theme of Christ as "the sent of verie lyfe," supplants the thorny landscape of the hunting analogy. Elizabeth attains the center of the *scala* when all mind and soul are "buzied" in "communication" with Christ — mental prayer is a way of salvation for a reasonable creature made in the image of God:

> in the booke of Canticles the Spouse discribeth his goodlinesse saying: *Dilectus meus candidus et rubicundus, electus ex millibus* [Cant. 5:10] . . . The same lykenes he hath and you haue, like body and lyke soule, touching his manhood, youre soule is also like vnto him in his godhead: For after the Image and similitude of it, your soule is made (*Works*, pp. 376-377).

The rest of the consideration "marvels" over a "commonplace" theme, the ordered beauty of the chain of being. The most rhapsodic passage in Fisher's prose, it temporarily erases the scene which the "Consolation" put before the eyes, the decay of fair-seeming beauty into a "sachell full of dunge" (*Works*, p. 358). The unifying theme of the two meditations emerges from the contrast between their central rhetorical commonplaces: when the faculties of the soul "behold" the beauty of creation and "inwardly consider that immortality is found in being kin to Wisdom" (Wis. 8:17), then the decay of the senses and death itself is no longer a fearful spectacle:

> Finally his good and gentil maner is all full of pleasure and comfort so kinde, so friendly, . . . so dulcet and sweet in communication. For as scripture saith. *Non habet amaritudinem conuersatio vel tedium conuictus*

*illius, Sed letitiam et gaudium* (Wis. 8:16; *Works,* p. 377).

In the seventh consideration, a stark meditation on the Passion, the proof of Christ's personal love for Elizabeth, restrains this mystical celebration of the Bridegroom reminiscent of St. Bernard's *Sermons on the Canticle of Canticles.* The metaphor of the soul as a mirror which receives and reflects divine love more fully as it is polished, a favorite motif with Hilton and other mystical writers, serves in the eighth consideration as an emblem for the "way to perfect religion" through methodical devotions like the tract itself. Recalling how Lucifer and Adam fell from grace though they were created perfect, the ninth consideration cautions Elizabeth to live and pray "in the wildernesse farre from any worldly comforte," as Mary Magdalene supposedly did after Christ's death (*Works,* p. 384). At the close of the tenth consideration on the "Martirs innumerable" who have suffered for the love of Christ, Fisher directs Elizabeth to fall on her knees and say the final prayer to the Spouse with all her "hart and mynde" (*Works,* p. 385). The theme text of this colloquy confirms "his good and gentil maner" and the value of prayer as a true way of salvation: "what person so euer commeth vnto me, I wil not cast him away" (John 6:37). The second meditation discovers the friend who does not seek his own "profit" and whose promises are binding.

The rhetorical structure of "The Wayes to Perfect Religion" approximates the three divisions of Ignatian meditation.[11] The exordium with its hunting metaphor is equivalent to the composition of place which employs the visual imagination or memory; the logically ordered considerations resemble the lessons systematically derived by the understanding; the concluding prayer, like the final colloquy in Ignatian meditation, marks the full response of the will and affections to the fire of divine love. Fisher's exercise, like those of Ignatius and many spiritual writers, "perfects" the image of God "mirrored" in the soul by engaging all its faculties, memory, reason, and will, which were traditionally thought of as being analogous to the Trinity.

Fisher's love for his sister and his special desire that she perfect her religion through systematic devotions are evident in a brief epilogue to the tract. He urges her to employ the "meditation of death, which I send you here before" when the latest gift fails to stimulate "any dulnesse of mynde." This technique of alternating between "diverse melodies" of dread and hope, an ancient homilectic practice, also determines the structure of the *Treatyse* on the penitential psalms (*Works,* pp. 71, 113-114) and the Passion sermon. The epilogue closes with seven aspirations to Jesus, one for each day of the week, intended to busy the mind amidst present distractions: "For thus you may in your hart shortly pray what companie so euer you be amongest" (*Works,* p. 387). His greatest "comfort" now hopes for her future, "merueylouslie" kindled in "good religion," Fisher ends his ministry and leaves Elizabeth to the company of her heart.

Unlike the "Spiritual Consolation" and "The Wayes to Perfect Religion," the meditation on the Passion published with them is a sermon to the laity. This juxtaposition reflects in minature the transition between the devotional guides of the Middle Ages written primarily for contemplatives and layman's handbooks like Erasmus' *Enchiridion.* The pre-Reformation desire for books of practical piety was nourished by the spiritual exercises of the *Devotio Moderna* of the low countries and by English tracts like Hilton's *Letter on the Mixed Life* of contemplation and action or a *Werke for Householders,* by Richard Whiteforde, friend of Erasmus and More. Fisher fashions the systematic steps of his meditation for laymen from the schematic structure of the medieval scholastic sermon, a shift from dialectical to rhetorical discourse characteristic of humanistic writings. The sources of the sermon, which have not been pointed out before, further illustrate the curious amalgam of medieval and Renaissance elements in his work. The exordium is modelled after Erasmus' exhortation to the study of scripture, the *Paraclesis,* the most quoted, and most moving statement of his "Philosophy of Christ."[12] The body of the sermon derives in part from the *Legenda Aurea,* an extremely popular medieval sermon manual printed frequently in the sixteenth century, a reservoir of the apocryphal saints' lives and biblical stories which Erasmus felt polluted the *limpidissimos fontes* the preacher should draw from directly.

Fisher was primarily attracted to the meditations on the cross attributed to St. Bernard in the *Legenda,* liii, "De Passione Domini."[13] Like Donne's "Good friday, 1613. Riding Westward," the sermon is a classic example of Cistercian meditative technique in which the Passion is made visually "present" to the memory, eliciting a total emotional response to Christ's suffering humanity.[14] A series of six visualizations of the Passion in the Cistercian manner begins in the protheme of the sermon, and they are spaced at intervals through the divisions of the body. Since this is one of Fisher's most artfully designed sermons, I will outline its structure in the scholastic form (statement of theme, protheme or exordium, bidding prayer, division, and schematic development) before proceeding to an analysis of its themes:

Statement of theme, Ezech. 2:9, *Lamentationes, Carmen, et Vae.*
Exordium, an imitation of Erasmus' *Paraclesis,* or *Exhortation to the Study*

*of the Philosophy of Christ* (cf. *LB*, V, 139B-140C)

The "marvel" of the philosophy of the Christian people, the first visualization of the Passion (*Works*, pp. 388-390)

St. Francis' method of studying the book of the crucifix: "Quis tu, et quis ego domine?" (*Works*, pp. 390-393)

An analogy between the crucifix and a book, the second visualization of the Passion (*Works*, pp. 393-396)

Bidding prayer; restatement of theme; and division (*Works*, pp. 396-397)

   *Lamentationes*, subdivided into four "affections":

     Fear (*Works*, p. 397-399)

     Shame, the third visualization of the Passion, taken from St. Bernard (*Works*, pp. 399-403; cf. *Legenda*, p. 226)

     Sorrow (*Works*, pp. 403-405)

     Hatred of Sin (*Works*, pp. 405-407)

   *Carmen*, subdivided into four "affections":

     Love (*Works*, pp. 407-409)

     Hope, the fourth visualization of the Passion, taken from St. Bernard (*Works*, p. 409-412; cf. *Legenda*, p. 230)

     Joy, subdivided into three points from the *Legenda:*

      1. The cross reconciles us to God (*Works*, pp. 413-414; cf. *Legenda*, p. 228)

      2. The cross overthrows Satan (*Works*, p. 414; cf. *Legenda*, p. 230)

      3. The cross erases the "handwriting" which records our sins, Col. 2:14 (*Works*, p. 415; cf. *Legenda*, pp. 230-231)

     Comfort, the fifth visualization of the Passion (*Works*, pp. 415-420)

   *Vae*, the sixth visualization of the Passion, ten comparisons between Christ's agonies and the pains of hell (*Works*, pp. 420-428)

The art of "marveling" which Fisher explains to his congregation in the exordium of the Passion sermon closely resembles the method of mental prayer he teaches Elizabeth. Like the devout person figured by the Hunter "buzied" in heart and mind, St. Francis provides an examplar for the congregation to imitate. Shutting out other "company," he converses with Christ in a single aspiration of ultimate significance. Though the devotional ideal descends from the Cistercian mystical tradition, the systematic way Fisher adapts the technique to busy laymen outside the cloister reflects the practical piety of Hilton and the *Devotio Moderna*.

Fisher's immediate source for the impulses of the new devotion is the famous passage in the *Paraclesis* which the Protestant Reformers cited to support their doctrine of *sola scriptura*. In a notable example of the art of imitation practiced by humanistic writers, he applies all the elements of the concept of study which Erasmus continually opposes to scholasticism to the study of the cross: the idea that a certain internal disposition of simplicity and faith is a prerequisite of Christian scholarship; that "fruitful" knowledge is the ultimate goal of *studium*; and that through diligent application both learned and unlearned can attain their level of perfection if the way is made "easy."

> Thus who that list with a meeke harte, and a true fayth, to muse and to maruayle of this most wonderfull booke (I say of the Crucifixe) hee shall come to more fruitefull knowledge, then many other which dayly studie vpon their common bookes (*Works,* p. 390; cf. *Paraclesis, LB,* V, 139F-140A).

> [This] lesson is so playne, and so common, that euerie man (be he neuer so simple,) may somewhat profite in it. And agayne, it is so hygh, that fewe can attayne to reach to the specyall fruite of it (*Works,* p. 391; cf. *Paraclesis, LB,* V, 140A-B).

> A man may easily say and thinke with himselfe (beholding in his hart the Image of the Crucifixe), who arte thou, and who am I. Thus euerie person both ryche and poore, may thinke, not onely in the church here, but in euery other place, and in hys businesse where about hee goeth. Thus the poore laborer maye thinke, when he is at plough earyng hys grounde, and when hee goeth to hys pastures to see hys Cattayle, or when hee is sittyng at home by hys fireside, or els when he lyeth in hys bed waking and can not sleepe. Likewyse the rich man may do in his businesse that concerneth him. And the poore women also in theyr businesse, when they be spinning of their rocks, or seruing of their pullen. The ryche weomen also in euerie lawfull occupation that they haue to doe. It is an easie thyng for any man or woman to make these two questions wyth them selfe (*Works,* pp. 391-392; cf. *Paraclesis, LB,* V, 140C).

The rest of the exordium develops the second of the six visualizations of the Passion in the sermon, an analogy between the crucifix and a book, the scroll in Ezechiel. The analogy is a variation of a favorite figure of medieval iconography, the Scroll of Charity or Testament of Christ which seals in blood the pledge of reconciliation with the father. The comparison has the same function as the composition of place in Jesuit meditation. The detailed correspondences between the crucifix and the binding, parchment, and letters of an open book fix the scene in the imagination throughout the course of lessons derived from it.

The three divisions in the body of the sermon come from the writings in the scroll, *Lamentationes, Carmen* (interpreted as a song of gladness rather than in its biblical sense as a dirge), and *Vae.* The first two members are subdivided to form a rising scale of emotions. Fear, shame, sorrow, and hatred of sin *(Lamentationes)* are replaced by love, hope, joy, and comfort *(Carmen)* through the alchemy of the cross. As each visualization of the cross makes the sinner more keenly aware of Christ's agony, the subdivisions of *Lamentationes* and *Carmen* systematically foster a more profound affective response to St. Francis' unaoidable question, "Quis tu et quis ego domine?" Through a sequence of biblical allusions to fallen women who have turned their faces from God in shame (Jer. 3:3, Ezra 9:6, John 8:3, Ezech. 16:8), the congregation is gradually led to identify itself with a second exemplar, Magdalene at the foot of the cross. In a movement which recalls Donne's

"Good friday. 1613, Riding Westard," the psychological climax is reached in the subdivision on hope, when the penitent can return (Jer. 3:1-3) and gaze on the image of the crucifix committed to the memory (*Works,* p. 411). Like the bitter scroll which turned to honey in Ezechiel's mouth, the book of the crucifix becomes increasingly sweet if it is "accepted" and consumed in the meditations of the first two members of the sermon. The two references to Ezechiel's book in the Apocalypse reinforced the analogy. Only the Lamb slain in sacrifice can open the enigmatic scroll containing the first series of seven visions (Apoc. 5:1-10). By contrast, the last member, *Vae,* on the tortures of hell, corresponds to the "little book" of Apoc. 10:10 which turned from sweetness to bitterness in John's belly because it contained God's judgment against the damned. Their "doom" is epitomized in the final text of the sermon which is ruminated in all its senses: Ps. 48:15, *Mors deposcet eos,* "death shall bee theyr continuall meate" (*Works,* p. 427).

In this sermon Fisher brings the medieval art of extracting the whole substance of the discourse from the scriptural implications of the initial text to consummate perfection.[15] As in Ignatian meditation, the reason strives to exhaust the significance of the biblical theme through logical analysis. Although he retains the intellectual precision of the scholastic sermon, Fisher simplifies the schematic development so that the overall structure is devotional, a juxtaposition of traditional "commonplaces" — "diverse melodies" of hope and dread. Thus the structure of the meditation for laymen closely approximates the sequence formed by the "Wayes to Perfect Religion" and the "Spirituall Consolation." After the exordium sets the scene with a striking analogy, the meditation proper mounts a scale of perfection divided exactly between a purgative half *(Lamentationes),* which inculcates "hatred of sin," and a "mystical" half *(Carmen),* in which the "honey" and "scent of life" hidden in the theme text is discovered in Christ's personal love for the sinner. The last member, *Vae,* is equivalent to the "Consolation" which Fisher advises Elizabeth to read periodically. By systematically reviewing the opposing commonplaces, the devout person "perfects religion."

Fisher's practical devotional method is "mystical" in a sense that can be applied to a tradition of mental prayer which remained part of the English consciousness from Walter Hilton to George Herbert. They felt that the interior life of all Christians followed the same path in cycles upward, refreshed by intimations of a friend "so sweet and pleasaunt, that the conversacion of him hath no bitternes (*Works,* p. 377). These cycles alternate, as in Herbert's *Temple,* around the bitter-sweet "Sacrifice" of the Good Friday service, and each visualization of the Scroll of Charity "dost anneal in glasse thy storie,/Making thy life to shine within" ("The Windows," 1. 6-7).[16] Toward the end of the *Temple,* Herbert's colloquies increasingly take the form of short aspirations like those which Fisher appends to "The Wayes to Perfect Religion" so that in her heart Elizabeth can "shortly pray what companie so euer you be amongest." The poem "Bitter-Sweet" distills the Cistercian tradition that inspired Fisher into a "compendious" prayer that any English "laborer maye thinke, when he is at plough earyng hys grounde."

> Ah my deare angrie Lord,
> Since thou dost love, yet strike;
> Cast down, yet help afford;
> Sure I will do the like.
>
> I will complain, yet praise;
> I will bewail, approve:
> And all my sowre-sweet dayes
> I will lament, and love.

Herbert and Fisher practiced the presence of Christ, attuning their lives to the *Horologium Sapientiae,* the fall and rise of the hourglass emblem of "Easter-Wings." As ministers they instructed their closest loved ones and their congregations in the "science" which Eternal Wisdom taught the Dying Man, "putte my passyone bitwix the and my dome" (*Seven Poyntes,* p. 364). This teaching is patterned into the "affliction-joy-affliction" sequences of the *Temple* and into the methodical structure of *Lamentationes, Carmen, et Vae,* and the Tower meditations. The Image of the Cross, fixed in the memory, effaces the "Spectacle" of death, as in the closing poems of the *Temple,* "The Forerunners," "Death," and "Dooms-Day." The practice of the presence of Christ, the "fruitfull business" of Herbert's "Employment I and II," transforms all time and space into the *Temple.* A man may best find "plesynge seruise" in the last hour when "there is no place to flee" (*Works,* p. 359, 1.35; *Seven Poyntes* p. 360, 1.38; p. 358, 1.43).

By its posthumous publication, the little book of spiritual exercises by the martyred Bishop of Rochester became part of Counter Reformation literature. In a quiet, devotional tone it surveys most of the doctrines and practices which were harshly defended and attacked in the period: the veneration of the crucifix, purgatory, the communion of saints, the value of the cloistered life, and the basic assumption that, like the saints of the Golden Legend who served as vivid exemplars, every man had sufficient freedom of the will to be able to perfect religion through good works of action and prayer.[17] Somewhat ironically,

Fisher's last book brought together two essentially gentle traditions available for spiritual renewal which did not temper the bitterness of either faction of the church: the affective spirituality of St. Bernard, St. Francis, Henry Suso, and Walter Hilton, and Erasmus' pacific "Philosophy of Christ."

Fisher's meditations have a greater affinity with the mystical temper of the Cistercian tradition than with the more ethical orientation of Erasmus' biblical humanism. There is a difference between a way to perfect religion which leads into "hourly" communion with Christ, and a *ratio vivendi* which teaches us how to "arrive at a mentality worthy of him." In Erasmus' devotional method, the mystical half of the *via* precedes the purgative half. The canons on the mystical sense of scripture in the first part of the *Enchiridion* anticipate the fuller revelation of the Divine Image in the central section of the book, which deals with the literal sense of the New Testament. Christ is the sole exemplar, the *scopus* which the down-to-earth rules of moral conduct in the prosaic second half of the book refer back to. After Erasmus opens the Silenus, the *Enchiridion* loses some of its interest, and one is not apt to reread the last sections with pleasure — a reaction which "The Wayes to Perfect Religion" or the *Temple* does not elicit.

The Cistercian technique of initiating meditation with a visual image, passed on by the spiritual exercises of the Counter Reformation, profoundly affected poets like Donne and Herbert. Here again there is an essential contrast with the biblical humanism of Erasmus, who stresses in the central section of the *Enchiridion* and again in the last sentences of the *Paraclesis* that the divine teachings of the New Testament reveal the complete Image of Christ. No painted likeness or relic, Erasmus warns, can "establish the mystery of the cross within your heart" as readily as his own words.[18] For Fisher and More, the crucifix, beheld inwardly in the Cistercian manner, is the *viaticum* for both the common man and the contemplative. Perhaps Fisher meant to emphasize this difference in attitude by his adaptation of Erasmus' *Exhortation to the Study of the Philosophy of Christ.* In any case, the elements of his spiritual temperament come together most characteristically when he opens St. Bernard's book for his congregation, with a muted echo of the irony Erasmus directed at the followers of Aristotle who inquire into the secrets of nature:

> And so by dyligent searche and inquisition, they came to great knowledge and cunning, which cunnyng men call Philosophie naturall. But there is another higher Philosophie which is aboue nature, which is also gotten with marueyling. And this is the verye Philosophie of Christian people (*Works,* pp. 388-389; cf. *LB,* V, 139B-E).

157

In the *Paraclesis* the Protestant Reformers found the proper emphasis on scriptural study as the path to Wisdom beyond the reaches of science. The devotion of the Counter Reformation maintained the customary ways to the "Philosophy of Christ," including meditation, or "marueyling" on the common images of tradition.

Despite significant differences, Cistercian and Erasmian spirituality both taught that an authentic religious experience is inward and totally transforming. Fisher chose Ezechiel's text for meditation, but he also understood Erasmus' favorite figure for the goals of a true theology:

> Among the human disciplines, different disciplines have different ends. With the rhetorician you are concerned to speak copiously and splendidly; with the dialectician to reason subtly and to entrap your adversary. Let this be your one and only end, perform only this vow, only this one thing, that you be changed, that you be seized, that you be breathed, that you be transformed into those things which you learn. Only then is the food of the mind useful, not if it remains in the memory or the stomach, but if it is conducted to the emotions and the very viscera of the mind.[19]

# NOTES

1. My references, cited hereafter in text, are to the edition of S.T.C. 10899, "A spirituall consolation . . . " in *The English Works of John Fisher*, ed. John E. B. Mayor, E.E.T.S., E.S., XXVII, 2nd ed. (London, 1935), pp. 349-428. The facts of publication are not known. The date suggested in the S.T.C. [1535?] seems unlikely. For another discussion of these works, see Edward Surtz, S.J., *The Works and Days of John Fisher* (Cambridge, Mass., 1967), pp. 373-383.
2. Walter J. Ong, S.J., *Ramus, Method, and the Decay of Dialogue* (Cambridge, Mass., 1958), pp. 231-232.
3. Trans. Donald B. King and H. David Rix, *Medieval Philosophical Texts in Translation*, No. 12 (Milwaukee, 1963), pp. 17-18; *De Copia*, I, ix, *LB*, I, 7B.
4. British Museum MS. Cott. Cleop. E. VI, fols. 168-68ᵛ; *Letters and papers, Foreign and Domestic of the Reign of Henry VIII, 1509-47*, ed. J. S. Brewer *et al.* (London, 1862-1910), VII, 1563 (p. 583).
5. For a complete English translation of the *Little Book of Eternal Wisdom*, see the *Exemplar: Life and Writings of Blessed Henry Suso, O.P.*, ed. Nicholas Heller and trans. Sister M. Ann Edward, O.P. (Dubuque, 1962), II, 6-127. For the Latin text of Suso's meditation on death, see the *Horologium Sapientiae*, ed. Josephus Strange (Cologne, 1861), pp. 155-169. Caxton's edition, ". . . seuene poyntes of trewe loue and wisdame . . . " is included in S.T.C. 3305 [The Book of Divers and ghostly matters]. The work is cited here as *Seven Poyntes*, and references are to K. Horstmann's edition of Caxton in *Anglia*, II (1888), 357-365. The meditation on death in Caxton is a close translation of the Latin. For information on the imitation and circulation of Suso's meditation, see Sister Mary Catherine O'Connor, *The Art of Dying Well: The Development of the Ars Moriendi* (New York, 1942), pp. 19-20, p. 173, n. 10.
6. *Scale of Perfection*, ed. Evelyn Underhill (London, 1923), I, xli (pp. 94-95). For other evidence that Fisher read Hilton closely, see my article, "Some Parallels Between Walter Hilton's *Scale of Perfection* and St. John Fisher's *Penitential Psalms*," *Moreana*, IX (Feb., 1966), 13-27.
7. The Introduction to Nicholas Harpsfield, *The Life and Death of Sir Thomas More*, ed. Elsie V. Hitchcock, E.E.T.S., O.S. CLXXXVI (London, 1932), cxxii.
8. *Enchiridion Militis Christiani*, *LB*, V, 1. *The Enchiridion of Erasmus*, trans. and ed. Raymond Himeleck (Bloomington, Indiana, 1963), p. 37. For a discussion of the etymological metaphor of "method" as a "way leading somewhere," see Ong (p. 255); Neal W. Gilbert, *Renaissance Concepts of Method* (New York, 1960), pp. 28-9, 107-108. See also *Ratio Verae Theologiae*, *LB*, V, 75C.
9. Sister Joan Marie Lechner, *Renaissance Concepts of the Commonplaces* (New York, 1962), pp. 143-145. See also Ong, pp. 119-120.
10. The *loci communes* were thought of both as "topics" of arguments and as "little orations," "speeches-within-a-speech" for the purpose of amplification or persuasion (Lechner, p. 3).
11. For a discussion of Ignatian meditation, see Louis L. Martz, *The Poetry of Meditation* (New Haven, 1954), pp. 25-43.
12. See the English translation in John C. Olin ed., *Christian Humanism and the Reformation* (New York, 1956), pp. 94-97. References to the Latin (*LB*, V, 139B-140C) are cited in text.
13. Jacobus de Voragine, *Legenda Aurea*, ed. Th. Graesse (Dresden, 1848), pp. 226-230. Cited in text as *Legenda*.

14. Pierre Pourrat, *Christian Spirituality,* trans. W. H. Mitchell *et al.,* II (London, 1924), 168-170; Etienne Gilson, *The Mystical Theology of Saint Bernard,* trans. A. H. C. Downes (New York, 1940), pp. 79-84.

15. Etienne Gilson, *Les Idées et les lettres* (Paris, 1932) pp. 113-114. See also R. W. Blench, *Preaching in the Late Fifteenth and Sixteenth Centuries: A Study of English Sermons 1450-c.1600* (Oxford, 1964), pp. 81-85.

16. Rosemond Tuve, *A Reading of George Herbert* (Chicago, 1952), p. 43. See the same author's *Allegorical Imagery: Some Medieval Books and Their Posterity* (Princeton, 1966), p. 163 and figures 42 and 43.

17. Father Surtz (p. 520, n. 9) draws attention to the parallel between Fisher's meditations and Luther's Tower Experience.

18. *Enchiridion Militis Christiani, Caput* VIII, *Canon* V, (*LB,* 31F-32B); Himeleck, pp. 112-113. Contrast More's view in *A Dialogue Concerning Heresies,* in *The English Works of Thomas More,* ed. W. E. Campbell *et al.* (London, 1927), II, 121F-G (pagination of the facsimile edition, *Complete Works,* Rastell, 1557).

19. *Ratio, LB,* V, 77B. This translation is by Richard McKeon, "Renaissance and Method in Philosophy," *Studies in the History of Ideas,* III (1935), 75.

159

# Prudentius and Sixteenth-Century Antiquarian Scholarship

*Robert W. Gaston*

During the sixteenth century the study of the early Church was established as one of the primary fields of historical scholarship.[1] The present essay is concerned with one aspect of this development: the use of literary sources for the clarification of archaeological evidence. Our focus will be the scholarly use made of the writings of Aurelius Prudentius (348-c. 405 A.D.). The Spanish born poet, who visited Rome towards the end of the fourth century, is one of the few ancient witnesses to leave us descriptions of catacombs and the cults of the martyrs buried in them.

The choice of Prudentius is not an arbitrary one. The first published account of the cemetery of the Giordani after its discovery in 1578 gave an eloquent appraisal of the poet's significance for the study of the catacombs. Cardinal Cesare Baronio, in the second volume of the monumental *Annales ecclesiastici,* printed in 1593, vividly recalled his impressions of entering the catacomb twelve years previously. He concluded with the observation that scholars like himself who had read about the catacombs in manuscripts of Prudentius and Jerome, or had seen the parts of the ancient cemeteries still exposed to view, were able immediately to understand what they could now see with their own eyes.[2]

Throughout the Middle Ages Prudentius had been the most widely read Christian Latin poet of the Roman period. His popularity from the fifth to the fourteenth century is evident not only in the several hundred surviving manuscripts of his works, but also in the number of references to him and quotations from his poems in medieval books. We still lack a satisfactory account of the reading of Prudentius in the Middle Ages. The philologists have been predominantly interested in the verbal imitation of Prudentius by later authors.[3] Also, philologists and art historians have understandably been preoccupied with the *psychomachia* theme,[4] which had an immensely fruitful afterlife in the art and literature of most European countries. Haskins and others have drawn attention to the use of Prudentius in medieval school curricula,[5] where he played a rather minor role in the study of grammar. Prudentius appeared quite frequently in the *libri manuales* and *florilegia* [6] from the Carolingian period onwards; however, he was clearly not regarded as an indispensable author for Christian education, as were Vergil, Ovid, and Statius.

But what happened to Prudentius during the Renaissance? Did he maintain his pre-eminence among the Christian poets, or did he fall by the wayside, a victim of changing tastes and priorities in literature? The humanist scholars of the fourteenth and early fifteenth centuries showed little enthusiasm for Prudentius or the other early Christian poets, Arator, Juvencus, Sedulius, and Paulinus of Nola. Sabbadini[7] demonstrated that the libraries of the leading humanists were nearly always stocked with patristic manuscripts as well as classical ones, though the Christian poets did not fare as well as the prose writers, the preference being for Augustine, Ambrose, Jerome, Lanctantius, and Gregory, and more rarely Tertullian, Salvian, Cyprian, and Orosius. Among the Greek fathers, Basil, John Chrysostom, Gregory Nazianzen, Gregory of Nyssa, and Eusebius were the most commonly read.[8] Although Petrarch owned a manuscript containing several works by Prudentius, he had scant interest in its contents.[9] Boccaccio admitted to an appreciation of Prudentius, Sedulius, Arator, and Juvencus, particularly because the first two had revealed sacred truth *sub tegumento*.[10]

In Prudentius' case the stumbling-block was his style. While it was granted that he was *lyrico insignis carmine,*[11] it was altogether exceptional in these years for his style to be called elegant.[12] This stylistic obstacle was to prove most embarrassing for the Christian humanists of the Renaissance. They were keen to disseminate the pedogogic content of Prudentius' religious poetry, but as scholars of grammar nourished on a diet of classical literature they were acutely aware of the anti-classical tendencies of Prudentius' Latin. Erasmus, for example, oscillated between two extremes in his attitude to Prudentius. It is unlikely that he had become acquainted with the poet while at school in Deventer, since he was there more than a decade before an edition of Prudentius was printed there (see below). After 1484 he moved to Steyn, where he entered the monastery of the Augustinian canons and remained until 1492. Béné proposes that Erasmus' renewed friendship in the monastery with his schoolfriend from Deventer, Cornelius Gerard, was the key event in his initial acceptance of Prudentius.[13] However, we still lack the proof. In any case, there is the prefatory letter to Erasmus' 1497 edition of the poems of Guillaume Hermans, in which he attacked the "modern versifiers" who chose as models Catullus, Tibullus, Propertius and Ovid, rather than St. Augustine, Paulinus of Nola, Prudentius, Juvencus, and even rather than David and Solomon, "as if they were ashamed of being Christians."[14] However, by 1519 Erasmus had modified his position. Now he disagreed with Latomus' recommendations that the obscene pagan poets be ousted by the early Christian poets. His reasons were clear enough: "as if one could profit any from Juvencus in the formation of one's style; or from Paulinus, who wrote only one or two poems; as if Prudentius could be read by anyone other than a theologian!"[15] Yet by 1528, when Froben printed Erasmus' *Ciceronianus* at Basel, the master was at least prepared to concede that he would much prefer one hymn by Prudentius to three books of Sannazaro.[16] Erasmus' change of heart had been signalled four years earlier in his edition of Ovid's *Elegies,* dedicated to the two children of Thomas More and including for their benefit two hymns by Prudentius on the Nativity and the Epiphany.[17]

In prescribing Prudentius for the religious edification of More's children, Erasmus had fallen into stride with a number of Christian educators in England and on the Continent. Dean Colet of St. Paul's had recommended Prudentius, along with Sedulius, Juvencus, Baptista Mantuanus, and Lactantius, for his school's Latin course as early as 1512, as examples of "good auctors suych as have the veray Romayne eliquence joyned withe wisdome."[18] This development had its beginnings around the turn of the century and is bound up with the printing of the first complete editions of Prudentius' works. We are much in need of a detailed study of the early editions of Prudentius; the existing catalogues of early editions of the poet are incomplete and tend to give a distorted picture of the geographical distribution of his works. Identifying even the *editio princeps* remains problematical since the contenders for this honour do not bear dates of publication. However, it is likely that the first collected edition is among the group of undated exemplars prepared by Rodolphus Langius and printed by Richard Paffroet at Deventer, all of which predate April 1498. They have been variously dated 1490-97.[19] There is no evidence for the existence of a Deventer edition of 1472.[20] The Deventer group were published without commentaries,[21] so we have little in the way of direct information about their origins.

We do know more, however, about Paffroet and the contemporary scene at Deventer. Rudolph of Langen, (died 1519) was a student of the Brethren of the Common Life at Deventer and eventually became provost of the house at Munster. A number of the early editors and commentators of Prudentius who were born north of the Alps — the list includes Langius, Agricola, Wimpfeling, Reuchlin, Celtis, and Erasmus — had either been schooled at Deventer or had some degree of contact with the Brethren of the Common Life and the Devotio Moderna.[22] The press managed by Paffroet and Jacobus de Breda at Deventer between 1477 and 1500 had the largest output among the Dutch and Belgian presses. The establishment had intimate connections with the Brethren, whose school seems to have been the major consumer of the predominantly theological and edificatory works chosen for printing.[23] It is probable that Prudentius was here first used as a schoolbook in printed form.

I

The intentions of the Christian humanists in "rediscovering" the early Christian poets are clearly expressed in the preface to Aldo Manuzio's collected edition of Prudentius (along with Prosper of Aquitaine and John Damascene) published at Venice in 1501.[24] Aldo mentions that his manuscript had come to him from Britain, "where it had remained hidden for eleven centuries." He had published the Christian poets as a substitute "for the lies and the books of the ancients," for the benefit of youth, "and to distinguish the true from the false," putting youth in touch with orthodox teaching and the virtues. "My intention was," he wrote, "to see these works in our schools, where the tender spirits of our youth are instructed, and brought into contact with pious men." He added to the volume a life of Prudentius, a brief but original study which became appended to most sixteenth-century editions of the complete works.[25]

If the humanist printer's claims to have brought Prudentius to light after a thousand years of darkness seem to us mere hyperbole, then we are in danger of overlooking the fact that genuine discoveries were made during these years in connection with Prudentius manuscripts. Not every Quattrocento library possessed manuscripts of Prudentius.[26]

Professor Kristeller's meticulous survey of Quattrocento library hold-ings has shown, on the other hand, that there may have been more copying of the poet's manuscripts in fifteenth-century Italy than one would have expected.[27] There are occasional hints of a lively interest in Prudentius manuscripts in the 1490's. In 1493 Matteo Bossi of Verona sent to Angelo Poliziano in Florence a manuscript in a pre-Caroline script which contained works by Ausonius and Prudentius. Later in the decade exploratory visits to the library at Bobbio and to libraries of the Milanese monasteries by Merula and Galbiate, and after them by Aulo Parrasio, uncovered other Prudentius manuscripts whose identity today is difficult to establish.[28] The discovery of new and sup-posedly better manuscripts of Prudentius continued throughout the sixteenth century, and nearly all of the subsequent editors in the North were able to amend the Aldine text (for better or for worse) with the help of a *codex antiquissimus.*[29]

It was in the North, and particularly in Germany during the first three decades of the sixteenth century, that a genuine learned enthusi-asm for Prudentius came to the fore. There is evidence that Prudentius was introduced into university curricula in Germany. Jacob Wimpfel-ing began his summer course of 1498 at the University of Heidelberg, where he was professor of rhetoric and poetry, with lectures on St. Jerome's letters and the poetry of Prudentius.[30] Petrus Mosellanus, in his jocular book, *Paedologia* (1518), completed an account of the com-ing semester's course at the University of Leipzig in these words:

> Lastly, a few books of Virgil's poems will be expounded, doubtless in order that this fine poet, as Augustine says, fixed in youthful minds, may remain throughout all life. In addition to these things, since it is not fitting that Christians should be all wrapped up in pagan books in these days when we are celebrating feasts, we should also hear the most splendid and solemn hymns of Aurelius Prudentius, that grave and saintly man, or if they are not satisfactory, the *Enchiridion militis Christiani* of Erasmus Roterdamus studiously commented on.[31]

Here was a thinly-veiled hint that Prudentius' style could be rather too turgid for a university literature course.

At Leipzig in 1499 Jacob Thanner printed a separate edition of the *Liber historiarum* which ran to two more editions in 1503 and 1505. Johannes Murmellius edited Prudentius' hymn on St. Romanus at Cologne in 1507, and in 1508 the hymn on St. Cassian was published there too. An edition of the *Cathemerinon,* prefaced with a letter from Petrus Mosellanus to Matthew Meyner on the educational merits of Prudentius, appeared at Leipzig in 1522. A decade later, from the same press of Nicolaus Faber, came the curious little book of poems by Prudentius and Virgil set to music (*Melodiae Prudentianae et in Virgilium magna ex parte nuper natae,* Lipsiae 1532 or 1533?). Presses at Augsburg, Erfurt, and Schlettstadt also printed Prudentius during these years, and there is a single edition of the *Hamartigenia* in folio which appeared at Nuremberg as early as 1475.[32]

Austrian and Swiss humanists also contributed their talents. Johann Cuspinian's earliest work was an edition of the *Cathemerinon* (Vienna 1494?);[33] another, including a preface by Agricola, was printed in 1515. A number of editions appeared at Basel after Sichard's of 1527. In the Low Countries we find a single printing of the *Psychomachia* at Zwolle of c. 1500, and several editions of the *opera* at Antwerp from the 1530's onward.[34] In France, the main centres of interest in Prudentius were Lyon, Paris, Poitiers, and Avignon.[35] In Spain, Antonio of Nebrija published editions at Logroño and Salamanca,[36] and his commentaries became integrated to later editions in the North. The *Peristephanon* was printed by Mathias Scharffenberg at Cracow in 1526.

Italy alone seems to have remained satisfied with the Aldine edition of 1501. Goldschmidt was right in suggesting that "the humanist tendencies of the Italian schoolmasters" were opposed to experiments introducing the post-classical poets to school curricula. Judging by his preface to Prudentius in the *Poetae Christiani,* Aldo Manuzio's pedagogic ideals were not far removed from those of the Northern humanists who championed Prudentius. In October 1502, Manuzio wrote to Johannes Reuchlin, sending him, among other books from his own press, "Prudentius the Christian poet, with some others written in Greek, and also Sedulius, with Juvencus and Arator . . . "[37] Reuchlin's Germany was to prove a more fertile soil.

Space will not permit further investigation of the widespread interest in Prudentius shown by Northern humanists and printers. I have noted additional material of importance in the writings of Joachim Vadian, Thomas Murner, Nikolaus Mameranus, the two Pirckheimers, Konrad Celtis, Amerbach, Aventinus, Theodore Poelman, Victor Ghisselinck, Laevinus Torrentius, and Petrus Nannius.[38]

## II

Concern for the historical information afforded by Prudentius' poems lagged far behind the textual developments. The humanist antiquarians of the fifteenth century had not been entirely unaware of the value (and limitations) of patristic writings in dealing with the intricacies of Roman monumental remains. Biondo Flavio produced a dazzling array of patristic texts in his disputes with Bartolomeo of Sassoferrato and Giacomo Tolomeo regarding the placement of the statues of SS. Peter and Paul along the new access-stairs to the Vatican basilica.[39] Cyriac of Ancona had sought out literary sources from the early Church to clarify the details of his journeys in the eastern Mediterranean.[40] But on the whole, the fifteenth-century scholars did not pause to gather the scattered passages in the fathers dealing with Roman topography and monuments[41] in order to substantiate or test the more familiar evidence in the classical authors. Cyriac of Ancona carefully wove into his narrative couplets from the classical poets bearing on topographical matters: where else could one find historical evidence expressed in such succinct and artistic form? Yet we will search in vain throughout the treatises of the fifteenth-century antiquarians — and even those writing directly on the monuments of the early Church in Rome — for a similar use of Prudentius.

The *Catalogus* of Trithemius provided scholars in the early sixteenth century with a moderately detailed biographical survey of the fathers of the Church. Trithemius' medieval predecessors had rarely devoted more than a sentence or two to Prudentius and the other Christian poets; nor were their brief notices always correct.[42] The first comprehensive, chronologically systematic history of the Church (at least of the first thirteen centuries) to be produced during the Reformation was the Magdeburg *Centuries.* Published between 1559 and 1574 at Basel and researched by a team of Lutheran scholars, the *Centuries* worked laboriously through the historical-biographical details of the developing Church, seizing upon Roman "errors" at every turn and propagating a Protestant viewpoint on major issues. There are few references to Prudentius in the seven folio volumes of the *Centuries.* The Roman martyr Lawrence is mentioned in *Cap.* XII of the third century: the authors quote Prudentius' hymn on the saint in its entirety. In *Cap.* X of the fourth century we find a brief sketch of Prudentius' life and works which includes selections from his poems on dogmatic issues, on the cult of the martyrs, and on the struggles against heretics. There is a note on the meaning of the *Dittochaeum* which acknowledges Aldo's 1501 edition as the source of information.[43] Here, then, Prudentius is examined primarily for the needs of the dogmatic historian, and Trithemius' bare account has been fleshed out to this end.

The most important antiquarian studies of the early sixteenth century do not use Prudentius as an historical witness. Andrea Fulvio (*Antiquitates Urbis,* 1527) and Giovanni Marliano (*Urbus Romae topographia,* 1534) do not mention him, although both use a range of patristic authors, and Fulvio has a brief chapter on the Roman cemeteries. Prudentius is also mysteriously absent from the writings of Conradus Brunus, one of the stalwarts of German Catholicism during these years. Prudentius does not appear either in his *De caeremoniis* (in which part of Lib. IV dealt with Christian burial customs) or in his *De imaginibus,* in which he cited Athanasius, Nilus, Eusebius, Gregory of Nyssa, John Chrysostom, and Basil.[44] Martin Luther himself was attracted to some of Prudentius' hymns, and included one in his *Christliche Geseng leteinisch und deutsch zum Begrebnis,* printed at Wittemberg in 1542.[45]

## III

Prudentius enters the main stream of antiquarian scholarship in the works of Onofrio Panvinio. Panvinio, who had devoted his early studies to Roman imperial history, was the first scholar to compose a separate treatise on the Roman cemeteries. While his acquaintance with the Roman catacombs was limited to the few accessible sites, his research into the literary evidence had the flavour of originality. In the *De ritu sepeliendi mortuos apud veteres christianos* of 1568, Panvinio used Cyprian, Ambrose, Eusebius, Augustine, Sozomen, Gregory, Gregory Nazianzen, Gregory of Tours, Tertullian, Origen, Chrysostom, Epiphanius, Basil, Jerome, Socrates, Damasus, Ignatius, John Damascene, Isidore, Rufinus, Gregory of Nyssa, and a range of Carolingian and later medieval writings touching on the subject. Three times he quoted Prudentius at length to illustrate early Christian burial customs. A decade earlier, in his *De civitate Romana,* Panvinio had drawn attention to Prudentius' valuable account of the Vestal Virgins' role in late-Roman state religions.[46]

In 1568 Johannes Molanus, theologian at the University of Louvain, published a revised edition of the ninth-century *Martyrologium* of Usuardus. In his text Usuardus had made four references to Prudentius in connection with the feasts of SS. Agnes, Vincent, and Hippolytus, three of the many saints and martyrs honoured with poems in the *Peristephanon.* Bede may have been the first to include Prudentius as a witness in a *martyrologium.* He was followed in this respect by Rabanus Maurus, and the short notices found their way into Usuardus' version. Molanus did not augment Prudentius' role in his edition of the text. However, two years later, in his *De picturis et imaginibus sacris,* Molanus demonstrated an easy familiarity with both Prudentius and Paulinus of Nola, quoting or citing Prudentius on the use of the sign of the cross on the forehead, on the existence of pictures of SS. Cassian and Hippolytus in the early Church, on the use of lamps in churches, and on the Magi.[47]

Molanus' *De picturis* had a profound impact on Cardinal Gabriele Paleotti, archbishop of Bologna, who addressed himself to the issue of sacred images in a lengthy discourse published in 1582. An original attempt to set out the Church's teaching on images for the benefit of his own diocese, Paleotti's *Discorso intorno alle imagini* was fully documented with patristic sources. Prudentius figured in two significant entries, one on the virtues and vices, and another where the source is not specified. This is in a discussion of decorum *(onestà)* in sacred art where Paleotti considers "Pitture fiere et orrende." He argues (Lib. II, cap. XXXV) that one of the rare cases in which gross cruelty is justified in religious painting is when the subject depicts the patient sufferings of the Christian martyrs:

> . . . daily we see the dreadful torments of the saints represented and, expressed in detail, the wheels, razors, iron hooks, fiery ovens, gridirons, racks, crosses and an infinite range of the cruellest tortures.

This catalogue of tortures betrays Paleotti's acquaintance with the *Peristephanon* of Prudentius.[48] Paolo Prodi has added another dimension to our understanding of this section of the *Discorso* in demonstrating Paleotti's close dependence on the ideas of the classicist and scientist Ulisse Aldrovandi. The Bolognese scholar maintained that the skilled painter should familiarize himself with the classifications of natural and man-made objects in consultation with experts like himself. While Paleotti's *Discorso* was in press, Aldrovandi composed a treatise for the archbishop on this subject, observing that:

> . . . the painter should converse with the most excellent anatomists and study carefully all the sections of the human body, both internal and external, so that he can know how to represent the heart, the liver, the spleen, the intestines, the stomach, the throat, the brain; so that when he happens to paint a martyrdom like that of S. Erasmus and others like it . . . he will be able to depict it in a natural manner.[49]

It would be surprising if Paleotti, his learned friends, and perhaps even the artists in the diocese who took commissions depicting scenes of early martyrdoms, were not aware of Prudentius' brutally realistic accounts of torn, burned, and broken bodies in the *Peristephanon*. Further research into the genesis of late sixteenth-century paintings depicting the deaths of martyrs to whom Prudentius dedicated hymns in the *Peristephanon* may throw light upon the origins, literary and otherwise, of the visceral, almost obscene realism which characterizes much of the religious painting of those years.

In 1588 Pompeo Ugonio published at Rome his *Historia delle Sta-*

*tioni di Roma,* dedicated to Sixtus V. In this work we encounter the first attempt to use fully Prudentius' information about the Roman churches of his day. Some examples will indicate the importance of Ugonio's contribution. In his discussion of the tribune of S. Sabina, Ugonio dealt with the numerous meanings of the term *tribunal* in antiquity, using Prudentius' *Perist.* XI, 225-26 to demonstrate how *tribunal* could mean a raised pulpit in an early Christian basilica.[50] In topographical matters Ugonio could use Prudentius to give his interpretations an aura of preciseness which, for the most part, eluded his predecessors. Here is his account of the exact location of the martyrdom of St. Lawrence:

> Those who have composed books on the antiquities of Rome, like Fulvio, Pomponio Leto, Biondo, Marliano and others, put the Baths of Olympiadis in this part of the Viminal hill. Having said this, following the writers of the Martyrdom of S. Lorenzo, they say that he was martyred in the aforesaid baths. This is then the place where the most illustrious and glorious saint was crowned in martyrdom . . . The Christian poet Prudentius indicated this place when naming the different parts of Rome where the holy Martyrs were massacred, and named there the Suburra, which as I have said, stood in this part of the Viminal hill, and he doubtless alludes to the martyrdom of S. Lorenzo.[51]

No scholar before Ugonio thought of comparing Prudentius' topographical notices on martyrdom with those preserved in the *Acts* of the Roman martyrs. Moreover, Ugonio seems to have been the first to adduce Prudentius' evidence on the location of the Suburra.[52] Ugonio's most brilliant application of Prudentius was in his description of the interior decoration of S. Paolo fuori le mura. Here, quoting *Perist.* XII, 49 ff., he used the text to elucidate two features of the decoration whose early date and character could only be explained by reference to Prudentius:[53]

> In the arches which span from one column to another in the central nave, and on the bottom and outside, the most beautiful foliage is worked in stucco on a green background, and perhaps that of which Prudentius spoke in the following verses: "Then [the emperor] covered the curves of the arches with splendid glass of different hues, like meadows that are bright with flowers in the spring."
> In some places the walls show signs of having had inlaid marble tablets. But the soffit was already covered with gold plate, as Prudentius also shows, when he says: "He laid plates on the beams so as to make all the light within golden like the sun's radiance at its rising."[54]

In the same year, 1588, Baronio published two works of astounding erudition: the first volume of the *Annales* and his revision of Molanus' edition of the *Martyrologium Romanum.* In their treatment of Prudentius' evidence, both works call for comparison with their earlier rivals, the Magdeburg *Centuries* and the 1568 *Martyrologium.* Baronio's works were immeasurably more systematic and thorough in their exploration of the patristic evidence. In the *Annales* the early Christian poets, especially Gregory Nazianzen and Prudentius, were used on a scale never before envisaged in historical research. In Tom. I alone, Baronio extracted a wider range of information from Prudentius than any previous writer. The poet was cited or quoted at length on the following issues: the types of animals present at the Nativity; the star of the Magi; the anointing of martyrs' bodies; the use of chrism in administering sacraments; exorcism; the effects of image prohibition in fourth-century Spain; paintings of martyrs Cassian and Hippolytus; the frequency of feasts for the saints; the use of musical instruments to accompany the singing of hymns; the martyrdom dates of SS. Peter and Paul; the place of Peter's crucifixion; Peter's inverted cross; Peter's burial in the Vatican area; prodigies in Nero's reign; the odious habits of Jews; the locations of martyrdoms under Domitian.[55] We may smile at Baronio's historical *naïveté* in reinforcing the New Testament accounts with evidence from fourth-century poets. We can be more in sympathy with his occasional forays into mature source-criticism, as in his demonstration (in Tom. II, Anno 229) that Prudentius had confused three separate men, each named Hippolytus, in his poetic tale of the martyr's death (*Perist.* XI).[56] In the first six tomes of the *Annales,* Baronio consistently used' Prudentius to substantiate arguments that he first proposed on the basis of other literary evidence. However, in the *Martyrologium* the poetic evidence of Prudentius was given a more autonomous role. Baronio ransacked Prudentius for passages bearing on the Roman calendar of martyrs, blending this evidence with selections from Damasus, Paulinus of Nola, Venantius Fortunatus and material from the prose writers, to produce a closely-woven tapestry of documentation.[57] In this rather specialized context, Prudentius and the other hagiographic poets came into their own as witnesses of Roman *consuetudo.*

Cardinal Baronio's researches constituted a watershed in patristic studies in the last years of the sixteenth century. In the field of Christian archaeology, activities were confined to the collection and examination of the evidence in the catacombs; a substantial summary of that evidence would only appear in print in Bosio's book of 1632-34. In the meantime, Antonio Gallonio published two studies at Rome in 1591 which gave Prudentius his due as leading witness to the hideous deaths of the early Christian martyrs. In his *Historia delle Sante Vergini Romane,* and particularly in the *Trattato degli instrumenti di martirio e delle varie maniere di martoriore,* Gallonio exploited Prudentius' evidence to the fullest extent, and in the latter work illustrated the text with a series of engravings showing the types of deaths suffered by the martyrs.[58] The engravings literally depict many of the episodes so vividly recounted by Prudentius, and it was fitting that they were chosen in the nineteenth century to accompany the Migne text of Prudentius' *opera*.

The culminating point of the developing interest in Prudentius among sixteenth-century antiquarians actually lay in Bosio's posthumous *Roma sotterranea*. Although Bosio's use of Prudentius deserves a lengthy study in itself, a few brief comments are appropriate here. First it must be pointed out that the editor, Giovanni Severano, considerably reduced the documentation of the manuscript for publication. Bosio had worked from a massive compilation of patristic evidence (now four folios in the Bibl. Vallicelliana) which, in De Rossi's words, contained all that was shown to Bosio's age for the study of the catacombs and their decoration. In the *Roma sotterranea* Prudentius was quoted repeatedly as an unimpeachable observer of the cult of the martyrs in its heyday. It would be difficult to find a passage in Prudentius touching on the martyrs, burial customs, and the cemeterial topography of Rome that was not quoted and assessed by Bosio in the light of other evidence.[59]

Prudentius was now firmly enshrined as a source for early Christian antiquarian studies. In Bosio's book and in the less-distinguished Latin translation by Aringhi (*Roma subterranea novissima*, 1651), the preliminary reports on the catacombs were carried all over Europe to scholars of all denominations. During the next three centuries the findings and conclusions of Bosio and his contemporaries would often be subjected to scrutiny and, in some cases, would be rejected in favour of new interpretations as archeological method became more scientific. Today we recognize Prudentius as one of the primary and indispensable sources for the study of early Christian archeology. It remains one of the major achievements of the sixteenth-century pioneers of Christian archeology to have searched deeply into the literature of the early Church and to have drawn out authors like Prudentius, who might otherwise have remained unfashionable curiosities.[60]

# NOTES

1. See the following studies on aspects of patrology in the Renaissance: C. Dejob, *De l'influence du Concile de Trente sur la littérature et les beaux-arts chez les peuples catholiques,* Paris 1884. P. O. Kristeller, "Augustine and the Early Renaissance," *Review of Religion,* VIII (1944), pp. 339-58. E. Wind, "The Revival of Origen," *Studies in Art and Literature for Belle da Costa Greene,* Princeton 1954, pp. 412-24. D. P. Walker, "Origène en France au début du

XVIᵉ siècle," *Courants religieux et humanisme à la fin du XVᵉ et au début du XVIᵉ siècle*, Paris 1959, pp. 101-19. S. L. Greenslade, *The English Reformers and the Fathers of the Church*, Oxford 1960. P. Fraenkel, *Testimonia Patrum. The Function of the Patristic Argument in the Theology of Philip Melanchthon* (Travaux d' Humanisme et Renaissance, XLVI) Geneva 1961. R. Peters, "The Use of the Fathers in the Reformation Handbook *Unio Dissidentium*," *Studia Patristica*, IX (Berlin 1966) pp. 570-77. Natalie Davis, "Gregory Nazianzen in the Service of Humanist Social Reform," *Renaissance Quarterly*, XX (1967) pp. 455-64. P. Petitmengen, "Le Codex Veronensis de saint Cyprien," *Revue des Etudes Latines*, XLVI (1968) pp. 330-78. A. Hufstader, "Lefèvre d'Etaples and the Magdalen," *Studies in the Renaissance*, XVI (1969) pp. 31-60.

2. *Annales ecclesiastici*, II, Rome 1594, p. 81; in the Lucca edition of 1738, pp. 117-18: further references are to this edition.

3. Still indispensable are the indices of M. Manitius, *Geschichte der lateinischen Literatur des Mittelalters*, I-III, Munich 1911-31. Also, E. B. Vest, *Prudentius in the Middle Ages*, (unpubl. Ph.D.) Harvard 1932, using Manitius' references but almost entirely concerned with *loci similes*. For the manuscripts, see J. Bergman, "De codicum Prudentianorum generibus et virtute," *Sitzungsberichte der Phil. — hist. Klasse der kaiserl. Akad. der Wiss. in Wien*, 157 (1908) Heft 5; M. Lavarenne, *Prudence* (Coll. Guillaume Budé) I, Paris 1951, Introduction. H. Silvestre, "Aperçu sur les commentaires carolingiens de Prudence," *Sacris Erudiri*, 9 (1957) pp. 50-75; A. Kurfess, s.v. "Prudentius," Pauly-Wissowa, *Realencyclopädie der klassischen Altertumswissenschaft*, XXIII, 1, 1957, esp. cols. 1068-70 on Prudentius' influence; recently, the edition of the *Carmina* by M. P. Cunningham, (Corpus Christianorum, Ser. Lat. 126) Turnholt 1966, with an up-to-date bibliography.

4. See C. Gnilka, *Studien zur Psychomachie des Prudentius* (Klassisch-Philologischen Studien, 27) Wiesbaden 1963.

5. C. H. Haskins, *The Renaissance of the Twelfth Century*, Cambridge, Mass. 1927, pp. 82, 113, 116. In Ruotger's *Life of Bruno*, archbishop of Cologne (late 10th-early 11th cent.), we hear that Bruno began his education in grammar with Prudentius (*M.G.H. SS.* IV, p. 256). E. Garin notes that Prudentius' so-called *Dittochaeum* (identified in the Middle Ages by the incipit *Eva columba*) was included in some collections of instruction texts in the scholastic period (*L'educazione in Europa 1400-1600*, Bari 1957, p. 72, note 45).

6. See Eva M. Sanford, "Classical Latin Authors in the Libri Manuales," *Transactions of the American Philological Association*, LV (1924) pp. 190-248. Prudentius appears 29 times in the 414 manuscripts described, but Sanford's list is neither detailed enough in the entries nor wide enough in scope to give a clear idea of Prudentius' role. Cf. also B. L. Ullman, "Tibullus in the mediaeval Florilegia," *Classical Philology*, XXIII (1928) pp. 128-74; G. Billanovich, " 'Veterum vestigia vatum' nei carmi dei preumanisti padovani," *Italia medioevale e umanistica*, 1 (1958) pp. 155-243, esp. 160. Among the highpoints in the scholarly use of Prudentius which require further attention are Bede's inclusion of him in his *De arte metrica*, perhaps his earliest appearance in a schoolbook; in the seventh century, Julian of Toledo's peculiar interest in Prudentius' *Dittochaeum*, then read as allegorical excerpts from Scripture; in the ninth century, Dungalus' application of proof-texts culled from superlative manuscripts of Prudentius and Paulinus of Nola, in his *Responsa* to bishop Claudius of Turin, an important episode in the western side of the iconoclastic controversy; and in the twelfth century, Prudentius' role in the *Libelli de lite*, whose polemically-slanted use of patristic proof-texts significantly prefigured the Reformation debates on *consuetudo*.

7. *Le scoperte dei codici latini e greci ne'secoli XIV e XV*, Florence 1905, and *Nuove ricerche col riassunto filologico dei due volumi*, Florence 1914.

8. See the illuminating study by E. F. Jacob, "Christian Humanism," in *Europe in the Late Middle Ages*, ed. J. R. Hale *et al.*, London 1965, pp. 437-65. The memoirs of Vespasiano da Bisticci indicate the continued and lively interest of his princely clients in patristic literature that was either rare or not easily accessible. The rediscovered writings of the fathers were given a new significance in religious education by scholars like Lefèvre d'Etaples. See E. F. Rice Jr., "The Humanist Idea of Christian Antiquity: Lefèvre d'Etaples and his Circle," *Studies in the Renaissance*, IX (1962) pp. 126-60.

9. P. de Nolhac, *Petrarque et l'humanisme*, Paris 1907, p. 103 on the manuscript, now Paris, Bibl. Nat. fonds lat. no. 8500; cf. pp. 210-11. On the Paris manuscript and related codices, see R. Weiss, "Ausonius in the Fourteenth Century," in *Classical Influences on European Culture A.D. 500-1500*, ed. R. R. Bolgar, Cambridge 1971, pp. 67-72.

10. *Genealogia deorum gentilium*, Lib. XIV, cap. XXII. (Ed. G. Ricci, Naples 1965, pp. 1056-58). The passage was quoted in Giovanni Dominici's *Lucula Noctis* of 1404; see Sabbadini, *Nuove ricerche*, p. 177. See also Salutati's letter to Dominici, in F. Novati, *Epistolario di Colluccio Salutati* (Fonti per la Storia d'Italia, Epist., Sec. XIV) Rome 1905, p. 232. Giovanni Colonna (born c. 1265) knew the *Psychomachia* and *Dittochaeum* (Sabbadini, *ibid.*, p. 55); Amplonius Ratinck (born c. 1365) owned a Prudentius codex, along with Sedulius and Prosper (*ibid.*, pp. 15-16).

11. As he was described by Nicola de Clemangis (born c. 1360); cited by Sabbadini, *ibid.*, p. 80.

12. Domenico de' Bandini (1335-1418) named only Prudentius as a Christian poet: (Sabbadini, *ibid.*, p. 185, note 36). Du Pin wrote at the end of the seventeenth century: *Prudentius* is no very good poet, he often useth harsh Expressions not reconcilable to the Purity of *Augustus's* Age (*Nouvelle bibliothèque des auteurs ecclésiastiques du premier au 17ᵉ siècle*, Paris 1690-1723, cited from the London translation of 1693, III, p. 5).

13. Ch. Béné, *Erasme et saint Augustin* (Travaux d'Humanisme et Renaissance, CIII) Geneva 1969, p. 47. Cf. C. Reedijk, *The Poems of Desiderius Erasmus*, Leiden 1956, p. 100.

14. See A. Renaudet, *Préreforme et humanisme à Paris pendant les premières guerres d'Italie 1494-1517*, Paris 1916, p. 278; the phrase "comme s'ils rougissaient d'être chrétiens" probably came to Erasmus from his reading of Gregory Nazianzen's *Discourses*, where the emperor Julian is described in similar terms.

15. Béné, *op. cit.*, p. 319.

16. A. Gambaro, *Desiderio Erasmo da Rotterdam, II Ciceroniano*, Brescia 1965, pp. 278-79.

17. E. E. Reynolds, *Thomas More and Erasmus*, London 1965, p. 137.

18. Quotation from E. W. Hunt, *Dean Colet and his Theology*, London 1956, p. 3; see A. M. Stowe, *English Grammar Schools in the Reign of Queen Elizabeth*, New York 1908, p. 109. Prudentius was prescribed as late as 1583 at Saint Bees school (p. 111).

19. The following provide incomplete lists of early editions: F. Didbin, *An Introduction to the Knowledge of Rare and Valuable Editions of the Greek and Latin Classics*, Vol. 2, 3rd ed., London 1808, pp. 180-83; A. Dressel, *Aurelii Prudentii . . . Carmina*, Leipzig 1860, p. XXV ff.; A. Palau y Dulcet, *Manual de librero Hispanoamericano*, XIV, Oxford/Barcelona 1962, pp. 237-40; E. P. Goldschmidt, *Medieval Texts and Their First Appearance in Print*, London 1943, p. 43. On the dating, see M. F. A. G. Campbell, *Annales de la typographie neérlandaise au XVe siècle*, The Hague 1874 ff., no. 1456; L. Polain, *Catalogue des livres imprimés au quinzième siècle des bibliothèques de Belgique*, III, Brussels 1932, no. 3263; A. Thurston and C. F. Bühler, *Check List of Fifteenth Century Printing in the Pierpont Morgan Library*, New York 1939, no. 13432; F. R. Goff, *Incunabula in American Libraries*, New York 1964, p. 509 ff. The only detailed study of the Deventer press known to the author does not consider the dating of the Prudentius editions: L. A. Sheppard, "Printing at Deventer in the Fifteenth Century," *The Library*, 4th Ser., XXIV (1944) pp. 101-19.

20. See J. A. Fabricius, *Bibliotheca Latina*, II, Venice 1728, p. 288, and the rebuttals of Dibdin and Dressel ( *loc. cit.*); J.-C. Margolin, *Erasme, Declamatio de pueris statim ac liberaliter instituendis*, Geneva 1966, p. 349, note 434, refers to such an edition.

21. In May 1493 Paffroet published the *Liber Cathemerinon* with an *Interpretatio* by Antonius Liber; see *Short-Title Catalogue of Books Printed in the Netherlands and Belgium . . . in the British Museum*, London 1965, p. 173.

22. However, one must acknowledge the tenuous nature of the evidence for the influence of the Brethren and the *Devotio* on these scholars. R. R. Post argues that of this group only Erasmus had "any contact of importance with the Devotio Moderna . . . Agricola, Wimpfeling and Mutian may also have absorbed a little influence from a distance" (*The Devotio Moderna*, Leiden 1968, pp. 10-12). On Langius, see Jöcher, *Allgemeines Gelehrten-Lexicon*, Leipzig 1750, *s.v.* Lange.

23. On the printing activities of the Brethren themselves, see E. F. Jacob, "The Brethren of the Common Life," in *Essays in the Conciliar Epoch*, 3rd rev. ed. Manchester 1963, pp. 121-38.

24. See A. Firmin-Didot, *Alde Manuce et l'hellénisme à Venise*, Paris 1875, p. 186 ff.; cf. P. Renouard, *Bibliographie des impressions et des oeuvres de Josse Badius Ascensius, Imprimeur et Humaniste, 1462-1535*, II, Paris 1908, p. 507, for comments by Badius Ascensius.

25. Sixteenth-Century scholars frequently used the account of Prudentius' works in the *Catalogus Scriptorum Ecclesiasticorum* of Johannes Trithemius, printed in 1494 and often reprinted (*Opera Historica*, Frankfurt 1601, p. 210 ff.); following Gennadius, Trithemius wrongly attributed to Prudentius a work *In hexameron lib. 6*, and even "epistolas . . . non paucas." Prudentius won a brief mention in G. I. Vossius' *De historicis latinis*, Lyon 1527, p. 190.

26. Prudentius does not appear in the 1411 inventory of the papal library at Avignon; however, only 648 of the 882 codices are actually described in the document. See Anneliese Maier, "Der Katalog der päpstlichen Bibliothek in Avignon vom Jahr 1411," *Archivum Historiae Pontificiae*, 1 (1963) pp. 97-178. Yet the catalogue of the same library for 1379 does list a manuscript containing Terence, Prudentius and Macrobius; see F. Simone, *Il rinascimento francese*, 2nd ed., Turin 1965, p. 17. Nor does Prudentius figure in the fifteenth century inventories of the Vatican Library; see E. Müntz and P. Fabre, *La bibliothèque du Vatican au XVe siècle d'après des documents inédits*, Paris 1887. Prudentius does appear in the catalogue of a private library in Cremona: G. Mainardi, "Due biblioteche private cremonesi del secolo XV," *Italia medioevale e umanistica*, 2 (1959) p. 450. He was listed in the 1470 inventory of Hieronymus Münzer's personal library (E. P. Goldschmidt, *Hieronymus Münzer und seine Bibliothek*, London 1938, p. 134); and later, to cite one of many examples, in both manuscript and printed form (the Aldine edition) in Fulvio Orsini's library (P. de Nolhac, *La bibliothèque de Fulvio Orsini*, Paris 1887, pp. 368, 388).

27. P. O. Kristeller, *Iter Italicum*, I, London/Leiden 1965, pp. 73, 157, 272, 412; Vol. II, 1967, pp. 128, 129, 197, 318, 326, 395, 490, 558. Also, Johannes Murmellius listed the following commentaries: "In Prudentiam Rudolphus Agricola, Hermannus Buschius Hadrianus Barlandus, Johannes Murmellius" (A. Bömer, *Des münsterischen Humanisten Johannes Murmellius De magistri et discipulorum officiis Epigrammatum liber*, Münster 1892, Heft V, p. 144).

28. Sabbadini, *Le scoperte dei codici*, p. 154, 159-60, 170; Weiss, *art. cit.*, pp. 69-70; G. Soranzo, *L'umanista canonico regolare lateranense Matteo Bossi di Verona (1472-1502)*, Padua 1965, p. 188.

29. See, for example, P. Lehmann's comments on Sichard's 1527 edition of Prudentius' *Opera*, in which he emended the Aldine text using a Strassburg manuscript, and derived his scholia "ex codicibus vetustioribus" (*Iohannes Sichardus und die von ihm benutzten Bibliotheken und Handschriften*, Munich 1911, p. 48ff. and 184).

30. See P. Adam, *L'humanisme à Selestat*, Schlettstadt 1962, p. 39; O. Herding, *Jacob Wimpfelings Adolescentia*, Munich 1965, pp. 71-72, 89, 314.

31. R. F. Seybolt, *Renaissance Student Life: The Paedologia of Petrus Mosellanus*, Chicago 1927, Dialogue 9, p. 29; the preceding part of the curriculum included Cicero, Quintilian and Terence.

32. For the German editions see Dressel, pp. XXVII-XXX; Palau y Dulcet, pp. 237-40; G. Bauch, *Geschichte der leipziger Frühhumanismus*, Leipzig 1889, p. 71 ff.; D. Reichling, *Johannes Murmellius*, Freiburg i. Br. 1880, pp. 64-65, 142-44. On the Augsburg *Psychomachia* printed by Oeglin in 1506, see Dressel, p. XXVII; Palau y Dulcet, p. 238. Goldschmidt, *Medieval Texts*, p. 43, notes the existence of a "single title" edition at Erfurt, but I have not seen another reference to one. On the Schlettstadt *Cathemerinon* published by Spiegel in 1520, see A. Horawitz and K. Hartfelder, *Briefwechsel des Beatus Rhenanus*, Leipzig 1886, pp. 221-22; cf. also on Prudentius pp. 18, 235, 607-8; E. König, *Konrad Peutingers Briefwechsel*, Munich 1923, pp. 214, 447. The Nuremberg edition is noted in W. A. Copinger, *Supplement to Hain's Repertorium Bibliographicum*, I, London 1895, no. 13437; Palau y Dulcet, p. 238; Goff, *op. cit.*, p. 510, for American copies.

33. H. Ankwicz von Kleehoven, *Documenta Cuspiniana*, Vienna 1957, pp. 90-91, for the dating 1494. On the Basel editions see Lehmann, *op. cit.*, p. 49; Dressel, pp. XXX-XXXI.

34. Palau y Dulcet, p. 237, lists editions of 1536, 1540, 1545, 1546, 1564, 1594.

35. See J. Baudrier, *Bibliographie Lyonnaise*, 7 Ser. Lyon/Paris 1908, pp. 8-9; 11 Ser. 1914, p. 487; Palau y Dulcet, pp.

237-38.
36. Dressel, pp. XXVIII-XIX; C. Haebler, *Bibliografia Iberica del Siglo XV*, New York 1903 ff., no. 599; J. Lycell, *Early Book Illumination in Spain*, London 1926, p. 286. On the influence of this edition in Spain, see D. W. McPheeters, *El Humanista español Alonso de Proaza*, Valencia 1961, p. 117 ff. On patristic studies in early 16th century Spain, and notes on the poets, see F. Rubio, "Don Juan de Castilla y el movimento humanístico de su reinado," *La Ciudad de Dios*, CLXVIII (1955) pp. 55-100; M. de Riquer, *L'humanisme Català* (1388-1494), Barcelona 1934, esp. pp. 14, 47, 57; C. Lynn, *A College Professor of the Renaissance. Lucio Marineo among the Spanish Humanists*, Chicago 1937, esp. pp. 178, 181 on Sedulius; Palau y Dulcet, p. 238.
37. See C. Dionisotti, "Aldo Manuzio umanista," *Lettere italiane*, 12 (1960) pp. 375-400, esp. 383; E. K. Quaranta, "La formazione culturale di Aldo Manuzio ed il suo criterio nella scelta dei testi," *Studi Bibliografici: Atti del Convegno dedicato alla storia del Libro Italiano nel V Centenario dell'introduzione dell'arte tipografico in Italia*, Florence 1967, pp. 147-58; also Firmin-Didot, *op. cit.*, p. 235.
38. See W. Naf, *Vadian und seine Stadt St. Gallen*, St. Gall 1944, pp. 208, 285; P. Lehmann, *Mittelalterliche Bibliothekskataloge Deutschlands und der Schweiz*, I, Munich 1918, p. 59 ff. P. Scherrer, *Thomas Murners Verhältnis zum Humanismus*, Basel 1929, p. 5. N. Didier, *Nikolaus Mameranus*, Freiburg 1915, pp. 213-14. A. Reimann, *Die alteren Pirckheimer*, Leipzig 1944, p. 117; J. Pfanner, *Briefe von, an und über Caritas Pirckheimer (aus den Jahren 1498-1530)*, Landshut 1966, p. 78. H. Rupprich, *Der Briefwechsel des Konrad Celtis*, Munich 1934, pp. 121, 527; Celtis owned a Prudentius manuscript and lent it to his friends: it is now Cod. Vind. 247, and is described by H. J. Hermann, *Die deutschen-romanischen Handschriften*, VIII, II Teil, Leipzig 1926, p. 33. Celtis signed the manuscript in 1507. A. Hartmann, *Die Amerbachkorrespondenz*, II (1514-1524) Basel 1943, no. 956, p. 469. J. Turmair, *Aventinus, kleinere historische und philologische Schriften*, Bd. I, Munich 1881, pp. 521, 545-49; Bd. VI, p. 79. On Poelman, see H. de Vocht, *Cornelii Valerii ab Auwater, Epistolae et Carmina*, Louvain 1957, p. 402. On Ghisselinck, see *ibid.*, p. 488, and H. de Vocht, *Literae virorum eruditorum ad Franciscum Craneveldum, 1522-1528*, Louvain 1928, pp. 543, 600-01. Marie Delcourt and J. Hoyoux, *Laevinus Torrentius Correspondance*, III, Paris 1954, p. 263. A. Polet, *Une gloire de l'Humanisme belge. Petrus Nannius (1500-1557)*, Louvain 1936, pp. 177-78.
39. B. Nogara, *Scritti inediti e rari di Biondo Flavio* (Studi e Testi, 48) Rome 1927, pp. 202-07; for patristic sources, see pp. 109, 153, 162, 167, 178 ff. In the *De Roma triumphante*, posthumously published at Basel, 1559, Biondo uses Augustine, Eusebius, Jerome, Ambrose, Cassiodorus and Chrysostom, but seems not to have known Prudentius' important evidence on the *vestales*, in the *Contra Symmachum*. R. Weiss noticed that Biondo "was too sharp to overlook the fact that Christian and medieval writers had also something to contribute." (*The Renaissance Discovery of Classical Antiquity*, Oxford 1969, p. 67).
40. *Kyriaci Anconitani Itinerarium*, Florence 1742, esp. pp. 3-4, 55, 66.
41. There are a few flashes of interest in the patristic evidence. Giovanni Cavallini used Lactantius and Isidore in his *Polhistoria de virtutibus et dotibus Romanorum* (R. Valentini and G. Zucchetti, *Codice topografico della città di Roma*, IV, Rome 1953, pp. 29-30, 43, 46, 54). In his *Descriptio urbis Romae* of 1430 Nicolo Signorili listed his sources, among them the two Christians Augustine and Orosius (*ibid.*, pp. 162-63). Cola di Rienzo appears to have been in some doubt as to whether the fifth crown for his coronation as Cavaliere should be of olive as Prudentius intimated (Ore columba refert ramum viriditatis olive/in gaudium pacis date), or of laurel, as Isidore (and the *Graphia aureae urbis*) had it; see A. Gabrelli, *Epistolario di Cola di Rienzo*, Rome 1890, p. 247; cf. Valentini-Zucchetti, III, p. 99.
42. See, for example, Ekhard's *Chronicon universale:* Anno 399. Huius tempore Claudianus et Prudentius poetae insignis habentur (*M.G.H. SS.*, VI, p. 134). Sigebert's *Chronica:* Anno 393. In Hispania Prudentius lyricus poeta claret. Anno 407. Prudentius quoque poeta luculento metrici operis libello blasphemias Simmachi refellit (*ibid.*, pp. 305-05). Conrad of Hirschau used Gennadius' account in his *Didascalon;* see Manitius, III, pp. 317-18; further examples in *M.G.H. SS.*, XXIII, p. 512; XXI, p. 128. John of God mistakenly speaks of "Prudencius Equitanensis," in his *Cronica: M.G.H. SS.*, XXI, p. 310.
43. On the genesis and method of the *Centuries*, see E. Feuter, *Geschichte der neueren Historiographie*, Munich/Berlin 1911, pp. 249-53. For Prudentius in the *Centuries*, see Cent. III, pp. 297-301, Cent. IV, pp. 1180, 1186-87.
44. *D. Conradi Bruni . . . De Caeremoniis Libri Sex*, in *D. Conradi Bruni . . . Opera Tria nunc primum aedita*, Mainz 1548, pp. 97-105. Nor does *Lib.* V, *cap.* II on church singing mention Prudentius.
45. See *Works of Martin Luther . . . The Philadelphia Edition*, 6, Philadelphia 1932, pp. 280-81; cf. *Table Talk* (same ed., 54, 1967, p. 147); also *D. Martin Luthers Werke, Kritische Gesamtausgabe* (Weimarer Ausgabe), 54, p. 34; cf. G. Sixt, "Eine Prudentiusübersetzung Adam Reissners (1471-1563)," *Blätter für Hymnologie*, VII (1889) pp. 170-73.
46. On Panvinio, see G. Ferretto, *Note storico-bibliografiche di archeologia cristiana*, Vatican City 1942, pp. 91-99. The *De ritu sepeliendi* was first printed at Cologne 1568; edited by G. Jogh, Frankfurt/Leipzig 1717 (this ed. cited here); see pp. 14-15, 16-17, 18. *Onuphrii Panvinii Civitas Romana*, Venice 1558, in J. G. Graevius, *Thesaurus antiquitatum romanarum*, Leiden 1694-99, I, cols. 230-31. Cf. also Panvinio's *De ecclesiis Christianorum, cap.* III, in Mai *Specilegium Romanum*, IX, Rome 1843, pp. 147-48, 150, 179; and the *De rebus antiquis . . . Basilicae Sancti Petri, Lib.* II (ibid., esp. pp. 226-27).
47. *Usuardi Martyrologium quo Romano Ecclesia ac permultae aliae utuntur . . . et Annotationibus*, Louvain 1568; see under Jan. 22, Feb. 30, Dec. 17. *De picturis et imaginibus sacris, liber unus*, Louvain 1570, pp. 23, 29, 63-4, 88; Molanus also used Paulinus of Nola extensively; a 2nd rev. ed. appeared in 1594. See esp. P. Prodi, "Ricerche sulla teorica delle arti figurative nella Riforma cattolica," *Archivio italiano per la Storia della Pietà*, 4 (1962) pp. 121-212, esp. 139-40.
48. See Paola Barocchi, *Trattati d'arte del Cinquecento fra Manierismo e Controriforma*, II, Bari 1961, pp. 417, 460. Cf. Prudentius' *Perist.* I, 55-57; III, 116-20, 144-50; IV, 137-38; V, 109-12, 206-08, 217-20; VI, 33; X, 108-10, 756-59.
49. See Prodi, p. 166 ff.
50. *Historia delle Stationi*, p. 8ᵛ.
51. *Ibid.*, p. 75ʳ.

52. For recent opinion on the ancient location of the Suburra see A. von Gerkan, "Zum Suburaproblem," *Rheinisches Museum für Philologie*, 96 (1953) p. 69 ff. Fifteenth century opinion is indexed in Valentini-Zucchetti, IV, p. 600.

53. See L. Martínez Fazio, "Un discutido testimonio de Prudencio sobre le ornamentación de la basilica ostiense en tiempos de Innocencio I," *Archivum Historiae Pontificiae*, 2 (1964) pp. 45-72.

54. Cf. also pp. 73ʳ, 88ʳ⁻ᵛ on the burial places of Peter and Paul, 174ʳ⁻ᵛ on the Temple of Roma on the Via Sacra, 227ᵛ-228ʳ, 229ʳ⁻ᵛ, 233ᵛ, 236ʳ all on St. Paul and his church.

55. Lucca ed. 1738: I, pp. 2, 12, 218, 228-29, 408, 458-59, 525, 575, 629-30, 635-37, 639, 676, 747; II, pp. 117-18, 125, 286, 474, 481; III, pp. 12, 93, 127, 147, 370, 455, 506 ff., 523, 524-25, 527, 532; IV, pp. 57, 67, 187; V, pp. 36, 48, 357-58, 553, 570, 577, 607-08; VI, pp. 49, 52, 92-93, 143, 149, 176, 180-81, 272, 435. In Tom. I Baronio also cited Paulinus of Nola on the dress of John the Baptist (p. 68), Juvencus on Judas' death (p. 141), Arator on Peter's miracles (p. 208), etc. He obviously thought the poets were close enough in time to the events to be cogent witnesses.

56. II, p. 481.

57. *Martyrologium Romanum ad Novam Kalendarii Rationem, et ecclesiasticae historiae veritatem restitutum;* a 3rd ed. appeared at Antwerp in 1589, and I cite the latter: on Prudentius, pp. 2, 4, 22, 37, 40, 42, 43, 54, 59, 104, 128, 136, 169, 196, 223, 250, 287, 328, 339, 347, 357, 378, 487, 510, 541.

58. See the *Historia*, p. 24, and the *Trattato*, pp. 34, 36, 37, 38, 45, 47, 62, 63, 83, 107.

59. See Bosio, *Roma sotterranea*, Pref., where Severano outlines his editorial approach; cf. G. B. De Rossi, *Roma sotterranea cristiana*, I, Rome 1864, p. 31 ff. De Rossi calls the Vallicelliana manuscript "questo stupendo tesoro di testi illustrante la sacra antichità." However, none of the patristic sources was as important to Bosio as the inscriptions from the catacombs which he discovered in his explorations. On Prudentius, see Bosio pp. 4, 6, 7-8, 10-14, 15-19, 22-23, 27, 45, 297, 398-99, 417, 477, 547, 601, 613, 629, 655.

60. I wish to thank Professor Charles Mitchell for his valuable criticism.

# Wyclif's Political Theory: A Century of Study

*Lowrie J. Daly, S.J.*

"**P**ROBABLY NO CHARACTER in English history has suffered such distortion at the hands of friend and foe as has that of John Wyclif."[1] These words of Dom David Knowles are true not only of judgments about Wyclif and his influence in general but also about those regarding his political theory and political importance. Nevertheless, during the past one hundred years there have been interesting developments in the evaluations of Wyclif's political theories and influence. This essay will try to show them by means of a brief survey of the important books and articles dealing with his political theory.

Back in 1873, C. V. Lechler's two-volume biography of John Wyclif initiated a movement towards a more historical presentation. Lechler felt that "his great works . . . the three books *De Civili Dominio,* his work *De Ecclesia* and others leave upon the reader the strongest impression of a warm patriotism — of a heart glowing with zeal for the dignity of the Crown, for the honour and weal of his native land, for the rights and constitutional liberty of the people,"[2] and he was of the opinion that Wyclif came into national prominence at the time of the Parliament of 1366, and he was sure that he was a member of the Parliament in 1376 or 1377. In taking this position Lechler had to give Wyclif some share in the Good Parliament of 1376; and as a consequence he was faced with the dilemma of admitting that he had acted openly against his patron, John of Gaunt, or that he was not a member of the majority group whose actions gave the assembly its popular name. In one of his relatively few passages about the political theory of Wyclif, Lechler noted that Wyclif denied the cogency of the argument of the "Two Swords" as "a leap from the literal sense to the spiritual." He pointed out that Wyclif extended the dominion of the State, and that he "recognizes, as attaching to the State, both a right and a duty even in the internal affairs of the Church."[3]

In 1884, Reginald Lane Poole published a brief but very significant essay on Wyclif's doctrine, in which he summarized the main principles of Wyclif's *De Divino Dominio,* which he was to edit some years later. Dominion, a habit of reasonable nature, is of the essence of nature, but God's dominion surpasses all other dominion. With regard to man's dominion, "no one in mortal sin has any right to any gift of God, while on the other hand every man standing in grace has not only a right to, but has in fact all the gifts of God."[4] Augustine had remarked that men who sinned were as nothing, and Wyclif went on to conclude that they had nothing. For possession, he reasoned, depends on a title, and that goes back to God's good pleasure; but God cannot be thought to approve their title; therefore they possess nothing. The wicked only share in outward membership; their possession is not really worthy of the name. In brief then: the righteous man has all things; the wicked has nothing, and what the wicked man seems to have, he has only by usurpation.

Dominion is founded on grace, and human ordinances are accidental or indifferent and a consequence of the Fall of man. Even if a people should select a ruler, it does not follow on that account that he is rightly their ruler. Although Wyclif prefers a monarchy, he does not clearly commit himself to choosing or following a hereditary principle. The reverse side of the dominion theory is the responsibility it involves of service to the subject. In this "we find the only check recognized by Wycliffe upon the action of kings: they have a responsibility not — we may infer from the tenour of his argument — to the people over whom they rule but to God from whom they derive their dominion."[5] Since all are lords and all servants of one another and God alone has dominion unqualified, then "all that we call property must belong in common to all." But the good man, he who alone has true dominion, who is truly lord of all things, cannot assert possession against civil right or disobey the civil ruler because he is wicked; no, God permits these things.

With regard to the source of these theories, Poole made clear in the appendix to his volume of *De Civili Dominio* Wyclif's dependence on Ralph Fitzralph, Archbishop of Armagh, by means of the partial translation of that author's *De Pauperie Salvatoris.* He also indicated its connection with feudalism: "For the most ideal scheme of polity conceived in the middle ages, and the furtherest removed from practical possibility, was also one modeled closely on the organization of feudalism. This is the Doctrine of Dominion suggested indeed by a previous English writer, but so appropriated and matured by John Wycliffe that he may be fairly considered its author."[6]

In this volume for the series "Epochs of Church History," some years later, Poole penned a judicious review of the main facts in the life of Wyclif and incorporated much of the political material from his own *Illustration of Medieval Thought and Learning.* He agreed with Gregory XI, who averred that some of Wyclif's principles were already contained and condemned in the work of Marsilius of Padua. He noted that "like Ockham, Wycliffe feels too strongly the necessary infirmity of all human institutions to be able to lay down any fixed scheme of government," and that he "suspects all principles almost in the same degree, the popular will, hereditary or elective monarchy and seems to give a grudging preference to monarchy of the hereditary class chiefly because it was the system under which he lived and which he found on the whole to work well."[7]

These essays of Poole were very influential writings and have largely determined the common opinion about Wyclif's political theory. Lechler had referred in generalities to Wyclif's patriotism, even to his zeal for the rights and constitutional liberty of the people, phrases which perhaps belong more to the nineteenth than to the fourteenth century. But in the writings of Poole one finds a clear grasp of Wyclif's dependence on Fitzralph and of the central importance of the concept of dominion to his theories, as well as a recognition that Wyclif gave only a cautious approval to hereditary monarchy. Poole saw the similarity of some of Wyclif's opinions to those of Marsilius of Padua, as had Gregory XI centuries before and also his Ockham-like scepticism of all human systems of government.

In 1896 something of a scholarly bombshell was dropped in Wycliffian circles with the appearance of a short article in English by the German historian, Johann Loserth, who contended that Wyclif's tract, the famous *Determinatio,* should be dated 1376-1377. He reasoned that Wyclif could not have propounded at the earlier date the type of argument contained in the tract; for instance, the proposition that every ecclesiastic, even the pope himself, can be compelled by the laity to the performance of his duty, would scarcely coincide with his own appeal to the pope. He pointed out that although parallel passages from the *De Dominio Divino* can be found for the first Lord's argument in the *Determinatio,* arguments of the others are only to be found in Wyclif's later works, *De Ecclesia* and *De Civili Dominio.* Loserth concluded that before 1376-1377, it is a "mistake to suppose that Wyclif . . . held any fully developed opinion in regard to questions of ecclesiastical politics." He further remarked that the words of the *Determinatio* suggest this: "If the possession of temporalities is burdensome to the church, they must be taken away from it. But whether the church at the present day is in such a case it is not my business to inquire; that must be left to politicians to determine."[8]

In 1899 appeared G. M. Trevelyan's *England in the Age of Wyclif.* He gives a brief sketch of Wyclif's treatise, *De Officio Regis,* which he characterizes as Erastian, and he noted that this implied "a daring proposal . . . for an English Church governed by the king and co-extensive with the State."[9]

In 1920 H. B. Workman, the authority probably most often quoted on Wyclif, published the article about him in Hasting's *Encyclopedia of Religion and Ethics,* and followed this, six years later, with a two-volume biography.[10] He dated Wyclif's entrance into politics at about 1372 and minimized his importance on the Bruges delegation. In his remarks about Wyclif's political theories he relied heavily upon Poole's work, again noting that Wyclif's doctrine would have led to anarchical consequences if he had not distinguished between dominion which belongs to the righteous man alone, and power which the wicked may have by God's permission. In the *De Officio Regis,* the "dignity of the king is immediately from God . . . and as God's vicar the king has supremacy over the clergy." "Episcopal jurisdiction is from the king and the king may inquire into all sins and must withdraw temporalities from those in sin and . . . even tyrants must be obeyed." "Henry VIII could have asked no more thoroughgoing defense of Erastianism or of the divine right of kings against the Church and pope than this treatise . . . Considered as a statesman, Wyclif was unfortunate in that there was no deep national movement with which he could ally himself."[11] His conception of the church was too Erastian, his claim for royal supremacy too absolute, and he made the church a mere department of the State.

In the volume *Social and Political Ideas of the Middle Ages,* F. J. C. Hearnshaw wrote the final chapter, "John Wycliffe and Divine Dominion." For him, Wyclif "was not an original thinker; he followed Plato in his exaltation of Ideas . . . Fitzralph in his theory of dominion . . . What was original in him was the intellectual fearlessness which he pushed premises to their logical conclusion."[12] Wyclif's ideal was a national State with a national Church subordinate to it, and Hearnshaw thought that his exaltation of the State and the ascription to it of sovereignty anticipated the *Prince* of Machiavelli, the *Republic* of

Bodin, the *Von Weltlicher Oberkeit* of Luther, and the *Leviathan* of Hobbes. Wycliff agreed with Augustine and the Fathers generally that the Fall of man caused the institution of the State, and in the actual sinfulness of the world Wyclif thought a strong monarchy was essential.

In 1932 C. H. McIlwain's important *Growth of Political Thought in the West* was published. It contains one of the few treatments of Wyclif written by a political theorist. Speaking of the doctrine of dominion, McIlwain wrote, "there is scarcely one significant point in it which had not already been elaborated again and again in writings resulting from the great controversy within or concerning the Franciscan order." He found an interesting indication of the growing spirit of nationalism in the decrying of Roman law; while the comparison of Wyclif's doctrine on dominion with that of Fitzralph shows how "little there was really new in Wycliffe's statements . . . though the practical inferences drawn from it are in many cases different from those of all his predecessors." In reviewing the content of the *De Officio Regis,* he states that for Wyclif the king "is vicar of God in temporal matters as the priest is in spiritual and he should put down rebellion . . . God Himself instituted both powers immediately and not in the sense that one of them should institute or authorize the other." Wyclif's views regarding the nature of the office of king are not different in any marked way from those generally current in his time.[13]

Here we may well pause and see where the research has led us so far. Loserth's dating of Wyclif's tract, the *Determinatio,* to 1376-1377 was influential in curtailing the extent of Wyclif's political activity timewise and bringing it into sharper focus. The writings of Workman, although at times tending to be more evangelical than historical, due perhaps to an overuse of historical imagination,[14] put before the reader a good deal of data hitherto scattered about. But he also restricted Wyclif's political activity and saw "anarchical possibilities" latent in the dominion theory unless very carefully distinguished, one might almost say distinguished away. The Erastian element of Wyclif's church-state doctrine was unhesitatingly admitted, and the patient acceptance or tyrannical rulers was noted. The lasting influence of Poole's conclusions upon subsequent writers (Erastianism, his dependence on Fitzralph) is evident even in the few quotations selected. However, the remark of McIlwain that Wyclif's ideas of kingship are not markedly different from those held by his contemporaries seems a clear departure from the view of Workman that Henry VIII could have found no better defender of Erastianism than Wyclif.

In 1936 appeared the final volume of the classic work of A. J. and R. W. Carlyle. The treatment of Wyclif's political doctrine is in their usual judicious and lucid style. Wyclif has the traditional medieval concept that coercive authority "was accepted by the custom and consent of the people as being approved by reason, for as St. Paul says in Romans xiii, 4 the ruler bears the sword not without a cause;" but though Civil law was instituted "by man on account of sin, it does . . . derive its authority from God;" and Wyclif decides that "it is better in view of man's sinful nature to be governed by kings." To the question whether man should obey a tyrant, Wyclif answers that it seems so.

In the *De Officio Regis,* they find that Wyclif again says that political authority was made necessary by sin and that monarchy is the best form of government. "He also set out in clear terms that the authority of the ruler is founded on the election of the community and that this was the case both in England and in other kingdoms." Thus far the position of Wyclif is ordinary, but when it comes to the extent of royal authority, he leaves the normal medieval position. Perverse rulers, too, have authority from God; hence, we must patiently submit to personal injuries; and, if the action is against God's law, we must resist to death but in patience. He who resists by force or fraud is guilty of a great sin. The king obeys the divine law in "compulsory subjection," but to his own law he owes "voluntary subjection." Still, there is no legal right in the community against the king."[15]

The Carlyles believe that Egidius Colonna (Giles of Rome) held a much more revolutionary doctrine on this matter of dominion than did Wyclif. Speaking of both Fitzralph's and Wyclif's theory of dominion, they maintain "that their conception . . . added little or nothing to the medieval theory of political authority and of private property, that is that neither of these belong to the state of innocence, but that they were the results of the fall and remedies for it." But "when we turn to the conception of the nature of this authority (political authority), we find that Wycliffe asserted that concept of the duty of absolute obedience to the prince and of the wickedness of resistance, which as we have often pointed out, was dogmatically stated by Gregory the Great but had practically disappeared in the Middle Ages . . ."[16]

In 1952 Joseph Dahmus published his study, *The Prosecution of John Wyclif* (New Haven, 1952). This book is one of the best studies so far written on Wyclif, but it is restricted to his relationships with ecclesiastical authorities. In 1954 a helpful and timely collection of readings was made available in the *Medieval Political Ideas* of Ewart Lewis (2 vols. New York, 1954). Wyclif is discussed under the heading of "Property and Lordship," and his dependence on Fitzralph is noted. Professor B. Wilkinson in the third volume of his extensive *Constitutional History* has clearly summarized several aspects of Wyclif's political theory and finds him an extremist in matters of religious reform but a moderate in politics. He was a cautious royalist with views probably similar to those of John of Gaunt. Wyclif believed in a king limited by feudal consent, but found that he had to adapt this concept to the growing national monarchy in whose times he lived.[17]

The article of T. J. Hanrahan, C. S. B. on "John Wyclif's Political Activity," is a fine piece of historical exposition, investigating the different reasons for the various dates of Wyclif's political activity. The author concludes that Wyclif's political career "started in 1374 in the field of diplomacy, was renewed in late 1376 with a great commotion in the pulpits of London [and] exploded into the fireworks of trials, charges and countercharges and considerable public disturbance." Wyclif took "his last fling at politics in the Gloucester Parliament of October 1378," where he defended the royal officers who had been excommunicated for violating the right of sanctuary in Westminster Abbey.[18]

In 1962 the author of this article published *The Political Theory of John Wyclif* based on the three works basic to an understanding of Wyclif's political theory, the *Tractatus de Officio Regis,* the *De Civili Dominio* and the *De Dominio Divino.* Limiting the discussion strictly to political theory, the author sees Wyclif as much more of an Augustinian than an Aristotelian and more of a theologian than a philosopher. The theory of dominion is central to all his political theory, while his conviction that civil dominion was sinful caused him to rule it out for clerical users. Wyclif in these works held the usual concept of one ecclesia in which there were two powers, the temporal and the spiritual; indeed the "interaction of the members of the two 'arms' of the ecclesia is very necessary for Wyclif's argument that the temporal lords can punish the evil-living clerics by confiscating their goods."[19] Wyclif's emphasis on the Gelasian formula of the two divinely ordained powers, one spiritual and the other temporal, was united to the medieval concept of a single *respublica christiana.* In advocating that the secular power take away the possessions of clerics who were suffering from an overdose of this world's goods, Wyclif based his argument on fraternal correction and the mutual aid that each part of the ecclesia owed to the other.

The discussion about a form of government finds Wyclif in the ideal order preferring aristocracy since it resembles more the state of innocence; in this state, as he envisions it, men would be ruled according to the laws of God by means of judges. But in the present sin-laden world monarchy is to be preferred, for civil rule needs an enforcer and God approved kings in the Old Testament. As to the type of monarchy, Wyclif devotes much space to arguments for and against both elective and hereditary monarchy, but seems cautiously to affirm that hereditary monarchy is "melius simpliciter." With regard to English nationalism, one finds that Wyclif has no hesitation in affirming that the kingdom of England is in no way subject to the emperor, because the emperor did not live as he should but acted against the religion of Christ by endowing and allowing a bad clergy, nor did he prevent his dominions from being despoiled, and besides England cannot be ruled by imperial authority since it is so far away.

Professor Kaminsky in a thought-provoking article, "Wyclifism as Ideology of Revolution," deals with various aspects of Wyclif's doctrines about the Church (which for Wyclif is the collectivity of the predestined to salvation), on the secular kingdom, the Law of Christ and the state, and the reduction of the civil order to the divine order. By depriving the status quo of the objective sanctity which earlier religious thought had allowed it and "by transvaluing every element of social and political reality into a constituent part of the church militant," Wyclif, he feels, pioneered an ideology of revolution.[20]

Edith C. Tatnall in a carefully documented article, "John Wyclif and *Ecclesia Anglicana*,"[21] shows how much English nationality Wyclif professed to find in the English church of his time. Investigating Wyclif's references to English law, the English kings, the early English church, and his selected examples of some later English bishops (Becket, Pecham, and Grosseteste), she finds that his use of such English sources provides strong evidence that he had a concept of a distinctly English ecclesiastical tradition. As Wyclif saw it, too many of his contemporary churchmen departed from it and he strove to call them back. To remedy the situation he constantly contended that the king and lay lords could take away the abused properties of the "Caesarian" clergy, and a good deal of his use of various English sources was to buttress that particular contention.

When one considers that a century has past since Lechler published his biography, a work which can be said to have begun a more historical approach to Wyclif, it may seem that only a few books have appeared since then dealing with his political theory. This is correct. Although the Wyclif bibliography is a relatively large one, there are not many books that discuss his political theory in depth, and this is unfortunately true of recent books as well as of the older ones. Probably one of the chief reasons for this may well be the Latinity of Wyclif himself. He is not easy to read, and he is both loquacious and repetitive. The declining percentage of younger medieval researchers able to use Latin easily may be another reason for a lack of interest in the various aspects of Wyclif's political theory. This is unfortunate because Wyclif is one of the few late scholastic writers whose works have been edited in such quantity with the earliest ones dating back to the 1880's, all due to the zeal of the Wyclif Society. Yet with all these original works lying at hand, the actual number of works which draw heavily upon such documentation is not large, and when we turn to those actually dealing with his political theory, the number dwindles even more.

Bearing these restrictions in mind, one can see some lines of development in the century of study that has past. The general effect has been some clarification of his doctrine and the reduction of the extent of his direct influence in the political arena. The latest article on his political influence, that of Hanrahan referred to above, begins his political career in 1374 with a more intense activity from 1376, and ends it as early as 1378. It has become more evident that Wyclif's influence depended much more on his authority as a theologian than on any political skill. As long as Wyclif was criticising evils of contemporary ecclesiastical life and customs and centered his attack upon the "Caesarian clergy," he found that he was far from being alone in the field. But when he began to expound what were considered erroneous or heretical theological doctrines, then his influence in political matters as well as his friendship with Gaunt both received serious shocks. This has been made clear by the writing of Dahmus, for instance.

When one evaluates recent opinions about his political theories, it seems evident that the results of the researches have been to place Wyclif more in the context of his own time and fit him in with the various contemporary political, philosophical, and theological trends. His position within late medieval scholasticism seems more clearly defined, and the conservatism in some of his viewpoints, which may come as somewhat of a surprise, seems plain enough. His position within the Augustinian school for many of his doctrinal themes has also been clarified. Whether Wyclif had a system or whether his "tracts for the times" represented a more scattered intellectual approach is still in controversy. The placing of Wyclif in his intellectual environment has been tremendously helped by the intensive research which has been devoted to scholasticism in the past few decades, but it must also be admitted that very much of this effort has concentrated on the thirteenth and early fourteenth century. The large number of works of fourteenth and fifteenth-century scholastic writers which are still in manuscript attest to the need for much further probing and offer rich research possibilities for those interested.

The theory of dominion is central to Wyclif's political philosophy even though it may seem somewhat fantistic to the modern mind. The essay of A. Qwynn, already referred to (n. 16), is a must for anyone who wishes to understand the background and development of this theory which was exploited in quite disparate ways by both Wyclif and Giles of Rome. Wyclif believed that civil dominion was involved with sin, and this was quite a sufficient reason for him to forbid it as far as clerics were concerned. Monarchy in the present world was the preferred form of government, but his espousal of the hereditary form was a rather cautious one. With regard to English nationalism Wyclif had no hesitation in affirming that the kingdom of England was in no way subject to the emperor, because the emperor had acted against the religion of Christ by endowing and permitting a bad clergy. Besides England was too far away from the imperial court to be ruled effectively anyway.

The Erastianism which several scholars have noted in Wyclif's approach is mitigated when placed within the context of the medieval concept of the *ecclesia* with its two powers, the spiritual and the temporal. The interaction of its two "arms" was a necessary foundation for Wyclif's argument that the temporal lords can and should punish the evil-living clerics by confiscating their goods. He was not unique in his constant and carping criticism of the "Caesarian" clergy; but until he openly advocated what was considered a heretical doctrine regarding the Eucharist, he was probably regarded in academic circles more as a brilliant, somewhat erratic, and sarcastically-critical theologian than as a dangerous heretic.

Some aspects of Wyclif's political theory still need investigation, and the following problems should be answered by careful comparisons with his various books, even though some of these books can only be dated approximately. For instance, how much in the years 1380-1384 did Wyclif deviate from the political theory to be found in his earlier works such as the *De Divino Dominio* or the *Tractatus de Officio Regis?* Again, how much did his developing anti-papalism actually affect his overall traditional concept of the medieval *ecclesia?* To what extent can these various later passages be reconciled with his earlier works, or are we to infer that in Wyclif there was an earlier and a later

186

political theorist? Despite the studies of the past these are problems whose answers would certainly help us today to gain a clearer picture of Wyclif's political theory and by means of this a deeper understanding of his entire doctrine both philosophical and theological.

# NOTES

1. David Knowles, *The Religious Orders in England* (Cambridge, 1955), II, 98.
2. G. V. Lechler, *Johann Wyclif und die Vorgeschichte der Reformation* (2 vols.; Leipzig, 1873); translated and abridged (by translator and author) by Peter Lorimer, *John Wyclif and His English Precursors* (2 vols.; London, 1878), I, 194-195.
3. *Ibid.,* II, 32, 82.
4. Reginald Lane Poole, *Illustrations of the History of Medieval Thought and Learning* (London, 1884). Quotation is taken from the second edition (1920), p. 255.
5. *Ibid.,* p. 261.
6. *Ibid.,* p. 247, note 1. It is interesting to note Bellarmine's remark, written centuries before, pointing out the same dependence: "De Ricardo Armachana . . . Consulat lector Thomam Valdensem, qui errores Armachani et Jo. Wiclefi, qui ab Armachano aliqua accepit, diligenter refutat; consulat etiam si placet, quae nos scripsimus lib. *de Monachis,* cap. 45, 46." *De Scriptoribus Ecclesiasticis, Opera Omnia* (Paris: Vives, 1891), XII, p. 459.
7. Reginald Lane Poole, *Wycliffe and Movements for Reform* (London, 1902; first published, 1889), p. 92. See the letter of Gregory XI to Sudbury and Courtenay, a translation of which is in J. H. Dahmus' *The Prosecution of John Wyclyf* (New Haven: Yale University Press, 1952), p. 39.
8. J. Loserth, "The Beginnings of Wyclif's Activity in Ecclesiastical Politics," *English Historical Review,* XI (April, 1896), 327.
9. G. M. Trevelyan, *England in the Age of Wyclif* (London, 1899), p. 98.
10. H. B. Workman, "Wyclif," *Encyclopaedia of Religion and Ethics,* ed. James Hastings, XII (1922), 812-23. *John Wyclif* (2 vols.; Oxford, 1926).
11. *Ibid.,* XII, 819. Workman had written earlier in a similar vein in his *Dawn of the Reformation* (London, 1901).
12. F. J. C. Hearnshaw, ed., *The Social and Political Ideas of Some Great Medieval Thinkers* (London, 1923), p. 200.
13. C. H. McIlwain, *The Growth of Political Thought in the West* (New York, 1932), pp. 315-317.
14. See the review of Workman's *John Wyclif* by J. P. Whitney in the *English Historical Review,* XLIV (1929), 466.
15. R. W. and A. J. Carlyle, *A History of Mediaeval Political Theory in the West* (6 vols.; London, 1903-1936), VI, 51-56.
16. *Ibid.,* 61-62. In A. Qwynn, *The English Austin Friars in the Time of Wyclif* (Oxford, 1940), there is an excellent chapter on "The Augustinian Theory of Lordship and Grace." Although he does not treat Wyclif's political theory to any extent, Dom David Knowles in his volumes on the religious orders in England gives an excellent summary of Wyclif's part in the earlier disputes between the mendicants and possessioners and his later controversies with orthodox theologians in general (*The Religious Orders in England* [3 vols.; Cambridge, 1948-1959], II, chiefly 67-73, 88-89, 94-95, 98-111).
17. *Constitutional History of Medieval England 1216-1399,* (3 vols.; London, 1948-1958), III, 92-94.
18. *Mediaeval Studies,* XX (1959), 162.
19. L. J. Daly, *The Political Theory of John Wyclif* (Chicago, 1962), p. 82.
20. *Church History,* XXXII (March, 1963), 57-74.
21. *Journal of Ecclesiastical History,* XX (April, 1969), 19-43.

# Classical and Medieval Rhetoric: Three Recent Studies

*John Conley*

George Kennedy, *The Art of Rhetoric in the Roman World, 300 B.C.-A.D. 300.* Princeton, New Jersey: Princeton University Press, 1972. Pp. xvi, 658. $18.50.

James J. Murphy, ed. *Three Medieval Rhetorical Arts.* Berkeley, Los Angeles, and London: University of California Press, 1971. Pp. xxiii, 235. $7.50.

James J. Murphy, comp. *Medieval Rhetoric: A Select Bibliography* with a preface by John Leyerle. Toronto: University of Toronto Press, 1971. Paper. Pp. xvi, 100. $4.95.

WRITTEN TO SUPERSEDE M. L. Clarke's *Rhetoric at Rome* (1953), *The Art of Rhetoric in the Roman World* is a comprehensive work, the second volume of a projected three-volume history of rhetoric. One of the virtues of this study is its emphasis on the prestige of speech among the Romans, who "were taught to regard" it "as the noblest human act" (p. 307). In general Professor Kennedy's interpretation follows the standard one: rhetoric was gradually perverted to sophistic. Or in his words: "My basic theme is that the Romans imitated from the Greeks an art of persuasion which gradually developed into an art often more concerned with what I call the secondary characteristics of rhetoric: not persuasion, but style and artistic effect" (p. xv). Contrary to the implication of another prefatory statement, what Professor Kennedy stresses when treating the period of the principate is not the "effort made by a number of writers to recover some of the powers of persuasion" lost at the battle of Actium but, rather, the deplorable dominance of recitation and declamation.

To adapt Professor Kennedy's comment on "Augustanism" (p. 404), *The Art of Rhetoric in the Roman World* is "probably worth the effort." Although intended for "students of classics and speech," it will also be valuable to scholars because of the ample documentation and the detailed discussions, sometimes disproportionate, of various standard questions, such as the date and authorship of the *Rhetorica ad Herennium,* known in the Middle Ages by alternate titles, the *Rhetorica secunda* and, later, the *Rhetorica nova.* To this discussion, as to others, Professor Kennedy offers his own carefully argued solution.

Unfortunately, however, he dislikes rhetoric except in the forms of deliberative and forensic oratory, and even here he is not much interested in technique, which he identifies with the "rules" and hence academicism, though he himself is a prominent academic. Though he refers, for example, to the famous reply of Demosthenes — "Delivery" — "when asked what was first, second, and third most important in speaking" (p. 122), when treating delivery in the *Ad Herennium,* which contains some memorable precepts and observations concerning this matter, Professor Kennedy is perfunctory and censorious, remarking that "the whole account . . . is rather pedantic and like some of the other additions to rhetoric bears the stamp of the schoolmaster" (pp. 122-23). In fact, one of the defects of this study is the inadequate treatment of delivery; as in the instance of the *Ad Herennium,* little use is made of the material on this topic in Quintilian, and no use is made of the material in Marcus Aurelius, who describes "how he himself had declaimed Fronto's speech *[On Foreign Wills]* (with appropriate gestures) to the Emperor Antoninus Pius" (p. 595).

I have noted two extraordinary statements. A perverted conception of rhetoric "continually lurked in the subconscious of even the noblest rhetoricians and orators" (p. 641). Such anachronism accords with the romantic statement that Quintilian "wants to produce a natural style, he wants a speech to grow naturally and organically" (p. 499).

As a rhetorician Professor Kennedy is proficient in *dispositio* but weak in *elocutio.* His favorite rhetorical device, which readers may find bruising, is *exclamatio* (two examples occur on p. 199). Journalese is not shunned: "spell out" (p. 227), "along the lines of" (p. 234), "political football" (p. 11), "thought control" (p. 427), "philosophy of disengagement" (p. 405), "entered into the picture" (p. 502), and "lurid-minded" (p. 271). In practice Professor Kennedy is indeed no purist: we find "masterful" in the sense of *masterly* (p. 524), "rather unique" (p. 502), "skilled at" (p. 55), "very interested" (p. 485), and "humanist" in the sense of one concerned with "the whole man" (p. 498).

The second study under review, *Three Medieval Rhetorical Arts,* edited by James J. Murphy, presents the following treatises: Anonymous of Bologna's *The Principles of Letter-Writing (Rationes dictandi,* 1087), translated by the editor; Geoffrey of Vinsauf's *The New Poetics (Poetria nova,* c. 1210), translated by Jane Baltzell Kopp, and Robert of Basevorn's *The Form of Preaching (Forma praedicandi,* 1322), translated by Leopold Krul, O.S.B. Because of the importance of Aristotle's *Topics* and *On Sophistical Refutations* as textbooks in the Middle Ages for "the training in language" afforded by "the university course in dialectica," excerpts from these works are included in an appendix. There is also a selected bibliography. In the introduction the editor, a well-known American scholar of rhetoric in the Middle Ages, outlines what he calls the "Western preceptive tradition" of rhetoric. "The basic principle of medieval rhetoric," he observes, "is a frank pragmatism, making a highly-selective use of ideas from the past for the needs of the present" (p. xiv).

This collection is obviously useful but less so than one would reasonably anticipate. The present translation of the *Poetria nova* is the third one in print; the first one, which the editor elsewhere describes as "good," has been available, in paperback, since 1967. Meanwhile, we lack, for example, a translation of Matthew of Vendôme's *Ars versificatoria* (a. 1175) though I understand that one is making the rounds. As for *The Principles of Letter-Writing* and *The Form of Preaching,* neither seems altogether suitable as an introduction, for the modern reader, to the respective arts. Apparently the former was chosen because it is short and also because it "was the first" such treatise "to set forth what became the standard medieval doctrine of five parts for a letter" (p. xvi). It contains no assortment of model letters, and the treatment of the five parts is very brief except for the salutation, which is inordinately long. On this point we have the unhelpful editorial comment that "the length of the treatment is of course further indication of the important [sic] attached to Salutations" (p. 4). The kind of comment needed in this instance is one on the importance in *dictamen* of one of the offices of rhetoric, persuasion (see *Principles of Letter-Writing,* p. 17 of *Three . . . Arts*). *The Form of Preaching,* a work of virtuosity, has an interlaced structure featuring a list of twenty-two ornaments. Again the intended reader may be put off. Yet in the same collection from which the text of the *Forma praedicandi* was taken — *Artes Praedicandi* by Th.-M. Charland, O.P. — there is a straightforward treatise, *De modo componendi sermones* by Thomas of Waleys. Strictly speaking, the work is unfinished, but nothing essential is lacking. Concerning Professor Murphy's collection one infers, indeed, that it was not so much planned as assembled. For the translations of the *Poetria nova* and the *Forma praedicandi* derive from doctoral dissertations; they were available, in other words.

Though there are examples of questionable phrasing, I have not noted any errors in Professor Murphy's translation, *The Principles of Letter-Writing.* Mrs. Kopp's translation of the *Poetria nova* contains a few errors. Three of these also occurred in Margaret F. Nims's translation and were pointed out by A. Brian Scott in a review (*Medium Aevum,* XXXVIII [1969], 189). They concern "in studio" (Faral, line 442, and *Three . . . Arts,* p. 49); "imago prioris" (Faral, 1362 but actually 1367, and *Three . . . Arts,* p. 82); "voluit" (Faral, 1448/1453, and *Three . . . Arts,* p. 84). "Praemetitur" (Faral, 45) is construed as passive (p. 34); "adhuc" (Faral, 440) is rendered as "still" (p. 49); and "ostia" (Faral, 1363/1368) is rendered as "gates" (p. 82). The translation of *The Form of Preaching,* by Father Krul, tends to be mechanical. Thus "discretio" is translated as "discretion" (p. 179), and "genus" is translated simply as "genus" (p. 164) in a passage that, like many other passages in this work, calls for a note. "Casus" is duly translated as "case" (p. 163), but the reading is plainly corrupt; "status" is presumably meant. On p. 129, line 15, *precept* is preferable to "reason." As already indicated, the notes on *The Form of Preaching* are generally inadequate.

Except for the section containing *The New Poetics,* which was apparently proofread by the translator, misprints abound in *Three Medieval Rhetorical Arts.*

*Medieval Rhetoric: A Select Bibliography,* compiled by James J. Murphy, belongs to a series of medieval bibliographies being published by the University of Toronto Press and edited by John Leyerle. Every student or scholar of medieval studies will be grateful for this bibliography, which is much needed. Once gratitude subsides, one will of course be critical of various omissions pertaining to one's special interests. Ernest Gallo's valuable study of *The Poetria Nova and Its Sources in Early Rhetorical Doctrine* (Mouton: The Hague, 1971) is missing, though it was accepted as a doctoral dissertation in 1965. Karl Young's important article on "Chaucer and Geoffrey of Vinsauf" is also missing, as if hopelessly discredited (*Modern Philology,* XLII [1943-44], 172-82; the compiler refers to it in *Three Medieval Rhetorical Arts,* p. 29, with the author's first name given as "Earl" and the volume number as "XLI"). There is no reference to Nicolaus Dybinus (Tybinus) despite Karel Doskočil's study, *Mistr Dybin, retor doby Karlovy* (Prague, 1948). Again, though the cut-off date of the bibliography is unclear, one wonders why Harry Caplan's "Memoria: Treasure-House of Eloquence," in *Of Eloquence* (1970) is not listed, especially since the compiler's *Three Medieval Rhetorical Arts,* which was published a year later, turns up. The inclusion of the *artes poetriae* under grammar *(ars grammatica)* reflects the compiler's well-known polemics against "the cult of Vinsauf." In a few instances reviews are cited; why not regularly? Richard McKeon's review of J. W. H. Atkins' *English Literary Criticism: The Medieval Phase* (listed on p. 49 and in "A Basic Library," p. 87) is one that should have been included (*Modern Philology,* XLII [1944-45], 59-60). The date of *Studies in Rhetoric and Public Speaking in Honor of James Albert Winans* (p. 78) is 1925, not 1962. But enough: a salute to the compiler!

# Mimesis and Persuasion From Aristotle Through the Eighteenth Century: Some Recent Studies

*P. Albert Duhamel*

John D. Boyd, S.J. *The Function of Mimesis and Its Decline.* Cambridge, Mass.: Harvard University Press, 1968. Pp. 317. $7.50.

Russell Fraser. *The War Against Poetry.* Princeton: Princeton University Press, 1970. Pp. 215. $7.50.

Annabel M. Patterson. *Hermogenes and the Renaissance.* Princeton: Princeton University Press, 1970, Pp. 240. $10.00.

Ａ S LONG AS critics, both *periti* and *virtuosi,* continued to concur in Hamlet's belief that man could be "the paragon of animals," and Lear's confession that "pomp" must share its "superflux" with "looped and windowed raggedness" to "show the Heavens more just," so long could all men agree with Hamlet's reminder to the players that "the purpose of playing, whose end, both at first and now, was and is, to hold as 'twere the mirror up to Nature" (III, ii, 23-25). But, as Father Boyd demonstrates in *The Function of Mimesis and Its Decline* — almost with "overkill," the relationship between the conception of the function of imitation as the nature of art and the definition of the nature of man are so closely inter-related that any identification of man with the "quintessence of dust" must necessarily imply a demeaning of the function of art. The best proof is his interpretation of what happened to the conception of mimesis from its magisterial formulation by Aristotle down through the decline of its hegemony in eighteenth-century England. His approach is not philosophic because many of the critics he must include in his discussion were not systematic philosophers, but rather "noetic," explaining their concepts "against the background of the general psychological and cultural orientation of the critic's thought and of his age" (p. 3).

Though Renaissance critics never went beyond thinking of art as imitation, in some form or other, they represented a wide range of opinion about the purpose to be realized by imitation. According to Russell Fraser, in *The War Against Poetry,* the humanist justified the imitation of poetry as "an ethical discipline." In these terms, poetry could be considered useful, and "utility, very amply construed," became "the master motive informing the judgment of poetry and the theatre" (p. 5). It was this useful function of mimesis which Hamlet seemingly had in mind when he reminded the players that the purpose of drama was "to show virtue her own feature, scorn her own image, and the very age and body of the time its form and pressure" (*loc. cit.* 24-27). But, as Professor Fraser shows with wit and stunning choice of quotation from countless, contemporary sources, as the seventeenth century developed, the demand became increasingly strident that this imitation be practical, pointed and pertinent. To wring the most out of Hamlet's advice to the players, the play was not "to make the unskilful laugh," which would have made "the judicious grieve," and it was their censure which, in the allowance of the players, must "o'erweigh a whole theatre of others" (*loc. cit.* 27-31).

By the middle decades of the seventeenth century, "the Puritan . . . the devotee of naked truth, who refuses the bone for the marrow, who wants the kernel and is discontent with the shell" felt sufficiently in control that he could suppress the representations of secondary manifestations, the plays in the theatres, in favor of the encouragement of the study of primary manifestations, the scientific study of nature. So, in a sense, "Modern science enters Oxford in the train of the New Model Army" (p. 172). The increasingly pragmatic definition of mimesis, as a corollary of an increasing commitment to science, was one of the most important reasons, according to Father Boyd, for the decline in the vitality of the concept of art as imitation. With the passing of the humanist's and the Schoolman's metempirical view of nature, the concept of mimesis was increasingly little understood. "The old world passed with Newton" (p. 86) and with it the proper understanding of the concept of the function of imitation.

As he views the history of criticism from Aristotle to Sam Johnson, "Opinions," about the function of mimesis, can "be found to vary within the polarity of autonomous, pleasurable contemplation outlined by Aristotle and the notion of pleasure as a means of persuasion espoused by the far greater majority of the critics studied" (p. x.). His own concern is almost exclusively the coherent, detailed explication of the Aristotelian position of disinterested contemplation as the function of mimesis, and he refers to what might be considered its antithesis, the identification of the function of imitation with persuasion usually only as an explanation of the dialectic which developed between the two extremes. A consideration of one of the strong forces which made for the identification of the function of imitation with persuasion is to be found in Annabel M. Patterson's *Hermogenes and the Renaissance.* "The main concern," of this long-needed study of the second century A.D. Greek rhetorician's definition of different styles, "is to define the scope and influence of Hermogenic Ideas on the European Renaissance, and to show that they filled a great gap in the art, not of Invention, but of Persuasion" (p. 6). The two books thus tend to supplement each other, with Father Boyd's concentrating on a tradition which viewed the product of imitation as "an autonomously meaningful structure," and Mrs. Patterson's on another where the function of poetry, in the largest sense, is "more rhetorically conceived" and viewed "as an instrument for molding opinion or moving an audience to action" (Boyd, p. x.).

So these three recently published books, though never intended to be mutually complementary, do, when taken together, provide a detailed, convincing demonstration of the inter-relatedness of the definition of the nature of imitation with the conception of the nature of man and the implications of stressing either the cognitive or pragmatic values to be realized by imitation.

For Father Boyd, the point of departure for any understanding of the implications of the Aristotelian definition must be the Greek mind which he views as "outward going," living in "an object-centered world which, for all its irony and mystery, was considered ordered, substantial and stable" (p. 5). With this as background and following Gerald F. Else's reading of the *Poetics (Aristotle's Poetics: The Argument.* Cambridge: Harvard University Press, 1957), he sees the poet as an imitator insofar as he is a maker of plots. He imitates nature by shaping the action of his play towards its goal in somewhat the same way nature shapes our ends in real life (p. 23). Like Polixenes justifying all forms of art in *The Winter's Tale,* "Nature is made better by no mean// But Nature makes that mean" (IV, iv, 89-90). Imitation is thus the discovery of something already there, and the proper pleasure of art is the contemplation of this newly perceived relationship as valuable for its own sake. Consequently, "From Aristotle's realistic noetic, his conception of structural realism, and his notions of the organic union of insight and pleasure for the audience of poetry stems all Western realistic critical theory down to the demise of the Neoclassical tradition" (p. 33).

In this tradition it is the structure of the art work which is its guarantee of integrity and its sufficient reason for being. The poet or dramatist is a creator because he is a maker of structures, and what he makes becomes part of the truth which all men desire to know for its own sake. The structure of the individual art work is neither a physical thing nor merely an abstract idea, but a thing of meaning in being a thing made and existing in the mode peculiar to all literary forms. Mimetic structure draws "form from nature into the poem to present it to the audience, with due respect for the autonomy it deserved in all three states: in nature as 'the given,' in the poem as what was significant, and in the mind of the audience as what was pleasurable contemplation" (p. 126).

Granting Father Boyd's assumptions and Aristotelian definitions, his interpretation of the history of the concept of the function of mimesis is not only consistent but it goes beyond the eighteenth century limits of his study and sheds some light on problems which have preoccupied the so-called New Critics. He has trouble getting Sam Johnson under his tent for, as he observes, Sam's "Classical bias for the universal" and "his personal psychological and religious bent" made him veer "now and then in the direction of a narrow moralism" (p. 290). More serious is his tendency to dismiss the relevance of any contribution the Neoplatonic critics might have made to the clarification and preservation of a metempirical view of imitation. Beginning with the observation that Plato "never successfully coped with the place of the arts in his own system" (p. 17), he later goes on to explain "I have not thought it necessary to spell out the noetic implications of Neoplatonism, because for our purposes they were essentially the same as the Platonic" (p. 100). With due respect for the force of that word "essentially," it seems that it might be observed that the noetic implications of Neoplatonism were essentially the same as the medieval noetic, at least in so far as a respect "for analogy as a pervasive habit of mind" (p. 231). It is the passing of this recognition of the relevance of analogy which had provided what he calls "the needed perilous balance" (p. 248) which, in his opinion, prevented later eighteenth-century critics from understanding the function of imitation in the true classical sense.

The limitation of the conception of invention to the stimulation of "new thought about matter already found in the raw material of experience" (p. 196) and not to the seeking of new material seems to me unnecessarily restrictive of critics like Rosemond Tuve (*Elizabethan and Metaphysical Imagery*. Chicago: University of Chicago Press, 1947). As he reads the Neoplatonic texts, poetry in that tradition is an art "in which imagination or invention merely clarifies, praises or adorns an idea or a purpose" and thereby "removes the precisely creative activity from forming the very heart of the poem, from its cognitive and structural center" (p. 197). Surely Sidney, Castiglione, and Ficino can be read so that poetry can be distinguished from rhetoric.

Admittedly the Church Fathers did not distinguish very successfully between poetry and rhetoric. It was only when poetry was rhetorical that it was acceptable. As Russell Fraser points out in *The War Against Poetry,* they inherited from Plato the belief that "the same person will hardly be able to play a serious part in life, and at the same time be an imitator" (p. 102). Some were so close in their beliefs to Plato that Jerome remarked, "Either Plato philonizes, or Philo Platonizes" *(loc. cit.).* The Elizabethan clergymen who inveighed against poems and plays were heirs of Augustine who looked upon all art as imitations and all imitations, by definition, but secondary and lesser truths. Consequently they could conceive of attendance at plays as worshipping "another Veale" or "golden calf," and all traffic in "metaphors, allegories and such figurative, superlative terms and so much vain eloquence as yielding 'no fruit at all' " (p. 4). The only justifiable pleasure was to be taken from a study of the essence; the study of accidents and derivations was idle and foolish. So, by the middle of the seventeenth century, "The connoisseur of first and last things, in his character of militant salvationist, seeks to banish the poet and playwright because, in their commitment to the phenomenal or merely figurative representation, they are involved with no more than a cantle of the truth" (p. 179). In pursuing the metaphorical way, poet and playwright "abandon the real world for the *selva oscura* of fable and romance" (p. 180).

Puritan demands that all art be useful forced critics to defend poetry as persuading to virtue. By the eighteenth century, explanations of the Horatian formula that art should delight and teach tended to place less and less emphasis on delighting and more and more on instructing. To instruct effectively required knowledge of the techniques of persuasion, and one of the popular manuals of rhetoric, much better adapted to the practical criticism of style than the *Poetics,* was Hermogenes.

A well-known authority during the Renaissance, Hermogenes has been little read since. On the last page of her study (p. 216), Mrs. Patterson points out that as authoritative a writer as J. W. H. Atkins could, in the article on "Concerning Ideas" in the *Oxford Classical Dictionary,* dismiss the treatise as "notable for its obscure terminology, its endless classifications, distinctions, definitions, and rules, which added but little to the vital appreciation of style . . . It gave rise to a system which had disastrous effects on literature for centuries to come." She, on the contrary, maintains that "There are certain features of English poetry in this period (the Renaissance) which require knowledge of the Ideas of Hermogenes as a necessary ingredient for total understanding . . . " (p. 68). She, far from concluding that the study of Hermogenes had disastrous effects on literature for centuries, attributes the appearance and development of the heroic ode in English to Hermogenes' suggestions on how to write in the Grand style. Many elements of the sonnet she attributes to his definitions of Beauty and Verity. The epic would never have become what it did without Hermogenes' stipulations about the requirements of a Grave style and the importance of decorum.

Hermogenes was available to Renaissance critics in some twenty editions beginning with the *editio princeps* of Aldus Manutius of 1508. The *Art of Rhetoric,* a compendium title, consisted of four treatises: Concerning Statusm, Concerning Invention, Concerning Ideas, and (possibly spurious) On the Method of Gravity. The third treatise, Concerning Ideas, was the most popular part of his work and consisted of expositions of seven ideals of style: Clarity, Grandeur, Beauty, Speed, Ethos, Verity, and Gravity. Each idea of style was described as having its appropriate subject matter, its appropriate method or principle of organizing that subject matter, its proper diction, its suitable schemes and tropes, its peculiar members or phrases of appropriate lengths to be used in the construction of its periods, its right texture of sound patterns, as well as correct cadences and rhythms. A thorough demonstration of the effect of Hermogenes' ideas on any given poet would require a detailed analysis of how his style reflects the use of all these devices as Hermogenes considered them appropriate for the Idea of style he was trying to realize. Something in the order of Sister Miriam Joseph's *Shakespeare's Use of the Arts of Language* (New York: Columbia University Press, 1947) would prove that any author in question had read Hermogenes and followed his directions carefully in putting together his work. What we find in *Hermogenes and the Renaissance* is not a detailed analysis of how cadence, rhythm, method, and sententiae in a canzone conform to Hermogenes' prescriptions, but an explanation of how the broad definition of a style in the rhetoric book seems to have guided a poet in the organization and disposition of his materials.

What seems to have happened to the literary historian is what she observes may have happened to Edmund Spenser: "Indeed, one could argue that if the influence of the Seven Ideas is to be felt in the poem *(Faerie Queene)* as a whole, it consists less in modulations in style (though these are important) than in modifications of the concept of a few Ideas with which Spenser was particularly concerned" (p. 210). Her illustrations of how Hermogenic conceptions of stylistic grandeur and decorum may have influenced Spenser in what he included and excluded from his epic are most stimulating. Her explanation of how the ideal of Verity in style may have been the reason why Sidney, in *Astrophel and Stella,* repeatedly professes his determination to eschew all artifice, and how Shakespeare, in his *Sonnets,* repeatedly claims that he cannot acquire the stylistic polish he needs (p. 135) will, from now on, have to be considered as adequate an explanation for the content of these sonnets as the traditional explanation of anti-Petrarchanism. Overall, however, what her study shows is that Renaissance writers were more influenced by Hermogenes' general observations than by his detailed prescriptions. As Sturm put it: "Hermogenes was not only a Rhetorician, but also a philosopher, and a Platonic philosopher at that," (p. 36) and Hermogenes the philosopher was as influential as Hermogenes the rhetorician. Indeed, the "the seven Ideas of Hermogenes came to be associated with the Ideas or forms of Platonic philosophy" (p. 35).

When Hermogenes' definitions came to be taken as absolute prescriptions, as Aristotle's heuristic principles came to be taken as prescriptive in the eighteenth century, then the effect of "Seven Ideas of Style" was indeed to foster a kind of formalism. The formalism of the seventeenth-century and early eighteenth-century rhetoric boc`s, when taken into consideration in the context of growing demands from Puritan and other moralists that art be purposeful, tended to encourage a reaction to an esthetic of emotionalism or sentimentalism. Poetry then began to be judged in moral terms and form was isolated from content. It was no longer "thought of as deriving from the inner movement of the poem or as closely enough related to it, but rather as a kind of form or value in itself" (Boyd, p. 209).

In addition to the depreciation of the relevance of the imitation of poetry consequent upon the development of a formalism and the growing demands that all art be practically relevant, seventeenth-century belief in the value of imitation was further eroded by the rapid development of the mathematical sciences with their stress on clarity as the norm of reliability and the elaboration of cosmological theodicies. This constellation of forces was steadily driving devotees of the value of artistic imitation to less and less defensible positions. By the eighteenth century, critics like Dennis were reduced to defining the form present in the art work which provided the cognitive element in the structured imitation as derived from a very superficial level of nature and, consequently, no longer defensible as expressive of the probable. Critics also found themselves increasingly calling attention to formalistic elements as the source of the beauty of the art work and unable to explain how painting and music could also be considered as imitative. Gradually they were beginning to think of all art, not only music and painting, as self-expression, and the concept of the function of art as imitation was well into decline (p. 98). Though many critical discussions would still develop within the skeletal framework imposed by Aristotelian definitions, the assumptions which were vital to a continued belief in the substance had been replaced, and sentimental or rationalistic criteria were now the readiest way to justify the function of poetry. Art, no longer defensible on its own assumptions, as it had been as long as the commitment to a conception of imitation as creative had been possible, was now dependent for its acceptance upon its adaptability to other ends. At least that is the way these three books see the history of a concept from Aristotle to Wordsworth.

# Shakepeare's History Plays: The Romantic or the Heroic View

*Irving Ribner*

Robert Ornstein. *A Kingdom for a Stage: The Achievement of Shakespeare's History Plays.* Cambridge, Mass.: Harvard University Press, 1972, Pp. xi, 231. $11.00.

David Riggs. *Shakespeare's Heroical Histories: Henry VI and Its Literary Tradition.* Cambridge, Mass.: Harvard University Press, 1971. Pp. xi, 194. $6.50.

SHAKESPEARE'S ENGLISH HISTORY plays were generally regarded as formless, chaotic works of little artistic merit until E. M. W. Tillyard in 1944 published his *Shakespeare's History Plays.* With this work began a new wave of interest in these plays, and Tillyard was followed by other writers who drew heavily upon him while extending his work in new directions and amplifying it in many ways. Among the most important of these scholars were Lily B. Campbell, J. D. Wilson (who were actually working along the same lines at the same time as Tillyard), and M. M. Reese. The present writer drew heavily upon Tillyard, Campbell, and Wilson in relating Shakespeare's history plays to the large corpus of historical drama which virtually dominated the English stage during the last decade of the sixteenth century. Out of these books, and the hundreds of articles (and new introductions to editions) which followed them, emerged what might be considered a kind of orthodoxy in the treatment of the history plays, although it must be stressed that no one of these critics was exactly like any other and that there was thus a very wide diversity in their points of view. Generally they tended to stress the importance as a framework for the plays of a providential view of history developed by Tudor historians and called the "Tudor myth," to relate the plays to the contemporary historical writings which were their sources, and to emphasize the importance of the morality play tradition in the evolution of the Tudor history play as an identifiable dramatic phenomenon. On the other hand all of the important critics recognized that Elizabethans themselves had no conception of the history play as a separate dramatic genre, somehow separate from comedy or tragedy, and that any definition of it which we may evolve must be a twentieth century construct.

There are few critical orthodoxies, however, which can survive two decades of repetition and inclusion in standard textbooks and histories. In 1964 S.C. Sen Gupta in *Shakespeare's Historical Plays* attempted to attack Tillyard's essential assumptions. Now the attempt has been made again in Robert Ornstein's *A Kingdom for a Stage.* At the same time David Riggs in *Shakespeare's Heroical Histories* has tried, somewhat more modestly, to approach the plays from a direction quite different from that of Tillyard. We may well be on the verge of a new burst of writing on Shakespeare's historical plays, with all of the usual attempts at reevaluations and assertions of originality where little, in fact, exists.

Ornstein has taken up the 1953 suggestion made by F. P. Wilson in his *Marlowe and the Early Shakespeare* that Shakespeare, for all we know, may have been the very first person to write an English history play. Wilson was concerned with emphasizing that we cannot date with precision any of the plays drawn directly from the English chronicles and free from morality play abstractions, which have generally been taken to be earlier than Shakespeare's *Henry VI* plays. Ornstein would extend this to argue that there was no tradition of historical drama at all when Shakespeare began, for his early history plays have no roots in medieval drama; hence, he argues further, earlier critics were wrong in stressing the morality play as contributing to them. Ornstein holds, and few would disagree with him, that Shakespeare wrote about history because he was deeply interested in the subject and approached it in the same manner and with the same spirit that he approached his comedies and tragedies, probing the motives of men and the intricacies of events without regard to any special system of belief. Ornstein is concerned with an independent aesthetic criticism of the plays as drama. This is an important and worthwhile objective. He is a keen and intelligent critic, and he has much to say about the plays which is perceptive and illuminating. He is especially good — as in his chapter on *Richard II* — in his exploration of the complexities of human character in difficulty and trying political involvements, and he offers some keen insights into Shakespeare's use of language. It is unfortunate, however, that he feels the need to establish his work as antithetical to that of Tillyard and his followers, because in actuality it is not that at all.

As Ornstein recognizes himself and acknowledges in his preface, his book is built upon the foundations laid by the earlier critics. In his quite unnecessary attempt to establish an independence which does not really exist, he offers in his initial chapter a view of earlier criticism of the history plays which greatly oversimplifies, and sometimes badly distorts, the work he is describing by lumping diverse critics together as some kind of homogeneous "they." I doubt that many of those "earlier critics" whom he sees himself as opposing would disagree with him when he writes that "I do not think that Shakespeare was content to serve as the spokesman for an official version of history in the tetralogies" (p. 31). None of them ever called Shakespeare a propagandist, and some of them have pointed to more specific unorthodoxies in Shakespeare's political plays than Ornstein himself is able to suggest. Nor would they deny that the elements of heroic romance which he finds in the early histories, for instance, echoes of the courts of love and of Malory, are present, for all of these were elements which went into what the "earlier critics" recognized as probably the most diverse and heterogeneous of Elizabethan art forms. But Ornstein assumes a heavier burden of proof than he can sustain when he states categorically that there is nothing of the influence of the morality play in Shakespeare's *Henry VI* plays. That the plays themselves are moralities no one would claim, but neither can we deny the neat formalism of the character parallels, the traditional motifs of comic vice in the Jack Cade scenes, and dozens of other elements which critics have long pointed to as having their origins in the earlier native dramatic tradition. In general, while Ornstein has much of interest and value to say about what is in Shakespeare's history plays, his sometimes arbitrary statements about what is not in them carry far less conviction. The value of his book is not at all enhanced by its polemic quality.

Tillyard, it must be remembered, was delineating a frame of reference for the history plays at a time when this had never been done before. He never suggested that Shakespeare merely echoed the platitudes of dull political moralists. No serious critic of the history plays has ever suggested that Shakespeare did not go far beyond any of his inherited materials, that he did not explore the ambiguities and complexities inherent in his subject matter, or that he created his characters in terms of morality play stereotypes. That Ornstein can find no separate tradition of historical drama before Shakespeare's *Henry VI* plays need surprise no one who has read F. P. Wilson. It is not in plays like Shakespeare's that the tradition lies. The point has been made repeatedly that Elizabethans never conceived of the history play as a separate dramatic genre. The evolution of the history play is that of the drama in general. What sets it apart is that it uses all of the elements which had been developed by the English drama so as to do what was done by writers of history in non-dramatic forms. As drama its chief characteristic is diversity, not exclusiveness of form. *Gorboduc* and *Cambises,* whose importance to the history play Ornstein questions, are significant because they contributed, each in its own special way, to an evolving dramatic tradition which Shakespeare inherited, and they happen to have done so by using historical subject matter. Bale's *Kynge Johan,* whether it was known to later historical dramatists or not — and Ornstein concludes that it was not because there are no specific references to it and because it was never printed — is important because it shows how the abstractions of the morality drama could easily evolve into actual historical figures. This is the first play, moreover, to present in drama a special Reformation view of King John which was later to appear in *The Troublesome Reign of John* and to furnish the material out of which Shakespeare fashioned his own special vision of that particular monarch.

"Can we believe," Ornstein asks, "that Shakespeare was so shallow in his assessment of the temper of his countrymen, and so fearful of the threat of incipient anarchy, that he wrote play after play to persuade his audience of the need for order and obedience?" (p. 25). But this is not at all what earlier writers on the history play have maintained. That the plays assert the evils of rebellion and are generally orthodox in their support of the Tudor monarchy is obvious; they could scarcely have been staged had they done otherwise. Ornstein is not the first writer to suggest that it may not have been for its orthodoxies that *Richard II* was chosen for private performance on the eve of the Essex uprising. The terms of political obedience are probed, however, in a way which no kind of literature dedicated to persuading an audience could ever attempt. Earlier critics have pointed out that Shakespeare's concern with politics extends to all of the relations between human beings within a social structure, the duties and responsibilities of subject to king, of king to subject, and of both to God. Again, earlier critics have found in the plays a probing of the relation of public duty to private morality, of how the duties of kingship impinge upon the moral nature of individual man, and thus of just what kind of man may be capable of bearing the burdens and executing the responsibilities of a king. These are the issues found by the most important of earlier writers on these plays, and their work cannot be dismissed in the simplistic terms with which Ornstein treats them.

Ornstein is often equally cavalier in his treatment of Tudor history itself, drawing most of his notions from a few secondary sources and somewhat oversimplifying the background against which Shakespeare's plays were written. In his discussion of opposition to Elizabeth's government and the advocacy of rebellion against her, which he attributed in the 1590's to "a very small and fanatical group of Catholic exiles," far too little attention is paid to the steadily mounting puritan opposition. His assertion that "the fear of subversion was largely unfounded" at this time carries little conviction in the light of the long series of actual plots against the queen and the final terror of the Gunpowder plot only three years after her death. I doubt that the comparison of subversive-hunting in England of the 1590's with that of the McCarthy era in America, on the ground that both were in reaction to an entirely imaginary threat, is a valid historical analogy. That Shakespeare in *Henry IV, Part II* is capable of envisioning the rigor and cruelty of the law as well as its necessity, provides no evidence that he "could see that the fear of Catholic subversion and the harshly repressive measures passed against Catholics in the 1590's posed a greater threat to the unity of England than did the fanaticism of Catholic extremists," thus endowing him with the author's own questionable vision of Tudor history, derived from the perspective of four hundred years of hindsight. To argue also that under Henry VIII the crown was a symbol "of Protestant defiance of a hated Papacy" is to distort the religious conflicts of that time out of all proportion. Particularly difficult to understand is the final sentence of Ornstein's book, which suggests that Queen Elizabeth, rather than the warlike Henry V, was a Shakespearian ideal of rule: she "won the praise of her wisest subjects because for nearly half a century she kept her beloved England at peace." There was scarcely a year of her reign when English armies were not fighting abroad — in Ireland, in France, in the Netherlands; English fleets raided the Coast of Spain, and her subjects were pressed into service as ruthlessly as Falstaff's recruits, to be dismissed after their service to beg or to steal like Pistol. Far too often in reading Ornstein one gets the feeling that the author's emphatic statement of a proposition is the only proof of its validity that he expects his readers to demand.

While Ornstein is concerned with denying the existence of a tradition of historical drama earlier than Shakespeare, Riggs goes to the very opposite extreme in attempting to establish one. The main thrust of his argument is that there is a rhetorical and heroic tradition of historical writing which reached its apogee in Marlowe's *Tamburlaine*, and that this play is the principal impetus behind Shakespeare's earliest history plays. This notion need surprise no one, for the heroic elements of the history play were argued by Schelling in 1902 and Briggs in 1914; and in 1911 Tucker Brooke called Marlowe's *Tamburlaine* the "source and original" of the Tudor history play. Unfortunately Riggs shows no awareness of the writings of any of these scholars, whose work, in fact, furnished the basis upon which Tillyard and his own successors built.

Riggs's attempt to define and identify a tradition of heroic history plays earlier than Shakespeare's *Henry VI* plays rests upon some extraordinary assumptions about the dates of the plays he places in this tradition and often upon his treating as fact what are no more than remote possibilities. The famous reference to Talbot in Nashe's *Pierce Pennilesse* of 1592, for instance, is taken to be an indication that Shakespeare's *Henry VI, Part One* was merely the best of many similar plays, now lost but known to Nashe. Riggs then lists fourteen such plays which he assumes, without evidence, to be earlier than Shakespeare's, and which, he finds, display the "worthy and memorable" acts of aspiring conquerors. The dates he assigns to some of these plays we may accept as probabilities, but others are highly questionable. It is difficult to find much that is "worthy and memorable" in the career of the hero of *Selimus* (which he dates in 1592, a reasonable guess, but no more). *The Famous Victories of Henry V,* however, he places without reason or explanation in 1586 and *Edward III* in 1590; he dates *Cambises,* "a medieval *de casibus* tragedy," without explanation in 1571, whereas the only reasonable evidence we have as to the dating of this play suggests that it was performed at court during the Christmas season of 1560/61.

Riggs begins, moreover, by asserting some ancient ideas which recent scholarship has pretty well discarded. To repeat Malone's old notion that Greene is accusing Shakespeare of plagiarism in *A Groatsworth of Wit* is rather hazardous in the light of the work of J. S. Smart and Peter Alexander. To argue that Shakespeare in the *Henry VI* plays was imitating "a kind of history play that Greene and his contemporaries brought to fruition" is to assume a certainty about the dates of the *Henry VI* plays to which few scholars before him have aspired, and to write about plays which may not even exist. To just what plays by "Greene and his contemporaries" is Riggs referring? Surely not to

*James IV,* a play as unlike Shakespeare's *Henry VI* plays as any play can be, and which, in any case, could have been written later than Shakespeare's. Peele's *Edward I,* a romantic hodge-podge also quite unlike Shakespeare's history plays, could possibly be earlier than the *Henry VI* plays, but we cannot be sure of that. Shakespeare's earliest history plays have always been a dangerous quagmire for scholars, and one cannot conclude that Riggs has successfully escaped their perils. Nor can we have much confidence when he writes of an official view of history which "Puritan preachers were seeking to superimpose on the fabric of historical literature" (p. 25). I know of no Puritans ever concerned with propagating an official view of anything, let alone history.

Nevertheless, in spite of such lapses, Riggs in many ways provides a useful corrective to Ornstein's more personal and less historical critical method. Riggs's purpose, as he explains it, "is to introduce new readings, not to question old ones" (p. 30). He delineates the relation of Elizabethan historical writing to principles of classical rhetoric as they were taught in the Elizabethan grammar schools, and he shows that this rhetorical tradition, devoted to celebrating the virtues of heroic men, affected Shakespeare's history plays. He does these things with a considerable display of learning, making discriminating use of the great quantity of material that has been written about his subject in the past. However, there is a limited single-mindedness in Riggs's effort which sometimes causes him to miss the woods in seeking the trees. Surely he cannot really believe that Shakespeare or any of his mature contemporary writers of history ever devoted themselves to a "pure history," analyzed by the rhetorical methods of Aphthonius as taught in the grammar schools, and "untouched alike by the medieval effort to construct a theodicy and the Italian school of political analysis." No amount of schoolboy exercise could ever erase the medieval heritage of Shakespeare's age, or alter the fact that the special use of history by writers like Machiavelli and Guicciardini was a vital part of the intellectual climate in which they lived. If Shakespeare's *Henry VI* plays are simply examples of heroic eulogy in the stylized manner of Renaissance rhetoricians, there is little more reason for us to read them today than there is for us to study the *Apophthegmata* of Erasmus or *The Forest* of Thomas Fortescue. The readings of the plays themselves do not suggest any such belief on Riggs's part, and they seem, in fact, to be somewhat at variance with the rigid ideological framework in which they are introduced. Despite all this, he accomplishes a useful purpose in reminding us of one of the crucial elements in the development of the history play, one which has not been emphasized sufficiently in recent years.

# Government and Culture in the Renaissance City-State: Three Recent Studies

*Julius Kirshner*

William M. Bowsky. *The Finance of the Commune of Siena 1287-1355.* Oxford: Clarendon Press, 1970. Pp. xx, 379. $16.00.

Anthony Molho. *Florentine Public Finances in the Early Renaissance, 1400-1433. (Harvard Historical Monographs,* 65) Cambridge, Mass.: Harvard University Press, 1971. Pp. xiv, 234. $10.50.

Donald Weinstein. *Savonarola and Florence, Prophecy and Patriotism in the Renaissance.* Princeton: Princeton University Press, 1971. Pp. xi, 399. $13.50.

D URING THE LAST two decades we have been inundated by a profusion of studies centering on late medieval and Renaissance Tuscany. If this outpouring was rendered possible by the fabulously rich Tuscan archives, its torrential force stems from a romantic as well as scholarly commitment to mapping the material and spiritual resources of Lorenzetti's Siena, Medicean and Savonarolan Florence, and so on. The first wave of scholarship, emphasizing political and social history, was preoccupied with testing Marxist and Burckhardtian dogmas against new archival discoveries, and has successfully altered older perceptions of the Renaissance. While such research shows no signs of waning, some recent studies are aiming their critical sights at many theses minted in the fifties and sixties by Fiumi, Becker, Herlihy, Baron, Garin, and many others. This shift is discernible in the monographs written by Bowsky, Molho, and Weinstein.

Bowsky's study of Sienese public finance under the oligarchic regime of the Nine is an impeccable piece of scholarship and a welcome contribution to the ever-growing literature on Tuscan economic history. His principal conclusions are these: mounting expenditures for public work projects, territorial acquisition and aggrandizement, alms for the dispossessed, the purchase and stockpiling of grain to

211

meet acute food shortages, and above all, defense and military campaigns increased the communal budget from £140,000 in 1288 to £400,000 in 1351 and over £320,000 during the first half of 1354 alone; unlike the *classe dirigente* of other Tuscan cities, especially Florence, which favored indirect over direct imposts, the oligarchy of Siena did not shy away from the *dazio* (even though its members felt the brunt of direct taxation more than the lower echelons of Sienese society), but relied upon a mix of taxes and loans to meet the city's fiscal obligations; while the tax burden upon the *contado* certainly constituted a hardship, it was not "crushing," and supporting Fiumi, Bowsky rejects outright the thesis advanced by Salvemini and Caggesse and followed by Schevill that the Nine consciously and willfully sought to oppress and exploit the rustic population of Siena. If the author finds the economic managers of Siena relatively astute, uncorrupt and efficient, he notes a conservative stance on their part for not establishing a consolidated public debt, as Venice, Genoa, and Florence had done.

Bowsky admits that his conclusions are tentative, under a cloud of conjecture. Despite his diligent examination of a staggering number of documents, the sources are too uneven and fragmented to permit highly focused generalizations. His conclusions are also delimited by the starkly public and legalistic nature of the material. As a result, the crucial nexus between private and public finance remains to be elaborated. Although hampered by a shoreless sea of evidence, the author, I believe, could have made his arguments more comprehensible, and derived more from his material than he has. There are multiple references to the socio-political foundations and effects of Sienese taxation. Unfortunately, these fleeting allusions are not dealt with in a systematic manner. The absence of such an analysis is not simply a matter of patchy documentation, but is linked to the author's assumption (p. vii) that "One must unravel the system of taxation in order to fathom the network of political relationships that formed the commune itself" — a point of departure which allows him to portray the *haute bourgeoisie* of Siena as economic managers singlemindedly committed to efficiency and to balancing the budget, surely an anachronistic distortion of the passions of fourteenth-century politicians. And Bowsky's expressed sympathy for the Nine leads him to underestimate the benefits the ruling groups garnered from their own tax policies. Citing statutory exclamations that direct taxes will be imposed fairly and equitably — each citizen shouldering his share according to his taxable wealth — the author asserts (p. 112) that "We cannot discount this as a

platitudinous wish . . . Inequality there was to be sure, as in any society. But the rulers of Siena must have believed that this was the sort of
government and system of values expected of them . . . The Nine
were not Jakob Burckhardt's Constantine, and fairness and equality
were more than slogans." Without doubt, taxation in the name of
equality (distributive justice) was expected, in fact demanded, but this
is not so peculiarly a Sienese phenomenon as the author thinks. The
same theme is found in other Tuscan cities and in the commentaries
on taxation of *trecento* jurists. Equality as a political principle and its
relationship to an oligarchic form of government must be examined in
a much wider context than is presented here. For all the cant concerning equality of taxation, it most assuredly did not exist in Siena, nor
anywhere else in *trecento* Tuscany. As Bowsky himself demonstrates,
the monied groups of Siena reaped handsome profits from the farming
of gabelles and from interest running as high as 60% on well-guaran-
teed state loans. In Siena the principle of *equalitas* served as an ideological ballast for the ruling class.

Toward the close of his book, Bowsky exhorts the Florentine historical lobby to produce a work modeled after his. Actually, scholarship
on Florentine public finance has a long pedigree. It began with Canes-
trini, Barbadoro, and Sapori, continued with Becker, Herlihy, and de
la Roncière, and now we can add to that list Molho's cogently written
and factually packed volume. Although the latter has devoted his ener-
gies to reconstructing the budget of early-*quattrocento* Florence, his
work invites comparison to Bowsky's. As in Siena, Molho singles out
warfare as the chief culprit in boosting the net indebtedness of Florence from 450,000 florins in the 1340's to 2,500,000 in the 1420's. The
propertied groups in Florence, he confirms, favored gabelles and inter-
est-bearing forced and voluntary loans over direct taxation, but he
concretely demonstrates that the swollen public debt *(Monte Comune)*
and its astronomical carrying charges — approximately 200,000 florins
by the 1420's — cast a pall over the prosperity of the Florentine mer-
cantile and banking community. If Molho agrees with Fiumi and
Bowsky on the question of the exploitation of the contado, he offers
fresh evidence in support of Becker's thesis that the territories under
Florentine rule, as well as the populace of the city, suffered heavily as
the tax burden mounted in the late *trecento* and *quattrocento*. The
theme of equality runs like a thread through Florentine fiscal legisla-
tion, but Molho rightly views rhetorical statements about the elite's
self-abnegation with proper suspicion. He does argue, however, that
the *castasto* introduced in 1427 did inject a greater measure of equity

into the tax system than before. He is less impressed with the administrative abilities of cameral officials than Bowsky, and he makes an obvious but valuable observation (p. 89): "The concept of an annual anticipated budget decided upon by the communal authorities was entirely unknown in Renaissance Florence. As the need arose, expenses were met on a month to month basis." The originality of Molho's work hinges on this point. Instead of projecting his own rational calculations to *quattrocento* administrators, he deftly shows how titanic impersonal economic and demographic currents overwhelmed the well-honed plans of Florentine statesmen, and how in the early 1430's the government, in order to remain solvent, was pathetically reduced to relying upon a handful of banking houses, the most important of which was Cosimo de'Medici & Co. These forces, coupled with military disasters in the 1420's-30's, he suggests, provide a partial explanation for the erosion of the city's republican constitution and the pressures which led to Medici rule.

I have only a few minor criticisms to offer about this admirable book. Table 10 (p. 147), listing foreign investments in the public debt, is probably misleading, since the figures given are based on the amounts the Commune authorized foreigners to invest, and may not reflect the amounts they actually invested. Molho writes (p. 142) that foreign investment in the *Monte Comune* was safe and lucrative, and that interest payments were promptly disbursed, but this was not the case with the investments of the king of Portugal, Pope Eugenius IV, and the Orsini family of Rome. It remains to be seen whether investment in the *Monte Comune* in the third half of the *trecento* was as profitable as Molho believes. Finally, his statement (p. 71) that "credits of the Venetian public debt were quoted at uniformly high levels" does not hold true after her War with Genoa (1380).

For all its significance, public finance remains only one dimension of the Florentine experience. In his book on Savonarola, Weinstein reminds us that political crises appeared in all shapes and colors in the *quattrocento,* and were often tinted with religious elements. The author subjects earlier scholarship on Savonarola, running from Villari through Spini and Garin, to tender scrutiny. He lavishes praise on his predecessors for being eloquent and brilliant, but finds their work deficient in connecting the central motifs of Savonarola's life as they converge during his sojourn in the Arno city (1490-1498): his personal religiosity; the nature and sources of his prophecies; his role as a spiritual and political reformer in the wake of the downfall of the Medici government in November, 1494; and the quality of his political thought.

In dealing with these themes, Weinstein has written a remarkable book, in which the dynamic interplay between Savonarola the man (his frustrations, opportunism, and apocalyptic fantasies) and the political and social milieu of late fifteenth-century Florence is brilliantly illuminated.

Weinstein rejects the position that the adolescent Savonarola was a mature prophet and reformer. Convincingly, he shows that as a young man Savonarola was tormented by a conflict between flesh and spirit, reminiscent of the crisis St. Augustine underwent, and that he entered the Dominican Order not to reform the world, but to resolve his personal dilemma. The author admits that Savonarola's eschatology was touched by Joachite and Chiliastic currents, but that he did not elaborate a consistent eschatology of his own until 1492, when he was in Florence. In response to the spiritual yearnings of the Florentine *bourgeoisie,* and under the spell of Florentine civic humanism and what Weinstein calls "the Myth of Florence" (the idea that the Florentines were a chosen people, and that the City of the Lily has a special spiritual and temporal destiny), Savonarola's apocalyptic visions were transfigured. From 1492 on, Savonarola began to blend Florentine fantasies with his own, to produce a unique prophecy in which the Florentines are the latter-day Israelites, whose election and glorious future were foretold in Holy Scripture. Savonarola's political thought, Weinstein proposes, underwent a similar transformation. Initially, it derived from St. Thomas; yet combined with Florentine political ideology and myth, it becomes Savonarolan. Moreover, Savonarola was neither a reactionary spokesman for the patriciate, nor a supporter of radical political reform and democracy; his political instincts appear to be cautious and conservative. He did not enter the Florentine political crisis of 1494 as a leader, armed with a program of reform, but as a peacemaker. If events swiftly prodded him to assume the role of leadership, he was not, as some have asserted, the architect of the new government. He supported the *governo libero,* with its promise of greater civic participation than under the Medici, because he believed it would stem the tide of civil discord. As high priest of Florence, Savonarola's moral exhortations and prophecies dominated the lives of the citizens, and as Weinstein reveals, were echoed throughout the early decades of the *Seicento.* The author concludes rather questionably that the Savonarolan episode could not have taken place anywhere else in Italy, except in Florence. As Savonarola was the father of his movement, so Florence was its mother. The subtle chemistry of Florentine piety delineated by Weinstein will probably be debated by scholars who have the pleasure of reading his fascinating book.

# From Complaint to Satire: The Art of the Confessio Amantis*

*Paul M. Clogan*

IT IS ONE of the paradoxes of literary history that the writings of John Gower, counselor of Richard II and Henry IV and respected friend of Chaucer, were much admired in fifteenth-and sixteenth-century England but subjected to charges of timeserving in the eighteenth and claims of dullness in the nineteenth century. The fifty odd manuscripts of the *Confessio Amantis,* Gower's major English work, commissioned by the young king Richard, and their deluxe appearance suggest that the poem was well received in courtly circles. Sir Thomas Bodley was pleased to receive a copy of the poem for his new library two centuries later, and the Chorus of *Pericles* indicates that Shakespeare knew at least the last book of the *Confessio.* The early twentieth-century scholars who discussed Gower's writings claimed that he simply lamented in a traditional way social and political problems and that his complaints lacked wit, humor, and specificity.[1] Eventually, the claim that Gower's writings had no direct relation to his time was corrected most notably through the work of George R. Coffman, Arthur Ferguson, Mary Wickert, John H. Fisher, and a half-dozen studies published since 1953.[2]

Yet all these studies are curiously limited to Gower's didactic works: *Mirour de L'Omme,* a collection of love-ditties written in his youth and composed in twelve-line stanzas of French octosyllabics; and *Vox Clamantis,* Latin elegaics describing society in the reign of Richard II and containing an account of the Peasants' Revolt (1381) and of Richard's reconciliation with the London Commune (1392). These studies are primarily concerned with the content of Gower's social and political ideas, or at best with his political consciousness, and not with his

217

poetry. They emphasize his role as a moralist and present to us a picture of a fearless critic of the corruption of his time and an exponent of moral philosophy, which remains consistent throughout his three major works. The limited view of Gower's poetic art has only recently undergone a corresponding reassessment.[3] The work of Derek Pearsall on Gower and the English Chaucerians and the new editions of his poetry for the modern reader by J. A. W. Bennett in the Medieval and Tudor Series and by Russell Peck in the Holt, Rinehart and Winston series allow us to present Gower to our students in a less formidable and more attractive format. In this paper, I would like to examine briefly some of the satiric elements in the *Confessio Amantis,* to suggest that the poet transformed traditional themes of rebuke from complaint to satire, and to submit that some of the weaknesses in the structure of this lengthy poem can best be understood in the context of its satiric elements.

Much of the misunderstanding of the structure of the *Confessio* perhaps stems from too ready acceptance of John Peter's contention of the dominance of complaint over satire in the Middle Ages. In 1956 for his study of the development and evolution of *Complaint and Satire in Early English Literature,* Peter drew a basic distinction between complaint, which is said to be impersonal, conceptual, Christian, corrective, and unsophisticated and satire, which is identified as being personal, sophisticated, flexible, and only superficially corrective in aim. As early background material for his study of satirical poems and plays which appeared in England at the turn of the sixteenth century, Peter discussed Jerome and Tertullian and considered the former rather satirical. However, Bernard of Cluny, Peter Damian and Aldhelm are considered serious Christians and, therefore, given to complaint. Peter based this distinction on the old Wells' *Manual of Writings in Middle English* compound of satire and complaint in referring to medieval sermons, but he separated the two terms and distinguished complaint from satire as a mode of social criticism in the Middle Ages. He further claimed that the taste of satire virtually died out from the time of St. Jerome until it was revived in the Renaissance. He included under complaint that vast body of medieval literature of reproof which ranges from comprehensive works like *Handlyng Synne* down to lyrics and epigrams a few lines long. This distinction between complaint and satire is not really useful and does not consider the influence of the Fourth Lateran Council which decreed reform in the preaching and teaching of moral themes and especially the Seven Deadly Sins. The distinction overlooks *Piers Plowman, Speculum Stul-*

*torum, Roman de Renart,* and *Ecbasis Captivi,* as well as a great amount of splendid satire in French, Provençal, and Latin which, if examined, could reveal a theory of satire during the Middle Ages. Instead, complaint appears as a formless and vague classificaiton including almost everything which Christians censured and satire appears as a form of "art for art's sake" colored with romantic paganism. As a result, Peter argues, complaint dominated satire during the Middle Ages and is said to have little literary value. The *Confessio Amantis,* which "aims at being a sort of *codex* of the rules of Courtly Love, is so confused by the sombre temper of its 'moral' author as to be rendered almost unreadable."[4] Moreover, Gower is said to be "mixing oil and water" and thus setting for himself an almost prohibitively difficult task. It is in view of the medieval habit of Christianizing secular tales that Peter can finally understand how Gower could write so many heavy complaints.

Certainly Gower did include many traditional moral themes of complaint in the Prologue and parts of the tales. There are the usual attacks on the clergy, Lollards, and usurers; on the rich, social upstarts, and nationalities; and on the themes of death and judgment, fallen man, and nostalgia for the past. Yet it must be emphasized that in the course of the *Confessio,* whose major theme concerns regal responsibility, these traditional moral themes are not simply photostats of cliché morality, but they become part of a larger scheme of satire. The *Confessio* begins as an allegory of love, but it ends by rejecting love as unsuited to the hero, *senex amans.* Gower's original purpose was a combination of courtly love and serious morality, and this may have evolved out of his relationship to Richard II, who had commissioned the work in a barge on the Thames. The manuscripts of the *Confessio* provide us with three different dedications: the first was a tribute to Richard and Chaucer, the second was addressed to Richard alone, and the third replaced both the tribute to Richard and Chaucer with a new dedication to Henry, who later supplanted Richard and five weeks after his coronation awarded Gower for life "two pipes of Gascon wine." These dedicatory changes may well have been the result of new presentations of the *Confessio,* but they may also reflect variations in Gower's theme of the reconciliation of love and morality. As Fisher noted: the poem's "anomaly is that instead of urging the Lover on to sexual intercourse and procreation, in the *Confessio* Venus and Genius are the advocates of their moral enemies, reason and self-discipline."[5]

In the course of the poem, the complaint conventions achieve very little, for it is only through his personal education by Venus that the Lover is taught the way to salvation. Gower's satirical approach is seen in his use of the penitential tradition, and particularly in the confessional framework of the poem, which is a parody of the ever popular manuals of penitential instruction.[6] Venus, the goddess of earthly love, has her servant-priest, Genius, hear the Lover's confession of errors in love by examining him regarding a list of potential sins and by telling tales to illustrate the nature of the sins. At times, Genius' interrogations seem oblivious to the plight of the long suffering penitent, and the tales narrated by the priest as admonitory exempla frequently seem inappropriate to the sin and the teller. Indeed, the elaborate and varied tales of Genius and his enthusiasm for his subject are clear indications of the satirical dimension of the poem. As both the universal figure of generation and potency and as Venus' priest, Genius must constantly praise love and at the same time teach the lesson of the Seven Deadly Sins.[7] The ironies multiply when Genius is viewed as both the priest of Venus and as the allegorical figure of generation. Gower is satirizing both the confessor and the penitent, and Genius signifies the only sin which the Lover does not confess.

The courtly and penitential character of the Lover and the nature of this satiric role are central to the poem's literary achievement.[8] In Book I, he confesses that he has sinned against obedience by not obeying his lady in two ways: he talks constantly about love against her wishes and he cannot believe her when she says that he will never be rewarded; in Book IV, the Lover refuses to demonstrate his love with feats of arms because leaving his lady would probably mean losing her; and again in Book V while speaking of Avarice, the Lover violates the courtly love tradition by claiming that his lady "is guilty of usury in love." Genius, of course, admonishes the Lover for each violation of the courtly tradition, but the total effect of this satiric characterization reveals that the foolish Lover is not a sincere penitent and the attempt to combine courtly love with serious morality ends in failure. Moreover, Gower develops this satiric portrait of the Lover and his indifferent lady with dramatic effectiveness and with a wry sense of humor. Specific scenes of his courting are described in Books IV, V, and VI. *Senex amans* becomes the counterpart of Chaucer's January as he tries to possess his young wife who "passeth al the lust of Maii." Obviously, his lady is indifferent to his complaints (V, 4749ff; VI, 711ff), and there seems to be little hope for this tired old Lover. As a result, his confession is often timid, rueful and pathetically wistful.

The structure of the *Confessio* uses a dramatic framework of the

Lover's confession to present the Seven Deadly Sins as a criticism of man's nature. Enlarged by a satirical treatment, these elements become part of a design of criticism of Estates or King as well as of divine love. The themes of the *Confessio* trace a spiritual progression from physical to ascetic love, as the satiric treatment of the poem progresses from a satire on the complaint and penitential literatures to a satire on the courtly love tradition. The Lover reveals the limitation of the courtly and moral traditions, which cannot help him. Since he is not a selfless courtier, his complaint of physical love will not be answered, and his confession is an anticipation of death and not earthly love. In the last book of the *Confessio,* many of the satiric elements reappear as the futile quest of *senex amans* reaches its climax. The physical love he desires is shown to be the cause of division in the world, and divine love, which was identified in the Prologue as charity, is the only way to salvation. Gower has rightly been called a moral poet as the final meaning of his poetry is strongly Christian. Yet his writings can also be labeled moral because their satirical view of the world ranges from ironic contrasts to a burlesque dignity. Gower included in the *Confessio* specific political, religious, and social criticisms and these have been thoroughly examined by John Fisher and others who trace the three major works of Gower from sin, though justice, to law. They assert that Gower displays an increasing "interest in the establishment of ruling forms of order in the *Confessio.*" Yet I would caution against placing too much significance on the political and social views since the *Confessio* is essentially concerned with the divine perspective in human affairs. The specific criticisms of his times are indeed evident in the poem, but they are part of a larger web of contrasts which bind the poem together.

In the dynamics of the final irony, it is Venus who prescribes the Lover's penance for his confession: instead of seeking personal gratification, he should think of the "common profit" of mankind. He is encouraged to pray for peace, to follow reason as his guide, and to seek moral virtue (VIII, 2908-2927). In a very different manner from what he had anticipated, the Lover is shriven of the desires of love. After the anguished soul-searching is concluded and the masturbatory fantasies put to an end, *senex amans* can draw breath and find something almost like relief. The courtly and penitential character of the Lover and the nature of this satirical role can, I submit, help us to understand better some of the visible weaknesses in the structure of the *Confessio.* The unexpected renunciation of *fins amor* at the end of the confession, the symbiotic framework of the narrative, and the effusive abundance of tales are part of a larger web of contrasts which bind and unite the poem. Gower's rejection of love as unfit for an aging poet becomes the moral conclusion of the commissioned work which was undertaken "In englesch forto make a book Which stant betwene ernest and game (VIII, 3108-09).

# NOTES

\* This article is based on a paper delivered at the Middle English Group of the Eighty-Sixth Annual Meeting of the Modern Language Association of America.

1. S. M. Tucker, *Verse Satire in England before the Renaissance* (New York, 1908), p. 44; and R. M. Alden, *The Rise of Formal Satire in England* (Philadelphia, 1899), p. 12. For the text of the *Confessio Amantis*, I use *The English Works of John Gower*, ed. G. C. Macaulay, vols. 1-2 (Oxford, 1900-01; rpt. 1957).
2. G. R. Coffman, "John Gower in His Most Significant Role," in *Elizabethan Studies and Other Essays in Honor of George F. Reynolds*, (Boulder, Colorado, 1945), pp. 52-61; *idem*, "John Gower, Mentor for Royalty," *PMLA*, 69 (1954), 953-64; Arthur B. Ferguson, *The Articulate Citizen and the English Renaissance* (Durham: Duke University Press, 1965); Maria Wickert, *Gower Studien* (Kölner Universitäts Verlag, 1953); and John H. Fisher, *John Gower, Moral Philosopher and Friend of Chaucer* (New York University Press, 1964).
3. See Peter Fison, "The Poet in John Gower," *Essays in Criticism*, 8 (1958), 16-21; and Derek Pearsall, "Gower's Narrative Art," *PMLA*, 81 (1966), 475-84.
4. (Oxford, 1956), p. 52.
5. Fisher, p. 182.
6. For a survey of penitential literature, see W. A. Pantin, *The English Church in the Fourteenth Century* (University of Notre Dame Press, 1962), esp. p. 227; and John J. McNally, "The Penitential and Courtly Tradition in Gower's *Confessio Amantis*," in *Studies in Medieval Culture*, ed. John R. Sommerfeldt (Western Michigan University, 1964), pp. 74-94.
7. E. C. Knowlton, "The Allegorical Figure of Genius," *Classical Philology*, 15 (1920), 380-84; *idem*, "Genius as an Allegorical Figure," *Modern Language Notes* 39 (1924), 89-95.
8. For Gower's treatment of the conventions of courtly love, see C. S. Lewis, *The Allegory of Love* (Oxford, 1936), pp. 198-222.

# Review Notices

James Hurt, *Aelfric*. (Twayne's English Authors Series, 131.) New York: Twayne Publishers, Inc., 1972. Pp. 152.

Kenneth Jackson. *The Gaelic Notes in the Book of Deer*. (The Osborn Bergin Memorial Lecture 1970.) Cambridge: Cambridge University Press, 1972. Pp. xv, 164. $10.00.

Elisabeth Okasha. *Hand-List of Anglo-Saxon Non-Runic Inscriptions*. Cambridge: Cambridge University Press, 1971. Pp. xv, 159. $35.00.

Peter Clemoes' essay "Aelfric" in *Continuations and Beginnings* (ed. Eric Gerald Stanley, London, 1966, pp. 176-209) is the best available introduction to Anglo-Saxon England's great homilist and teacher, but it is only thirty-three pages long. Therefore James Hurt provides a fuller guide for the non-specialist in this volume of Twayne's English Authors Series. His book is a sensibly organized selection of facts about the background and character of Aelfric's works, one which medievalists can read with pleasure and recommend to their students, although a few cautions and quibbles may be in order. Professor Hurt's numerous quotations from Old English need proofreading, as do names like *Vita Patrum* and *Admonition ad Filium Spiritualem* in the index and *Brihtnoth* and *Ecclesiastical History of the English Church and People* in the text proper. Some of the bibliographical items are carelessly cited; for example, all the articles appearing in *English Studies* are cited as appearing in the journal *Englische Studien*, while titles of works by Otto Funke, Karl Jost, and G. I. Needham are inexactly quoted. The author's statements about Aelfric's use of his sources would have benefitted from a consideration of J. E. Cross's recent essays on Aelfric and memory, while the value of the entire book would have been greatly increased by a consideration of the Aelfric homilies published for the first time in John C. Pope's EETS editions of 1967 and 1968. By excluding this fresh material from his study Hurt missed a chance to be first in the field with an original assessment of Aelfric's stature as it is newly revealed in Pope's monumental editions.

MS no. i.i. 6.32 in the Cambridge University Library is a partial Gospels manuscript in which are entered the earliest specimens of the Gaelic language spoken in Scotland — a series of twelfth-century notations including an account of St. Columba's journey from Iona to northeastern Scotland, his acquisition of land for a monastery there, and his conferral of the name *Deer* on the foundation when he noticed that the new abbot, St. Drostán, shed tears (Gaelic *déra)* at his departure. This quaint fable, which Kenneth Jackson suggests may have more historical foundation than most scholars have allowed (p. 3), is followed by six other accounts of land grants and immunities, the last in Latin. These seven notations — less than a thousand words all told — are exhaustively edited by Professor Jackson, who provides a fresh description of the Gaelic hands (but unfortunately no facsimiles), diplomatic as well as edited texts, a translation, and 115 pages of historical, linguistic, onomastic, and paleographical commentary along with an introduction and three indices. At several points the discussion necessarily becomes speculative, but the genuineness and cultural significance of the *notitiae* are convincingly established, while Professor Jackson's resourceful handling of linguistic questions heightens one's anticipation of his forthcoming history of the Gaelic languages.

The most important of the three books under review is Dr. Okasha's *Hand-List*. This is "a corpus of all known Anglo-Saxon, non-runic, inscribed objects" which contain Old English texts, Latin texts including Old English names, and exclusively Latin texts found in the Old English speaking area (unless they contain names indicating Celtic rather than Anglo-Saxon origin). The 158 inscriptions recorded in the *Hand-List* occur on altars, caskets, crucifixes, sundials, weapons, and other objects; only coins and seals are excluded. Famous items are the Alfred jewel ("Identification with King Alfred the Great has been asserted but not proved" — p. 49), the Brussels cross, St. Cuthbert's coffin, the Franks casket, and the Ruthwell cross. Many have runic as well as non-runic inscriptions. The dedication slab of Benedict Biscop's church at Jarrow, dated ca. 685, is the earliest non-runic inscription; the latest are twelfth-century specimens. Most of the stone inscriptions were found in the north of England, most of the others in the south. Five were found on the Continent. The longest vernacular inscription is the forty-eight word legend on the sundial at St. Gregory's Minster, Kirkdale. The inscription on the Sutton brooch is in verse. Altogether, Dr. Okasha's book provides an excellent starting point for further linguistic and historical work on the non-runic inscriptions. She dates and briefly describes each object, indicates the circumstances of its discovery, lists full bibliography, transcribes and translates each text, and, if the object itself is still extant, supplies at least one photograph of it.

When Dr. Okasha's *Hand-List* is joined on the shelf by R. I. Page's forthcoming Corpus of Old English Runic Inscriptions, these two works will constitute a record of virtually all known Anglo-Saxon inscriptions, both runic and non-runic, vernacular and Latin. The present volume is therefore an important reference work which every serious library must order. It is also one through which medievalists and philologists might profitably browse at leisure; more is the pity then that the high cost of the photographic plates (which are not always as revealing as they might have been) has driven the price of the volume beyond the range of most scholars.

*Fred C. Robinson*
Yale University

Robert R. Newton. *Medieval Chronicles and the Rotation of the Earth.* Baltimore and London: The Johns Hopkins Press, 1972. Pp. xvii, 825.

A surprise awaits those readers who anticipate the subject matter of this volume to be medieval discussions of the possible daily axial rotation of the earth in the manner of Nicole Oresme and Jean Buridan. The primary concern is solar eclipses. The author's original research interest was to devise means for improving our ability to predict the positions of satellites for use in navigation. Central to this problem are the tides, which exercise a direct retarding effect on the motion of the moon and the rotation of the earth and, consequently, affect the positions of the satellites indirectly. "In principle," however, "one can use astronomical data from ancient times, deduce from them the changes that have occurred in the lengths of the day and month, and hence deduce properties of the tides that will test some of the results obtained from artificial satellites" (p. 2). Since for this purpose solar eclipses are valuable, Robert Newton has collected and carefully examined all instances of solar eclipses between 400 and 1200 A.D. that were recorded in the British Isles, continental Europe, the Byzantine Empire, and the eastern Mediterranean. Drawing upon a large number of published (only one manuscript was used) annals (the most important single source), chronicles, and histories of this period, Newton identified 2000 instances of recorded solar eclipses. Of these, two-thirds were eliminated as obvious copies, leaving 629 for further study, of which 379 were judged independent of other known sources.

Most of this work, which consists of eighteen chapters and nine appendices, is devoted to an assessment and evaluation of the solar eclipses themselves, stressing such factors as source, data, place of occurrence, reliability of data, and astronomical analysis. From all this, the author concludes that the properties of tides altered drastically around 700 A.D., the approximate time of the separation of Mont St. Michel from the coast of Normandy.

Although the appeal here will be primarily to historians of medieval astronomy and professional astronomers, medievalists will find the second and third chapters of more general interest. In Chapter II, Newton summarizes ecclesiastical and astronomical problems associated with the historical development of the determination of Easter. A critical evaluation of "Annals, Chronicles, and Histories" forms the subject matter of Chapter III, where among other things, R. L. Poole's claim (p. 52) that annals are derived from Easter tables is rejected (Newton allows only that Easter tables "furnished a convenient medium for the keeping of annals" [p. 47]), as is Poole's assertion (pp. 55-56) that the English discovered the concept of a "Christian era" which "made the revival of historiography possible."

*Edward Grant*
Indiana University

Maurus of Salerno, *Twelfth-Century "Optimus Physicus," with His Commentary on the Prognostics of Hippocrates,* transcribed and translated by Morris H. Saffron, M.D. (Transactions of the American Philosophical Society, N.S., Vol. 62, Part 1, 1972, pp. 1-104). $4.00.

Maurus, head of the medical school of Salerno, died in 1214. Among the more than eighty physicians listed in the Necrology of the Cathedral of San Matteo at Salerno, he alone was called *optimus fisicus.* Whether Maurus deserved such regard will not be determinable until all his writings, as well as his possible sources (like Musandinus), will have been satisfactorily published.

Meanwhile M. H. Saffron contributes an edition of Maurus' work on Hippocrates' *Prognostics.* In this commentary Maurus analyzes sleep, vomit, elimination, coughing, fevers, abscesses, and convulsions, to derive signs favoring or not favoring recovery. Saffron's booklet gives the Latin text and critical apparatus, preceded by an introduction discussing the school of Salerno, Maurus, and his commentary. Following the Latin text are an English translation, notes, bibliography, and indices.

Saffron's work is not flawless. He mentions fleetingly Vatican lat. 4477 as containing an expanded version of the commentary and Paris BN lat. 7102 as containing a fragment (p. 3). He offers no description, not even a date, for either manuscript. He sometimes cites the Vatican text in his apparatus but does not say whether he is indicating its variants consistently or only on occasion. He seems to be unaware of the fragments of the text preserved in Paris BN lat. 7040 and Nouv. acq. lat. 481 (as reported to me by the Institut de recherche et d'histoire des textes). He often fails to record erroneous readings of the manuscript upon which he based his text, BN lat. 18499, like *contradictione* for *contractione* (p. 34 line 48) and *coloris* (corr.) for *odoris* (p. 40 line 51). He certainly misread his basic manuscript in a number of instances, for example: particularis: particularia *MS.* (p. 24 lines 45-46), etiam: enim *MS.* (p. 24 line 49), equaliter: equalis *MS.* (p. 31 line 45), perficit: perfecte *MS.* (p. 38 line 25), medicum: medicus *MS.* (p. 53 line 12). These faults may seem trivial, but *corde* misread for *corpore* (p. 35 line 2) is significant indeed in a medical work.

One must deplore the fact that whereas the Latin text is arranged in two columns of about fifty-five lines to the page, line-numbering is not offered to ease citation. Also, the critical apparatus employs no siglum for the Paris codex, and so it is difficult to decide whether a reading is unclear in the manuscript or represents a conjectural emendation when one sees typically '*fortasse* maximum *vice* maxime' (p. 23 n. 6).

Furthermore, a translation, especially of a scientific work, should be as precise as possible, and Saffron sometimes misinterprets his text. Thus "Medicus laudem et gloriam et amicorum sibi comparat copiam" is not "The physician will acquire for himself and for his colleagues great praise and glory" (p. 54) but "The physician acquires for himself, praise, glory, and an abundance of friends;" "In odore consideratur: fetidus declarat corruptionem humorum, grauis membrorum" is not "As to odor: it is thought that a fetid odor indicates a serious corruption of the parts" (p. 61) but "In odor there is this consideration: the fetid smell declares a corruption of the humors, a heavy smell declares a corruption of the limbs." Similarly, "ipsius preceptiones dimittendo" is misunderstood. The phrase expresses fear that a physician might dismiss the instructions of Hippocrates, but Saffron translates "he [i.e. Hippocrates] dismisses us with the following precepts" (p. 90).

M. H. Saffron merits credit, however, for publishing a work that is equally important for the *Nachleben* of Hippocrates and for the history of medieval medicine, with notes which are full of modern medical insights.

*M. L. Colker*
University of Virginia

Edward J. Kealey. *Roger of Salisbury: Viceroy of England.* Berkeley: University of California Press, 1972. Pp. 312. $13.50.

Professor Kealey, presently Associate Professor of History at the College of the Holy Cross in Worcester, Massachusetts, has, in *Roger of Salisbury,* made a substantial contribution to the growing body of literature devoted to the reigns of Henry I and Stephen. Roger of Salisbury has long been regarded as one of the more important figures of that period, but a full-scale analysis of the man and his accomplishments has never been attempted. The present work was designed to remedy that omission.

The author has been diligent in his research, gathering an impressive body of documentary evidence, supplementing it with numismatic and archaeological material, and visiting many of the sites discussed. His efforts have made possible two valuable appendices to the work, a detailed itinerary and an edition of thirty-one of Roger's writs and charters.

The organization of the body of the work is somewhat complex. The author does not attempt to develop a single connected narrative until the events of the year 1126. Roger's activities prior to this time are discussed topically, and the first 150 pages are devoted to a consideration of his various roles: "new man," Justiciar of the Realm, officer of the Exchequer, bishop of the diocese of Salisbury, and prelate of the Church. Approximately the last fifty pages recount the events leading to Roger's arrest and despoilment at the hands of Stephen.

The net result of this biographical treatment is curiously unsatisfactory, however. Professor Kealey's efforts fail to produce a convincing portrait of Roger of Salisbury either as a man or as an administrator. It is easy enough to claim, as the author does, that Roger was "one of England's greatest statesmen." It is far more difficult to cite specific accomplishments which might entitle Roger to such a distinction. The truth of the matter appears to be that Roger of Salisbury was one of those administrators whose object it is to leave no wake behind them. It is their function to promote quiet and orderly development, equally devoid of controversy and personality. If Roger was indeed a great administrator — and there is far more evidence to the contrary than

Professor Kealey would admit — then his success is measured in direct proportion to his personal obscurity. It is suggestive in this regard that Roger emerges into the full light of historical record only at the moment of his sudden fall from power. He may well have been a significant figure of his age, but he was of the sort that makes adequate biographical treatment extremely difficult.

This is not to suggest that the book is a failure. Professor Kealey has used the many-sided Roger of Salisbury as a point around which to organize an effective discussion of the many complex themes of a turbulent and often obscure era. This is, in itself, a substantial accomplishment. That Roger of Salisbury remains a shadowy and enigmatic figure is less a reflection of the abilities of the author than of the limited and often contradictory evidence with which he has had to work.

*Lynn H. Nelson*
University of Kansas

Edwin Brezette DeWindt. *Land and People in Holywell-cum-Needingworth. Structures of Tenure and Patterns of Social Organization in an East Midlands Village, 1252-1457.* (Pontifical Institute of Medieval Studies, Studies and Texts, 22; Toronto, 1972.) Pp. vi, 299.

Agrarian historians of medieval Europe today are shifting their interest away from the legal and economic structure of the manor and toward the peasant village, which was by no means dominated and formed exclusively by manorial discipline. The author of this present work, E. B. DeWindt, a student of J. A. Raftis, is fully aware of these new tendencies and warmiy sympathetic toward them. To illustrate changes in peasant society from the middle thirteenth through the middle fifteenth century, he has focused his attention upon a small community of the English midlands, Holywell-cum-Needingworth. A dependency of Ramsey abbey, the village included at its maximum medieval size perhaps 300 persons. The manor rolls and court rolls, through which its history must primarily be reconstructed, are fairly complete, although the inevitable gaps within them cut from the historian's view some topics and leave some decades in obscurity.

DeWindt subjects these series to the kind of careful and exact examination which has characterized Raftis' own work. In the first half of his book (two out of four chapters), he explores changes in "structures and patterns of tenure" across the two centuries of his interest. The theme he principally develops is the emergence of a class of substantial peasants, loosely tied to the manor. DeWindt calls them "proto-yeomen," and identifies the group with the nucleus of the full-fledged Tudor yeomanry of the sixteenth century. This social change in the countryside is studied in close relationship to population movements and to changes in the manorial structure. He then goes on to explore families in Holywell-cum-Needingworth and the role they assumed in the community. In the last chapter, he studies the "group quality" of village life, by which he apparently means the manner in which the component families cooperated with one another and thus helped shape social life and institutions.

There are several, small points of criticism which could be made concerning DeWindt's methods of analysis. The court rolls form a principal foundation of his work, but he does not inquire into whether or how the business of the court may have changed over the two centuries. He notes, for example, a growing incidence of trespassing in the community in the fifteenth century, and attributes this to "an attitude of indifference to the physical state of the village as well as to any deep sense of communal responsibility." He seems to believe that this evidence is enough to show that a capitalistic spirit of individualism had invaded village life. But of course, the business of the court could be affected by factors other than the spirit of the villagers, such as the policy of the court itself, a desire to raise income from fines, or the changing economy of the area. In other words, an examination of the character of this basic source seems essential before safe conclusions can be drawn concerning society. So also, in tracing families, DeWindt identifies persons with the same surname as members of the same family, even when the persons were separated in time by several decades. Although the community was small, the reader may wonder if this procedure is always safe. Were not some surnames unstable? Were not others quite common, shared by more than a single lineage? Does not the subject at least deserve extended attention and discussion? The doubts raised by this use of the sources weaken the last part of the book, when DeWindt deals with families and attempts to reconstruct cultural attitudes. The evidence cited does not support the conclusion that the behavior of the peasants had become, by 1457, "strikingly particularistic, independent and even impersonal."

These objections do not, however, undermine the real interest of the study, which in many respects is a pioneering work. In the Preface, J. A. Raftis announces that this is the first of a series of studies to be devoted to medieval village life. DeWindt's book has given this important new series an auspicious beginning.

*David Herlihy*
Harvard University

F. D. Blackley and G. Hermansen, edd. *The Household Book of Queen Isabella of England, for the Fifth Regnal Year of Edward II, 8th July 1311 to 7th July 1312* (The University of Alberta, Classical and Historical Studies, I). Edmonton: The University of Alberta Press, 1971. Pp. xxvii, 255. $15.00.

This volume includes an edition (by G. Hermansen) and translation (by F. D. Blackley) of British Museum, Cotton MS Nero C VIII, fols. 121-152, the household account prepared by the keeper of her wardrobe for Edward II's wife, Isabella, for the period 5 Edward II (8 July 1311-7 July 1312). As the editors point out, this is the first household account of an English queen to be published; as such, it marks a welcome addition to the small number of similar and roughly contemporaneous texts in print, including accounts of King Edward I for 1294-1295[1] and 1299-1300[2] and of two late thirteenth-century ecclesiastics, Richard de Swinfield, bishop of Hereford, and Bogo de Clare.[3]

The value of these texts for students of administrative and social history is well known. The earliest surviving roll, that of Eleanor de Montfort, countess of Leicester, for 1265 (British Museum, Add. MS 8877) was used by Margaret Wade Labarge for her *A Baronial Household of the Thirteenth Century* (London, 1965), and the present account was one of the main sources for Hilda Johnstone's studies of the administrative organization of queens' households in later medieval England.[4] In their introduction the editors discuss the main segments of the text and provide brief analyses of some of the more noteworthy points of information it contains on administrative personnel and politics — for this was the year the antiroyalist movement culminated in the Ordinances and the downfall of Peter Gaveston.

By far the greatest importance of the text, however, will be for the social and economic historian, and perhaps for the student of popular devotion and piety as well. The value of the account is somewhat limited because the complimentary roll of daily expenses, such as that of the countess of Leicester manuscript, is no longer extant; but its topical organization will facilitate its use on such matters as details of fiscal procedure, gifts and purchases in support of the noble way of life, and the complex structure of social relationships and etiquette hidden in (and sometimes between) its matter-of-fact lines. The routine, incidental character of the account conveys not only the realities, but also the sense of ordinariness, of daily life, even of the highest strata of society. This is perhaps its most general and enduring value.

Scholars will be grateful for the care and thoroughness with which the editors have gone about their job, and for the handsome production of the volume by the University of Alberta Press. Both augur well for the new series of which this volume is the first to appear.

1. *Book of Prests of the King's Wardrobe for 1294-5, Presented to John Goronwy Edwards*, ed. E. B. Fryde (Oxford, 1962).

2. *Liber Quotidianus Contrarotulatoris Garderobae Anno Regni Regis Edwardi Primi Vicesimo Octavo* (London, Society of Antiquaries, 1787).

3. *A Roll of the Household Expenses of Richard de Swinfield, Bishop of Hereford, during Part of the Years 1289 and 1290*, ed. John Webb (Camden Society, old series, vols. LIX, LXII, 1853-1855); "Wardrobe and Household Accounts of Bogo de Clare, 1284-1286," ed. M. S. Giuseppi, *Archaeologia*, LXX (1918-1920).

4. See especially "The Queen's Household," in *The English Government at Work, 1327-1336*, vol. I, *Central and Prerogative Administration*, edd. J. F. Willard and W. A. Morris (Cambridge, Mass., Publications of the Mediaeval Academy of America, no. 37, 1940), pp. 250-299.

*Michael Altschul*
Case Western Reserve University

B. Rekers. *Benito Arias Montano (1527-1598)* (Studies of the Warburg Institute, vol. 33). London: The Warburg Institute, University of London, and Leiden: E. J. Brill, 1972. Pp. xi, 199. Gld. 42.

Benito Arias Montano was a central figure in what scholars have come increasingly to recognize as the rich and complex culture of Counter-Reformation Spain; but as Dr. Rekers remarks, he has been very little studied, and none of his writings have been printed or re-edited since the sixteenth century. Apart from brief literary analyses by Aubrey Bell (1922) and C. Doetsch (1928), Arias Montano is known only, at least outside the circle of Hispanicists, through incidental references to his Biblical and Hebraic studies in such standard authorities as Otis Green's *Spain and the Western Tradition* (1963-1966). Rekers' account is squarely based on hitherto little-used and largely unprinted correspondence. His work is doubly welcome, for it places Arias Montano firmly in the context of political and religious life in later sixteenth-century Spain and the Spanish Netherlands, and it will serve as the necessary prelude to, and hopefully incentive for, a larger study of his more strictly literary and philosophical importance.

Fully one-third of the book is taken up by the Appendices. These include a full list of Arias Montano's prodigious writings, both published (in Antwerp by Plantin) and unpublished; but by far the most important Appendix is that containing the full texts of 117 letters to, from, and about Arias Montano (pp. 131-166). In a sense, Rekers' own study is a running commentary on, and partial translation of, these letters. He has skilfully used them to build up a picture, not entirely uncritical, of Arias Montano's involvement in what J. H. Elliott *(Europe Divided, 1559-1598* [London, 1968], p. 392) has called the "strange third world" between the extremes of dogmatic Spanish Catholicism and dogmatic Calvinism. Sent by Philip II to Antwerp in

1568 to supervise the Polyglot Bible project, Arias Montano shortly began, in a brief career as political counsellor to Alba and his successor Requesens, to espouse a policy of Spanish toleration for Flemish autonomy. Of more lasting significance for his own career, he apparently converted — partly through intellectual sympathy with men such as Plantin, partly because of the cool reception afforded the Polyglot Bible in Spain and in Rome — to the antidenominational sect of the *Familia Charitatis,* a secret movement practicing outward conformism but marked by a pervasive influence of Stoicism and Erasmianism, a profoundly personal and allegorical approach to Scripture, and distinct affinities with the earlier Northern tradition of the *Devotio Moderna.* Rekers cautions against an automatic or excessive sympathy with Arias Montano, by showing the elitist nature and limited value of the Familists, and in particular his own lack of appreciation for the genuine bases or criticism brought against his Biblical work by the notorious León de Castro and the more scholarly Juan de Mariana. From 1576 to 1587 Arias Montano served as librarian and censor at the Escorial, where he introduced Familism and simultaneously preserved a tradition of Biblical scholarship and Erasmianism. Among his small number of converts, the most important were his successor, José de Sigüenza; his secretary and literary executor, Pedro de Valencia; and the Hebraist Lucas de Alaejos. Rekers' last chapter is largely concerned with the details of their careers.

None of the causes with which Arias Montano identified himself had much lasting influence in later Spanish history; but the careful demonstration of their importance and vitality in the later sixteenth century, at least, is a welcome corrective to standard emphases on the authoritarianism and conformism of Spanish intellectual life in this period. Arias Montano emerges as an essentially lonely, and thus sympathetic, even pathetic, figure; his unique qualities have now been fully and sharply etched in this splendid study.

*Michael Altschul*
Case Western Reserve University

Juan Ruiz. *Libro de buen amor.* Edited with an Introduction and English Paraphrase, by Raymond S. Willis. Princeton: Princeton University Press, 1972. Pp. 479. $20.00 cloth, $9.50 paper.

Professor Willis, whose academic credentials as an editor of medieval Spanish texts have long been recognized as impeccable, here distinguishes himself as a humanist. A humanist in the fundamental sense of employing his philological skill and knowledge in the service of human beings. In this case, the human beings who will profit most from his labors may well be medievalists in other fields, long unaware that Spain possesses in the *Libro de buen amor* a 14th-century poem entirely worthy of being classed with the *Roman de la rose* and the *Canterbury Tales*. It was a task that could not have been accomplished until recent years. For until the analysis of Juan Ruiz' "sotil" poetic technique undertaken by Americo Castro (*España en su historia,* Buenos Aires, 1948) and until the appearance of two new critical editions in 1964 (by G. Chiarini, Milan-Naples) and 1967 (by J. Corominas, Madrid), Spanish medievalists, let alone students of Chaucer and Jean de Meung, had not fully realized the import of the text. The witty ambiguities, the poetic sophistication, and the immensely significant portrayal of human life (conceived of, not in transition between Heaven and Hell, but as a process of living in the intimate company of all life, animal, vegetable, and verbal) which characterize quatrain after quatrain were obscured by inappropriate autobiographical and didactic interpretations. But I have no space here even to begin to present a proper "defense et illustration" of the masterpiece. Those who desire such, and they will include any lover of poetry who knows the two languages, as well as professional philologists and students of allegory (the allegorical sections are utterly unique) can do no better than to read Willis' learned and charming introduction. As for the paraphrase, I am not in full accord with every one of Willis' renditions. For example, I would not translate "con buen servicio vencen caballeros de España" as "by serving well the knights of Spain win victories" (pp. 168-69, quatrain 621), even though that is what the Spanish says. From the context (everything can be achieved by artful flattery), it would appear that Juan Ruiz here, as elsewhere, treats the rather decadent knights of his time with sarcasm. This is not made clear in Willis' straight military version. "Victories by Spanish Knights are (now) achieved through service" would seem to me more adequate. This is, among other things, a subtly satirical poem in which very little can be taken at face value. Yet the paraphrase will be immensely useful even for our colleagues in Spanish. They know only too well the many lapses of the standard Cejador edition, and they will be able to save much time and eyesight which otherwise might have been spent pursuing the typographically obscure annotation of the new critical editions. Willis has done much work for us by consistently choosing the most likely variant and by explaining it in clear and unpretentious English. The students in my graduate seminar found this to be immensely helpful. In short, Willis has proferred us an irresistible invitation to the joys of "buen amor" on every level from *eros* to *agape*.

Stephen Gilman
Harvard University

Don Cameron Allen. *Mysteriously Meant: The Rediscovery of Pagan Symbolism and Allegorical Interpretation in the Renaissance*. Baltimore: The Johns Hopkins Press, 1971. Pp. 354. $12.00.
Frank L. Borchardt. *German Antiquity in Renaissance Myth*. Baltimore: The Johns Hopkins Press, 1971. Pp. 356. $12.50.

These two studies of myth in the Renaissance are quite different in their scope — Allen traces various literary and philosophical approaches to classical myth from the fifteenth to the eighteenth century in western Europe; Borchardt limits himself to German myths of national origin and of empire from 1350-1530 — but both contribute to our general knowledge of the Renaissance and both provide detailed summaries of Renaissance sources that are not readily available. They will be most valuable as reference works.

Allen follows "the Renaissance search for Christian origins" among philosophers, sacred historians, and commentators on classical poetry. In the sixteenth and seventeenth centuries, historical connections were sought between Greek and Hebrew cultures; classical myths were thought to be a corruption by later generations of the "perfect theology" Adam had possessed. Some believed that the sons of Cham turned biblical figures into idols with the names of Greek Gods, worshipping Adam as Saturn, Cain and Jupiter, and Eve first as Rhea and later as Venus. Others thought that Homer had read Moses and studied Jewish theology in Egypt and then disguised the doctrines in poetic fables. By the eighteenth century, myth was treated more as a natural human expression than as a proof of universal theology; the Christian interpretation of pagan myth was slowly superseded by scholarly studies of pagan religion or of the literary influences of classical literature. Allen gives detailed accounts of major and minor Renaissance works which touch in any way on classical thought or even on antiquarian objects like coins. In his last chapter, he surveys the various and changing attitudes towards classical myth of poets and philosophers from Pico to Pope. This is the least successful part of the book because so much is covered so briefly.

The emphasis in this study is so distinctly on the development of Renaissance ideas that little attention is given to medieval back-

235

grounds. There is a brief survey of early Christian attitudes towards pagan philosophy in the first chapter, but after that medieval interpretors are rarely mentioned. With remarks such as "Martianus Capella, Fulgentius and Isidore had medieval imitators but the original texts of these followers were not printed in the Renaissance," Allen virtually leaps from the sixth to the fourteenth century. He makes nothing of the various writers connected with Chartres in the twelfth century, although they commented on the same secular works of poetry and philosophy that interested Renaissance writers. These men may not have influenced Renaissance interpretation directly, but they were important enough in their own time to affect later thought at least indirectly. Guillaume de Conches is not named, though he, like Bernard Silvester, gives many of the readings Allen considers classical or Renaissance, e.g. the identification of the Gods with the elements. Bernard's commentary on the *Aeneid* is mentioned but not discussed because it was not published during the Renaissance although, as Allen himself notes, it was known. (Incidentally, the Bernard whose commentary on the *Aeneid* John of Salisbury mentions is not Bernard Silvester, but Bernard of Chartres [fn. 21, p. 140]).

Allen's attitude towards medieval commentary is evident in various passages: he speaks of the "revitalization in the Renaissance of allegory (made tired and tiresome by fifteen centuries of monkish endeavor)," and says of typology: "The custom pursued to a sacred nausea had become tritely sterile. It was so comically boring . . . " Certainly there are boring and perhaps even ridiculous commentaries from the Middle Ages, but the implicit comparison with Renaissance methods does not hold. It is difficult to see much difference between medieval commentaries and the Renaissance interpretations that Allen cites. The major distinction that does emerge from this study, and it is significant, lies in the origin of classical myth. For medieval writers, if Christian truth could be found in pagan myth, it had been put there by the Holy Spirit for those who held the key. Renaissance writers, more aware of cultural differences, tried to find historical reasons, however fabulous, for a human transmission of ideas. There is a great deal to be gotten from this study, and it is, no doubt, unfair to criticize a work that covers so much for not covering more. It includes an extensive bibliography, particularly of early sources.

Borchardt discusses a more narrow but quite interesting subject, the German historical myths of national origin and political myths of empire. One might at first question his pairing of the two, but connections emerge in the course of the study; increasing national consciousness is at the heart of both. The myth of empire has four parts: it is Roman, German (by direct transmission), sacred, and supreme. The end of the empire will mean the end of the world and the rise of Antichrist. The last emperor will be Frederic II, believed never to have died. (One wonders why Borchardt does not mention the similar belief about Arthur, since a connection seems likely; he does refer to legends about Nero, which reinforce the Roman thesis.) The empire moved from Rome to Greece (Constantinople) and finally to Germany with the coronation of Charlemagne. Borchardt finds indications of the wide diffusion of such beliefs in medieval literature and in official documents: Innocent III claimed papal responsibility for the translation of the Roman empire from the Greeks to the Germans in the person of Charlemagne; in the thirteenth century, there were French attempts to distinguish the King of the Germans from the Emperor and to substitute *Gallici* for *Franci* in references to canonical texts.

The tendency to make everything German had led writers in some cases as far back as Adam to find the beginnings of the German people. Adam's language and Noah's were "all man's" or Alemannic — the Germans left Babel before the confusion of tongues. Borchardt offers many intriguing details of this kind, e.g. Bavarians, called "avari" by their enemies, tried to disguise the epithet with the *B;* Langobards are so named because they had their women tie their long hair under their chins to increase the apparent size of their armies. Borchardt is careful to note medieval sources for the material he covers. He emphasizes continuity rather than contrast, except in the rhetorical device of denying one version in favor of another, which he considers a distinctive feature of his Renaissance texts, although it occurs not infrequently in medieval writing. The conclusion of the study, once again, is less satisfying than the rest of the book, perhaps because Borchardt attempts to derive too general conclusions from the material covered, but the material remains valuable. There is no separate bibliography, but much useful information can be found in the footnotes and in an appendix on secondary sources for German historiography during the Renaissance

*Joan M. Ferrante*
Columbia University

James D. Tracy. *Erasmus The Growth of a Mind.* Geneva: Librairie Droz, 1972. Pp. 258. Bibliography; index.

The title of this book may suggest that it is simply one more study that traces Erasmus' intellectual development through his formative years and then settles down to analyze his mature thought within predetermined categories. Such, however, is not the case. Tracy insists on seeking for the interrelationships of Erasmus' personal life, educational, literary, and religious ideals throughout all stages of his career. Consequently, he describes the evolution of his subject's beliefs and recommendations for reform from his earliest schooldays until his deathbed.

As a Princeton dissertation, Tracy's study presented Erasmus' program of humanistic and religious reform primarily in the light of three concepts: allegory, *libertas,* and *simplicitas.* To these is added a fourth, *humanitas,* in the published version. Although Erasmus tended to apply it less frequently after his "Reformation crisis" in the early 1520's, allegorical interpretation, particularly of Scripture, was a cornerstone of his program. For in his mind, as Tracy remarks, "the Christian who reached the spiritual sense of a verse, and perceived the truth of which the literal sense was an image, found a source of sweetness and delight which could help to make Scripture efficacious in his life" (p. 103). Hence the guests of Eusebius in the "Convivium religiosum" engage in an ideal humanistic activity when they expound the Old Testament verse "The heart of Kings is in the hand of the Lord." The other three terms represent concepts which permeate Erasmus' writings, and which both shaped, and were shaped by, the circumstances of his own life. For him, *humanitas* meant man's gentle, peaceloving qualities, to be drawn out by proper cultivation; *libertas,* freedom from artificial constraints to allow the qualities of *humanitas* to develop properly; *simplicitas,* use of language which is "above all sincere and without artifice."

While an author courts the dangers of mechanical categorizing or tendentiousness in trying to encompass the intellectual career of so complex a figure as Erasmus within a few, however broadly conceived, terms, this book avoids both pitfalls. Tracy succeeds because he uses the work of his scholarly predecessors judiciously, because his biographical approach prevents him from simplistic analysis in terms of his selected topics, and because he writes lucidly about complicated issues. In the chapter entitled "The Sweet Name of Liberty," for instance, he presents a succinct and lively account of the Dutch reformer's complex position with respect to Luther over the critical years from 1517 to 1523. The final chapter, "By the Rivers of Babylon," also demonstrates convincingly why, from 1523 onward, Erasmus seriously questioned his own earlier "ethical optimism" and fell back increasingly upon his religious faith and the "consensus Ecclesiae."

If one were to quarrel at all with this book, it would be merely to observe that Tracy appears to stress Erasmus the religious figure at the expense of other aspects of the growth of his mind. But the emphasis is understandable, given the thesis that Erasmus's thought never ceased developing. The one other cavil has to do with the printing: there are, unfortunately, numerous minor, yet annoying, typographical errors.

*Lawrence V. Ryan*
Stanford University

John B. Bender, *Spenser and Literary Pictorialism*. Princeton: Princeton University Press, 1972. Pp. viii, 218. $8.50.

This is a well written book with a sharply defined thesis. Mr. Bender begins by making a distinction between descriptive and pictorial poetry. Descriptive poetry "lacks pictorial force" because its catalogues, comparisons, and presentations of massive detail function "without compelling the reader to a fresh visualization and reevaluation of successive images in a developing context" (33). In short, the distinction is a psychological one, tied to the demands the different kinds of poetry make on their readers. Moreover, Bender asserts, the experience of reading pictorially imitates or parallels visual experience itself, which according to modern researchers (chiefly E. H. Gombrich, M. D. Vernon, Rudolph Arnheim, and James Gibson) is not a matter of instantaneous perception but "a process in time which depends very much upon conventional signs, systems of understanding, cues, and assumptions" (15-16). The psychological distinction also has an historical dimension. To the Middle Ages, writes Gombrich, "the schema is the image," while to the post-medieval artist, "it is the starting point for corrections, adjustments, adaptations, the means to probe reality and wrestle with the particular." It is Bender's thesis that "Spenser is so striking as a pictorial poet partly because elements of both the medieval and the post-medieval exist in his work, and at least in *The Faerie Queene* are often startlingly juxtaposed" (53).

The bulk of the book is given over to supporting and extending this thesis, and the argument is organized around three categories of perceptual experience: " 'Focusing' — reiterated visual imagery fixed into sequences analogous to the process of vision; 'Framing' — formally or spatially coherent visual fields suspended at points of marked interruption or reversal of action; 'Scanning' — rapidly juxtaposed image clusters and spatial fragments which shatter visual experience into sequential units" (4). These categories are not fixed, and the passages Bender discusses almost always fit more than one of them; but they do provide a continual reference point in opposition to the more static categories into which descriptive verse falls. They also provide the titles for Bender's three main chapters, each of which proceeds in the same way: a definition of the category, a series of examples illustrating it (often including comparisons with poets whose effects are less or differently pictorial) and an extended analysis of a set piece of pictorial verse (the approach to Lucifera, the Cave of Mammon, the Bower of Blisse). Bender's analyses are almost always convincing and illuminating, and they yield insights on a range of important matters, from the functioning of the narrative voice to the relationship between our perceptual experience and the special status of Faerie Land. The discussion of the stanza in which Acrasia is described (2. 12. 77) or, as Bender puts it, revealed, is particularly fine, but it is only one among many, and the delicacy and toughness of Bender's sensibility is evident on every page.

And yet, when all is done, the book is finally less than completely satisfactory, in part I think because its success is a function of its limitations. This is not a book about literary pictorialism (as Bender himself points out in the preface). There is no attempt to survey the vast field of perceptual theory; the few authorities Bender cites are used only to give some external support to his categories. The categories themselves are not the subject of the book, for they are, as he reminds us continually, only categories of organization. Nor is the book finally about the *Faerie Queene,* because there is no attempt to move from the discussion of local moments to some larger thesis about that extraordinary poem. (Indeed, the larger the unit, the less successful and original are Bender's analyses.) In the end, then, the analyses of individual stanzas constitute almost the entire value of *Spenser's Literary Pictorialism.* It may seem unfair, and even ungracious, to fault a book for what it has not attempted to do, especially when what it does do it does perfectly well, but as I read it I could not help but recall Angus Fletcher's distinction (in *The Prophetic Moment*) between exegetes of the labyrinth (Tuve, Alpers) and exegetes of the temple (Fowler, Frye, Nelson). Bender is certainly a member of the first group and his work continues and adds to the work of his predecessors. But what is needed, I think, is some way of joining the two strains in Spenser studies (Fletcher, himself, seeks that way, but does not in my opinion find it), and while the modesty of Bender's self-imposed limitations is in many ways admirable, it finally places his book in the category of "valuable, but not essential."

*Stanley E. Fish*
University of California,
Berkeley

Louis Green. *Chronicle into History: An Essay on the Interpretation of History in Florentine Fourteenth-Century Chronicles.* Cambridge Studies in Early Modern History, edd. J. H. Elliott and H. G. Koenigsberger. Cambridge: Cambridge University Press, 1972. Pp. vi, 178. $13.95.

In method, chronology, and genre this small volume works on the frontiers of that "historical consciousness" which has become a major theme in the search for the distinctive structures of early modern minds. Rejecting both well-worn antinomies of medieval vs. modern and easy exogenous triggers for the explanation of a fourteenth-century change in historical outlook, Dr. Green focusses on the gradual recombination of commitments and conventions of medieval historiography in response to their own internal contradictions. While the development of historical perspective has long been associated with fifteenth-century Italy and, more recently, with sixteenth-century France, Dr. Green examines its origins in fourteenth-century Florence. And where it has been credited to humanistic insights, techniques, and styles, Dr. Green traces it to the traditional world of chroniclers and chronicles.

The book is divided into chapters on Giovanni Villani, Matteo Villani, the later fourteenth-century chroniclers (Marchionne di Coppo Stefani and "Paolo Minerbetti"), and Goro Dati. Dr. Green analyzes the conceptual framework implicit in the historical interpretation of each figure, but also connects his chroniclers with "something of the effect of a slow-motion representation of the stages of a movement . . . " (153). In Giovanni Villani we are shown a many-layered identification of supernatural order, natural process, and historical event. Christian Providence, Aristolelian naturalism, astrology and animism, Florentine Guelphism and pragmatism — the disparate strata of Villani's mind and cultural inheritance — cohered to define good and evil in the actual workings of history. In the resulting "moral equilibrium" supernatural and natural forces combined to insure that Philip the Fair and Frederick II would come to a bad end and that Florence would be exalted. By the end of the fourteenth century the same intel-

241

lectual categories still existed, but supernatural and natural or merely contingent had separated in the mental universe of the chroniclers. Circumstances had forced the cleavage — the Plague, social troubles, and above all the failure of the temporal engines of cosmic design and moral purpose, Papacy and Empire. But so had the very nature of the historiographical mold in which supernature, nature, and event were made eventually to seem more incompatible by the emphasis on their congruity. Goro Dati's subjects could move in an earth-bound space, subject only to nature, their own moral fiber, and the uncertainties of chance. The way was thus prepared "for the separation of the human world into a self-sufficient universe of its own in which history, in common with other secular studies, could become a new, more selective inquiry into the natural course of events" (154).

With chronicles, even more than with other forms of historical writing, there are problems in this approach. On one hand, the analysis describes and labels high intellectual structures in a genre intellectually limited and conceptually inexplicit. On the other hand, it is concerned with change in an over-arching world view in works which were characteristically conservative, preoccupied with particulars, and composed in discrete moments by very different personalities. Dr. Green tries to pin down the abstractions by close, persistent reading of the texts. He is willing to take into account the impact of external forces and personal variation, though in rather general or half-hearted ways. Where he detects change, he keeps continuity in sight, even if it means considerable repetition. Difficulties remain, however. The comparability of Villani and Dati, universal chronicler and author of a "monograph" on Florentine history, is not as self-evident as Dr. Green assumes. We may wonder, too, whether the supernatural is so removed from the pages of the later fourteenth-century writers. Licensed by the approach, Dr. Green cannot resist the temptation to elaborate his categories at levels which leave such problems — and his chroniclers — behind him.

Whatever the limitations, and to some degree because of them in a field immersed in archival research, this is a valuable essay. Dr. Green's work complements the ongoing reinterpretation of the more mundane reaches of Florentine politics and society. It fills in the background to the historical outlook of humanism and deepens the sense in which the fourteenth century can be said to have experienced the breakdown of high medieval synthesis.

*Randolph Starn*
University of California, Berkeley

Ira O. Wade. *The Intellectual Origins of the French Enlightenment.* Princeton: Princeton University Press, 1971. Pp. xxi 678. $20.

This large volume is the first of two that Professor Wade plans to write on the French Enlightenment. Together with his recent monumental biography of Voltaire, they mark the culmination of an outstanding career of teaching and scholarship, much of it concerned with the Enlightenment in France.

The present volume, which aims to discover the "roots" of the Enlightenment, pursues the twin currents, conflicting and complementary, of free thought and systematic philosophy from the Renaissance to the end of the seventeenth century. Within its covers Professor Wade gives us studies, varying in length and detail from the thumbnail sketch to the monograph, of an immense range of writers and thinkers from Pomponazzi to Newton. The series culminates appropriately in a long essay of almost 100 pages on Bayle, seen as a kind of compendium or pandemonium of all previous philosophies. Perhaps only Professor Wade himself is competent to judge the erudition and the accuracy of all these accounts. Readers of less skill and experience must be content to admire and envy the ease with which he moves among so much literature.

My own comments on the book are of an historiographical nature and they concern Professor Wade's conception of his work. The assumption on which the enterprise rests is that the Enlightenment is an organic reality; it is the scholar's task to define it and describe how it came about, even though all attempts to grasp it in words and categories, which by their very nature are discontinuous and fragmentary, inevitably produce distortion. "To the very simple question: What is the eighteenth century? or better still, What is the Enlightenment? we can give partial answers but certainly no organic one. While developing the study of trends we have distorted the century's inner unity and even its vitality. And although such has not been our intention, we have done much to destroy the organic unity, the total effect, which that era certainly, in common with all eras, possessed" (p. xiii). Professor Wade's language is itself eloquent. In the section of Part I of the book, entitled "Some Attempts at Definition," the Enlightenment has significant attributes of a (pre-Freudian) person. It moves, it starts, it understands its task in a certain way, it wants.

The assumption that the Enlightenment is a real and organic entity cannot, however, it seems to me, be made as confidently as Professor Wade makes it. Many historians and writers on history (Kubler, Braudel, most recently Siegfried Kracauer) have questioned our idea of the homogeneity of historical time and consequently of the organic unity of historical periods. There is a time of natural history, a time of political history, a time of economic history, a time of the history of literature, etc., and the relations among these different time series are not easy to establish. Yet segments of chronological time cannot perhaps be adequately characterized except by the relations among their varying strata, by the peculiar and shifting pattern of their layers. The Enlightenment should therefore be thought of less as a reality that is given to us to apprehend (p. xvii) than as an historiographical category that allows us to order and interpret the materials and traces of history in a certain way. The analogy of the work of art, which Professor Wade introduces to clarify and support his conception of the Enlightenment, does not eliminate the questions we have raised: it duplicates them. The defining characteristic of the work of art need not be that it is an organic whole with an inner reality or form which provides the condition of every reading of it and is prior to that reading. Texts, for instance, may be thought of as multilayered in the same way that Braudel thinks of history as multilayered.

Professor Wade's conception of historical periods has determined in some measure the form of his work. "Hazard implied in the final summary of the *Crise,*" he notes, "that the roots of the Enlightenment extended to the Renaissance" (p. 52). But by organizing his study around a moment of *crisis,* Hazard escaped the problem of setting beginnings and ends, the infinitely receding ascent to origins and the difficult labor of placing a boundary stone in the flow of events. Traveling backward to the Renaissance (and why stop there? — cf. p. 62), Professor Wade has turned his study into something closely resembling a History of Modern Thought. Within this framework the studies of individual figures acquire a great deal of autonomy; the very richness of the author's erudition and the enthusiasm with which he debates interpretations with other commentators encourage the reader to concentrate on the particular case in hand. The genealogical investigation of the roots of the Enlightenment thus runs the risk of dissolving into a succession of loosely related studies of individual figures and groups of figures, arranged in broadly chronological order. The reader realizes that certain problems keep recurring and that all the writers under consideration had to come to terms with political, moral, scientific, and religious conceptions which no longer constituted an immediately perceived and coherent world view. The danger is that in Professor Wade's richly detailed account it is the individual struggles and solutions that command our interest rather than their significance for "the Enlightenment."

A final note on the style of this book. Professor Wade is sometimes obscure: he uses common words in a special and uncommon way to convey his own philosophical and methodological position, and he has some quirks of writing which are not found, as far as I recall, in his other works. Mostly, however, he is deceptively easy to read. Students will plunder his book with profit, but they should beware of his irony.

*Lionel Gossman*
The Johns Hopkins University

# BOOKS RECEIVED

This list was compiled from the books received between 15 January 1972 and 24 April 1973. The publishers and the editorial board would appreciate your mentioning *Medievalia et Humanistica* when ordering.

Economou, George D. *The Goddess Natura in Medieval Literature.* Cambridge, Mass.: Harvard University Press, 1972. Pp. ix, 213. $8.00.

Fish, Stanley E. *Self-Consuming Artifacts: The Experience of Seventeenth-Century Literature.* Berkeley, Los Angeles & London: University of California Press, 1973. Pp. xiv, 432. $12.50.

Forcione, Alban K. *Cervantes' Christian Romance: A Study of Persiles y Sigismunda.* Princeton: Princeton University Press, 1972. Pp. 167. $7.95.

Frank, Robert Worth. *Chaucer and the Legend of Good Women.* Cambridge, Mass.: Harvard University Press, 1972. Pp. ix, 219. $10.00.

Fraser, Russell. *The Dark Ages & the Age of Gold.* Princeton: Princeton University Press, 1973. Pp. xi, 425. $16.00.

Gilman, Stephen. *The Spain of Fernando de Rojas: The Intellectual and Social Landscape of La Celestina.* Princeton: Princeton University Press, 1972. Pp. xv, 559. $17.50.

King, P. D. *Law & Society in the Visogothic Kingdom.* Cambridge: Cambridge University Press, 1972. Pp. xiv, 318. $21.00.

Knoll, Paul W. *The Rise of the Polish Monarchy: Piast Pland in East Central Europe, 1320-1370.* Chicago and London: University of Chicago Press, 1972. Pp. x, 276. $11.00.

Marckwardt, Albert H. and James L. Rosier. *Old English: Language and Literature.* New York: W. W. Norton & Company, Inc., 1972. Pp. xviii, 394. $10.95.

Miner, Earl, ed. *English Criticism in Japan: Essays by Younger Japanese Scholars on English and American Literature.* Tokyo: University of Tokyo Press, 1972. Pp. xl, 306. $15.00.

Muscatine, Charles. *Poetry and Crisis in the Age of Chaucer.* Notre Dame and London: University of Notre Dame Press, 1972. Pp. vii, 168. $5.95.

Ristow, Walter W. *A la Carte: Selected Papers on Maps and Atlases.* Washington: Library of Congress, 1972. Pp. x, 232. $4.00.

Saville, Jonathan. *The Medieval Erotic Alba: Structure as Meaning.* New York and London: Columbia University Press, 1972. Pp. viii, 315. $17.50.

Schoenbaum, S. *Research Opportunities in Renaissance Drama: The Report of the Modern Language Association Seminar.* Evanston: Northwestern University Press, 1972.

Secret, Francois. *Guillaume Postel: Apologies et Retractions.* Nieuwkoop: B. De Graaf, 1972. Pp. 271.

Shippey, T. A. *Ole English Verse.* New York: Hillary House Publishers, 1972. Pp. 220. $3.75 paper.

Société Internationale pour l'Etude de la Philosophie Médiévale, ed. *Bulletin de Philosophie Médiévale,* No. 13. Louvain: Secretariat de la S.I.E.P.M., 1971. Pp. 230.

Talmage, Frank, trans. *The Book of the Covenant of Joseph Kimhi.* Toronto: Pontifical Institute of Mediaeval Studies, 1972. Pp. 88. $2.00 paper.

Uitti, Karl D. *Story, Myth, and Celebration in Old French Narrative Poetry: 1050-1200.* Princeton: Princeton University Press, 1973. Pp. ix, 256. $11.50.

Van der Werf, Hendrik. *The Chansons of the Troubadours and Trouvéres.* Utrecht: A Oosthoek's Uitgeversmaatschappij NV, 1972. Pp. 166. $15.00.

Weatherby, Harold L. *Cardinal Newman in His Age: His Place in English Theology and Literature.* Nashville: Vanderbilt University Press, 1973. Pp. xv, 296. $11.50.

Wetherbee, Winthrop. *Platonism and Poetry in the Twelfth Century: The Literary Influence of the School of Chartres.* Princeton: Princeton University Press, 1972. Pp. xii, 292. $12.50.

Winterbottom, Michael, ed. *Three Lives of English Saints.* Toronto: Pontifical Institute of Mediaeval Studies, 1972. Pp. 94.

Woolf, Rosemary. *The English Mystery Plays.* Berkeley and Los Angeles: University of California Press, 1972. Pp. 437. $16.00.